THE DRAMATIC STORY
OF
OLD TESTAMENT HISTORY

Portrait of Ḥammurabi

This contemporary of Abraham (Amraphel of
Genesis 14) was the Moses of the Babylonians of
the twenty-first century .(2123–2081) B. C.   He
gathered up and codified a body of laws of which
we to-day have 247 in written form.   Hammurabi
was also a remarkable leader and administrator,
who unified all Babylonia under one government.
His portrait is one of the oldest from that
faroff age.

The Dramatic Story
of
Old Testament History

By
IRA MAURICE PRICE, Ph.D., Ll..D.
The University of Chicago

WITH MAPS AND ILLUSTRATIONS

FIFTH EDITION

NEW YORK
Fleming H. Revell Company
LONDON

The Bible text employed in this volume, taken from the
American Standard Edition of the Revised Bible, copyright
1901 by Thomas Nelson and Sons, is used by permission.

New York: 158 Fifth Avenue
London: 16 Anerly Hill

To
My Wife,

ELIZABETH M. PRICE,

Devoted Companion and
Generous Helper in
Every Good Work.

Fig. 46. Jerusalem from Mount Scopus

(See Note on p. 9)

PREFACE TO THE SECOND EDITION

THE Old Testament is fast acquiring a fresh significance. Old Testament history has become incandescent with the wondrous archæological discoveries in Bible lands. Almost every period of that old Book has been flooded with a new light out of the ruins of the past. This lustrous halo has magnified and given added charm to many a character and event which formerly were prosaic and tame. Whole eras of Israel's career now throb with the pulsations of world movements and international activities. The Hebrews, though politically merely dust in the balance, played a significant rôle in scenes on the international stage of pre-Christian times.

This book aims to give the reader a rapid survey of the entire period of the Old Testament—with a pencil sketch only of the high spots as we sweep on. It also lights up the narrative with the choicest gleams of knowledge found in the ruins of the Near East. To appreciate the full import of the allusions and conclusions of the text, the reader should always read the references to the Scriptures. Then to avoid a serious case of chronological astigmatism, the Chronology should be consulted. That will give a correct idea of the synchronous character of the events of Israel and her neighbours. Don't let the riddle of the lengths of the reigns of the kings of Israel and Judah (from about 800 B. C. down to 700 B. C.) disturb you. The overlapping of regencies and formal reigns in that area was the normal method of computing length of reigns in that day. The several periods into which the entire expanse of time has been distributed, find their vindication in the very different character of each area in itself. The chapters commandeer and set off by themselves related groups of items and events. Each section is a unit, enshrining, as far as practicable, one clear idea. Such breaking up of the narrative into periods, chapters and sections, makes for conciseness, clarity, and a specific outline in the mind of the reader and student.

The spread of the treatment of a prophet through several non-consecutive sections of a chapter simply illustrates the wideness of his influence upon the everyday life of the Israel of that particular era.

The organization of the material used in the book lends itself either to rapid reading, or to use as a text-book. For the former, no precaution is needed, except that the reader familiarize himself with the Scriptural and contemporaneous background. For use as a text-book, teachers should insist on it that each pupil read the assigned Scripture texts, and perhaps one of the books on Old Testament history, or on contemporaneous history cited under §20. By the use of recitals and class papers, requiring a wider reading, the pupils can garner a rich harvest of biblical lore. For those who wish to explore the fascinating realms of contemporaneous history and literature, there are exquisite surprises just beyond their present horizon. Indeed, Old Testament history presents an open door into entrancing lines of study and research in ancient history, literature, and archæology.

The illustrations have been chosen to visualize persons, events, and crises, as we sweep on through successive periods. Of the many pictures available, only a few could be used. These, with the maps of Bible regions, will set up in our minds the scenery of the stage on which the Israelites played their rôle in the drama of those faraway days. The equipment of this volume, supplemented by that of its twin companion, *The Monuments and the Old Testament* (18th ed. 1925) cannot fail to localize and particularize the events and persons that protrude in all that stretch of time.

Do not overlook the little descriptions of the illustrations, maps, and plans, appearing under or near each of them. These, though in smaller type than the regular text, render a real service. They amplify the one-line captions, which are too often mere cryptographs. They sometimes round up and corral the characters in the text, whose part in the play would otherwise seem to be merely tangential. They open up gates into side avenues to the main highway through which we are driving. They throw on the screen some otherwise filmy and tenuous figures of the main drama. And they often bring us face to face with characters who dealt directly or indirectly with the Hebrews; and they impress us with the fact that those Hebrews were only one little folk in the midst of great nations who represented the most advanced civilizations of those pre-Christian centuries. Though politically small, these same Hebrews embodied within themselves moral and religious ideas that have survived the final downfall and destruction of those proud empires.

The author gratefully acknowledges his debt to his predecessors in this field, though it is obviously impossible to embody all such acknowledgments in the narrative. For the generosity of those who gave permission to use their illustrations and maps, acknowledgment is made in the List of Illustrations (pp. 19-27) under each title.

It is the hope and prayer of the author that this Nebo-like vista of Old Testament history may strike a spark of new inspiration toward acquiring a wider knowledge of that area of Holy Writ which is of such vital importance for a true understanding of the New Testament.

IRA MAURICE PRICE.

The University of Chicago.
May 6, 1935.

NOTE ON FIG. 46, page 6. Jerusalem from Mount Scopus: The one spot of Palestine that has seen all the history of that land from Abraham to Judas Maccabæus is Jerusalem. At first, it seems to have been a Jebusite fortress, though a city in the Amarna period (fourteenth century B. C.), from whose governor letters were sent in the Babylonian script to the king of Egypt. After its capture by David it became the Palestinian centre of the Hebrews until its fall in 586 B. C.

CONTENTS

PERIOD IV

TRIBAL ORGANIZATION: FROM THE SETTLEMENT IN CANAAN TO THE ESTABLISHMENT OF THE MONARCHY

PERIOD V

THE MONARCHY: FROM SAUL TO SOLOMON

PERIOD VI

DUAL MONARCHIES: FROM THE DISRUPTION OF THE KINGDOM TO THE FALL OF SAMARIA (931-722 B. C.)

PERIOD VII

Prophets Preaching: From the Fall of Samaria to the Fall of Jerusalem (722-586 b. c.)

PERIOD VIII

THE EXILES: FROM THE FALL OF JERUSALEM TO THE FALL
OF BABYLON (586-538 B. C.)

PERIOD IX

THE RETURNS: FROM ZERUBBABEL TO NEHEMIAH
(538-432 B. C.)

PERIOD X

JUDAISM EXPANDING

CONTENTS

NOTE ON FIG. 32, tailpiece below : " The superintendent of granaries " was an especially important official in Egypt. The real wealth of that land was its great crops of grain, which not only maintained its large population, but filled capacious granaries for crises at home and for sale to foreign peoples.

ILLUSTRATIONS, SKETCHES, AND PLANS
In Alphabetical Order.

MAPS

In Chronological Order.

INTRODUCTION

1. The Old Testament, Raw Material. The Old Testament is made up of a large body of raw material, out of which we may construct the history and daily life of the ancient Old Testament Hebrews. This material has been only partially organized by the ancient writers, and in each case to emphasize some particular thought that was in the mind of the writer. In almost every fragment of these writings we discover one permeating, prevailing fibre, and that religious. Indeed, that characteristic is usually bound up with certain well-established rituals and ceremonies of early origin and of commanding influence in the life of the people. In making proper use of the large mass of writings

NOTE ON FIG. 76, headpiece above: This *Scribe Accoupi* dates from the fourth to sixth Egyptian dynasties and is now found in the Louvre, Paris. It is said to be one of the best examples of portrait sculpture of that period. He is recording some transaction or inventory of goods. He usually sat thus on the ground, with a box of papyrus rolls at hand, a pen in hand and one in reserve behind his ear, and an opened sheet on which he was writing. The technique carried out was practically the same all down through the history of Egypt.

that have come down to us, we must so organize them and
their thought as to claim the high regard of reason and the
fealty of our spirits.

2. The Old Testament, a Source. The Old Testament is our main and chief source of information regarding
the ancient Hebrews. It embodies within it story, song,
annals, prophecy, poetry, law, genealogy and ritual. If
these sources are to be utilized to the best advantage, if we
are to construct a consecutive history out of them, our first
difficult problem is to place them in such an order that they
will present both the chronological growth of the Old Testament and the development of the Hebrews.

We must recognize at once that they were put together
by men, fallible though holy men, otherwise they would be
perfect with no need of any re-arrangement. When we
tackle that problem we must largely dismiss from our minds
our modern methods of writing books. We must take our
stand way back in the pre-Christian centuries, and go about
among the writers of that day and see their methods of
collecting and editing the materials available for their
purposes.

3. Antecedent Stories and Writings. The Old Testament Hebrews came late on the stage of action. Hundreds and thousands of years before the oldest writings of
the Old Testament there were written documents in Southwestern Asia and Egypt. These were inscribed on clay tablets, on stone, on metal and on papyri. Centuries before
Moses, or the date of Abraham, the learned men of Egypt
and Babylonia left us documents containing annals, records,
stories, folklore, myths and legends, connected with their
respective peoples. These ancient documents, unchanged
since they were first written, are now found in abundance
in many of the museums of Europe, Asia, Egypt, and in our
own country. In fact, the writings of the Old Testament,
compared with those of Asia and Egypt, are modern, and
have all the characteristics of the writings current in their
day. And the most romantic fact about these echoes of the

past is that we can now translate almost all of them into our own tongue and fit them into the niches of history where they belong.

4. Ancient Writers' Methods. Writing in ancient times was done by a special class of men called scribes. They were the masters of their own art and did as they chose. In our study of the records they have left we very soon discover with what liberty they treated their sources. They recorded oral stories, songs, legends, and events of their times with absolute freedom. They reproduced the style of a predecessor, his framework and even his phraseology with the liberty that was theirs at all times. This method is especially noticeable in the historical inscriptions of Assyria, where the succeeding annalist employs almost exactly the same form, the same words as his predecessors, and with no acknowledgements whatsoever. In Numbers 21:17 the author cites a folk-song which Israel sang at a well:

> " Spring up, O well, sing ye unto it;
> The well which the princes digged,
> Which the nobles of the people delved,
> With the sceptre, and with their staves."

In the same chapter, verses 27–30, we find proverbs recited which were current among the people of that day.

Besides oral story, song, and legend, they had written sources on which they freely drew for their purpose. Even in the Pentateuch we find a book unknown to-day quoted by the writer in his description of the journeys of Israel. That was the " Book of the Wars of Jehovah " (Numbers 21:14). In Joshua 10:12, 13, the author throws the responsibility for the statement that the sun stood still at the battle of Beth-horon on the " Book of Jashar." From the same book came " the Song of the Bow " put in the mouth of David in 2 Sam. 1:18–27, in his lament over Saul and Jonathan. Other books and annals are referred to occasionally in the histories, as, " Now the acts of David the king, first and last, behold they are written in the history of Samuel the seer, and in the history of Nathan the prophet, and in the history of Gad the seer " (1 Chron. 29:29). And again we read, " the rest of the acts of Jehu, and all that he did, and all his might, are they not written in the book of the chronicles of the kings of Israel? " (2 Kings 10:34).

The above-mentioned cases are merely samples of the methods by which the writers of the Old Testament employed and referred to their sources for the information they give, and for any further facts regarding the events or persons being described. In fact, there are twenty-four books quoted and referred to by name in the Old Testament which are unknown to-day.

5. Many Books of the Old Testament Compilations. We have seen that the writers of the Old Testament books used whatever narratives they had at hand, pieced them together as they saw fit, and they were not always particular to iron out all difficulties. Devout Christian scholarship has succeeded in detecting several of the sources they used, by their use of certain words, by their style, by their proper nouns, and by their very evident purpose.

More and more is it obvious that many of the books of the Old Testament have been compiled by men who were the most capable scribes of their time, men who revered God and used only such material as should promote the God-given purpose of their writings as they saw it.

These books were compiled from the best religious writings of their day, of the choicest sayings of the people, and of earlier attempts to record the events of the past (*cf.* Luke 1:1). These writers handled all this material with the freedom of the writers of their time.

`6. Authorship of Old Testament Books. Perhaps it may startle some of us to learn that the commonly supposed authorship of many of the books of the Old Testament was merely a conjecture of the Jewish Talmud (*Baba Bathra* 14b in *Jew. Encyc.*, Vol. III, 143) condensed. It asks and answers its own question:

" Who wrote them? Moses wrote his own book and the
section concerning Balaam (Num. 22:2–25:9) and Job.
Joshua wrote his own book and eight verses of the Penta-
teuch. Samuel wrote his own book and Judges and Ruth.
David wrote the book of Psalms, at the direction of ten
elders, viz., Adam, Melchizedek, Abraham, Moses, Heman,
Jeduthun, Asaph, and three sons of Korah. Jeremiah wrote
his own book and the Book of Kings and Lamentations.
Hezekiah and his Council wrote Isaiah, Proverbs, Song of
Songs and Koheleth (Ecclesiastes). The men of the Great
Synagogues wrote Ezekiel, the Twelve, Daniel and Esther.
Ezra wrote his own book and the genealogies of the Book
of Chronicles as far as himself."

Now read the above quotation again. The oftener you read
it the more unreliable it appears to be. If Moses wrote his
own book (the Pentateuch?) why should especial mention
be made of the Balaam episode? How could Samuel have
written his own book when he died at 1 Samuel 25,
while there remain 1 Samuel 26–31 and all of 2 Samuel which he could not have written? According to the
above, neither Isaiah, Ezekiel nor the Minor Prophets
wrote the books assigned to their names. Such late decla-
rations do not command our confidence as in any sense
trustworthy.

If we rule out of court this evidence of the Talmud regarding the authors of the Old Testament books we are
thrown back on our own investigations. The best Christian
scholarship of to-day is now practically agreed that, while
some of the books are in part compilations, we are able on
sound principles of study to differentiate in many places
between the different ancient writings which have been put
together by their compilers.

7. Great Names Used. About the time of the closing
of the Old Testament canon, we discover a tendency to
assign books to great names, in order thereby to increase
their popularity. This comes out in several of the apocryphal and pseudepigraphical books, as the " Ascension of

Isaiah," " The Wisdom of Solomon," and " The Apocalypse of Moses," none of which was composed by the great name embodied in the title.

Doubtless that was simply the custom which had been practiced by several of the compilers and writers of the Old Testament, when they used Moses, Joshua, Samuel, Solomon, Daniel, and other names mentioned in the above quotation from the Talmud.

8. Contemporaneous Sources. Besides the Old Testament itself we now have vast quantities of documents contemporaneous with those of the Old Testament which have been dug out of the ruins and mounds of ancient cities of Egypt, Babylonia, Syria, Asia Minor and Arabia. A majority of these were written in the Semitic languages, closely bound up with the vocabulary and syntax of the Hebrew of the Old Testament. Best of all for our purpose we find in these records many occurrences of the names of the kings of Judah and Israel as their vassals. Likewise many of the customs and manners current in Israel are found to be in vogue among their contemporary neighbours. These records are an unimpeachable evidence, as far as they go, to the truthfulness of the statements of the Old Testament regarding these contemporaneous peoples. They reveal, too, a very valuable source of material for the construction of the background of Israel's everyday life.

Another source, though a minor one, of material for Old Testament history is Josephus, whose *Antiquities* and *Wars*, when used with caution, give important sidelights on the history of Israel. And as supplementary we might add the apocryphal and pseudepigraphical writings of the period between the Testaments.

9. Purpose of the Old Testament. The Old Testament is not a textbook of history, it was never designed to be. History is merely incidental to the writer's real purpose. The political snarls in which Israel often found herself are sometimes dramatic and even tragic, but the writer's offhand and fragmentary manner of treating them leads us to conclude that his chief interest lay quite outside of politics.

Neither is he especially absorbed in the economic, social or civil conditions of his day. These features of individual, tribal, and national life sometimes creep into his records, but their comparative insignificance locates them quite outside the favourite trend of his aims.

The Old Testament was never intended to teach science. Its so-called science is merely the crude conception of those days touching the appearance of the heavens, the earth, and the forces and facts of nature that surrounded them every day.

A careful survey of the entire range of the Old Testament writings reveals to one that the pervading interest of the writer was religious. He was absorbed in the moral and religious phase of every event, of every aim, of every movement in the ongoing of the personal and national life of his day. Everything, history, poetry, prophecy, law are made subservient to this great theme,—the extension of the divine purpose among men.

10. First Part of the Bible. Especially significant is it that the Old Testament is only the first part of our Bible. It is the soil out of which grew many of the religious ideas and principles which have their fruition in the New Testament. It depicts the character and work of the Messiah with such faithfulness and fervour that we are drawn to pursue its counterpart into the New Testament under the form of the Christ. The close kinship of the two parts of our Bible is a compelling reason why we should so study the Old Testament that our background for the New Testament may be comprehensive, specific, and illuminating. It should foster in us a new conception of the unity that pervades all Holy Writ.

11. Basis of Our Beliefs. The basis of our ideas of God, of his love, mercy and faithfulness, have their roots in the words of Hebrew prophet and poet. The gradual growth of religious ideas through the Old Testament reveals to us the wise and inspiring process by which God has unfolded himself to adolescent mankind in all that old past.

Its great culmination in the revelation of himself in Jesus Christ, has its background in the Scriptures used by the Master himself, the Old Testament. So that if we expect to comprehend his teachings in their basal character we must study the Old Testament on which as a lad he was brought up, and which he quoted and interpreted throughout his ministry. More significant still is the fact that we find so much in the Old Testament that grips us, that responds to our highest desires and best moods, that seems to express our feelings and longings, that inspires us toward the noblest and best in life. The psalms and prophets have unfathomable depths of meaning that only the sincere and earnest searcher after truth can begin to understand and to feed upon. The New Testament writers and the early church fully appreciated these values.

12. Racial Background of the Old Testament. Thousands of years before the Old Testament Hebrews emerge, Asia and Egypt were peopled with great and small nations, some of them far advanced in the arts of civilization. Cities were built, kingdoms established, trade routes on land and sea laid out, and international relations negotiated. These peoples mustered armies, waged wars, were victors and vanquished, centuries before Abram migrated from Ur of the Chaldees. Egypt's armies repeatedly swept into Asia ages before the Hebrews wandered into Canaan.

Abram journeyed into the West, one Hebrew from an old Babylonian city, and migrated through countries long settled and populated by peoples whose tongue and worship were in the main familiar to him. When his descendants finally seized some of Canaan for a permanent abode they were wedging themselves into a world already thickly settled by civilizations whose remains are the wonder of today. So that the Hebrews were comparatively a small folk in the midst of mature and age-long peoples. Israel was an insignificant people whose racial background must be looked for among the complexity of nationalities who lived before and about them and in whose midst Israel moved, lived and had her being.

13. The Old Testament World. Nothing gives real-- ity to an event like acquaintance with a spot or site on which it took place. After one visits Jerusalem his mind's eye sees Solomon dedicating the temple, the Assyrian officers bantering the Hebrew defenders on the walls, or Nehemiah riding a burro down through the valley of Hinnom at midnight surveying the fallen walls of the old city.

To have a proper perspective of the chain of events of the Old Testament we must have more than a sketchy knowledge of the physiography of Bible lands. Compared with our present world the area occupied by the nations named in the Old Testament was very definitely circum- scribed. Its entire area, including land and water, from Persia on the east to Spain on the west, from the moun- tains of Armenia on the north to the south shores of Arabia, was approximately the same as the land area of the United States of America. But that Old Testament world con- tained less than one-half the land area of the United States; and of this land area about one-third was desert. The Old Testament world included the Mediterranean Sea in the west, the Red Sea in the southwest, the Persian Gulf on the southeast, all important waters for shipping purposes in the ancient world.

The great rivers of that world were the Nile in Egypt, flowing northward into the Mediterranean Sea; the Tigris and Euphrates in the Mesopotamian Valley emptying into the Persian Gulf; and the Orontes in North Syria debouch- ing into the Gulf of Alexandretta.

The central mountain range is the Taurus, located in Asia Minor, out of the eastern spurs of which rise the Rivers Tigris and Euphrates. Its southern projections wall in the Mediterranean Sea on the east under the name of the Leba- nons and extend south as far as Mt. Sinai in the desert.

The most significant bodies of land in the Old Testament world were Egypt,—the child of the Nile—fostering a civilization hoary with age; Mesopotamia-Babylonia, nurtured by the two splendid rivers, Tigris and Euphrates, sustaining civilizations that long antedated and were contemporaneous with the Hebrews of the Old Testament. Lesser though important lands of that day were Phœnicia on the upper east coast of the Mediterranean Sea; the Hittites in Asia Minor, the Elamites on the east of Babylonia, and Arabia, largest of all areas, though containing proportionately the least habitable land.

14. Palestine. But the little land of first importance in our survey is Syria-Palestine. Its location is on the east coast of the Mediterranean Sea, stretching to the Arabian desert on the east and south, and to upper Syria on the north. At most it embraced 50,000 square miles, about the size of the State of New York, but usually occupied only about 12,000 square miles, the size of Maryland, though the boundaries varied with the shifting of rulers. Into this bit of Southwest Asia the ancient and Old Testament Hebrews wandered, settled, came to themselves, and built up a kingdom and a nation that made itself felt among all the smaller and some of the greater peoples of their day.

Four physical parallels extending in general north and south, characterize this little land. The Mediterranean Seacoast with its attendant plains, Philistine, Sharon, and the opening to Esdraelon, cut by the projecting Mt. Carmel is the first. The southern extension of the Lebanons, the crumpled-up elevation of the country, in one cup of which sets Jerusalem, is the second parallel. The " fault " of the Jordan valley, holding in its embrace Lake Merom, the Sea of Galilee, the Jordan River and the Dead Sea, is a unique feature on the face of the earth. The fourth includes Hauran, the steppes of Gilead, and Moab on the east.

Each of its features deserves individual attention and study if we are properly to visualize the Old Testament events that sanctified the very soil and waters of this little spot on the earth's surface.

15. The Old Testament in Literature and Life. Our best literature is permeated, yea, often saturated, with the finest of the Old Testament. Shakespeare, Milton, Macaulay, Ruskin and hosts of others show their familiarity with some of the best principles of the Old Testament as well as with many of its most striking figures of speech. More than a few times have they acknowledged their debt to its language and thought. Even the editorials of our great daily newspapers echo the familiar similes and other idioms of the ancient Hebrew Bible. The common sayings and colloquialisms of ordinary conversation sparkle with the brilliant pictures of language that have their origin in the Old Testament.

16. Why and How Study the Old Testament? The " why " is stated briefly in the preceding sections, which are only a few of the many that could be written. The " how " is the problem before every writer of a book on the Old Testament. All agree on a few points. Such study should be thorough, comprehensive, reverent, open-minded, with a readiness to accept the truth when found. If these features characterize our study, we shall soon find ourselves interested, absorbed, enthralled, with the real spirit of the messages, and almost living in the presence of the great characters who quietly but truly mould the lives of their admirers. Such study of this part of Holy Writ will make it a new and inspiring world, and a real impetus toward a larger and more consecrated Christian life.

17. The Chronology of the Old Testament. No one system of reckoning time was current in Old Testament times. That scheme worked out and promulgated by Archbishop Ussher (died 1656) and first printed on the margins of Bishop Lloyd's Bible in 1701, is no longer usable. The discoveries in the tombs, tablets and mounds of the East have effectually laid it on the shelf as one of the ingenious but useless systems of the past. The Authorized

Version should discontinue its use, for its figures not only proclaim an erroneous interpretation of the origin of the universe, but form the basis of endless controversy among those who know nothing about the origin of this outworn system. The translators of the Revised Version recognized its falsity, and so discarded it.

18. Books and Chapters of the Bible. Is it worth while to learn the books of the Old and New Testament in the order in which they occur in our Bible? By all means. Too often do we see a young man or a young woman fumbling about in the early books of the Old Testament for Amos, or among the Minor Prophets for Joshua, or in Paul's Epistles for Mark. Put an end to such embarrassments and once for all learn to give the thirty-nine books of the Old Testament and the twenty-seven of the New Testament exactly in the order of the English Bible as it is printed to-day.

Do a little better and learn the number of chapters in each book. The writer has saved hours of time by knowing this little fact about each book. If, after you learn these figures, you should find a reference to Ruth 5:1, you know instantly it is an error, for Ruth has only four chapters; if Ezekiel 50:4 falls in your path, you can at once say, that is wrong, for Ezekiel has only forty-eight chapters.

19. Periods of the Old Testament.

I. A Pre-Hebrew Introduction: From the Creation to the Call of Abram.

II. Patriarchal Wanderings: From the Call of Abram to the Egyptian Bondage.

III. Israel's Bondage and Wanderings: Egypt and the Wilderness.

IV. Tribal Organization: From the Settlement in Canaan to the Establishment of the Monarchy.

V. The Monarchy: From Saul to Solomon.

VI. Dual Monarchies: From the Disruption of the Kingdom to the Fall of Samaria (931–722 B. C.).

VII. Prophets Preaching: From the Fall of Samaria to the Fall of Jerusalem (722–586 B. C.).

VIII. Exiles: From the Fall of Jerusalem to the Fall of Babylon (586–538 B. C.).

IX. Returns: From Zerubbabel to Nehemiah (538–432 B. C.).

X. Judaism Expanding: Life and Literature.

XI. The Greek Invasion and Judaism (333–161 B. C.).

20. A Modest Equipment. There are some indispensable articles of equipment for one who expects to do satisfactory popular work on the Old Testament. A few tools of the best temper and keenest edge skilfully used will accomplish vastly more than a larger number of a mediocre character, even though well handled.

A few necessary books:

The American Revised Version, 1901.

The Apocrypha—Revised Version, 1894.

Smith, G. A., *Atlas of the Historical Geography of the Holy Land*, 1915.

Bailey and Kent. *History of the Hebrew Commonwealth*, 1920.

Price, Ira M., *The Monuments and the Old Testament* (=MOT), 1925 edition.

Kent, C. F., *Biblical Geography and History*, 1911.

These works are desirable for further study:

ON OLD TESTAMENT

Kent, C. F., *History of the Hebrew People*, 2 vols., 1896.

Kent, C. F., *History of the Jewish People*—Babylonian, Persian, and Greek Periods, 1899.

Charles, R. H., *Old Testament Apocryphal Books*, 1917.

Josephus, *Antiquities* and *Wars*.

ON PALESTINE

Smith, G. A., *Historical Geography of the Holy Land*, 25th edition, 1932.

Macalister, R. A. S., *History of Civilization in Palestine*, edition of 1921.

Macalister, R. A. S., *A Century of Excavation in Palestine*, 1925.

Albright, W. F., *The Archæology of Palestine and the Bible*, N. Y., 1932.

Thomson, W. M., *The Land and the Book* (3 vols.), 1886.

Barton, G. A., *Archæology and the Bible*, 6th edition, 1933.

ON CONTEMPORARY HISTORY

Rogers, R. W., *History of Babylonia and Assyria*, 6th edition, 1915.

Olmstead, A. T., *History of Assyria*, 1923.

Rogers, R. W., *History of Ancient Persia*, N. Y., 1929.

Olmstead, A. T., *History of Palestine and Syria*, N. Y., 1931.

Breasted, Jas. H., *History of Ancient Egypt*, 1924.

Erman, A., *Life in Ancient Egypt*, 1894.

Hall, H. R., *Ancient History of the Near East*, 6th edition, 1924.

GENERAL

Hastings, *Dictionary of the Bible*, one vol. ed., 1909.

New Standard Bible Dictionary, 1926.

NOTE ON FIG. 37, tailpiece below: The Hebrews wrote their traditions, their annals, their contracts, their treaties, on papyrus, on clay, and probably in a few instances on stone. But their descendants used skins, and it is on these that we find our best biblical manuscripts to-day. Our illustration is such a Hebrew roll of a book.

PERIOD I

A PRE-HEBREW INTRODUCTION

From the Creation to the Call of Abram

CHAPTER I

GENESIS AND EARLY TRADITIONS

21. Purpose of the Genesis Stories. The first eleven chapters of Genesis form a kind of introduction or vestibule to the history of the Hebrews. They aim to present such a background for the future career of that people as to inspire in them a deep reverence for God as the creator of all things, and as the sustainer and guide of his creatures. And more, these chapters were intended to give Israel an assurance that God is all-powerful and can lead his people on to a noble destiny. And still more impressive, is the fact that the history of the chosen people is prefaced by such a divine origin of all life, as to lead Israel to see the essential goodness of God as distinct and separate from his creatures, yet closely associated with them in all their activities.

22. The Creation. The first account of creation (Gen. 1:1–2:4a) in our translation attributes the origin of the heavens and the earth to God (*Elohim*). Thence in the successive days we find the appearance of cosmic light, called day, and the darkness called night; the appearance of the clouds and mists above, with the waters beneath called heavens; the emergence of dry land, of vegetable life, of seed-bearing herbs and fruit-trees; the first appearance of the heavenly bodies (to one on the earth), establishing day and night, seasons and years.

On the fifth and sixth days we discover God creating sea-

43

monsters, filling the seas with marine life, and the air with birds that fly in the heavens; higher land animals and creepers on the ground culminate in the creation of man in God's own image; male and female he made them and put them

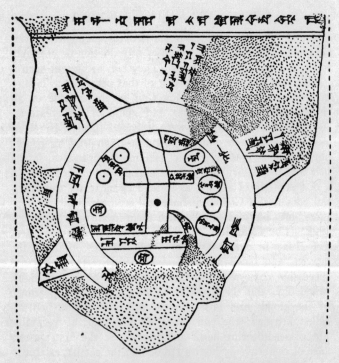

Fig. 100. The Babylonian Plan of the World

This Babylonian Plan of the World is sketched on clay. The earth is the round flat surface surrounded by the "bitter river," that is, salt-water. Within that circle, the parallel lines from top to near the bottom are the Euphrates River, emptying into swamps and marshes. The rectangle cutting across the bars above the dot contains the name, on the right, *tin-tir-ki,* "Babylon." The ellipse near the lower right hand corner of Babylon says, "country of Ashur." The conical projections outside the "bitter river" indicate districts,—a fascinating Babylonian plan of that part of the old world.

over all his creatures. On the seventh day God rested,—ceased from his creative activity.

In brief, this story tells us that God was the Creator of all things, that man was the climax of created things, and that God gave him dominion over all his creatures.

The Babylonian account of creation which has many features similar to the biblical though permeated with and saturated by a mythical and polytheistic element, clearly reveals their interdependence. Seven acts or stages in the creative process and the appearance of the different forms of life indicate that there must have been current among those two Semitic peoples the same traditions of their early origins. But the writer of the Hebrew record under divine inspiration has expunged the mythical and polytheistic features, and given us such a record as puts God at the centre of the cosmogony of the Old Testament. In other words, the real teaching of this narrative is religious, not scientific. It is in no sense a scientific description of creation as to the successive appearances of the different forms of life, and is not intended to be, for it does not agree with the latest and best findings of modern science.

23. The Creation of Man. The second story of creation (Gen. 2:4b-22) centers about man. The earth is prepared for him; he is made of earth and becomes a " living soul," he is related to the animal and to the vegetable world, and to woman. Man's chief distinction lay in his likeness to God: (1) a " living " or immortal " soul;" (2) an intelligent being; (3) with a conscience; (4) with a personality; (5) with a will; (6) with moral righteousness; (7) with affections;—with all these qualifications he was made ruler of all the earth.

This story locates the garden of Eden in close proximity to the great rivers Tigris and Euphrates, and two other streams, which some scholars have identified with two early irrigating canals of central Babylonia. " Sippar in Eden," has been found on a clay tablet discovered in 1885 in Babylon. Some theories of this garden's location in other parts of the earth are current, but Babylonia was more probably, in the mind of the writer of the story, the place of the Genesis Eden. Into this garden the man was put (1) "to dress it and to keep it;" (2) to eat of every tree of the

Fig. 18. The Sixth Creation Tablet

Of the seven tablets of the creation series our interest centres in the sixth, in which is recorded the creation of man. Ea, the god of the deep and of knowledge, said:

"My blood will I take and bone will I [make];
I will fashion man, that man may . . .
I will create man who shall inhabit [the earth],
That the service of the gods may be established and that
    shrines [may be set up]."

garden *except* "the tree of the knowledge of good and evil;" (3) to give names to "every beast of the field and every bird of the heavens," which "Jehovah God formed out of the ground." In all his communion with these marvellous creatures of God he found no one who could be a companion to him. To supply this lack Jehovah God formed a woman,—" taken from the man," and presented her to him, whom the man recognized as his own flesh and bone. So close was the relation established that we have the authoritative word (vs. 24), " Therefore shall a man leave his father and his mother, and shall cleave unto his wife " (cf. Matt. 19:5); (remnant of a matriarchy?).

This story of creation is quite different from the first one just described. Here we have no days of creation, an additional name for the creator (*Jehovah Elohim*), details of the creation of man and woman, and the character of the garden of Eden. This is evidently another story of creation which the compiler or editor did not try to harmonize with the first, but simply put it down as he found it in his sources. He gives the two stories with their fundamental teachings, that God is the originator and sustainer of all life on this earth, especially of mankind, and he is therefore able to guide his own creatures in the future.

24. The Temptation and Fall (Gen. 3). " Whence came sin and evil into this world? " With all his " image of God," and his mental and spiritual endowments, man was not invulnerable against the allurements of evil. His progress was marred by the subtle suggestions of an enemy. So insidious was the approach and so promising was the outcome, that the two intelligent Godlike personalities of the garden violated the only prohibition put upon them. Disobedience opened the eyes of their consciences and " they hid themselves." When discovered they passed along the blame, but were punished,—all of them: (1) the serpent to crawl; (2) the woman to bear children and to be subject to her husband; (3) the man to toil for his bread,—no more garden of Eden—and finally to return to the dust out of which he was made; (4) to perpetual enmity between the seed of the woman and the seed of the serpent,—symbolical if you like, but too explicitly true!

This narrative is not paralleled among other oriental

legends, but we have in early Babylonia a remarkable seal cylinder on which are found a tree on either side of which is a human figure, presumably a man and a woman; behind the woman we plainly see the form of a serpent with its head near the woman's head. This is often called the seal of temptation (See Price, MOT., p. 115).

This Genesis story is an attempt in a primitive way of accounting for the origin of sin; and also in quite a specific manner to give the real results of sin among men, especially as laid before us in the next half dozen chapters of Genesis.

But while regarding these disastrous consequences of disobedience we should note that the inspired writer inserted in the midst of this story of the sentence pronounced upon the serpent, whose evil character is often described in the Bible, a promise (3:15), " I will put enmity between thee and the woman, and between thy seed and her seed; he shall bruise thy head, and thou shalt bruise his heel."

This is the first so-called Messianic passage in the Old Testament, and is designated by scholars as the *Protevangelium*. The import of this verse is that victory over sin awaits man in the distant future; it is a promise that evil will be finally stamped out by the " seed of the woman,"— a distinct ray of hope in the very beginning of the fight with sin.

25. After Eden (Gen. 4). The sentence pronounced upon Adam and Eve began to be effective immediately after their expulsion from Eden. Their sons engaged in farming and sheep-raising, says the fragmentary record. Doubtless sacrifice to God had also been instituted long before this account was written, for each of the men brought offerings to Jehovah. Abel's was acceptable but Cain's was rejected, not because of the kind of sacrifice, but because of the attitude of mind of the two men (Heb. 11:4). Jealousy burst forth into anger, anger culminated in murder, and murder was followed by lying,—a picture of the shocking growth of sin into a horrible fruitage. Cain was marked, as a warning to others (peoples and neighbours) not to slay

him (in blood revenge), and was sentenced to a life of
wandering (Nod),—to a nomadic career where life is a
nightmare, where blood revenge is lurking in every shadow.

Among Cain's descendants we discover the first builder of
a city (4:17), the first named bigamist (vs. 19), the leader
of shepherds (vs. 20), the inventor of music (vs. 21), the
first smith (vs. 22) who made instruments of war and of
agriculture.

In this crude report of the organization of that early
world we discover the germs of the best elements of the
civilization of our day. Nevertheless, this little scrap of
ancient poetry (vss. 22–24) rings with the barbarity that
reigned when man had to defend himself by violence.

There are a few parallels among other peoples, of the
beginnings of the arts and of industry. Purged of their
mythical and polytheistic features, and given a sharp moral
turn our writer presents this rather cruel but still lesson-
teaching account of the consequences of disobedience.
Cain's descendants seem to have vanished with this old
record.

26. The Line of Seth (Gen. 4:25–5:31). The fatal
results of Cain's career and his virtual disappearance, bring
another leader on the stage. This third son of Adam and
Eve quite replaces Abel, for of his descendants it is said,
" Then began men to call upon the name of Jehovah."
Chapter five is a genealogical table based on a tri-verse
method of presenting the stories concerning each character
named except Enoch and Noah. Some significance is attached to the resemblance of the names of the descendants
of Cain (4:18–22) to those of Seth in this chapter. But it
is quite uncertain whether these represent the same original
list, the Cainites being differentiated as the originators of
the arts and industries of civilization, and the Sethites as
the originators of the worship of Jehovah.

The longevity of those patriarchs in chapter five has been
a problem down through the centuries; especially as the
Hebrew record of the years of life taken consecutively totals

9852

1656 years; the Samaritan numbers 1307 years; and the Septuagint (Greek) version, 2242 years. The span of life of the Old Testament characters varies from 969 years (Gen. 5:27) to 80 years (in Psalm 90:10). Of the plausible explanations of such variable longevity in the three ancient versions of the Genesis record we have these: (1) scribal errors; (2) a supposable difference in the methods of reckoning time, counting moons or seasons as years; (3) those long years cover the time, not of a single individual, but of a tribe over which he was the original head; (4) man's originally perfect body yielded slowly to the seeds of decay. The third explanation seems to be the most reasonable and plausible from every point of view, and was advocated by such a conservative scholar as the late Prof. William Henry Green, of Princeton.

The so-called parallels of this chapter in other traditions afford practically no assistance in explaining the problems here presented (see MOT., §87).

The chief purposes of the writer in preserving this chapter are seen in that wonderful verse 24: " Enoch walked with God; and he was not; for God took him;" and in the naming of Noah and his three sons, Shem, Ham, and Japheth, the presumed progenitors of the Old Testament Hebrews and their immediate neighbours.

27. The Deluge (Gen. 6:1–8:22). The fragmentary records that have come down to us fairly groan with the wickedness of the so-called " sons of God " and " daughters of men " who filled the earth with their lawlessness; but were " renowned " in the eyes of the men of their day. (Were the Titans of Greek mythology akin to these monsters?) Even Jehovah himself was so grieved that he had made man on the earth, that he determined to blot him " from the face of the ground " (vs. 7). But the goodness of old Noah caused him to retract that decision so far as that worthy and his own household were concerned.

According to specifications given by Jehovah, Noah built a boat (ark) on the best lines of that day; designed for the preservation of his family of eight persons, and of specimens of the available clean and unclean animals and birds, and for the storage of food for the period of their enclosure within the boat.

It took one week to embark with all the cargo, and close

Fig. 24. A Babylonian Deluge Tablet

The great national Babylonian epic of Gilgamesh contains twelve tablets, about 3,000 lines of text. The eleventh tablet, shown above, tells us the Babylonian story of the deluge. Most writing nations of early antiquity have left us a similar story. But the Babylonian carries the closest resemblance in every way to the biblical record in Genesis, chapters 6–8.

all the exits except air spaces. Thence the forty-day storm broke upon the earth. The boat was lifted up and floated by the floods while the struggling, cursing mob of drowning humanity and beasts of the field commingled in the awful cataclysm that engulfed them. After seven months of floating about, the boat was beached on Mt. Ararat, and after more than a year since embarkation, the entire living cargo disembarked; and Noah built an altar and offered up burnt-offerings of consecration to Jehovah.

Traditions of the deluge are found among others in the stories of the Babylonians, the Greeks, the Persians, the Scandinavians, the Welsh, and the Indians. There is considerable diversity in the character of the tradition in almost every case. But that one which most nearly resembles the Hebrew is the Babylonian. In fact, the presence of so many of the same features in both stories, such as the boat, the preservation of life, the sending out of birds, the sacrifice, leads devout scholars to the conclusion that the Hebrew account is scarcely more than the Babylonian purified of its crude, immoral and polytheistic elements.

The apparent inconsistencies of the story of the Hebrew deluge are doubtless due to the use by the writer of more than one primitive record of the event.

The extent of the deluge was probably limited to the area of the then known world, since the common sense arguments against a universal flood are positively overwhelming.

The writer's avowed purpose for the deluge, the minute details of which do not disturb his equanimity, was the judgment of God on the sin of mankind. Lawlessness and its penalty are the basal facts for the whole story. And, over against this, we discover the favour of God bestowed on obedience and faith in him, as exemplified in Noah and his household.

28. A New Beginning (Gen. 8:15–9:17). With the old sinners and their wickedness wiped out, Noah and his sons and their wives have an unprecedented opportunity for beginning anew. The patriarch started off well by offering a sacrifice to his Saviour God. So pleased was the Almighty that he vowed that he would never again bring such a dire disaster on the earth, but would cause the seasons to rotate in regular order without interruption. One evidence of his sincerity was that he set the bow in the cloud as a covenant between Noah and himself that no deluge should again destroy all flesh. As an assurance of his pleasure, he blessed Noah and his sons and commanded them to multiply. As in the beginning he gave them power over all living things. For food he was to use " every living thing that moveth," but flesh must be thoroughly drained of its blood, which is the life, before it is eaten.

Capital punishment was fixed as the penalty for man or beast for taking the life of a man. This was not mere blood revenge but the laying down of a principle for all men of whatever race or clime. The implication is that the writer of this record had in mind contacts with other races whose violence was shown on every hand.

In the midst of the genealogical table of Noah's sons we have a disgraceful episode given as a background for the poetical prophecy of Noah regarding the future of his sons' descendants (vss. 25–27).

Canaan, son of Ham, was to perpetuate the spirit of his father (cf. Deut. 27:16), and to be a servant to his brethren. " Blessed be Jehovah, the God of Shem," may God enlarge Japheth, and let him enjoy the hospitality of Shem (including the worship of his God).

29. The Table of Nations (Gen. 9:18–10:32). The so-called " Table of Nations " really begins with the recital of the names of the sons of Noah. To them the writer of this ethno-geographical table gives the credit of being the ancestors of the other known peoples of the earth. The names found in this chapter are not, as a rule, individual, but national. This is seen especially in the use of the plural form *im*, occurring several times as the final syllable in the names of certain peoples.

The writer of this chapter displays a marvellous knowledge of the so-called political geography of his age, presumably about the eighth century B. C. In the northern zone of the Old Testament world mainly about and south of the Black Sea, he located the descendants of Japheth, in Armenia, Media, Asia Minor, and also in Cyprus, and Greece in Europe. In the southern area, southern Babylonia, the southern and southwestern coast of Arabia and in Ethiopia he found Cush; Mizraim (Egypt) was northern Egypt, from Cairo to the Sea, and peoples along the south shore of the Mediterranean Sea; Put (Punt) on the shores of the Indian Ocean and the Red Sea; Canaan on the east coast of the Mediterranean Sea, including also the Phœnicians.

That zone which was of especial interest to him was the central or middle one in which the descendants of Shem were the chief figures. These nationals were found in the Elam highlands, east of Babylonia with its formidable 'fortified capital Shushan (Susa); Asshur, Assyria on the upper Tigris River; Aram, western Mesopotamia and Syria.

The author's omissions are quite as significant as his mentionings. He finds no descendants of Put, son of Ham; none of Elam, Asshur or Lud, sons of Shem. And the posterity of Peleg, ancestor of the Hebrews, is reserved for a later table (11:18 ff.). He does not discuss the question of migrations from some former racial or geographical centre, though he casually mentions the movement of Asshur towards the north (vs. 11). His chief interest seems to have been to depict a background for the rise, growth and expansion of the Hebrews as a people amid the peoples of the earth of that day.

30. The Story of Babel (Gen. 11:1–9). Chapter ten (10) gives us the location of the different races of men, and oriental-like in giving the result before the cause, the writer now tells how this dissemination came about. The problem of the origin of so many languages on the earth was doubtless a perplexing one. Its solution seemed to inhere in the popular derivation of the word Babel (" confusion ") in

Bab-ilu, " gate of God." The story as we have it was probably only a part of a longer one, and the writer has adopted only so much of it as he needed for his purpose, viz., to show that this entire story is fundamentally based on rebellion against God, which was both futile and disastrous to the best interests of mankind.

This is the last of the primitive stories that make up the introduction to the beginnings of the Hebrew people. As in all the other cases, the writer puts at the basis of his narrative the power and omnipotence, the faithfulness and favour, of this same God, who will direct, bless and instruct the Hebrews and make of them not only a chosen people, but a blessing to all mankind in the faroff future.

NOTE ON FIG. 15, tailpiece below : This tower of old Borsippa was built within twenty miles of the great Babylon on its northeast. The king of Babylon prided himself on its prosperity. Its temple Ezida, of the god Nabu, was one of Hammurabi's joys. The crumbling brick tower in the photograph was probably the ziggurat of that temple, which modern travellers have often called the ' tower of Babel.'

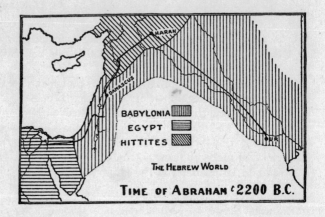

BABYLONIA
EGYPT
HITTITES

THE HEBREW WORLD

TIME OF ABRAHAM *c*2200 B.C.

PERIOD II

PATRIARCHAL WANDERINGS

From the Call of Abram to the Bondage in Egypt

CHAPTER II

ABRAM'S MIGRATIONS

31. Stories of the Patriarchs. We have just seen that the early chapters of Genesis were a sort of preamble to the history of the Hebrews as a nation. We should also note that the remainder of the book of Genesis is scarcely more that an introduction to Israel's growth and organization as a people. These stories, of course, were written at a very

NOTE ON MAP 1, headpiece above: Primitive population of Babylonia was Sumerian, now succeeded by Semites, who ruled to the Mediterranean Sea. The Hittites controlled Asia Minor, and Egypt was independent, holding part of the Sinaitic Peninsula. Abraham was at home under Babylonian sway.

much later age by men who gathered together the available information about their early heroes, and compiled for us a delightfully picturesque account of their achievements, their character, their customs, and the worship of their God. They made the most of the facts they had at hand, and gave them such a model treatment as doubly to enforce the real lesson they had in mind; viz., to show that God's dealings with his own were faithful and sure, that his providential care over them was characteristic of " Jehovah, the God of your fathers, the God of Abraham, of Isaac, and of Jacob " (Exod. 3:16).

So far as we are able to test the records these stories give us a faithful sketch of the age of the Patriarchs, though the background is very filmy and tenuous, and the patriarchs play their rôle on a stage especially devoid of actors. They lived much as did the people about them, with the same

Fig. 97. Ur Uncovered by Archæologists

The old mound of Ur has often been molested by archæologists. But it remained for the University of Pennsylvania and the British Museum to do a real job of excavation, to penetrate and uncover the old Sumerian civilization that ruled it in Abraham's day. This shows us the lower parts of the walls of the buildings, mainly of the homes of the Urites.

customs, the same habits of life, the same nomadic wanderings. Their religious beliefs and their faith, crude as they were, seem to have differentiated them from their pagan neighbours. Enough of the Hebrews, however, were true to the one God to perpetuate faith in him as the Creator and Sustainer of men.

32. Abram's Call and Response (Gen. 11:10–12:9). That the Old Testament beginnings of the Hebrew people may be properly introduced to the reader, the writer of this narrative goes back to Shem, the son of Noah, who was so marvellously saved from the deluge. He follows a single line of ancestry down in true genealogical order to Nahor, Terah, and Abram. This presentation opens the door to Ur (of the Chaldees—a late name of the territory about the Persian Gulf), the scene of the first act in the story of the patriarchs.

That there were other Hebrews dwelling in the Mesopotamian valley as far back as 2600 B. C. is abundantly attested by cuneiform documents of the age of Naram-Sin, preserved in the Hittite language. Also in the age of Rim-Sin, 400 years later, Hebrews are mentioned, where they seem to have been soldiers under the employ of the government.

The city Ur was located on the west bank of the Euphrates and was one of the prosperous cities of lower Babylonia about 2000 B. C. It is identified to-day as the modern Mugheir, now about 150 miles above the mouth of the Euphrates, though in early times it was not far from the shores of the Persian Gulf. Its population was composed of tradesmen, merchants, farmers who made their homes in the city, artisans, and the professional religious castes about the temple. The patron deity of Ur was the moon-god Sin (or Nannar). There were also other deities who were objects of worship, as seen in Josh. 24:2: "Your fathers dwelt of old time beyond the River, even Terah, the father of Abraham, and the father of Nahor: and they served other gods."

Of Terah's three sons, Haran, father of Lot, died in Ur. The old man Terah with Abram and Abram's wife Sarai, and Lot—four persons—with their flocks and herds and servants, migrated from Ur northwards 600 miles to "Haran" (Harran in the Babylonian), in Paddan-aram east of the Euphrates, the first lap of the journey to Canaan (11:31). Nahor probably followed at a later time (Gen. 24:15).

Now Harran was a great commercial centre, a kind of Semitic cross-roads in the northwest, where the moon-god Sin was revered in a notable temple whose ruins are still to be seen. These immigrants from Ur would be thoroughly at home here in language, culture and worship. Here the

Fig. 96. The Ruins of the Great Ziggurat of Ur

The centre of religious interest in each ancient city was its chief temple, and in that temple the ziggurat—the seven-staged tower on which was enshrined the symbols of its patron deity. The moon-god Sin was supreme in Ur, and on the top of the ziggurat, whose foundations are here seen, the devoted Sumerians worshipped.

patriarch Terah died. Abram, his son, heard a divine call
to separate himself from his pagan surroundings and go to
the land which should be shown him (12:1). He took his
wife Sarai (his half-sister, 20:12) and Lot his brother
Haran's son, and trekked down into Canaan among the
numerous peoples who occupied that country.

His course touched places that later became memorable
in Israel's history, such as Shechem, the oak of Moreh near
Bethel, where he built his first altar and called on the
name of Jehovah. Assurance that he was on the right
road came to him at Shechem in a message from Jehovah
and a kind of a covenant promise, " Unto thy seed will I
give this land."

33. To Egypt and Return (Gen. 12:10–13:18). One
of the semi-periodical famines of the country dropped down
on Palestine, and Abram and his clan followed the natural
trade-route into Egypt, the granary of those lands. His
kindly reception seems to have been due to the attractiveness of Sarai his wife (half-sister). When Pharaoh learned
that Abram had deceived him, he was angry and said to
Abram: " Behold thy wife, take her, and go thy way."
Why Abram was not punished beyond expulsion from the
land, we can only conjecture. But Pharaoh's men were
charged with the duty of seeing Abram and all his clan
safely across the border.

Their return to Canaan led them to the region of Bethel
near the spot whereon an altar was built when they first
arrived from Harran. But the greatness of their flocks and
the quarrels between their shepherds, forecast a separation
between Abram and his nephew Lot. The generosity of
Abram in giving Lot his choice of the land set a stamp upon
the fine character of the father of the Hebrews. Lot chose
the rich open spaces of the Jordan Valley, and Abram remained in the hill-country. On the repetition of the promise
of Jehovah for the third time, Abram removed with his
flocks, herds and clansmen to the region of Hebron (Kirjath-
arba), which he retained as his fixed abode; at the oaks of

Mamre he built another altar. Here he formed a kind of compact with Mamre, Aner and Eschol, who played a significant rôle a little later in Abram's career.

34. Abram at Home in Canaan (Gen. 14). The fourteenth chapter of Genesis is probably our oldest Old Testament scrap out of ancient history, of a time when the Elamites near the Persian Gulf had made conquest of Babylonia and the West to the Mediterranean Sea. The leader of those Elamites and their allies was Chedorlaomer (*Kudurlagamar*) King of Elam. Five vassal city-kings in the lower Jordan Valley are named as rebels against their eastern overlords; and chapter fourteen gives an account of this punitive expedition into the West. The eastern kings swept into the east-Jordanic highlands, scattering the Rephaim in Bashan, the Zuzim, and the Emim, and the Horites (cave-dwellers) of Mt. Seir; and by a swift turn, invaded Kadesh in the southland, and swung back to the Dead Sea, and fell upon the five Canaanite rebels. These insurgents were completely routed, and the Elamite allies plundered their cities and carried off as captives their population, including Lot and his possessions.

A swift messenger brought word to Abram. He hastily called out his own 318 trained servants and his confederates and started in pursuit of the Elamite army loaded down with captives and booty. Somewhere in the region of Damascus he overtook them, and by a surprise night attack effectually routed them and recovered Lot, the men and women prisoners, and the plunder.

On his victorious return Abram was met in the valley of Shareh by the (new) king of Sodom and by the mysterious Melchizedek, who was priest-king of Salem. Melchizedek blessed Abram, saying, " Blessed be Abram of God Most High, maker of heaven and earth." To him Abram gave one-tenth, tithes of all he had recovered; but refused to accept anything for himself, though he asked portions for his confederates who had helped him win the victory.

35. Abram Assured of an Heir and an Inheritance

(Gen. 15). There seems to have been some doubt in Abram's mind about the fulfilment of the promise of an heir. He thought he saw one of his own home-born slaves as heir to his rapidly increasing estate. To dispel that doubt Jehovah led him out at night where he might see the brilliant heavens of Palestine, and said, " Look now toward heaven, and number the stars, if thou be able to number them; and he said unto him, So shall thy seed be " (vs. 5). " I am Jehovah that brought thee out of Ur of the Chaldees, to give thee this land to inherit it." Abram's belief and faith expressed themselves, as was common in that day, in a bloody sacrifice to his God. The promise was expanded by stating that the seed should be afflicted 400 years, and afterwards should be given that land " from the river of Egypt unto the great river, the river Euphrates."

36. Hagar and Ishmael (Gen. 16). With no prospect of any direct heir to fulfil the promise in Genesis 15, Sarai, in accordance with good old Babylonian precedent (Hamm. §146) gave her Egyptian maid, Hagar, her own property, to Abram as a wife. Not long thereafter, jealousy sprouted up and bore strife which ended in the flight of Hagar into the wilderness, where she underwent the hardships of an unprotected life. She was assured by an " angel of Jehovah " (first mentioned here) that her son-to-be should be a man of the wilds, one of those free wandering characters found only far from the haunts of settled life. So remarkable was the message that Hagar called the well near where she heard it, Beer-lahai-roi (" the well of the living one who sees me "). In due time Hagar bore a son, and Abram called him Ishmael (" God hears "); Abram being eighty-six years old.

37. The Covenant Sealed with Circumcision (Gen. 17). In Abram's ninety-ninth year, Jehovah appeared to him and said, " I am God Almighty " (*El Shaddai*); and he gave him almost incredible promises regarding the future of his posterity. He also changed his name to Abraham (" father of a multitude ") and Sarai's name to Sarah

(" princess "). Among his posterity shall be nations and kings (as in the monarchy), though Ishmael shall produce only princes (vs. 20). Indeed, God will be with him, and his descendants shall inherit the land as an everlasting possession.

Circumcision, though a widely prevalent religious rite among primitive peoples, was adopted as a covenant and sign of the covenant by the Hebrews. It was a symbol of the bond that should bind every Hebrew to Jehovah. Abraham saw that all his male servants were circumcised. Henceforth every male child eight days old, the slave born in the house, and the foreigner purchased with money, shall be circumcised into the sacred family of the Hebrews, and thus bear the mark of God's everlasting covenant with them as a people. So essential was the observance of this rite that the penalty for its omission was either death or expulsion from the clan, according as we interpret the expression, " that soul shall be cut off from his people " (vs. 14).

38. Entertaining Angels (Gen. 18). Abraham was sitting in the entrance to his tent pitched under the terebinths at Mamre, when three strangers suddenly appeared before him. He hastened to greet them by bowing himself to the ground in true oriental fashion. They accepted his proffered courtesies and hospitality. The spokesman of the three seems later to have been Jehovah himself, who gave definite promise to Sarah that she, though " well stricken in age," should bear a son,—the long-promised heir of the covenant. Her joy at such a prediction broke out in laughter, for which she was rebuked.

Abraham's hospitable nature and suspicion of the real character of the men led him to accompany the angels as they went on their way. Jehovah, knowing that the posterity of the patriarch would be " great and a mighty nation," told him about the proposal to visit Sodom and Gomorrah to see whether it was indeed as wicked as reported. The proposition to wipe out those cities struck terror into Abraham, and he persistently interceded for their safety, doubtless because Lot, his nephew, was a resident of Sodom. Jehovah finally yielded and said that he would not destroy Sodom if ten righteous persons should be found in it. Thereupon the two separated, Abraham going back to the terebinths of Mamre, and the strangers to investigate the wickedness of Sodom (Note the humanlike character of Jehovah).

39. The Fate of Sodom and the Sodomites (Gen. 19). Those same strangers who had visited Abraham and Sarah at Mamre reached Sodom at dusk. Upon Lot's insistence they went home with him as his guests. In the course of the evening the men of the city besieged his residence to get access to the strangers. Lot's loyalty to the finest instincts of oriental hospitality was put to the test, and was victorious. The strangers proved their divine errand, and not only saved Lot's household from the shamelessness of the Sodomites, but smote the depraved " men of the city " with a blindness that defeated their aims. In addition, they revealed to Lot the fate that was in store for this wicked city, whose evil had reached high heaven. Lot's family,—four persons only—were hustled out of the city by the help of the messengers, and " Jehovah rained upon Sodom and upon Gomorrah brimstone and fire from Jehovah out of heaven " (vs. 24),—generally regarded as a volcanic eruption of some kind, possibly located at about the site of the present south end of the Dead Sea, where asphalt and sulphur are found in quantities at this day.

Lot's family barely escaped the fiery overthrow of " the cities of the plain." But his wife's curiosity to see what they had escaped, traditionally turned her into a " pillar of salt." He and his daughters fled to the mountains, lest even little Zoar, on the edge of the plain to which they were going, should fall in the same destruction. Either the Hebrews' hatred for the Moabites and Ammonites, or the desire of the latter to claim relationship with their more powerful neighbours, the Hebrews, is probably the explanation of the sordid story of the desperate method adopted by Lot's daughters to prevent the extinction of their family. Those Moabite and Ammonite tribes seem at least to have been related to the Amorites,—primitive peoples of the land.

NOTE ON FIG. 41, tailpiece below: We have here the Egyptian artist's profile of Hittites as they appeared to him either as captives or as allies. They do not differ greatly from the present-day Armenians, whose descendants they may partly be. In pre-Israelitish history they were a world-power in Asia Minor and southwestern Asia for more than 800 years.

CHAPTER III

Isaac's Brief Career

40. The Birth of Isaac (Gen. 21). After the burning of the cities of the plain, Abraham migrated with his family, his flocks and his herds, into the south country and became involved in relations with Abimelech king of Gerar. The compiler of those two chapters has left several frayed edges in his literary garment which we can scarcely explain.

The important and outstanding event that took place at Gerar was the birth to the aged parents, " Abraham being

Note on Fig. 40, headpiece above: This captive Hittite chieftain represents Egypt's trophy of victory. In the larger picture this captive is on his knees with a rope tied about his neck, part of which you can see. These Hittites gave Egypt trouble for several hundred years.

a hundred years old," of the long-promised son, whom they called Isaac ("laughing," 18:13). This birth was the beginning of the fulfilment of the oft-repeated promise of Jehovah to Abraham in emphatic and far-reaching projections into the future of his numerous posterity.

This new arrival in Abraham's household was circumcised on the eighth day as a mark of the covenant established between Abraham and God. On the usual weaning-day feast (Isaac being three years old), Sarah saw Ishmael playing with his little half-brother Isaac. That was too much familiarity for the son of the handmaid to show toward her own son, and she demanded the ejection of Hagar and Ishmael. Abraham reluctantly sent them away with food and a skin of water into the desert of Beer-sheba. In her distress God appeared to Hagar and said, " I will make him [Ishmael] a great nation " (21:18). In the desert they remained and he grew up an archer, and finally married a woman of Egypt.

And Abraham concluded a treaty with Abimelech at Beer-sheba ("well of the oath," or "seven"), and lived many days in that south country.

41. The Would-be Sacrifice of Isaac (Gen. 22). Abraham had received so many promises from God that they were now almost commonplace. To be certain that he fully appreciated their significance and gravity, God now subjected his faith to a supreme test. "Take now thy son, thine only son, whom thou lovest, . . . and offer him . . . for a burnt-offering." The prevalence of human sacrifice in devotion to a deity in that primitive age was well-known. This test was met with a willingness to obey God's command; in fact, Abraham's attitude was not only a trial of his faith in God's promises, but it was a test on God's part of the validity of his promises to Abraham.

With pathetic simplicity the writer describes the preparation, the journey, the dialogue between father and son, the building of the altar, the binding of Isaac, and the raising of the knife to slay him What suppressed emotion must have filled Abraham's breast during all those terrible three days' journey! In his heart the patriarch had already sacrificed Isaac to Jehovah. At the supreme moment, God, satisfied with Abraham's faith, called to him, " Lay not thy hand upon the lad, neither do thou anything unto him; for

Fig. 38. Hebron To-day

The oldest known city in southern Palestine, Hebron is rich in associations with Abraham, Caleb, David, and subsequent Hebrew history. Its home of earlier giants, and its rôle in the government of that region, and its cave of Machpelah make its site of prime interest to students.

now I know that thou fearest God, seeing thou hast not withheld thy son, thine only son, from me " (*cf*. Hebrews 11:17-19).

Thus foiled in his plan to slay Isaac, Abraham saw nearby a ram tangled in the bushes by his horns, which, without any express command, he took and sacrificed in place of Isaac, his only son whom he loved. Abraham's victory brought another repetition of the posterity-and-blessing-promise, but here emphasized by an oath of Jehovah (vss. 16-18). Then father and son returned joyfully to Beer-sheba; and not long thereafter removed about twenty-eight miles northeast to Hebron (Kirjath-arba), where Sarah died at the age of 127 years.

42. An Oriental Real Estate Deal (Gen. 23). Abraham up to this time had been a wandering nomad without owning any real property. Now that Sarah had died he needed a burial-place of his own. This section of Palestine was in possession of the Hittites, the powerful people of Asia Minor. When Abraham first approached them, oriental courtesy proffered him any burial-place he desired " as a gift." But the patriarch, wholly familiar with the pretentious generosity of those days as of these, in the Near East, engaged in a battle of wits, and tactfully ignored the free-gift proposal, which was really only an aversion to deed away any plot of ground. Abraham found the real man of authority, Ephron the Hittite, and appealed to him directly for the cave of Machpelah. Even Ephron made the same offer as a " free gift," but included the field about the cave, which Abraham had not requested. With the same persistent tactfulness, and desire to avoid any bitter disputes in the future, the patriarch asked the purchase price of both the cave and the field. The Hittite, courteously frustrated in his affectation of generosity, tried another characteristically oriental trick. He pretended that 400 shekels of silver, as between two such important persons as he and Abraham, was a mere bagatelle, though in reality it was a stiff price for the field, the cave and the trees thereabouts. Having won his battle, Abraham weighed out 400 shekels of silver, handed it over, and took acknowledgment of his possession in the presence of the people who passed through the gate of the city; and the property was thus made sure unto Abraham as a possession and a burying-place for that time and for the future.

Sarah was then buried in the newly purchased cave in the field, now held in fee simple by the patriarch Abraham, and for his successors.

43. Rebekah Found for Isaac (Gen. 24). Before Abraham should " pass on " he wished to make sure that Isaac should find a wife among his own Aramæan kinsfolk in Aram-naharaim. It tells us naïvely the customs of the day, how the head servant took an oath of fealty to his master's cause, met servants at the well, gave presents to the family, kin of Abraham, bargained for the return with him, of Rebekah, the family's attitude toward her departure, and the meeting and marriage of Rebekah to Isaac.

This is one of the finest bits of Hebrew prose-writing in the Old Testament. It's a full museum of ancient customs, manners, and rites. The writer does not attempt to harmonize several inconsistencies in the narrative, but sweeps right on until his whole story stands out before the reader in bold relief.

The underlying thought is the providential guidance of the Hebrews towards the fulfilment of their great destiny as the revealers of God to mankind.

44. Abraham's Death and Descendants (Gen. 25:1-18). Abraham, after the death of Sarah, took another wife. His new partner, Keturah, bore him six sons, whose names locate them in the land of Arabia, as the progenitors of some of the Arabs of later days. At 175 years of age he died, and by Isaac and Ishmael was buried in the cave of Machpelah by the side of Sarah his wife.

Ishmael's twelve sons were princes, the heads of tribes and peoples of Arabia, extending down to the border of

Egypt. They were likewise occupants of the lands and deserts of Arabia, more than likely commingled with the descendants of Keturah, Abraham's wife of his last days.

But the son of promise of Abraham was Isaac, whose Aramæan wife, Rebekah, was found in Paddan-aram, beyond the Euphrates, kin of the family that migrated from Ur of the Chaldees. Through Isaac the covenant given Abraham should be fulfilled.

45. Isaac's Career (Gen. 25:19–26:35). Isaac was the least significant of the three patriarchs. His career is really of minor importance. His marriage with Rebekah culminated in the birth of the twin brothers, Esau and Jacob, when Isaac was sixty years old. Although they were twins, and grew up in the same household, they differed greatly in character and tendency. Esau was " a man of the field," a skilful hunter, rough and ready; while " Jacob was a quiet man, dwelling in tents." Esau's proclivities developed along the line of the undisciplined, free-handed, rugged huntsman; Jacob followed the more regular, orderly life of the nomad as had his ancestors. Esau, on the other hand, lacked some of the meanest traits of character possessed by Jacob, especially in the earlier years of his long life. Jacob finally was purged of many of these streaks and developed a great capacity for growth in moral values.

As in so many other cases in the history of Israel, " a famine in the land " turned the tide of events. Isaac went to Abimelech, king of the Philistines (though these aliens did not settle on littoral Palestine until several centuries after the patriarchal age) unto Gerar. Here the covenant made with Abraham was renewed by Jehovah himself. Isaac, according to the story, saved himself as had Abraham, from anticipated death, by claiming that his wife was his sister. Though caught in the lie, he was unpunished by the king of Gerar. Following farming and animal husbandry he became so wealthy that his herdsmen quarreled with the men of Gerar. Peace was finally made and he removed to Beer-sheba, where we have substantially the same story as that regarding Abraham repeated, with another origin of the word, " Beer-sheba."

Esau's marriage with Hittite women was a natural consequence of his free and easy life " in the field," among the peoples who were dominant in this part of the land in that period. We remember that Abraham bought the cave of Machpelah from those same folk.

NOTE ON FIG. 56, tailpiece below: The cave of Machpelah was the centre of a deal between Abraham and Ephron, a Hittite land-owner. In this cave were buried Sarah, Abraham, Rebekah, Isaac, Leah, and Jacob. The interior of the cave, over which now stands a mosque, is supposed to contain the patriarchal tombs, though definite proof thereof has not yet been made public.

CHAPTER IV

Jacob's Dramatic Career

46. Isaac's Blessing Stolen by Jacob (Gen. 25:29-34; 27:1–28:9). The descendants of Esau and Jacob (Edom and Israel) were so diverse in their characters, that the writer inserts two stories of their origin. The first (25:29-34) tells the simple incident of the hungry, famishing Esau selling his birthright to his wily brother Jacob for a simple " red stew."

The second story involved the whole family of Isaac. True to the custom of the times, Isaac wished to bless his first-born, Esau, before he should " go to his fathers." As a natural prerequisite, probably a remnant of an earlier religious rite, the recipient of the blessing should prepare a sacrificial meal. Rebekah overheard Isaac's request of Esau. Being blind, he was unprotected against the wiles of deceivers. Jealous for Jacob's interests, Rebekah devised a

Note on Fig. 7, headpiece above: The left-hand figure is a north Aramæan of Aya near Afrin. On the right is an Aramæan of Merom. These Aramæans seem to have lived near the borders of the powerful Hittites, whose aggressiveness menaced them for several centuries. They were so prominent in the eyes of the Egyptians that they preserved for us these portraits.

73 ✓

heartless though clever scheme to divert her husband's blessing to her favourite son. Jacob, heartily co-operating with his mother, hastily carried out her suggestions and reinforced his deception by brazen-faced lies, and stole the blessing which his father Isaac had intended for Esau.

Esau's pathetic appeal to his father, whose first blessing was known to be irrevocable, wrung from him what was practically a curse when compared with what had been promised Jacob (in vs. 29). It should be rendered: " Far from the rich places of the earth shall you live, far from the dew of heaven above! ", that is, on the desert tracts of the earth he should live by his sword and be a servant to his brother who had stolen his blessing.

Esau's anger boiled, and he resolved in his mind to slay his contemptible brother. Rebekah, indifferent to any moral considerations, pressed Jacob's advantage to the extent of sending him to her brother Laban in Ḥarran, until Esau should forget it.

At this point (27:46–28:9) another story, leaving out Jacob's treachery, and Esau's wrath, tells how Isaac blessed Jacob and sent him to Paddan-aram to find a wife, because Esau had forfeited the blessing by marrying the inhabitants of Canaan.

The compiler of Genesis does not attempt to harmonize these two accounts, but gives the reader the advantage of possessing both of them. They testify at least to the different motives for the journey of Jacob to the land of Harran, where he formed friendships and contracted marriages that kept him in that country for a score of years.

47. Jacob's Flight to Harran (Gen. 28:10-22). The only safety for Jacob from the anger of Esau was in flight. With the urgent co-operation of his parents he started for distant Paddan-aram, or Harran. On one of the laps of his journey he spent the night at a place where he had a marvellous dream,—where he saw angels of God ascending and descending a stairs, at the top of which Jehovah stood and said,

" I am Jehovah, the God of Abraham thy father, and the God of Isaac; the land whereon thou liest, to thee will I give it and to thy seed; and thy seed shall be as the dust of the earth, . . . and in thee shall all the families of the earth be blessed. And, behold, I am with thee and will keep thee whithersoever thou goest, and will bring thee again into this land; for I will not leave thee, until I have done that which I have spoken to thee of " (vss. 13-15).

This realistic dream brought Jacob to himself in fear and trembling, with the remark: " this is none other than the house of God (Beth-el) and this is the gate of heaven." So overwhelmed was he that he vowed a vow that seems to be characteristically Jacobean and oriental.

" If God will be with me, and will keep me in the way that I go, and will give me bread to eat and raiment to put on, so that I come again to my father's house in peace, and Jehovah will be God, then this stone, which I have set up for a pillar, shall be God's house: and of all that thou shalt give me I will surely give the tenth unto thee " (vss. 20-22).

48. Jacob in Paddan-aram (Gen. 29 and 30). Jacob must have spent some weeks on that journey; he must have crossed the Euphrates River and have reached the Aramæans about Harran. The writer of this record without much ado leads him to the shepherds of the country near a well, where the flocks were to be watered. Among the shepherds and their flocks was Rachel, daughter of Laban, with her father's sheep. Thence the romantic story unfolds with a naturalness equalled only by the account of Abraham's servant's search in that same country for Rebekah (Gen. 24), who became the mother of Jacob.

The upshot of Jacob's presence was that he hired out to Laban, his mother's brother, as a shepherd for seven years for the hand of Rachel (his first cousin). On the completion of the seven years the tables are turned on Jacob (who had deceived his father Isaac), and Laban gave him in marriage his oldest daughter Leah, instead of Rachel, justifying the act on the basis of custom. Like a good sport,

Jacob went through the seven days of feasting; but at the end of that time called Laban to account for his ruse, and demanded Rachel. Laban consented on condition of seven more years of service, which Jacob accepted,—fourteen years of service in all for the two sisters.

At the end of the fourteen years, Jacob, seeing that he had made himself invaluable to Laban, and that his family had grown in numbers, proposed that he be sent away to his own country and to his own place. Laban protested that Jehovah had been with him (Laban) because of Jacob, and asked him to remain. Jacob, with true oriental cunning, emphasized the importance of his fourteen years' stay in building up Laban's flocks, and that now he should leave to care for his own house. When Laban asked for Jacob's wage for remaining longer, he replied, " Nothing at all,"— gratis, except the non-white that shall be among the sheep and goats (there were usually very few in an oriental flock). Laban carefully removed to a distance of three days' journey all such as were found at that time in his flocks.

Jacob was quite equal to the " gratis " proposition which he had made, and Laban had accepted. With all his flocks pure white in colour he subjected them to a perfectly well-known and established law of physiology (30:37-41). The hardier of the flock he employed in his devices and the weaker he set aside for Laban's share. " And the man (Jacob) increased exceedingly and had large flocks, and maid-servants and men-servants, and camels and asses " (30:43).

49. Jacob's Flight from Laban (Gen. 31). The words of Laban's sons and the countenance of Laban himself showed Jacob that his welcome had faded away. After conferring with Leah and Rachel, and while Laban was absent at his sheep-shearing, and at the command of the God of Bethel (cf. 28:10 ff.) Jacob, with his wives, children, servants, flocks, herds and all his substance started for his own country. How they crossed the Euphrates River, we are not informed,—heading toward Gilead.

Three days after their departure, Laban being informed of their flight, started in pursuit. After a seven days' chase he is said to have overtaken the caravan " in the mountain of Gilead " (a distance of more than 300 miles from Harran, an enormous stretch for such a train as Jacob's to have travelled in ten days). Immediately Laban fiercely attacked Jacob for his secret flight, for kidnapping his daughters, and for the theft of his teraphim; in reply Jacob elaborated the twenty years' hard work which he had suffered, and Laban's attempts to defraud him of his wages.

After all the affectation of lacerated feelings, of debased honour, and of fraudulent treatment, in which each attempted to outdo the other in his exaggeration of wrongs endured, Laban quietly cooled down and suggested that they make a covenant of peace between them. A stone was set up and a cairn of stones over which neither of the parties should pass with intent to injure the other. This was done in the presence of all the attendants of each. An all-night feast concluded the ceremony, after which they parted,—Laban returning to Harran beyond the river Euphrates, and Jacob going on southward. Inconsistencies in the narrative are not straightened out by the compiler of this story, but are left to the ingenuity of the readers.

50. Peace Made with Esau (Gen. 32–33). Twenty years had passed since Jacob had deceived Isaac and had stolen Esau's blessing. Jacob's conscience had lain dormant during all that time, but now his fear of Esau became so acute that he sent messengers to the country of Esau. Returning, the messengers reported that they had met Esau coming with four hundred men. Jacob's fear and prayer found a way to meet and greet his angry brother. He divided his families and flocks into two companies. After wrestling with an angel all night at Penuel (where his name was changed to Israel), Jacob won not only the favour of God, but the favour of Esau, in spite of his four hundred men of war.

After mutual proffers and good-wills, Esau, on Jacob's

insistence, accepted the present Jacob had set aside for him, and returned to Mt. Seir, his chosen portion of the country. Jacob crossed the Jordan River and camped near Shechem, where he bought a parcel of ground, and built an altar and named it El-Elohe-Israel (" God, the God of Israel ").

51. Jacob at Shechem and Bethel (Gen. 34, 35). Ancient Shechem is the modern Nablous, located between Mounts Ebal and Gerizim. The one pampered daughter of Jacob and Leah, Dinah, " went out to see the daughters of the land." Mingling with strangers about whom she knew next to nothing soon brought a scandal on the entire camp. The compiler has not harmonized the records at hand, so that the whole story is rather clouded. But the plain statement of the case finds Hamor, the Hivite prince of the land, negotiating for intermarriage between his house and Jacob's. The enraged brothers of Dinah took the matter into their own hands and with guile specified that intermarriage could be tolerated only on condition that Hamor's house should submit to the rite of circumcision,—really only a ruse to cripple Hamor's self-defence.

In good faith, the men of the city met the conditions imposed. On the third day, without any warning, Simeon and Levi, brothers of Dinah, treacherously entered the city and, in cold blood, slaughtered all the males without quarter, and rescued Dinah from the house of Shechem (34:26); after which all the sons of Jacob seem to have joined in the general looting of the city, taking captive women and children, flocks and herds and all their substance.

Jacob's rebuke of his sons and his alarm before the inhabitants of the land, and God's word to him, impelled him to demand his sons' purification and the surrender of the foreign gods among them, which gods he buried under a terebinth tree at Shechem. So drastic was the vengeance taken upon the men of Shechem that " a terror of God " (35:5) fell upon all the neighbouring cities; and Jacob was not pursued when he moved southward to Bethel.

The remainder of the chapter is rather fragmentary. It embodies a repetition for the most part of Jacob's blessing promised at Bethel when on his flight to Harran, a change of his name to Israel, reciting also the birth of Benjamin and Rachel's death and burial at Ephrath, a roll of the twelve sons of Jacob, and the death and burial of Isaac by his two sons Esau and Jacob.

Chapter 36 is a genealogical table of the descendants of Esau who lived in Mt. Seir, and on the edge of the Syrian and Arabian deserts.

NOTE ON FIG. 63, tailpiece below: One of the great sacred sites of central Palestine was Shechem, the modern Nablous, situated between Mt. Ebal on the north and Mt. Gerizim on the south. Here Jacob stopped awhile and dug a well, and had trouble with Hamor. Here Joshua gave his farewell address (Josh. 24). Jeroboam was here made king of the northern kingdom (1 Kings 12:25). Later it became the centre of the so-called Samaritan peoples.

PERIOD III

BONDAGE AND WANDERINGS

Egypt and the Wilderness

CHAPTER V

JOSEPH, SAVIOUR OF ISRAEL

52. Joseph's Sale to a Caravan of Midianites (Gen. 37). Jacob's clan occupied considerable territory in central Palestine. His sons were shepherds who followed their flocks wherever they could find plentiful pasture. Joseph, a lad seventeen years old, son of Rachel, was such a favourite of Jacob that he made for him a special garment. Joseph

NOTE ON FIG. 11, headpiece above: This notable picture, on the walls of his tomb at Beni Hasan, was painted by an Egyptian nobleman about 1000 B. C. It represents a caravan of Asiatic peoples, Canaanites or Aramæans, maybe merchants, coming from the hill-country of Absha. Note their dress, their weapons, their wares, and their features. They may have been of mixed blood, Hittite and Aramæan—possibly advance spies of the Hyksos invasion of Egypt.

was a sophisticated youth and had a couple of dreams that seemed to portend his supremacy over his parents and brothers. With an aggressive self-esteem he told these dreams to all of them.

As his brothers were caring for their flocks in the country about Shechem, Jacob sent Joseph to see how they fared. Their first sight of him stirred up their evil passions, and they planned to put him out of the way. Reuben, with the responsibility that usually belongs to an oldest brother, defeated that plan and had him dropped into a pit or dry cistern. A passing caravan of Ishmaelites, on its way to Egypt, gave Judah an opportunity to rescue him from his other brothers, Reuben being absent at the time. He negotiated his sale to this caravan for twenty pieces of silver,— the price of a slave—and it carried him into Egypt.

But what should the brothers report to their father? Judah knew what had become of him, and probably so did Reuben. But the others decided to practice such deceit as would not involve them in any guilt. By dipping the so-called " coat of many colours " in the blood of a goat they could thus deceive their father. The ruse worked, and Jacob in his distress seemed to believe that Joseph had been slain by a wild beast.

53. Joseph a Slave and Prisoner in Egypt (Gen. 39 and 40). While Jacob was mourning for Joseph as dead he (Joseph) was being sold in Egypt as a slave to Potiphar, captain of the guard. Jehovah was with him and gave him favour in the eyes of the Egyptian, and he made him overseer over all his estate. With full confidence in his character and integrity, he put into his hands the management of all his household and field work.

Taking advantage of her husband's absence, Potiphar's wife tried her wiles on the comely young man. Defeated in her craftiness, wherein she made a slighting reference to her husband as " he," her rebuff and chagrin blazed out into a woman's revenge. By falsifying the facts to her master, her lying intrigues threw Joseph into prison, where he was bound,—a very unusual punishment for such an alleged crime.

Within the prison Jehovah was with him (39:21), and he soon won the favour of the keeper, who gave Joseph large liberty and then responsibility. Among the prisoners whom the king consigned to that dungeon under Joseph were two court-officers, the chief butler and the chief baker. Each had a mysterious dream on the same night, and next morning both of them were downcast and sad. Upon inquiry Joseph was told that they had found no one who could interpret their dreams. Joseph's skill as an interpreter gave meanings to their dreams. In due time the interpretations of Joseph came true, but the fortunate chief butler, who had promised to commend Joseph to the king, forgot it.

54. Joseph's Release and Promotion (Gen. 41). Two years after Joseph had been falsely imprisoned, and forgotten by the ungrateful butler, the king himself had a kind of a double dream, which his magicians were unable to explain. The chief butler then, for the first time, came to himself, and recalled his own plight in the prison and his neglect of his promise to Joseph; and he now told the king about him. The Pharaoh sent for Joseph, and the king told him in detail his double dream. Modestly crediting God with the answer which he was about to give, Joseph told Pharaoh that this dream was one, that it foretold seven years of plenty to be followed by seven years of famine. He further advised the Pharaoh to "look out for a man discreet and wise, and set him over the land of Egypt" (41:33).

After taking counsel with his servants, the Pharaoh offered the position to Joseph himself, saying, "forasmuch as God hath showed thee all this, there is none so discreet and wise as thou: thou shalt be over my house, and according unto thy word shall all my people be ruled: only in the throne will I be greater than thou" (41:39, 40). The insignia of office were given him; an Egyptian name, Zaphenath-paneah ("revealer of secrets") was bestowed on

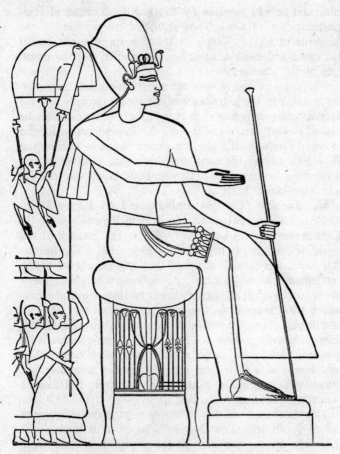

Fig. 72. Seated Statue of Ramses II

This is one of the scores of statues that Ramses II (1292-1225 B. C.) had prepared and set up of himself during his reign of sixty-seven years. His superiority and dignity are here symbolized by the representation of the necessity of having two tiers of fan-bearers to reach his normal height. He is apparently giving royal orders to some suppliant before his throne, possibly regarding the enslaved Hebrews.

him, and he was given as a wife Asenath, daughter of Poti-
phera, priest of On.   Thus equipped as premier of the
kingdom of Egypt, Joseph, at thirty years of age, assumed
his office and made a survey of the country, of the crops,
and of the storehouses.

The years of plenty were already at hand, and the country reveled in the abundance of its yield. Joseph had the
surplus grain stored in each city in such quantities that he
ceased to keep account of it,—all this in preparation for the
years of famine that were just ahead. Lack of rain on the
Blue Nile cut off the usual overflow; and, as often in history, that brought on a famine both in Egypt and its
adjoining lands.

55. Jacob's Distress and Appeal to Egypt (Gen.
42–45). The gnawings of the famine impelled Jacob in
Canaan, to send his ten sons to Egypt, the granary of the
world of that day, to buy food for their relief. The beautiful, lucid, free-flowing story of that trip cannot be safely
condensed without damage. So, follow those rough shepherds to the court of Egypt; listen to their truthful story,
watch their reaction to the harsh reception they received,
and observe how underneath all there was an awakened conscience regarding their evil past. After being figuratively
beaten about by accusations and delays, they were finally
sent home, with their food and their money remitted; but
Simeon was retained as a hostage to test their truthfulness
regarding their homefolks.

This food used up, the writer pictures a dramatic scene
before Jacob will allow Benjamin to go with them,—and
this only on the personal pledge of Judah. Upon their
second arrival in Egypt, the writer sketched Joseph the
ruler as still weaving a plot to retain Benjamin for himself.
But all his oriental craftiness is broken down by the irresistible plea of Judah. Joseph's protracted suspense, by
which he was really punishing his brothers for their past,
suddenly collapsed in the presence of Judah's pathetic picture of Jacob as they had left him for this second journey

(44:14-34). Joseph then revealed his identity, and credited the entire drama of the past few years to a gracious act of God for their preservation.

The entire royal house rejoiced in the celebration; and elaborate provisions were made for the transfer to Egypt of Jacob's clan with all its possessions. Five more years of famine were ahead of them, and only by such action could they be where Joseph could relieve all their necessities.

56. Jacob Went Down and Settled in Egypt (Gen. 46 and 47). The next dramatic scene occurs in Canaan when the eleven sons of Jacob reported that Joseph was still alive, and was ruler of all Egypt, and that he (Jacob) and all his house were to go down to that land of plenty.

Jacob delayed his departure to Egypt only long enough to visit Beer-sheba, to offer " sacrifices to the God of his father Isaac," where he received divine assurance that God would be with him and make of him a great nation. An uneventful journey brought them into Egypt. Judah had been sent ahead to arrange for their advent into the district of Goshen, which Joseph had already assigned to them, because it was in a section of the country, somewhat isolated from the Egyptians, who abominated shepherds. Jacob's entire family who migrated to Egypt is said to have consisted of seventy persons (46:27).

The pathetic meeting of Joseph and Jacob was followed by the latter's audience with the Pharaoh, who granted special privileges to the clan of his premier in the land of Rameses (47:11).

The duration of the famine impoverished the Egyptians and their neighbours, while it enriched the government of the Pharaoh both in cattle and in lands. Only the priests' lands were exempt from such transfer to the royal exchequer.

The Hebrews dwelt prosperously and peacefully in the land of Goshen, becoming rich in possessions and numerous in population.

57. The Last Days of Jacob (Gen. 48 and 49). Jacob

was 130 years old when he went down into Egypt, and had lived seventeen years in the land of Goshen. Knowing that he had only a few more years before him, he made Joseph swear that after his death he would carry him back to Hebron and bury him with his fathers in the cave of Machpelah. Ere this should take place the patriarch bestowed his blessing on Ephraim and Manasseh, the two sons of Joseph.

In chapter 49 we have a poetical characterization and forecast of the twelve sons of Israel addressed to each one of them individually, put into the mouth of Jacob on his death-bed. Sometimes called the " Blessing of Jacob," the picture is not always complimentary, but is quite frank in portraying some of the weaknesses of those sons which had brought anxious moments to their father, who here forecasts them as tribes in the distant future.

The historical situation pre-supposed by these verses would locate the composition of them some centuries later than Jacob's sojourn in Goshen. Compare with this sketch that presented in the thirty-third chapter of Deuteronomy.

58. Death and Burial of Jacob; Death of Joseph
(Gen. 50). At the conclusion of his blessing and charge, Jacob " was gathered unto his people." Being in Egypt, he was embalmed,—the process stretching over forty days. And the Egyptians wept for him seventy days. At the end of this period, at Joseph's request, Pharaoh sent his premier and a great host, a long caravan train, up to Canaan to bury the embalmed body of Jacob in the family burying-place, the cave of Machpelah, at Hebron.

Upon their return the consciences of Joseph's brothers became very acute, leading them to fear that Joseph, after the death of his father, and in accordance with oriental custom, would take vengeance upon them for their treatment of him when he was sold to a caravan of Ishmaelites. They quote an alleged death-bed request of Jacob (not elsewhere mentioned) that Joseph forgive them. Whether they told the truth or not, Joseph treated them kindly and cared for them in the land of Egypt.

Joseph lived eighty years in Egypt after he became premier, and the Hebrews prospered and multiplied in the land. At 110 years of age Joseph died, was embalmed and " put in a coffin in Egypt," and his bones awaited the time when they could be carried up to the land of his fathers.

We close the book of Genesis with the descendants of Jacob still in Egypt, when or under whose reign, we have no definite means of knowing. They had been there more than seventy-five years when Joseph died, probably engaged in the tasks of shepherds as had their forefathers, the patriarchs.

59. A New King over Egypt (Exod. 1). Who was that " new king "? There is some probability that Joseph became premier of Egypt sometime during the rule of the Hyksos Kings, assuming that these foreign potentates were Asiatics of the 13th to the 17th dynasties (1788–1580 B. C.). If that be true, then the " new king " is thought by many scholars to have been Ramses II of the 19th dynasty (1292–1225 B. C.), whose Hittite foes in North Syria compelled him to marshall all his forces to defend his country from their invasion. Recent excavations of the University of Pennsylvania at Beisan in Central Palestine discovered a tablet of Ramses II which states explicitly that he built the store city of Raamses in Egypt with Asiatic Semitic slaves. Not only cities, but fortifications, temples, tombs and public works all over Egypt were constructed by forced labour. Exodus (1:14) states that the lives of the children of Israel were made " bitter with hard service, in mortar and in brick,"—far from their former bleating flocks and lowing herds.

The precautions taken to prevent the further increase of the children of Israel, as a possible menace to the security of the government on the Asiatic border, were natural and seemingly necessary from the Egyptian's military point of view.

The most plausible " new king " seems, then, to have been Ramses II, whose rule covered 1292–1225 B. C., and about whom we have so many sources of information, and with whose personal granite figures Egypt is so abundantly supplied.

NOTE ON FIG. 71, tailpiece below: Ramses II of the Nineteenth Dynasty ruled Egypt sixty-seven years (1292-1225 B. C.) and is generally believed to have been the oppressor of the Hebrews. He was Egypt's greatest builder both of temples and cities, among them Pithom and Raamses. His treaty with the Hittites after the battle of Kadesh was the first comprehensive international document in history. His mummy was found at Thebes in 1881, and is now preserved in the National Museum at Cairo, Egypt.

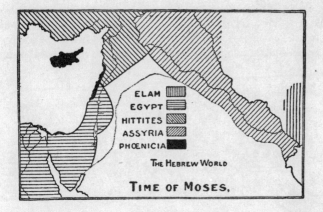

ELAM
EGYPT
HITTITES
ASSYRIA
PHŒNICIA

THE HEBREW WORLD

TIME OF MOSES.

CHAPTER VI

LEADERSHIP OF MOSES IN EGYPT

60. Birth and Royal Education of Moses (Exod.
2:1-10). The drastic means taken to prevent Israel's increase fired the inventive genius of the victims. Moses'
parents put him in a basket of papyrus, daubed it with
bitumen (as had the mother of Sargon I in Babylonia long
centuries before), and floated it among the flags on the bank
of the Nile. Pharaoh's daughter, on a bathing visit, found
it and rescued the child; and accepted as a wet nurse, a
Hebrew woman, in reality his own mother, adroitly suggested by the babe's sister, who was standing near the river.
Thus nursed daily by his own mother as long as necessary,
she left him to be reared in the royal palace of Egypt as
the adopted son of the Pharaoh's daughter.

NOTE ON MAP 2, headpiece above: Egypt had become master of Syria
up to Hamath when Moses was in his prime. The Hittites ruled Asia
Minor and part of Syria. Assyria was lord of Mesopotamia. Phœnicia was now entering on the control of the Mediterranean Sea, and
their Syrian coast cities.

As a prince in the royal house he was reared, instructed, and trained. Even the Acts (7:22) states that he " was instructed in all the wisdom of the Egyptians,"—a very large contract if carried out literally. That would mean

Fig. 17. Egyptian Brick-Makers

Action is the mainspring of these scenes, painted on the walls of a tomb. They represent the building of the most famous temple of all Egypt—Amon at Thebes. The workmen are Aramæan and Phœnician captives of Thutmose III, taken in his wars in southwestern Asia. In an inscription over the painting we read—" The taskmaster says to the labourers, ' The rod is in my hand; keep busy [be not idle].' " The workmen are burdened with only a minimum of clothing.

First Scene from the left : From a pond growing water lilies and surrounded by trees two men are carrying water; below, two are cutting off portions of mud; one is carrying it to the molder, who is turning a brick out of the mold; another is setting his cutter; another piling up the bricks to dry. The little inscription on the scene says: " for the new building of the storehouse of the god Amon of Apt, at Thebes."

Second Scene from the left : A man emptying a bucket of soft mud, being watched by a sitting taskmaster; two men carrying loads of brick with yokes and cords. A second taskmaster standing and " brandishing " his rod; one man carrying on his shoulder a vessel of mud; another returning with yoke and cords for another load of brick.

Fig. 73. Stela of Ramses II Found at Beth-Shean

The mound of Beth-Shean (Fig. 13) has been excavated for some years by the University of Pennsylvania. Among their notable finds none so far exceeds this stela. On it Ramses II boasts of his victories in the north about Hamath. For us the significant statement, if correctly rendered, says that he built the city of Ramses (Raamses) with Semitic labourers,—impliedly with Israelite slave labour.

in the language, the literature, the religion, the mythology, and in statecraft.

61. Practical Education of Moses (Exod. 2:11-24). Moses was doubtless familiar with the slavery of the Hebrews, whom he must have often seen as he rode about with his royal retinue. One day he strolled out alone and chanced to see an Egyptian slave-master beating a Hebrew. His loyal Hebrew blood boiled, and he slew the Egyptian and covered him with sand. The next day he went out again and saw two Hebrews quarrelling. His sense of justice led him to interfere in favour of the " under dog." Moses touched a live wire, for the rebuffed Hebrew said: " Thinkest thou to kill me as thou killedst the Egyptian? "

The sand had not hidden Moses' crime. News of it spread like wildfire, even to the royal palace. Pharaoh's anger sent out detectives to " get Moses." But the impetuous young prince fled the country, toward the east, toward Midian. There at a well, as in the cases of Abraham's servant, and of Jacob, destiny met him. The daughters of Jethro (Reuel), priest of Midian, reported him to tneir father, who employed him as a shepherd, and also made him his son-in-law.

What a sudden roundabout face for Moses! From a favourite son of the royal palace in Egypt he suddenly became a refugee in a strange land. From the luxuries of the court of the Pharaoh he was forced into the hardships and dangers of a shepherd in the wilderness of Midian. From the prospects of becoming a high officer in the Egyptian government, he is now glad to accept the menial service of a slave among the nomads of the desert. Henceforth his solitude became his instructor, and his meditation a source of strength.

62. Moses' Call and Return to Egypt (Exod. 3). Moses' meditation had now reached a point where, the king of Egypt having died, he had forgotten all his remorseful reflections. He now deliberated upon the dread bondage of his people and how they could be delivered. While deeply engrossed in thoughts of the possibility of such release and God's part in it all, " the angel of Jehovah appeared to him in a flame of fire out of the midst of a bush " (vs. 2). Out of the flame came God's message to Moses. The affliction and sorrow of the abused and oppressed Hebrew slaves had come up before him, and he had now come down to rescue them from the hands of the Egyptians, to take them to a good land and a large, flowing with milk and honey,—to the land now occupied by Canaanite, Hittite, Amorite, Perizzite, Hivite, and Jebusite.

How startled was Moses when God said to him: " Come now therefore, and I will send thee unto Pharaoh, that thou mayest bring forth my people the children of Israel out of Egypt! " Moses' modesty and reticence shrunk from any such huge task, even when God said to him: " I will be with thee."

But the Hebrews might ask him the name of the God who sent him unto them. To which he should reply, " I am " sent me unto you. Moses was so hesitant about assuming that responsibility that God and he engaged in a colloquy about methods and means of putting the plan into effect. Finally, Moses put up the plea that he was not eloquent, that he could not persuade Pharaoh to follow his suggestions. God quickly brushed aside any such pretext by naming Aaron as his spokesman.

Upon Moses' appeal to Jethro, his father-in-law, he was allowed to set out on his journey from the wilderness life, where he had spent so many years in virtual exile. His pretext for returning was to visit his brethren in Egypt to see whether they were still alive; but the men who had sought his life were all dead.

As he was passing along with his wife and two sons through the wilderness toward Egypt, Aaron, in obedience to a command of God, met him at the mountain of God (Sinai). The two brothers talked over the wondrous messages which they had received regarding their enslaved brethren, and then turned their faces toward Egypt to meet the God-given task which was theirs, confident and unafraid.

63. Moses and Aaron Face the Pharaoh (Exod. 5–9). On arriving in Goshen, the two brothers called together the elders of Israel for counsel. Filled with a divine courage, Moses and Aaron, conscious of God's presence and help and of their responsibility, made bold to face the ruling monarch of Egypt,—probably Merneptah, son of Ramses II.

Their first appeal fell flat. Pharaoh refused their request point blank, and made heavier the burdens of the slaves. Taskmasters and officers in a vengeful spirit drove the Hebrews with lashes into harder tasks.

Reassured of ultimate success, Moses and Aaron again ventured to enter the royal palace. God had predicted Pharaoh's continuous refusal to let Israel go, until the final test. One " wonder " after another, Nile turned into blood, frogs, lice, flies, murrain, boils, hail, locusts, and thick darkness, sometimes cowed the proud ruler; but removal of the pressure saw him rebound again and again into a more obstinate attitude of defiance. Five of the first nine plagues forced Pharaoh to call for Moses and Aaron, only to relent and defy them again. After the ninth plague, Pharaoh drove Moses and Aaron from his presence, refusing ever again to allow them to see his face.

The details of these plagues are vividly described, thus emphasizing the terrific severity of the pests on a people so strictly cleanly as the Egyptians. All these " signs and wonders " were known to the land in a small way, but their intensity, swiftness and severity not only humiliated the royal government, but insulted a god in the case of each individual plague. These first nine plagues were natural phenomena brought on in such rapid succession as to stagger the obstinacy of the Pharaoh.

NOTE ON FIG. 57, opposite: Ramses II's son and successor to the throne of Egypt was Merneptah. His accession was attended by political upheavals among all his subjects, so that within five years it was entirely possible for Israel to escape from the land of their bondage without serious risk to themselves. This is thought to have taken place about 1220 B. C.

Fig. 57. Portrait of Merneptah

CHAPTER VII

ESCAPE OF ISRAEL FROM EGYPT

64. The Passover and Last Plague (Exod. 11:1–12:36, 42-51; 13:1-10). As a preliminary to the tenth plague, the Israelites were "to ask" of their Egyptian neighbours jewels of silver and jewels of gold, which, it seems, they (the Egyptians) were quite ready to grant. Moses had been foretold that when Israel was allowed to go, it would be a sudden and speedy rush to freedom, that they would be driven out, although Pharaoh would not, after the ninth plague had cleared up, let them go.

On the night before the execution of the tenth plague, Israel's calendar year was determined. It was the first month (Nisan=March-April) of the year. On the tenth day of that month they should select a lamb without blemish. On the fourteenth day each family or two families should kill it at even, and sprinkle its blood on the side-posts and lintels of the houses. Already equipped for the march, they should eat it roasted, with bitter herbs and unleavened bread,—symbols of sorrow and haste. This was to be a perpetual memorial, observed annually on the same

NOTE ON MAP 3, opposite. The Delta and Sinaitic Peninsula: On a fertile little area, the land of Goshen, the children of Israel had been settled and had multiplied and had served. Thence they escaped under Moses through the Red Sea, about 1220 B. C., into the trackless wilderness of Sinai for their forty years' training.

Map 5. Canaan Apportioned to the Tribes of Israel

However and whenever the conquest of Canaan took place, the tribes received approximately these portions of the territory of Canaan, each accepting a few unconquered cities and strongholds of the Canaanites, —to test their martial and moral characters.

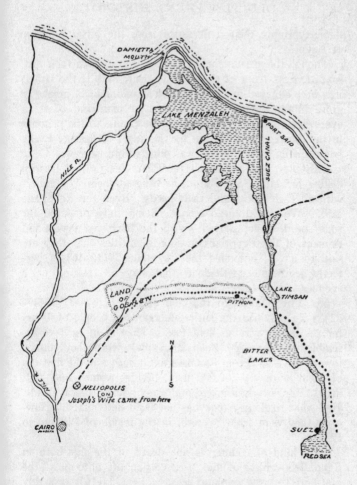

Fig. 31. Plan of Goshen and the Eastern Delta

The land of Goshen was a small district cut across by one of the smaller arms of the Nile, insuring perpetual water supply. From there eastward to the north extension of the Red Sea was an ancient canal on which ships sailed. Note the location of Pithom, so thoroughly excavated by Naville in 1883. The Hebrews crossed the sandy shallows somewhere east or southeast of that old city.

date, typifying their deliverance from the bitter bondage of Egypt.

Though the accounts are somewhat confused in their presentation the tenor of the story is clear. While the Israelites were engaged in their feasting at midnight, a great cry arose in all Egypt,—the first-born of man and beast in every home from the Pharaoh on the throne to the prisoner in the dungeon was smitten by the angel of death. Every home among the Egyptians was plunged into sorrow.

This blow was too much for Pharaoh's pride. Hastily calling for Moses and Aaron, he ordered them, " Begone," with all their flocks and their herds. Even the Egyptians said, " We are all dead men." Being fully prepared for such speed, Israel started,—with the borrowed jewels and raiment of the Egyptians in such quantities that they are said to have " despoiled the Egyptians " (12:36), a perfectly legitimate method in that day of treating one's enemies.

65. The March to the Sea (Exod. 12:37-41; 13:17-22). To mobilize the entire unorganized people of Israel for the march was no light task. They seem to have assembled at Raamses (Zoan, or Tanis), when they started toward the sea. From Raamses to Succoth was the first lap of their journey,—600,000 men, besides women and children. Hangers-on, a mixed multitude, joined the cavalcade. Just what road they took has not been determined. However, they went from Succoth, in the region of Pithom, to Etham.

As a kind of counter to the death of the first-born in Egypt Jehovah spake unto Moses, " Sanctify unto me all the first-born . . . of man and beast " (13:2, 11-16); probably spoken as they were on their march to freedom, to impress upon them the real significance of their escape from the sword of the angel of death.

We have no means of knowing just how much time was consumed in the mobilization and march to the sea. But their leaders were the pillar of cloud by day and the pillar of fire by night (13:22). From Etham they encamped "before Pi-hahiroth, between Migdol and the sea, before Baal-zephon: over against it shall ye encamp by the sea" (14:2).

By this time, Pharaoh had come to himself, and doubtless, being a kind of fatalist, he said, "It's no use to mourn over the dead. I'll get these slaves yet." With his choicest 600 chariots and troops he started in pursuit of the escaping Hebrews. The sight of the oncoming Egyptian warriors terrified the refugees, who were calmed down, however, only by the words of their leader, Moses, "Fear not, stand still, and see the salvation of Jehovah, which he will work for you to-day" (14:13).

Israel, encamped on the shore of the sea, was protected and hidden by the "angel of God" and the cloud in their rear from their pursuers, the host of Pharaoh.

66. Crossing the Sea (Exod. 14:21–15:21). The fleeing Hebrews trembled with fear as they were trapped between Egyptian chariots and the inexorable sea. At Jehovah's command Moses stretched out his rod over the waters, and an east wind blew all through the night and blew back the shallow waters, so that the sand was bared, and allowed the Hebrews to cross on the clean sand-shallows, with the deeper water on either side of them as a protection ("wall," cf. 1 Sam. 25:16) against a flank attack.

Screened by the cloud and fire from an onset in the rear on the part of the pursuing Egyptians, the tremulous host of Israel, with flocks and herds, reached the desert shore on the east. By the time the Egyptians had gotten well along over the sand-shallows, the wind having died down, the waters gradually came back to their normal level. Percolating through the sands, it now made the crossing a kind of quicksand, in which wheels, animals and men mired and sank. The Egyptians were caught in the rolling-in sea, and drowned to a man; and "Israel saw the Egyptians dead upon the seashore" (14:30). A similar baring of sands by wind is reported by Gen. Tulloch when a strong east wind

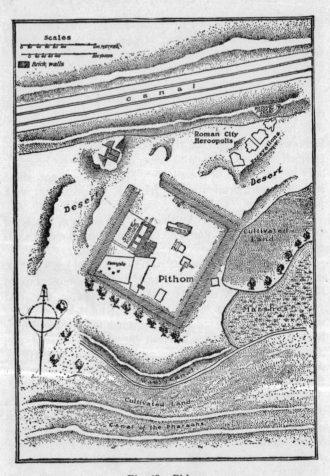

Fig. 69. Pithom

In his *Store-City of Pithom and the Route of the Exodus* (1888),
Naville tells his story of how in 1883 he uncovered this strategic
border, store-city of Ramses II. Surrounded by a thick wall, 750
feet long on each side, were great granaries, a temple, and other
attendant buildings. It was located on the southern bank of the
fresh-water canal that connected the Nile with the Red Sea,—
immediately in the line of escape of the Hebrew slaves.

drove back the waters of Lake Menzaleh seven miles (*Victoria Inst.*, Vol. 28, p. 267).

In celebration of their escape we have that wonderful pæan of victory in the poem of Exodus 15. It magnifies Jehovah, the incomparable, and his power in overthrowing the Egyptians, and in leading out of bondage into freedom his own people. It was composed to teach Israel their significance as a people under the leadership of God.

67. The Route of the Exodus (Exod. 15:22-27). The exact route taken by the fleeing Israelites has not been certainly fixed. It evidently was not near the head of the Red Sea, nor in the far north near the Mediterranean. Most probably the crossing was made at the modern Lake Timsah, or Crocodile Lake, a shallow body of water through which the Suez Canal passes. Before the cutting of the Canal it was " a mere pond of brackish water, and full of reeds,"—hence quite shallow. Its location just east of ancient Pithom, and between the guards of the frontier where no one would have suspected a place of crossing, seem to give us at least all the conditions necessary for locating this as the place of Israel's escape through the sea.

When the hosts of Israel had reached the desert they turned towards the southeast along the eastern shore of the Bitter Lakes (Marah). The " bitter " character of these lakes indicates that they were salt (sea) water. By turning towards the southeast the horde of escaping Israelitish slaves, with all their flocks, herds, hangers-on, and impedimenta would have gone south of any possible guards who might have been established opposite the usual crossing-places of merchants, travellers, and the omnipresent bedouin, who wandered into and out of Egypt. Scarcity of water in the desert raised the first murmurings of the miscellaneous mob. After sweetening the first undrinkable water and further flight to the southeast they came to Elim with its twelve springs and seventy palm trees,—all available for their needs. They had not yet sensed the situation into which they were plunged. The opulence of Egypt was

behind them, and the poverty of the desert before them.
The satisfaction of plenty to eat in the land of Goshen,
would soon be exchanged for the near-hunger of the desert.
The activities of a busy life, even though partly forced,
would soon be reversed in the idleness of a wilderness with
its scarcity of food and pasture. Even Moses himself was
not fully aware of the dread complaints and murmurings
that would soon break out in the host.

NOTE ON FIG. 43, tailpiece below: The "Israel" tablet of Merneptah
was found by Petrie in 1896 in the mortuary temple of Amenhotep
III at Thebes (a cut may be seen in MOT, p. 193). In this stela near
the bottom, we have in two lines the earliest known mention of "Israel," as translated in the text. After the word *Israel*, you see a man
and woman kneeling, and behind them three short lines in line,—a
plural sign, indicating them multiplied many times; that is, a great
number of Israel.

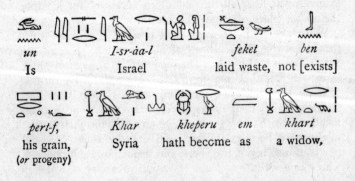

un   *I-sr-àa-l*   *feket*   *ben*
Is   Israel   laid waste, not [exists]

pert-f,   *Khar*   *kheperu*   *em*   *khart*
his grain,   Syria   hath become   as   a widow,
(*or* progeny)

CHAPTER VIII

THRILLS ABOUT SINAI

68. The Wilderness. Geographically the wilderness (desert) is one of the most interesting parts of the earth's surface. In the first place, its backbone and main peaks are the southern terminus of the mountain spur that projects southward from the Taurus and Lebanons in the far north. In the next place, it is partially wedged in between

NOTE ON FIG. 90, headpiece above: Since the sixth century this mountain, called by the Arabs *Jebel Musa* (Mount of Moses), has been regarded as the Sinai of Exodus. Geologically it belongs to the oldest epochs of earth history. Its granite and porphyry have defied the ravages of time, and rise to-day almost 8,000 feet above sea level. About its base imagination sees the escaped Israelites encamped for about a year, while they were being organized and trained under the leadership of Moses and his helpers in the laws of worship and life.

the Gulf of Suez on the west and the Gulf of Akabah on the east. It leans against Egypt on the west, Arabia on the east, and Palestine on the north. It is mainly desert with a few springs here and there that serve as centres for nomadic shepherds Its population has always been of the nomadic type, as it has had no sizable cities and no central government. Much of its western half had been tributary to Egypt through the early centuries, as it was a source of metals, and a route for caravans from the north and east. Its source of food was flocks and herds that occupied the possible pasturage localities over the entire area of its forbidding surface.

This, in brief, was the outlook for the mob of escaped slaves who were under the leadership of Jehovah and of Moses. With practically no food in sight except their accompanying flocks, this mass of a reported 600,000 men, besides women, children and hangers-on, were now face to face with this wilderness-desert.

69. In the Wilderness of Sin (Exod. 16 and 17). The vastness of the wilderness was broken up into several smaller subdivisions. From Elim, with its twelve springs, the host plunged into the wilderness of Sin on the 15th day of the second month. The pangs of hunger brought an outcry of the throng against Moses for having led them out into the wilderness to die,—far from "the flesh-pots of Egypt."

To meet the murmur and menace of the threatening people Jehovah rained upon the camp manna for the mornings and quail in the evenings, the manna to be gathered and used under strict regulations. This manna may have been similar to the exudations of certain trees or plants (*cf.* Num. 11:7-9) that are found to this day at some seasons in some parts of the desert, though not in sufficient quantity to supply the needs of a large multitude of persons. A burning thirst produced another murmur against Moses at Rephidim which Jehovah solved by ordering him to strike a rock in Horeb with his historic rod, whence poured forth water for all the host. Moses called the place Massah ("temptation") and Meribah ("strife").

Jealous of any intruders on their preserves, the Amalekites, a powerful desert tribe who were nearby, attacked these Hebrews with evil intent. At Moses' command Joshua drafted enough able-bodied men to meet their onslaught, and, finally, by the inspiration of Moses, Aaron, and Hur, he completely discomfited them. The fate of this same Amalek in the future was revealed to Moses and Joshua by Jehovah.

In this month also, Jethro, Moses' father-in-law, with whom he had spent long years in the great wilderness, made him a visit. A pious man, he offered sacrifices to God, and Moses gave a banquet for him with the elders of Israel. At his wise suggestion Moses organized the people into groups and gave a certain responsibility to the head of each group in all matters of dispute or cases at law. The probable outcome of the visit of Jethro for his own people was a kind of pact or alliance of the Midianites with Israel. Another record (Num. 10:29 ff.) seems to say that Hobab, son of Jethro, became Israel's guide through the mazes of the wilderness.

70. The First Doings at Sinai (Exod. 19). In the third month after their escape from Egypt, the Hebrews reached the wilderness of Sinai (named after Sin, the moongod of Babylonia), at the foot of the mountain, probably *Jebel Musa*, now a well-known peak. Moses is commanded to deliver to Israel this message—" Ye have seen what I did unto the Egyptians, . . . Now therefore, if ye will obey my voice indeed, and keep my covenant, then ye shall be mine own possession from among all peoples: for all the earth is mine: and ye shall be unto me a kingdom of priests, and a holy nation " (19:4-6).

In response the people covenanted with Jehovah to do all he required of them. Now Jehovah commanded a two-day purification, and on the third day he would come down on the mountain in full sight of all the people. Moses sanctified them and they beheld the clouds, and they all trembled before the awe-inspiring sights and sounds. Moses, called up to the mountain by Jehovah, was given a message and sent down again. Fearful that the people would be crazed by the overwhelming terrors, Moses warned them to stay outside the bounds set about the foot of the mountain.

71. The Ten Commandments (Exod. 20:1-17; 24; 34; Deut. 5:6-21). There are three or four accounts of the events of the stay at Sinai. In this first record the " ten words " seem to have been spoken by Jehovah directly to the people. While there is some confusion in the order and detail of events, they all agree that God spoke through Moses, that a covenant was established between Jehovah and his people, and that the laws presented a new and larger idea of God and of man's obligations to him, and of man's duty to man.

These so-called " words," commandments (mainly prohibitions) were the stepping-stones to the covenant between Jehovah and Israel. Of these two pentads the first defines man's duty to God, closing with honour to father and mother (Lev. 19:3). The second pertains wholly to our relations to our fellow-man. These ten are sometimes called the ethical-decalogue in distinction from the ceremonial or ritual one in Exodus 34 and elsewhere.

In their original form they probably consisted merely of a single line apiece, like the brief, short sentences of some law-statutes.

These " words " recognize the presence of other gods in those days; of images of things in the heavens and on the earth that were objects of worship; of adoration and worship of such images; of the jealousy of God for his own as over against those who hated him; and of his favour towards those who loved him and kept his commandments. The sacredness of the name of Jehovah is safeguarded by a prohibition against the profane use of that name. The sanctity of the sabbath day is maintained by the prohibition of any work on that day, either by a man or any of his own. As a corollary of man's duty to God the fifth commandment requires our honour of father and mother (*cf*. Lev. 19:3).

Duty to man is concentrated in five of the fundamentals of the moral life, closing with one that is wholly in the mind, intentional and not always apparent to the bystander. Jesus summarized them all in one double sentence: " Thou shalt love the Lord thy God with all thy heart, and with all thy soul, and with all thy mind. . . . Thou shalt love thy neighbour as thyself. On these two commandments the whole law hangeth, and the prophets " (Matt. 22:37-40).

In short, the God of the Hebrews was different from other gods whom Israel must have seen, and some had worshipped them in Egypt. He required reverence and honour; an observance of the sabbath; due honour toward parents. He prohibited murder, impurity, theft, lying, and covetousness. Banish all these acts and his demands would soon result in an ethical life such as was pleasing to him who would be their God, and they would be his people,—a holy nation (19:6).

The observance of these " words " by the Hebrews was so inadequate and impotent, that at times we could almost declare them inoperative in their lives. Polygamy, slavery, and many other evils of that day find no place in the list.

72. The Little Book of the Covenant (Exod. 20:22–23:33). Henceforth Moses was to be a mediator between Jehovah and Israel. Through him Israel should receive her orders. " An altar of earth," or of unhewn stone, was the only kind they were primitively to build and use for their offerings to Jehovah.

The " Little Book of the Covenant " is probably the earliest code of laws laid down for the Hebrews, and may have been partly compiled by Moses. Its more than thirty similarities to the Hammurabi Code (2123–2081 B. C.) point most probably to the existence among primitive peoples of many precedents or laws that were a common possession. We have embodied in this code those which would be most usable in the regulations of the life of the Hebrews, who had not yet entirely emerged from a crude and primitive state.

This group of laws is civil and not ritual or ceremonial. It specifies enactments that are applicable to a people living an agricultural rather than a nomadic life. Society, if such it could be called, was primitive in its methods; note especially the *lex talionis* (21:23, 24) enjoined as a punishment for crime. The old death penalty was dealt out for crimes that shock our sense of right, revealing a rude and heartless idea of justice. However, many of these so-called laws, civil and criminal, are to-day current among the Arabs of the desert.

The administration of these statutes was in the hands of judges whose decision was thought to be the sentence of God himself. Such administration would convince the people that behind all their doings there was a God of justice who would gradually lift them to higher levels of moral living, and prepare them for contact with other peoples in the future with whom they were not to make covenants nor pacts nor alliances. All these to insure them against falling into the service of other gods who would be a snare to them, and defeat the high purpose in store for Israel.

73. Set Feasts Established (Exod. 23:14-17; Lev. 23; Num. 28 and 29). The writer has added to the Covenant Code several specifications, among them that most important order for set feasts. "Three times thou shalt keep a feast unto me in the year" (Exod. 23:14-17): (1) On the 14th day of the first month "at even," is Jehovah's passover, and on the 15th, covering seven days, the feast of unleavened bread,—all in commemoration of the Exodus. (2) After entrance into the promised land, the feast of first-fruits of the harvest or weeks, or wheat harvest. This was celebrated fifty days after the feast of unleavened bread (Lev. 23:16), hence called pentecost,—a dedication of the first-fruits of their labours to Jehovah. (3) At the end of the harvest year the feast of ingatherings, or tabernacles, as a thanksgiving for the abundant yield of the season. This was observed on the 15th day of the seventh

Fig. 35. The Stela of Hammurabi

This diorite column, almost eight feet high, was found by the French expedition at Susa in Dec., 1901–Jan., 1902. It had been carved at Babylon and had been carried away as a trophy of victory by an Elamite army. It is now one of the prize stelae of the Louvre, Paris. On it are incised about 3,600 lines in the beautiful Babylonian script of the twenty-first century B. C. Hammurabi was the sixth king of the first dynasty of Babylon (2123–2081 B. C.).

month, originally seven days but extended to eight. These three feasts were to be observed each year by all males in Israel with all the sacrificial requirements specified in the law.

In addition there were other and minor feasts or fasts, such as the sabbath, the new-moon, the trumpets, the atonement and cyclic festivals of various kinds. Though generally observed in the periods of Israel's loyalty to Jehovah, they were not on the same plane with the three set feasts of the nation.

74. The Covenant Reaffirmed (Exod. 24). At the base of the mountain Moses built an altar, and burnt-offerings and peace-offerings were offered thereon. With half the blood he sprinkled the altar. Then having written down the words of Jehovah (for " Moses was trained in all the wisdom of the Egyptians ") their leader read out of the scroll " in the audience of the people: and they said, All that Jehovah hath spoken will we do, and be obedient. And Moses took the blood, and sprinkled it on the people, and said, Behold the blood of the covenant, which Jehovah hath made with you upon all these conditions " (vss. 7, 8).

As a confirmation feast, Moses, Aaron and his two sons, and seventy chosen elders went up above the people and " saw the God of Israel," and " they beheld God, and did eat and drink,"—a community feast of men and God, as seen among other peoples.

On the supposition that the people were dependable Moses made his fourth ascent into the mountain, with Joshua as " his minister," and left them with Aaron and Hur at the foot of it. Moses, covered by the cloud that crowned the mountain, remained there forty days and forty nights (vss. 18 and 34:28) in communion with Jehovah.

75. The Golden Calf (Exod. 32). The long absence of Moses and Joshua on the top of the mountain discouraged the people. They suspected their leaders had been lost, and God had forgotten them. With such an outlook for the future they gathered about Aaron and demanded a

Fig. 34. Hammurabi Receiving a Message from the God Shamash

At the top of the stela of Hammurabi we see these notable figures. The sun-god Shamash seated on a throne, wearing a robe with flounces, is handing some symbols, apparently a sceptre and a ring, to Hammurabi, the codifier of the laws, written on the stela. He rests his feet on what appear to be mountains. From behind his shoulders proceed rays marking him as the sun-god. His upper lip seems to be clean shaven, the custom of that time. He was the patron deity of the city Sippar.

god to lead them on their further journeys. Aaron, not able to resist the demand, speedily told them what to do. Out of their golden trinkets he fashioned a little metal calf, and even said, " This is thy god, O Israel, which brought thee up out of the land of Egypt." So devout was Aaron in this new service that he built an altar and proclaimed a feast to Jehovah, as represented by the molten calf. In their joy over their new visible god " the people sat down to eat and to drink, and rose up to play."

The golden calf must have recalled to the freed slaves what they had seen in Egypt, and doubtless what some of them had learned to reverence and even to worship. In doing this they had already violated the second commandment and broken their covenant made less than two months before.

While the Hebrews were celebrating their victory and rejoicing over their new god, Moses suddenly came down into the camp. Although already forewarned of God, he was not prepared for such an apostasy. Hot with anger, he dashed to the ground the two tablets of testimony which were in his hands, and seized the calf and ground it to powder and sowed that powder on the drinking-water of the people. Aaron, his brother, came in for a sharp rebuke for his part in the apostasy.

Moses, in his wrath, called for volunteers to defend the cause of Jehovah. The Levites rushed, armed, to his relief, and he ordered them to take vengeance on the violators of their sacred covenant with Jehovah. Three thousand of the guilty were slain in the onslaught on that day.

On the morrow, Moses renewed his plea, which he had already begun on the mountain, to save the rebels from complete extinction at the hand of their God with whom they had made the covenant. When Moses asked that he himself be blotted out of the book if God would not forgive them, Jehovah both relented, and promised to send his angel before Moses; but added, " Whosoever hath sinned against me, him will I blot out of my book " (32:33). The subsequent events that befell the people in their wilderness journeyings certainly verify this threat.

76. The Tent of Meeting (Exod. 25–31; 35–40). While Moses was on the mountain it is stated that Jehovah gave him the form and specifications for the Tent of Meeting with all its paraphernalia, its attendants and its place in their religious services and life. It was to consist of an enclosure or tabernacle, in which the tent was the main feature; divided into (1) the " holy of holies,' containing the ark, mercy seat, and cherubim, and to be accessible to the high priest only; (2) " the holy place," containing the altar of incense, table and vessels, and candlestick and vessels, both under one common roof. (3) " the court," containing the great altar and the laver of brass. The uniforms of the priests were specified in detail, and even the oil of anointing,—in fact all the services are laid out in minutiæ for this centre of the religious life of the camp, though pitched outside of it,—to be shielded by the cloud and glory of Jehovah.

Materials for the building of the Tent of Meeting were provided by the people: " whosoever is of a willing heart, let him bring it, Jehovah's offering,—gold, and silver, and brass, and blue, and purple," etc., etc. The construction of the Tent of Meeting was carried out by men who had understanding and knowledge in all manner of workmanship, in devising skilful work in gold and in silver, in cutting stones for setting and in carving wood,"—chief among whom was Bezalel (31:2 ff.). Under his leadership the entire task was carried through in every detail and the " sanctuary " dedicated with sacred and solemn ceremonies. Over it all hovered the cloud, and " the glory of Jehovah filled the tabernacle " (40:34).

77. The Priesthood (Exod. 28–30). About the time specifications were being given for the Tent of Meeting, Moses was commanded to set apart his brother Aaron and his four sons (28:1) to minister in the priest's office,—well-known functionaries among other religions in those days.

For these priests who should serve at the tabernacle elaborate vestments were required and designed. These were to be made by skilled workmen out of the most valuable materials. They included as characteristic features for Aaron, the ephod, the robe of the ephod, the breastplate with its settings of twelve precious and choice stones, a coat of checker work, a mitre (or turban) and a girdle.

After they were consecrated by sacrifices and offerings to the sacred duties that devolved upon them, Aaron was arrayed in the most gorgeous attire, and his sons in modest robes, at the door of the Tent of Meeting. There they were to officiate in the regular daily and the special sacrifices for themselves and for the entire congregation of Israel. More than this, Aaron and his sons " shall have the priesthood by a perpetual statute," throughout all generations,—of course with the usual proviso, that they remain faithful to Jehovah.

This divine appointment guaranteed the presence at the tabernacle at all times of the proper persons to officiate in all matters of sacrifice before Jehovah.

78. Moses Communes with Jehovah (Exod. 33 and 34). There are no more interesting revelations to Moses than those made in these two chapters, though somewhat confused in their presentation. Moses was commanded to take the people up to the promised land, but they on their part should strip off their ornaments during all their journey, and maintain a humble attitude before Jehovah.

The Tent of Meeting was pitched without the camp, and to this anyone came who sought Jehovah. When Moses himself went to the tent, the cloud came down and stood at its door, and all the people rose up and every man stood at the door of his tent and worshipped. " And Jehovah spake unto Moses face to face, as a man speaketh to his friend " (33:11).

Moses sought proof that Jehovah would lead up Israel hence to the promised land. And he was given it by a test of Jehovah's passing by while he (Moses) was hidden in a cleft of a rock, so that he could see his (Jehovah's) back

but not his face, " for man shall not see my face and live "
(33:20).

Chapter 34 is a ritual version of the ten commandments
(of 21:1-17), with amplifications and comments that give
those " words " a wide and practical application. Sand-
wiched in here and there are other items and orders that
often puzzle the reader, as, " Thou shalt not boil a kid in
its mother's milk " (vs. 26). This account represents
Moses as re-appearing at the foot of the mountain with the
two tablets of the testimony intact, and with such a brilliant countenance that he was obliged to cover it with a
veil when he approached the people; though he removed it
when he entered the Tent of Meeting to commune with
Jehovah,—symbolically representing the intimate relationship of Moses with the source of all his strength and
inspiration.

NOTE ON FIG. 61, tailpiece: Finished in 1545, Michelangelo's
Moses was designed to decorate
the tomb of Pope Julius II. It
now rests in the church of " St.
Peter in Chains" at Rome, and
is one of the great masterpieces
sought out by every lover of art
who travels to the imperial city.
The horns on the head are due
to an interpretation of Exodus
34:29, where the Hebrew reads:
" The skin of his face sent forth
beams " (Heb., " horns ").

CHAPTER IX

WEARY YEARS OF WANDERINGS

79. Departure from Sinai and on the March (Num. 10:11–12:16). In the second year, in the second month and on the twentieth day thereof, the cloud arose from over the "tabernacle of the testimony." And all the tribes and the tabernacle with its various parts proceeded in a specified order (10:12-28). The ark preceded that line of march by three days to find a suitable camping-place towards the wilderness of Paran, in the north, in the direction of Palestine proper.

NOTE ON FIG. 51, headpiece above: Dr. Ellis disagrees with a number of scholars in finding the real Kadesh-barnea, not at *Ain Kadis,* as did H. C. Trumbull in his *Kadesh Barnea* (1884), but at *Ain el-Guderat.* In this "fountain of Guderat" he finds abundant springs, ample surrounding plains, and all the space that seems necessary to accommodate the hosts of Israel during the thirty-eight years of waiting after the disappointing report of the ten spies. We are at the mercy of these travellers in reaching any conclusion on so disputed a point.

Even before Israel had reached Taberah, the first camping-place, where lightning slew the murmurers, they burst forth in complaints against Moses because of the monotony of their manna diet. " The mixed multitude " (hangers-on) with them raised a storm because " the flesh-pots of Egypt," the fish, the cucumbers, the melons, the leeks, the onions and the garlic, were merely a memory; " there is nothing at all save this manna to look upon " (11:6), they plaintively grumbled.

Moses was grieved and discouraged at the outlook. At the command of Jehovah, he appointed seventy elders to be officers over the people, to aid him in carrying the daily burdens of the dissatisfied host. At the door of the Tent of Meeting these men were set apart to their tasks, and when the spirit of Moses rested upon them they prophesied.

In answer to the outcry of the people for flesh, " a wind from Jehovah " blew over and into and around about the camp, bringing overwhelming multitudes of quails from the direction of the Red Sea. The people pounced upon them and doubtless, in their voracity, ate them only partially cooked and in such amounts that a plague scourged them and slew some of them. Kibroth-Hattaavah (" graves of the voracious ") was the name given that camp.

The next stop was Hazeroth, where the jealousy of Miriam and Aaron against the Cushite wife of Moses broke into a flame. Jehovah sharply rebuked their spirit and envy, and smote Miriam with leprosy. So invidious was her spirit that the appeal of Moses for her healing did not save her from the disgrace of being shut up without the camp for seven days. That quenched her jealous outbreak against her great brother and leader of Israel.

80. Spies Sent into Canaan (Num. 13 and 14). On the northern edge of the wilderness of Paran, in a better pasturage country than that about Sinai, was Kadesh-barnea (13:26), their next stop,—within sight of the

heights of the promised land. At the command of Jehovah, Moses sent out twelve men to spy out the land of
Canaan,—one from each tribe, "everyone a prince among
them" (13:2).

They were to view the land, the people that dwelt in it,
whether strong or weak, few or many; whether the land
was good or bad; what kind of cities they lived in, whether
they resided in camps or fortresses; whether the land was
fat or lean, whether they had timber or not;—also they
were to bring back samples of the products of the country.

After tramping, probably by twos, for forty days through
all the land from their starting-place to the approach to
Hamath, far north of Damascus, they returned to Kadesh,
bringing a mammoth cluster of grapes on a rod between two
as a sample of the fruits of the country.

Their report to Moses and the people was adroitly worded
to produce the proper effect: ' Surely the land floweth with
milk and honey, said they, and this is the fruit of it '
(13:27). But the people that live there are mighty and
their "cities are fortified and very great." And to our
horror we saw the giant children of Anak there. Amalek is
on the south, the Hittite, the Jebusite, and the Amorite live
in the hill-country, and the Canaanite by the sea and in the
Jordan valley.

Such a wave of disaffection swept over the listening multitudes that they let burst forth their keen resentment against
their leaders. Caleb, however, beckoning for silence, attempted to turn the tide for immediate advance into the
land. The ten spies with their dark report had poisoned
the minds of the crowd, and snowed under the favourable
words of Caleb and Joshua, who were nearly stoned because
of their minor though optimistic report.

The clamour of the people against Moses and Aaron was
outspoken and defiant. They went so far as to suggest their
own appointment of a captain to lead them back to Egypt,
rather than to let them die in the wilderness,—as they
seemed fated to do.

Jehovah came to the rescue of his leaders and would wipe out these rebels. Again, Moses' plea saved them temporarily; but (1) they shall wander forty years in this wilderness; (2) not one of those over twenty years of age who left Egypt shall reach the promised land except Caleb and Joshua,—who as spies brought back a favourable report.

While the people apparently repented of the evil they had done, they summoned their daring and courage, and in desperation started to fight their way through the Amalek- ites and Canaanites up into the promised land,—in the face of the punishments which Jehovah had pronounced against them. But they were ignominiously defeated and humili- ated, and driven back to serve out the sentences which had been pronounced upon them.

81. Korah's Rebellion (Num. 16). Moses and Aaron were buffeted about by almost every kind of disaffection on the part of the mercurial multitude. Probably while they were still at Kadesh, Korah, of the tribe of Levi, bidding for a place on the Aaronic priesthood, stirred up a religious revolt. Dathan and Abiram, descendants of Reuben, hatched a civil rebellion against the supremacy of Moses as their leader, on the ground of a claim that they were de- scendants of the oldest son of Jacob (Gen. 49:3 ff.).

These rebels, Korah, Dathan and Abiram, met a terrific death: " the earth opened its mouth and swallowed them " (16:32) and their families and their possessions. And the 250 men who dared to offer incense as priests were destroyed by lightning from Jehovah.

These fatal infractions against Jehovah were so ominous, that another kind of complaint came forth from the pagan crowd against Moses and Aaron,—that they had killed the people of Jehovah. The penalty for this outcry was a destructive pestilence in which 14,700 are said to have per- ished—and it would have wiped out the entire host had not Aaron made an atonement by a censor containing burning- incense. These were the days that severely tried the faith and endurance of Moses and Aaron, as well as the long-suffering and patience of Jehovah.

82. Miriam's Death and Moses' Mistake (Num. 20). Though Miriam had cherished a sister's jealousy of her brother's wife, she suffered her punishment, and was again restored to her former place of influence as one of the three who led Israel out of Egypt (Mic. 6:4). At Kadesh she died and there was buried.

Scarcity of water again brought complaints to Moses and Aaron. As at other times, they left the assembly and went to the Tent of Meeting and prostrated themselves before Jehovah. To Moses explicit directions were given to take the rod (Exod. 4:17) and assemble the people, " thou and Aaron thy brother," before the rock, " and speak ye unto the rock before their eyes . . . and thou shalt bring forth to them water out of the rock " (20:8).

They went out as commanded and gathered the people about the rock. But complaints and murmurs had worn down the patience of poor old Moses, and in his irritation he shouted: " Hear now, ye rebels; shall we bring you forth water out of this rock? . . . and smote the rock with his rod twice, and water came forth abundantly " (20:10, 11).

For this breach of faith and failure to obey on their part and to sanctify Jehovah in the eyes of the people both Moses and Aaron forfeited their right to lead the Hebrews into the land of promise.

83. Kadesh-barnea. Where was this stopping-place? Many conjectures have been made, and the one that seemed plausible was the location selected by H. Clay Trumbull in his work, *Kadesh Barnea*. But in 1926 Wm. T. Ellis, in *Bible Lands To-day*, claims to have found at *Ain el-Guderat* what he regards as far and away the most likely spot for Israel's encampment. It has all the requirements of the narrative for Israel's camp. As headquarters they could have ranged far and wide with their flocks and herds and have had plenty of pasture and water.

They probably reached this camping-place sometime in the second year after their escape from Egypt, having come by way of Sinai, after having endured many hardships and disasters. Following the events of the preceding section (82), that is, between verses 13 and 14, of chapter 20, we may have a blank space of about thirty-seven years with no intimation of what occurred in all that stretch of time.

No one can estimate the real importance of that period touching the character of the Israelites. Organized under the supervision of Moses and Aaron, they must have been severely tested in all that stiffens and hardens character. No doubt the laws laid down by Moses gave some of the people a training and a discipline that made for the development of their moral and religious fibre.

Then the fierce aridity of the desert and their exposure to raids and inroads, barbarous and cruel, of nomadic neighbours hardened their endurance and prepared them for future conquests. Weaned away from Egypt, they soon were compelled to practice a simple mode of living, such as always tends to simplicity of needs and invigoration of character. Without doubt, they became from necessity rough and ready soldiers. The severity of desert life gave them an austere idea of their God and his treatment of men.

84. Leaving Kadesh-barnea for Canaan (Num. 20:14–21:20). About the end of their sojourn at Kadesh Moses sent and asked permission of the Edomites for Israel to pass through their country on "the king's highway" (20:17); but they were flatly refused. About this same time Arad, a Canaanite, fiercely attacked Israel; he was not only routed but utterly destroyed, his cities and all.

Frustrated in their attempted short-cut to Canaan, Israel left Kadesh and started southward toward the Gulf of Akabah. On their stop at Mt. Hor, Aaron, at the command of Jehovah, was stripped of his official robes, which were put upon Eleazar, his son, and he (Aaron) died, being mourned by the people for thirty days.

They went " from Mt. Hor by the way to the Red Sea "
(21:4), to pass around the Edomite preserves. The same
old disaffection broke out against Moses because of the lack
of food and drink. And Jehovah let loose fiery venomous
serpents that bit the people and large numbers of them
died. At their repentance and the appeal of Moses, Jehovah
commanded him to put upon a pole a brazen figure of a
fiery serpent, at which, if anyone who was bitten looked, he
was cured of the bite. (This same serpent was supersti-
tiously reverenced at a later time until destroyed in Hezekiah's reforms (2 Kings 18:4).

Thence Israel, with all their handicaps, marched from
place to place until they reached the river Arnon, east of
the Dead Sea;—said Arnon being the southern border of
the territory of Moab. The list of stations of this march
(Num. 33) is rather confused in the different narratives, so
that we are not certain of the exact route taken, though we
know they reached the Arnon. The compiler finds in the
" Book of the Wars of Jehovah " presumably a collection of
descriptions of battles, poetical celebrations of victories, and
snatches of war-songs, in favour of the people of Jehovah in
fighting their enemies,—hence the enemies of Jehovah himself. This is the only original mention of such a book in all
literature. Out of this collection the compiler of these
records quotes a little ballad celebrating Israel's arrival on
the south bank of this border stream that flows from the
mountains east of the Dead Sea down into the briny waters
of that old sea. The ballad stands in these words:

> " Vaheb in Suphah,
>   And the valleys of the Arnon,
>   And the slope of the valleys
>   That inclineth toward the dwelling of Ar,
>   And leaneth upon the border of Moab " (21:14, 15).

From the southern bank of little Arnon Israel looked
northwards with trepidation, for the dread Amorites had a

reputation as fierce warriors. Their next duty was to face these peoples, whether friendly or hostile. They were their bar to advancement, and must be met.

NOTE ON FIG. 1, tailpiece below : Botanists find two varieties of trees in the desert that are designated " Acacia," probably of the same species, the *A. Seyal,* and *A. tortilis.* It is about 15–25 ft. high, with thick thorny branches. The wood is heavier·than water, very hard and fine grained. The sapwood is yellow and the heart brown. It is immune from attacks of pests. It grows in wadies and desert valleys, sometimes to two feet in diameter. It was a most suitable wood for the Ark of the Covenant, and other articles about the Tabernacle (Exod. 25 :10, 23, 28 ; 26 :15, 26 ; 27 :1 ; 30 :1).

CHAPTER X

In Sight of Canaan

85. Conquests East of the Jordan (Num. 21:21–22:1). Before venturing to cross the river Arnon, Israel sent messengers to Sihon king of the Amorites, to ask permission to pass through his country " on the king's highway." Sihon took the same attitude as had the Edomites

Note on Fig. 5, headpiece above: The Amorites were an ancient mountainous people who played no insignificant rôle in the development of the so-called " fertile crescent,"—stretching from the Tigris-Euphrates valley westward to the Mediterranean Sea. They were the *Amurru* who had some part in the government of Babylonia at the end of the third millennium B. C. The Hittite invasion of Syria put an end to their power. Egypt made vassals of them, and as a nation they gradually disappeared in the path of aggression of the Hittites; and were later appearing in scattered remnants throughout Syria. Sihon and his kingdom was wiped out by the Israelites (Num. 21).

at a similar request (20:21). He not only refused to permit it but backed it up by mobilizing his army and attacking the Israelites. The hardy wilderness-trained men of Israel, a new generation since Sinai, met the onset, defeated the Amorites and slew their chief Sihon on the field of battle.

With an invincible drive Israel took all the cities of Gilead even to the stream Jabbok, including Heshbon, the royal capital of the Amorites. The compiler has incorporated in his narrative a war-song (21:27-30), which refers either to Israel's victory over Sihon, or was some Amorite war-song composed when the Amorites conquered that land. Read it.

North of the Jabbok was another royal realm ruled by Og the king of Bashan. Of him Israel seems not to have asked any favours, but simply attacked him in the spirit of conquest. They swept victoriously through all his domain and took all his cities, including Edrei, the capital.

Both campaigns, if they can really be separated, opened scores of towns and cities for settlement of the Israelites on the east of the Jordan. The Moabites, through whose country Israel passed, had remained undisturbed by the Hebrew invaders. To forestall any possible attack their king, Balak, took precautionary steps, for the Israelites were encamped on the east bank of the Jordan.

86. Balaam and Israel (Num. 22:2–24:25). The stories of Balaam, while not consistent, still teach their lesson. Terror-stricken by the rapid unchecked advance of Israel which Balak had seen, he sent messengers to the far north, to Pethor on the Euphrates, where dwelt Balaam, a famous soothsayer; and implored him to come and curse a " people that came out of Egypt," and that " cover the face of the earth." Linked with the elders of Moab were the elders of Midian, who seem to have been settled together in the same area.

After a day and night spent with the great man, Balaam sent them back, saying, " Jehovah refuseth to give me leave to go with you " (22:13). On a second visit made by greater princes and noblemen, Jehovah gave Balaam permission to go, with the proviso that he should speak only the word that Jehovah would give him. On this journey Balaam and his ass met the angel of Jehovah, and the world-famed soothsayer met his humiliation and mortification.

On Balaam's arrival at the city of Moab, Balak met him and tried his charms on him. He gave Balaam presents, and took him up to Bamoth-baal (" heights of Baal "), whence he could see all Israel encamped down on the plain. At Balaam's order seven altars were built and sacrifices offered thereon; but the soothsayer gave Jehovah's message, —wholly favourable to Israel. From two other heights, contrary to Balak's request, Balaam pronounced a blessing upon the encamped Israelites. As a concluding stroke Balaam predicted what Israel would be in the future; how they would trample down and destroy their enemies in all that country, and would be the people out of whom would arise a star and a sceptre,—in other words, be the source from which there would arise a messianic ruler.

87. Israel Ensnared on Balaam's Advice (Num. 25). Failing to make use of his wiles and necromancy in his public messages, Balaam now seems, independent of Jehovah, to have advised the Moabites and Midianites to try another method of defeating and breaking down the morale of the Israelites (Num. 31:16),—a method not unknown in this century between opposing armies.

Connected with the worship of Peor of Baal and other divinities were the insidious and licentious practices that were especially attractive and dangerous to the worshippers. Israel being close at hand, was invited to worship the gods of these courteous and pleasing neighbours. Such invitations were accepted and there grew out of it all a fascinating familiarity, which soon yielded bitter fruits. Jehovah was forgotten and thousands turned to the seductive influences of the pagan gods of Midian and Moab.

So widespread and perilous became the defection that

Jehovah commanded Moses to hang up all the chief men of the people in the face of the sun, in order to turn away his fierce anger from Israel. More than that, each judge was ordered to slay every one of his men under him who had joined himself to Baal-peor. In addition, a plague,—whose character we do not know,—slew 24,000 of the Israelites. This malady was stayed only by the sanguinary act of Phinehas in his loyalty to Jehovah. The victims were so prominent in the life of Israel and Midian that the writer gives their ancestry and their names. And the plague ceased and the rest of the people were saved.

88. Israel's Vengeance on Her Traducers (Num. 26 and 31). After all of Israel's plagues, battles, and depletions, and as she was encamped on the east side of the Jordan, orders were given to number the present host of those twenty years old and above. At the end of the count there were found to be of fighting men 601,730, and of Levites 23,000 (*cf.* Num. 1–4). Command was given that out of these 1,000 from each tribe should be armed to go out to take vengeance on the Moabites and Midianites for their prostitution of Israel in the matter of Peor.

The 12,000 armed men of Israel made a drive against Moab and Midian and completely routed, defeated and destroyed every male and all their cities and villages, but saved their women and children and all their flocks and herds. Among the slain was that famous necromancer Balaam of Pethor on the Euphrates, who, in public had blessed Israel, and in private counsel had shown Moab how to undermine her.

Moses and Eleazar sharply rebuked the army for saving the women who had been the cause of Israel's plague. After these had been " dispatched," and the booty had been properly apportioned by the orders of Moses, the host rested in camp on the east bank of the Jordan.

89. Allotments of Land East of the Jordan (Num. 32). None of the territory conquered on the east of the Jordan had yet been assigned to any tribe. Noting that it was peculiarly adapted to grazing and animal husbandry, the leaders of the tribe of Reuben and Gad and the half-tribe of Manasseh requested that they, being shepherds, receive their allotments in this territory.

When the petition was presented to Moses, he suspected that the motive behind it was an evasion of further fighting for the possession of Canaan. To clear the atmosphere, he conditioned the granting of their request upon a solemn promise on their part that their armed men should cross the Jordan with the other tribes, and aid in subduing the land west of that river. And these two and a half tribes unhesitatingly accepted the condition and pledged their co-operation in the future warfare, and were granted their possessions on the east of Jordan.

After cleaning up some of the unconquered fringes and corners of their allotments they settled their families in the fortified and walled cities for safety's sake, while the armed men should be engaged in the campaigns for their brethren west of the river.

90. Last Words East of the Jordan (Deut. 1:1–4:43). While the host of Israel was encamped on the east bank of the river, Moses as leader gave them his farewell address. He spoke to them in words that became the introduction to the book of Deuteronomy.

His pathetic and thrilling review of the past forty years mirrored to them the reasons why they had not been wiped out by the wrath of Jehovah. And to prevent the ravages of blood revenge on the east of the Jordan, Moses named three cities of refuge at convenient locations in that territory.

While the so-called "Song of Moses" (32) sets forth some prophetic utterances it seems to be coloured by picturesque scenes of the desert wanderings, projected far back into the past. It may mark the end of their wanderings just as they are about to enter on a new life in a settled country.

The "Blessing of Moses" (33) abounds in pictures of war and victory, where Ephraim and Manasseh stand in the forefront as leaders and heroes. While each of the tribes receives its share of the glory and prosperity of the future, Jehovah is supreme in his protection and guaranty of Israel's supremacy (vs. 29).

91. The Death of Moses (Deut. 34). After Moses had given his last message to the encamped Israelites, of whom Joshua was henceforth to be the leader, he started up from the plains of Moab to face the penalty for his rashness in the wilderness. He would be permitted to see the land of promise but would not be allowed to set foot upon it. Up mount Nebo, to the top of Pisgah, opposite Jericho, he climbed, and Jehovah pointed out to " him all the land of Gilead, unto Dan, and all Naphtali, and the land of Ephraim and Manasseh, and all the land of Judah, unto the western (Mediterranean) sea, and the South, and the Plain of the valley of Jericho the city of palm-trees, unto Zoar " (34:1, 2). " This is the land which I sware unto Abraham, unto Isaac, and unto Jacob, saying, I will give it unto thy seed: I have caused thee to see it with thine eyes, but thou shalt not go over thither " (34:4).

Upon the conclusion of this mountain-top survey, " Moses the servant of Jehovah died there in the land of Moab, 120 years old, and was buried in the valley opposite Beth-peor, and no one knows his tomb unto this day."

The organization of Israel effected by Moses did not materially suffer with his passing, for its administration had been provided for on the advice of Jethro, his father-in-law, by the appointment of heads of divisions who were responsible for dispensing justice in those several divisions; the religious organization continued to function through the Aaronic priesthood and their attendant helpers in and about the Tent of Meeting,—the religious centre of the camp or tribes; the military organization had grown so increasingly efficient under Joshua's guidance that no fear for its future troubled any of the leaders prominent on the east bank of the Jordan. Thus from a military, a religious, and a civil administrative point of view, Moses left Israel in a very strong and desirable status. His personal influence permeated every fibre of Israel's life and left an impact that has never died away.

With his going there passed on the most revered and the greatest man in all Hebrew history. His patience, persistence and unwavering confidence in Jehovah, helped him to meet, combat, and deal with a mass of freed slaves in such a way as to make of them in the end an irresistible hardy army, able to cope with any of the smaller peoples of that day. In a modest, unselfish manner he gave himself unreservedly to the good of his people even when he himself suffered therefor. To him Israel owed her preservation from extinction at the hands of Jehovah more than once; and his genius and long-suffering gave her the beginnings of regulations which have been her guides all down through succeeding ages.

When we turn to the contemporaneous peoples of that day we find few if any characters that were to their people what Moses was to the Hebrews,—leader, lawgiver, chief justice, reconciler, teacher, and universal adviser. From his discovery in the basket of bulrushes to his view of the promised land from Pisgah, he had lived a dramatic and thrilling life. Reared in the court of the Pharaoh, and " instructed " at the feet of the teachers of Egyptian royalty, he had the intellectual background of the best men of Egypt. After having reached maturity his kinship with the Hebrews asserted itself, both in his sympathy with an abused Israelite, and by his slaying of an Egyptian taskmaster. This violent treatment of an oppressor of his own people forced him for safety's sake to flee to the wilderness-desert, where for forty years he endured the sharpest discipline,—preparatory to the very task which finally fell to

NOTE ON MAP 4, opposite. Canaan before the Conquest of Israel: Egypt ruled Palestine and Syria in the Amarna period,—fourteenth century B. C. Its city-state rulers reported to the kings of Egypt in letters written in the script and language of Babylonia. They announced that bands of people called Khabiri (Hebrews) were raiding the country.

his lot. With the modesty and reticence of a truly great man, Moses reluctantly undertook the supreme task of rescuing his people from their bondage to the Egyptian Pharaoh. With the resourcefulness of a thoroughly trained leader, a conscientious guide, a patient and God-fearing exemplar, he surmounted all stubborn obstacles, and brought that mass of Hebrews to the very gates of the promised land. Moses' patience and endurance in all that wilderness period are almost incredible. Only such a superb spirit and great man as he, could have reached that goal, and have opened to them the doors to their inheritance.

NOTE ON FIG. 9, tailpiece below: The sacred ark of the Egyptians as shown in this scene dates from the time of Amenhotep III (1411–1375 B. C.) of Egypt. The king is offering incense before the ark of the god Amon-Ra, which rests on poles on the shoulders of priests (*cf.* Exod. 25:13-15). The sacred symbol is in the form of a boat with a ram's head, symbol of the god, on both prow and stern. Of cedar of Lebanon was it made and overlaid with gold (*cf.* Exod. 25:10, 11). Immediately overshadowing the ark is the winged disc of the sun. Within or on the side of the ark is a beetle—a symbol of the sun— protected by two cherubic figures representing righteousness and truth (Exod. 25:18-20). On the boat are seen many sacred symbols. On the right is King Amenhotep holding an incense-vessel in his left hand, and with his right feeds incense into the flame. Behind the boat he appears in another capacity. When the Hebrews crossed the Jordan their sacred ark was carried before them by their priests.

PERIOD IV

TRIBAL ORGANIZATION

*From the Settlement in Canaan to the Establishment
of the Monarchy*

CHAPTER XI

JOSHUA'S CONQUESTS

92. Israel's New Leader, Joshua. Joshua was set apart to be the successor of Moses, at the command of Jehovah, by the laying on of hands in the presence of all the assembly of the people, and of Eleazar the priest (Num. 27:18-23). He was the son of Nun of the tribe of Ephraim. When the Amalekites attacked Israel immediately after her escape from Egypt, Moses appointed Joshua to lead the defense forces of Israel, and he won the day (Exod. 17:10 f.). He also attended Moses as " minister " on one occasion when he ascended the mountain (Exod. 24:13; 32:17). After the Tent of Meeting was erected Joshua was given general oversight of it. At the selection of one from each tribe to be sent to spy out the land, " Hoshea " was chosen from Ephraim, and Moses changed his name to Joshua (Num. 13:8, 16). When the spies returned from their journey, Joshua and Caleb were the only two who brought a favourable report. On account of his stand for faith in Jehovah he was granted a long life (Num. 14:38) and subsequent appointment as successor to Moses, his great leader from Egypt to the east bank of the Jordan.

93. Crossing the Jordan (Joshua 1:1-4:24). The records of the crossing are not harmonized by the compiler, so that we must be prepared for divergences in the story as

Fig. 49. The Jordan River

The Jordan is the longest river in Palestine. It drains the Sea of Galilee, and flows southward 65 miles in an airline, but in reality not far from 200 miles in its windings and turnings, to reach the Dead Sea. In that distance it falls 610 feet. By affluents on the way its volume is about doubled. Its waters are roily in appearance and justify the protest of General Naaman of Damascus against dipping himself in it seven times to heal his leprosy (2 Kings 5:8-14). By careful estimate it pours into the Dead Sea every day six million tons of fresh water.

presented. Uncertain as to what kind of a reception Israel would receive when they should cross the Jordan, Joshua sent over two men to spy out the land. Their success in Jericho and their subsequent return to the Israelites' camp with good news cheered the heart of Joshua.

Every preparation was made for an early passage over the river. The ark was carried by the priests more than a half-mile in advance of the people. When these officials came to the water's edge they stood still (3:8). In the next account we are told that when the soles of their feet reached the water's edge " the waters which came down from above stood, and rose up in one heap, a great way off, at Adam, the city that is beside Zarethan " (vs. 16),—almost twenty miles above the crossing-place. All the waters below flowed on down to " the sea of the Arabah, even the Salt Sea " (Dead Sea). This left a large space dry and available for crossing; and while the priests with the ark were standing in the middle of the bed of the former stream, the entire people were crossing over on dry ground.

In commemoration of this event, Joshua selected one man from each tribe to carry each a stone out of the bed of the stream, with which to build a memorial on the western bank of the river. At the same time twelve stones were gathered to erect a cairn where the priests stood in the midst of the Jordan,—of course, it could be only a temporary mark.

At the head of the almost unnumbered Israelites, in ranks and files, were the 40,000 warriors of Reuben, Gad, and the half-tribe of Manasseh, whose pledge to Moses they were making good by leading in the conquest of Western Canaan (Num. 32:31, 32). As soon as the multitude of the people, the flocks, and the herds had crossed, Joshua commanded the priests with the ark to come up out of the bed of the Jordan. When they reached the west bank of the river the waters from above came rolling down and gradually went up over all its banks as before.

The Jordan is a swift river and often undermines its banks, sometimes causing great landslides to occur. The word Adam means " reddish ground." It is thought by some historians that this name is represented by the modern Tell ed-Damieh, just below the confluence of the river Jabbok with the Jordan. But the notable thing we wish to mention is that a dependable Arab historian tells us that in the year 1257 A. D. the Sultan Bibers had to dispatch work-men to repair a bridge at this point, to save the retreating Moslem army. The spring floods being on, they regarded the task as impossible, but when they reached the place they found the river bed empty. By speeding up, they made the necessary repairs before the waters came rushing down from above. Such a favourable condition they regarded as an interposition of Providence, until they discovered that the entire damming up of the river had been caused by an enormous landslide some distance up stream. Such phenomena are by no means unknown in our day in other parts of the earth,—notably in Switzerland.

94. First Encampment in Canaan (Joshua 5). Report that the hosts of Israel had crossed over on the dry bed of the Jordan into the land west of the river reached the ears of the kings of the Amorites and the Canaanites. Their hearts quailed with fear and their spirits melted away. The invincible hosts of Jehovah's people were threatening their safety and security.

As soon as Israel became settled in camp, Joshua, at the command of his God, Jehovah, circumcised all the males who had escaped attention during the long years of wandering, indifference, and apostasy in the wilderness. This covenantal ordinance was followed by the observance of the passover on the regular date, and that by the feast of unleavened bread. On the day after the passover, when they had begun to eat of the produce of the land, manna ceased to fall.

Now that they were ritually consecrated, were enjoying the fruits of the new land, they were ready for the next step in the campaign. At this juncture Joshua had a vision of a prince of the hosts of Jehovah, who was to be their commander-in-chief. This was a signal for Joshua to prepare for the conflict that was immediately ahead of him. All the land was to become theirs only after they should do their part to secure possession of it.

95. Ancient Jericho. About six miles west of the Jordan, at the foot of the first range of hills, only a few feet above the plain of the Jordan, reposed the old Canaanite town Jericho. The ruins to-day are oval-shaped, lying almost north and south, about 1,100 feet long by about 550 feet wide. It covers about twelve or thirteen acres. Its height is about forty feet above the ground about it. It is surrounded by a wall which is almost precipitous on the eastern side. Out from beneath this eastern stretch flows the fountain of Elisha (*Ain es-Sultan*). German excavations here in 1909 revealed many interesting features of that old walled town. Considerable portions of the wall were uncovered. Parts of it were found intact and in excellent preservation, revealing some good masonry. In places it was six to eight feet thick and sixteen feet high, of stone of various sizes. On the top of the stone wall was built another wall of burnt brick six to seven feet thick, and in the ruins about eight feet high. On the north end there was a citadel probably three stories high, with a stone stairs to the top. Some of the walls the German excavators identified as having been built by the Hebrews.

Such a walled city in that day was well nigh impregnable. Carefully guarded by warriors behind parapets on walls thirty to forty feet high and six to eight feet thick, Jericho was thought to be able to withstand a siege of long duration.

96. Jericho Captured (Joshua 6). The most formidable obstacle to Israel's first drive into Canaan was this fortified city Jericho, not far from the Jordan and near the first entrance to the hill-country. Their first task was to strike at this stronghold. They carefully organized their forces and for seven days terrified the inhabitants by their trumpet-blowing and their marchings around its walls. On the seventh day at the great shouting of all the people the walls are said to have fallen down flat (marg., " in its place "), and the people went up into the city, every man straight before him, and they took the city (vs. 20). That is, there was no formal siege, it succumbed at the first real onset, and Israel was the victor. Did these six to eight foot walls fall down flat, or is this a poetic figure for the inhabitants of Jericho's inability to withstand the terrific hosts of

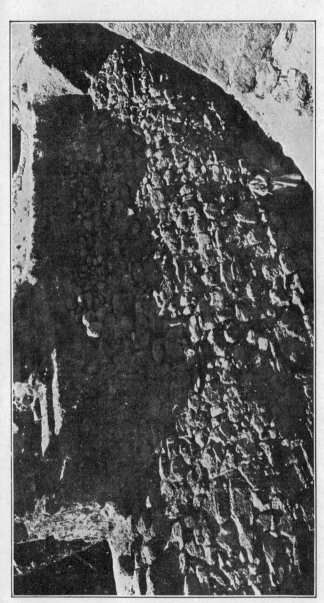

Fig. 44. An Israelitish Wall of Old Jericho

Jericho had been occupied by many peoples before the advent of Israel into Palestine. The German excavator of Jericho in 1909, Sellin, discovered among the many kinds of walls in those ruins, this one, which he definitely fixed as having been erected by the Israelites. It is bound together neither by cutstone nor mortar. It is held in place by weight and height only, differing greatly from other walls uncovered in that great mound.

Jehovah? However that may be, the city fell before Joshua. Its population was " devoted " to Jehovah and completely wiped out,—men, women, children and animals; and all the treasure was turned in to the treasury of Jehovah. Such complete slaughter among Semites was a common occurrence and was regarded as the highest devotion to one's god. And a curse was then pronounced upon anyone who should rebuild Jericho (vs. 26; cf. 1 Kings 16:34).

True to their oath, the two spies who had been saved by Rahab, now sought out and rescued her from the carnage of life and property. She and hers were not only saved but were so incorporated into the stock of Israel that subsequently she became an ancestress of David (Matt. 1:5).

97. The Drive into the Hills; the Fall of Ai (Joshua 7 and 8). Jericho now wiped out of the pathway of Israel's advance, Joshua planned to drive up into the hill-country through a pass, at the upper end of which stood the city Ai. By the common ancient tactics of ambush and feigned retreat the city was taken, the army destroyed and the inhabitants of it " devoted " to Jehovah, that is, slaughtered to the last one.

These two cities, Jericho and Ai, out of the way, Israel had an open road into the plateau or hill-country, whence they could strike in any direction to capture the land.

As if in gratitude for the abundant entrance of Israel, Joshua later built an altar to Jehovah, God of Israel, in Mt. Ebal, and offered burnt-offerings and peace-offerings thereon. Here he read all the words of the law of Moses in the hearing of all the host of the Hebrews, thus reminding them of the covenant and the statutes that they were to obey in their new homeland.

98. The Biter Bit (Joshua 9). The fame of the undefeated army of Israel had spread like wildfire throughout all adjoining lands. The inhabitants trembled before the doom that seemed to face them. Joshua was not the only strategist in that motley array of peoples. A company of weary travellers, with old clothes and mouldy bread, staggered into the camp of Israel at Gilgal. They had come from a " far country," and having heard how the God of Israel had blessed them, wished to make a covenant and treaty of peace or an alliance with Joshua. Their dilapidated condition and their pathetic appeal caught Joshua napping, and he made a covenant and peace with them.

At the end of three days, Joshua, in humiliating dismay, discovered that the " far country " was Gibeon and three neighbouring towns (vs. 17), less than ten miles west of Ai. So chagrined was the host of Israel at the deception that they wished to deal out to the Gibeonites the same fate as that which had fallen upon Jericho and Ai; but the elders fortunately realizing the sanctity of an oath taken in the name of Jehovah, refused to touch them. However, as a penalty for their mendacity, Joshua sentenced them to a life of servitude not only to Israel's people, but to the service and ritual of Israel's God.

99. The Great Battle at Gibeon (Joshua 10:1-28). Angered at the perfidy of Gibeon in deserting their cause against a common enemy, Adoni-bezek, king of Jerusalem, summoned his neighbouring friendly kings of the south, of Hebron, of Jarmuth, of Lachish, and of Eglon, to join him in a war on such traitors. Gibeon, thoroughly frightened at the strength of the hostile combination, dispatched swift messengers to the camp of Israel at Gilgal. By a night march Joshua and his warriors rushed up the pass and came upon the hosts of the Amorites of the hill-country, in camp before Gibeon, at break óf day. The suddenness of the onslaught, with Jehovah's help, gave Israel the victory. The five kings with their armies fled down the western slopes of the hills past Beth-horon, where Jehovah rained great hailstones upon them, killing more thereby than with the sword. On they fled, down the valley of Aijalon as far as Makkedah in the foothills. Having trapped the five enemy kings in the cave of Makkedah, Joshua and his men slew them and hanged them on trees until evening, when their bodies were taken down and thrown into the caves in which they had taken refuge.

At this point in the narrative the compiler introduces a piece of an old war-song from the " Book of Jashar " (vss. 12, 13), his only authority for that remarkable incident:

> " *Sun, stand thou still upon Gibeon;*
> *And thou, Moon, in the valley of Aijalon.*
> *And the sun stood still, and the moon stayed,*
> *Until the nation had avenged themselves of their enemies.*"

100. Conquests in the South (Joshua 10:29-43). We have two accounts of the conquest of southern Palestine. The first, following the defeat of the central alliance against Gibeon, is carried out by Joshua and his exultant troops. Immediately following the execution at Makkedah, they attack and capture Libnah and destroy it with the identical thoroughness with which they had treated Jericho and Ai. The same fate was visited upon Lachish, Eglon, Hebron and Debir (Kirjath-sepher), all important cities in southern Palestine in that day.

The second account in Judges 1 credits the subjugation of the south to Judah and Simeon, with the aid of the Kenites and those affiliated with Caleb. We are told that Hebron was taken by Caleb and that the giants, Sheshai, Ahiman and Talmai were driven out of it (Joshua 15:14). While Judges (1:10) credits Judah with smiting them; and Joshua (10:36, 37) with wiping out all the population. Othniel, a kinsman of Caleb, took over Debir, or Kirjath-sepher, which Joshua (10:38, 39) is said to have devoted to Jehovah.

It is evident to any careful reader that we have here, at least, two records of the entrance into and conquest of the country. The compilers of Joshua and Judges seem to have made no effort to harmonize the records. They give us what they found, and out of those fragments we must construct our view of how and when Israel entered into and conquered Canaan. The records in Joshua seem to recite a straightforward campaign commanded by Joshua, while the record in Judges may refer to a somewhat desultory and unorganized entrance into and capture of the country, perhaps stretching over a considerable period of time.

101. Conquests in the North (Joshua 11:1–13:6). The report of Joshua's victories in the central and southern zones of the land had penetrated to the far north end of the country. Terror seized the Canaanitish kings, who formed an alliance under Jabin, king of Hazor, to bar the invaders. Fearful of an immediate movement against them, they mobilized their troops near the waters of Lake Merom. Joshua, by a sudden drive, fell upon them unawares, routed them, and pursued them even unto great Sidon in Phœnicia. All the people were slain, but the animals and booty were taken for themselves, and places fortified on a hill were not destroyed. They embraced in the main those towns and cities of which use could be made in the future. Their horses were hamstrung, probably with the falchion hook on a pole, and their chariots were burned. This concludes the first reported wars of conquest conducted by Joshua.

After the battle of Merom, Joshua is said to have kept up his warfare and pursuit of the enemy until he had destroyed thirty-one kings and their subjects in the territory west of the Jordan. Among these were the Hittites, the Amorites, the Canaanites, the Perizzites, the Hivites, and the Jebusites,—a mosaic of peoples who had wandered into this land during the past centuries.

But there remained many strongholds that were too much for the troops of Israel. These were found in the main on the plains of Philistia, on the sea-coast in the north, and among the Sidonians.

102. Why Exterminate the Canaanites? The orders of Jehovah to Joshua to slaughter the Canaanites, man, woman and child, and in some cases, animals, has been a perplexity to many readers. Why? Because those readers have carried back into those crude, barbarous and savage times the ethical principles and refinements of the New Testament. On the other hand, they must carry themselves back in mind, to an age where inhumanity, violence and brutality were the accompaniments of all warfare, where mercy was almost a stranger. In fact, each nation looked upon its god as requiring such treatment of the devotees of its enemy's god.

When Jehovah commanded the wiping out of the Canaanites (Joshua 6:17, 21; 8:26; 10:40), he was doing, according to their view of devotion to him, only the necessary and logical thing, and obedience to that command was a mark of true loyalty to him, as they understood him.

Another reason sometimes given is, that providential history so-called proceeds with seeming indifference to the sanctity of life,—such as storms, floods, earthquakes, pestilences, and famines. If those powers of nature have any providential guidance at all, it rarely appears in manifestations recognized by man.

Still another explanation of the reason for such wholesale slaughter of those old inhabitants of the land has been seen in the wisdom of God for the future of his chosen people. This is inferred from subsequent references to the character of those whom the swords of Israel put out of the way (Judges 3:5, 6; 1 Kings 14:24; 2 Kings 16:3; 21:2, etc.). If Israel had simply conquered the peoples and settled down among them in the land and become amalgamated with them, how long would they have existed as a nation? They would have gone down into the quagmires of superstition, corruption and paganism, and have disappeared from history. Dr. Arnold, in his *Sermons*, Vol. 6, 35 f., says: " The Israelites' sword, in its bloodiest executions, wrought a work of mercy to all the countries of the earth to the very end of the world."

103. Allotments of the Tribes (Joshua 13–21). After the conquest of considerable portions of the land there still remained in the hands of the native population many fortresses and strongholds. These were assigned by lot to the respective tribes for their own ouster proceedings, as part of the future cost of their territory.

Reuben, Gad, and the half-tribe of Manasseh, at their own request, had already received their portions (13; Num. 32:1-38) on the east of the Jordan. Caleb of Judah, the twin spy with Joshua, who brought back a faithful report, was given as his own the city Hebron in the hill-country. All the southern section of the land extending to the river of Egypt, was assigned to Judah (15:1-63), in whose territory stood Caleb's Hebron.

The powerful Joseph tribes were given the central backbone of the country: Ephraim the middle territory with the half-tribe of Manasseh on the north reaching to Mt. Carmel, and its projection eastward to the Jordan.

We have no means of knowing how much time was consumed in the allotments and assignments of the tribes,—but the writer describes the remaining rather unequal divisions as the result of a survey made by twenty-one men. On the basis of their report and allotments we find the following portions of territory designated:

Benjamin, north of Judah and south of Ephraim (18:11-28), with all its cities, including Jerusalem.

Simeon, within the southern section of that already allotted to Judah, as if this weak tribe required the protection of the stronger. In later times Simeon seems to have been wholly absorbed by the powerful Judah.

The entire section north of the western half-tribe of Manasseh, Issachar, covering the plain of Esdraelon to the Jordan, Zebulun embracing Galilee, Asher stretching up the sea-coast as far as Tyre, and Naphtali bordering the Jordan, the sea of Galilee and as far north as the sources of the Jordan. The last surveyor's lot fell to Dan, and it lay between Benjamin and the Mediterranean Sea, including Joppa and some Philistine strongholds. Joshua's chosen city was Timnath-serah in the hill-country of Ephraim.

Cities of refuge as a check on blood revenge were named

west of the Jordan as follows: Kedesh in Galilee, for the far north; Shechem in Ephraim, in the centre; and Hebron in Judah in the south. Those on the east of Jordan were Bezer in Reuben for the south; Ramoth-gilead in Gad for the centre, and Golan in Bashan for the far north.

The Levites were not allotted any portion of the country as were the other tribes. To them by divine command all the tribes gave by lot forty-eight cities and their pasture-lands about those cities (Joshua 21). They were quite evenly distributed throughout all the country, so that they might be available wherever needed for service. Among those cities we find Hebron, Libnah, Debir, Gibeon, Ana-thoth, Shechem, Gezer, Aijalon, Taanach and Kedesh, west of the Jordan; east of that line there were Golan in Bashan, Bezer, Ramoth-gilead and Heshbon.

It will be noticed that the Levites possessed all the six cities of refuge and many other important centres of the land, whence they could exercise a most salutary influence, if they were so inclined.

104. Last Acts of Settling Down (Joshua 22). Lest Israel should forget Jehovah their God, Joshua assembled all the congregation of the people at Shiloh, and set up the tabernacle, as a centre of service to Jehovah. As soon as all the tribes had been provided for, Joshua called together the soldiers of the two and one-half tribes from over the Jordan, who had fought side by side with the western war-riors, and commended them for their loyalty to their pledge made to Moses, and for their services in the conquest of the land. He also charged them to give diligent heed to the commandments and law delivered by Moses. Then he blessed them and sent them back to their homes east of the river.

On reaching the Jordan they decided to build an altar both as a witness to Jehovah, who had preserved them dur-ing all the time of their military service with their brethren, and as a mark of their common loyalty to the God of their nation. The tribes on the west of the river heard of this altar-building and, suspecting their motives, dispatched Phinehas and ten princes to investigate the meaning of it all. When the real explanation was given, Phinehas and his commission returned fully satisfied with the reason which inspired the erection of the altar-memorial.

105. Joshua's Last Words (Joshua 23 and 24). Some years after Israel's quiet settlement in their allotted territory, Joshua called together the chief officials of the nation. He was far-sighted and keen-witted enough to realize the imminent dangers that threatened the moral safety of Israel. He saw that the men of his age and rank, as Caleb and Eleazar, were soon to pass on without leaving successors adequate to cope with the situation. The increasing familiarity between Israel and their ought-to-be-enemies inspired him to take what steps he could to hold up the hands of the weaklings, and to re-pledge those regarded as pillars in the religious life of the people. Then in his address he reminded them that he was old and had only a few more days to live. He also pointed out that they still had some land unsubdued, whose inhabitants were a menace to Israel's faithfulness and loyalty to Jehovah. They were not to mingle with them nor even to name their gods, much less to swear by them. Disobedience would bring swift punishment and early extinction.

Another record (24) pictures all the tribes coming together at Shechem to hear Joshua's final message. He began with the migration of Abram, and scanned the peaks of history down across the years to his own day, especially emphasizing their providential preservation throughout all that long past. He challenged Israel to serve Jehovah, the God of Israel. The people pledged their faithfulness to him, renewed their covenant at Shechem, and protested against the possibility of their falling away to or bowing down to the gods which their fathers had served beyond the river (24:14-16). On the completion of the pledge Joshua sent away the people, each to his inheritance.

Soon thereafter Joshua died, being 110 years old, and

was buried in his estate at Timnath-serah, in the hill-country of Ephraim. The writer adds that the bones of Joseph, which had been carried up from Egypt, were buried in Shechem in a parcel of ground which Jacob had bought from Hamor. Eleazar also died and was buried in Gibeah of Phinehas.

Joshua's unswerving faithfulness to Jehovah and his unimpeachable character made an indelible impression on all the Hebrews. Their pledge and covenant to remain true to such a God was kept through all the years of Joshua and all the days of the elders that outlived Joshua. The co-operation and commingling of Hebrews and Canaanites immediately following the settlement in the land could have been forecast by any careful student of neighbouring nationalities. But even Joshua with all his past experience seems not to have measured the strength and adhesive power of the proximity of the two peoples. The speed with which they almost amalgamated, and the character of that combination, reveals the weakness of the hold which the service of Jehovah had upon the Hebrews. Their subsequent lapses into all the abominations of the Canaanites are simply the natural outcome of their devotion to the Canaanite ritual and customs. Their pledges to follow Jehovah soon faded away, and the appeal of the gods of Canaan and of their devotees quietly and fascinatingly led the Israelites into forbidden paths. Is this what we are to expect of the generations that followed so great and noble a character as Joshua? If the power for righteousness of such a life as Joshua's so soon faded away, what can we say of the crudity, the shallowness, the hypocrisy of the people who were regarded as worshippers of Jehovah in that day? They were little if any better than the pagans by whom they were surrounded, and who finally pulled them down to their own level. The book of Judges is a pathetic revelation of the character of the Hebrews underneath the religious veneer that seems to have been theirs during Joshua's life. Next to hopeless was the task of the few pious judges who arose as their saviours from complete obliteration before the fascinating power of the Canaanites. That story awaits us in the next chapter.

NOTE ON FIG. 30, tailpiece below: Gezer has been more thoroughly excavated than any other ancient city of Palestine. Its mound stands on the uplands between the Philistine plain and the hill-country of Judah. Its rôle in the history of this area was continuous from 2500 B. C. to the Christian era. Macalister's excavations of that old centre of civilization have opened a new volume in the history of Canaan. A single instance gives the place a romantic past, viz.: Pharaoh of Egypt conquered the city and gave it to his daughter, one foreign wife of King Solomon, in the tenth century B. C., and her husband was, of course, impelled to make it attractive, and built it into a place of beauty.

CHAPTER XII

THE DARK AGES OF THE JUDGES

106. Israel's Precarious Position. Israel had wedged her way into Canaan by force of arms extending over a considerable stretch of years. Some parts of the country had been brutally wrested from the population and occupied by the conquerors. Some strong cities remained un-

NOTE ON FIG. 39, headpiece above: The High Place was the site of ritual worship of the early peoples of Palestine and Syria, and was used by the Hebrews more or less during the entire Old Testament period. Our picture is that of the so-called "cathedral-altar" on the chief summit inside the city Petra. In the top of the rock a platform with an area of 20 ft. x 47 ft. was sunk. Two altars were chiseled out, the main one in the right centre of the picture with steps leading up to it. On the top a hollowed-out place was for libations. The altar on the left has a deep pool cut out, probably for washings. Further back is a round altar for bloody sacrifices, also let down into the rock.

The Old Testament high places were usually on high hills, under green trees, with accompanying stone pillars or wooden figures.

148

attacked and unharmed. Some city-states had protested against the invasion of the foreigners, but kept safely within their walls.

When the territory of Canaan was allotted to the various tribes, each received some share of the unconquered cities and strongholds. On the southwest there lay on the plain of the seashore several powerful Philistine cities; farther south were the hostile Amalekites of ancient fame; and on up the coast some strong Canaanite centres. On the north and northeast were the Aramæans of Damascus, and also to the east thereof. East of the Jordan were the Amorites and south of them the Moabites. South of the Arnon River lay the Edomites, who refused Israel's passage through their land. In the northwest the Phœnicians seem to have paid no attention to the invaders; as they had no reason as yet for attacking them.

With all these cities and centres of population, thrifty and prosperous, and still unconquered, the tribes were to meet the test of their strength and character. One or the other must go down; or, both might be amalgamated; or one might be absorbed by the other.

A real danger which faced these Israelites was the social contact. Indeed, there was the possibility that the Hebrews would be content with their present foothold, and not wage warfare against the native population to extermination or even to conquest. In such case, they were liable to live side by side, first, in tolerance of each other, then in trade relations, and then in friendly intercourse. Common customs and manners would in themselves be an easy introduction, and the same language (Isa. 19:18) would speed up their good-will and familiarity. Finally they would cross the boundary line of their pledge to Joshua (Joshua 23:12, 13), and intermarry with their former enemies, but now friendly neighbours. This would result in part in an amalgamation with their should-be foes, and a disappearance of their tribal identity, and an ultimate submergence.

A still more subtle danger that lurked in their offing was

the religious one. They were living in every day contact with a system of worship widely different from the pure religion of the Jehovah who had brought them safely thus far. The land was full of sacred trees, springs, stones, and high places devoted to baals of various kinds. These symbols and the accompanying licentious rites made an especial appeal to the already weakening Israelite, and too often enticed him away from the more spiritual and less tangible Jehovah-worship of the wilderness and the nomadic life of their fathers.

The new settled life carried with it certain requirements. The Hebrews, except the two and one-half tribes east of the Jordan, were largely forced to change their occupations, their mode of living. Instead of being wandering nomads with flocks and herds, they had to settle down in one place, and become farmers, tradesmen, mechanics and labourers. Instead of living in tents they had to learn to make their homes in villages, towns and cities, with all their impairment and depletion of the physical man. These changes carried with them a shifting and rearrangement of their former customs of everyday life. Such breaking down of former regulations sometimes jeopardized their future habits and morale, especially in face of the quite different life of their new neighbours.

But another great problem that they as a nation must face, was how to effect a unified organization, how to maintain their identity in the face of so many disintegrating elements. If all the unconquered strongholds and cities should unite in a simultaneous attack on them they would be exterminated. But with that as an improbability, and with faithfulness to Jehovah their God, they fully expected to win out in the long run, though depleted in strength, and weakened in morale because of the many apostasies which would eat into their vitals, in the course of the future.

107. The Period of the Judges. Years of close contact and intermingling with the native population dulled the glow of the best of Israel's worshippers of Jehovah. The

Canaanites had taught them the necessity of gifts and offerings to local gods if they (Israelites) expected crops and flocks. Israel had quickly fulfilled the conditions by honouring such local baals, and had also worshipped Jehovah as their national God. This commingling of worship both corrupted the Hebrews, and gradually let slip from their lives the wholesome effect of their conception of Jehovah. In other words, the nature-worship of the Canaanites, with all its symbols and depraved rites, by degrees, displaced the sincere and whole-souled service of Jehovah taught by Moses and Joshua, and threatened the extinction of the people who were in this training-school of Jehovah their God.

Just how much time was covered by this period we have no definite means of figuring out. The number of years assigned to certain stretches of peace are so mechanical that they leave us where we started. Several of the judges may have been contemporaneous, and thus have shortened the entire period by many years. Probably the period covered not over 150 years, and may not have been that long. The chaos and conquests, the drag-down and the resiliency give us a continual shifting of scenes from loyalty to Jehovah to apostasy and captivity, and a subsequent rescue.

108. The Function of the Judges. The widely separated units of the tribes of Israel and their lack of national organization worked to their disadvantage while living among the Canaanites. More than this, the small nations bordering on the land of Canaan, such as the Aramæans, the Moabites, the Midianites, the Ammonites, and the Philistines, were a constant menace to Israel's endurance and continuity.

The writer of Judges says: " Now these are the nations which Jehovah left, to prove Israel by them, even as many as had not known the wars of Canaan " (3:1); that is to say, the new generation born after Joshua's conquest of the land.

The narrative pathetically tells us over and over again: " And they forsook Jehovah, and served Baal and the Ash-

taroth " (2:13). And Jehovah was angry with them, " and
he delivered them into the hands of spoilers that despoiled
them; and he sold them into the hands of their enemies
round about." When they became so sick at heart and down-
trodden by these enemies that they cried out to Jehovah for
relief, then he raised up saviours to deliver them. These saviours he called " Judges." Among the Phœnicians such officers were administrators of commissions. But these chosen
saviours were sometimes men of God, whose valour not only
rescued the Hebrews from oppression, but perpetuated their
leadership in times of peace. The religion of Israel as over
against the paganism of their enemies, was under their
guardianship. They stood for the worship of Jehovah, even
if at times their conception of him was crude, cruel, and
primitive. They were in a way the personification of the
conscience of Israel in that period of the world, while they
had no fixed rulers or guides, where " every man did that
which was right in his own eyes."

109. Israel's First Three Oppressions (Judges 3:7-
31). The Aramæans on the upper Euphrates had made a
raid down through the southwest and exacted tribute from
their victims for eight years. Among these unfortunates
were the Israelites. Othniel (first judge), a nephew of the
noble Caleb, already prominent in history, was raised up by
Jehovah, as a saviour of the Hebrews from their exacting
oppression; "and he judged Israel " (3:10),—the land
having respite from oppression for forty years.

The Moabites on the east side of the Jordan had suffered
no little at the hands of the Israelites. The name Balaam
recalled to them their slaughter on one occasion by these
same peoples. Now they felt strong enough to even up the
score. With the help of Ammon and Amalek, their allies,
their king, Eglon, crossed the Jordan and took that same
old Canaanite city Jericho, the city of palm-trees. From
this place as his capital he exacted taxes from the subjugated Israelites for eighteen years.

Upon their importunate cry to Jehovah he raised up Ehud

(second judge), a left-handed Benjamite, to deliver them. After turning over the usual tribute, Ehud, by a bit of treachery, secured an audience with Eglon in his summer palace. On the pretext of delivering a message from God direct to the king, he thrust him through with a dagger, and escaped to the hill-country of Ephraim. There he blew a trumpet, and the oppressed people, who were expectantly waiting, rushed down into the Jordan valley, seized the fords of the Jordan, and cut down every Moabite who attempted to escape over the river. Ten thousand fell that day; and Israel was complete victor and had rest from that direction for " eighty years."

The Philistines on the southwest also had sorely over-ridden the rights of Israel until Shamgar (third judge), the son of Anath, apparently a giant, slew of the same Philistines, with an ox-goad, 600 men, and rescued suffering Israel. This might have occurred contemporaneously with either of the last two oppressions.

110. The Canaanite Oppression (Judges 4 and 5). The Canaanites of the north had gradually gained the whip-hand over the tribes settled among them. Joshua's battle at Merom (Joshua 11:1-14) was merely temporary in its results. Jabin, king in Hazor, so heavily trampled down all the Israelites in his realm, that they groaned under their burdens. Even the highways were infested with brigands and the byways were unsafe for travel. Israel implored Jehovah for relief.

Deborah (fourth judge), a prophetess, was then judging Israel in the hill-country of Ephraim between Bethel and Ramah. Word having reached her of their desperate condition, she called to Barak in Kedesh-Naphtali and appealed to his loyalty and commanded him forthwith to mobilize 10,000 men to strike for freedom. He promised to undertake the task if she would accompany him. She consented. Her moral courage was equal to any emergency that might arise.

Barak marshalled his 10,000 men on Mt. Tabor on the

north side of the plain of Esdraelon. Jabin's forces were in charge of his commander-in-chief, Sisera, who was stationed at Harosheth of the nations,—an oak forest bottling up the northwest end of the plain of Esdraelon, except the cut made between it and Mt. Carmel by the river Kishon, that flows northwestward to the bay at Haifa. Sisera's strategy was to drive through the length of the plain toward the Jordan River and thus cut off any possible juncture of the army of north Israel with that of the south. With his 900 chariots of iron and mobile troops, Sisera drove through this plain on the highway, forming a mighty military line through Megiddo, Taanach and Beth-shean, thus solidifying his army and cities. This strategic movement was in plain view of Barak and his army on the top of Mt. Tabor. At the command of Deborah, spokesman for Jehovah, Barak, at the head of his 10,000 men, charged down the south side of Mt. Tabor against Sisera's centre. The suddenness and roar of the onset struck terror into the enemy. At the same time, 'the stars from the heavens fought against Sisera' (5:20) and the rain fell in torrents. The soft soil of the plain was turned into a morass. The plunging horses and the sinking chariots threw the Canaanites into disorder, and after a first set-to, into defeat,—attributed to the storm as the work of an angry god. The rising waters of the Kishon added peril to the awful carnage that fell upon the Canaanite troops and chariots.

To avoid capture, Sisera leaped from his mired chariot and fled on foot, and went toward the tent of Heber the Kenite. Jael, the wife of Heber, cunningly invited him into her tent, where as guest his person should have been inviolable. When, in sheer weariness, he had fallen fast asleep she treacherously slew him; and went out and reported her act to the pursuing Barak. Israel, with God's help, wholly subdued the Canaanites on that day, and continuously until Jabin's kingdom had been destroyed.

The poem of chapter 5 is among the oldest pieces of Hebrew literature, and may have been written immediately after the battle. At any rate it gives a few stirring glimpses of actors in that great tragedy. Barak's army was composed of the men of Zebulun, Issachar and Naphtali of the north, of Ephraim and Benjamin of the centre, while Judah and Simeon of the south are not mentioned. East of the Jordan, " Great resolves of heart," mark Reuben's attitude toward the campaign, while Dan and Asher risked nothing, but remained in their ships on the sea. Jael's treacherous deed is praised and immortalized at a time when perfidy and cruel barbarity were in good standing. The methods of dividing spoil are celebrated in the final verses of this marvellous poem of a crude and cruel age.

Similar battles in history are full of interest to the student of ancient times. Read the record of the battles of Cressy, and of Timoleon against the Carthaginians.

111. The Midianite Oppression (Judges 6–8). The several variant records of this oppression give us substantially these facts. While Israel was wandering in the wilderness they probably made a pact with the family of Jethro the Midianite, father-in-law of Moses. Their nomadic character and life carried them wherever they could find pasturage. Located east of the Jordan in this period, they, with the Amalekites, made annual raids west of that river into the territory of the central plateau and plain of Esdraelon, just following the wheat harvest. These yearly forays so terrorized the Israelites that they hid in caves, dens and strongholds, while the raiders gathered up the harvests and drove off their flocks and herds.

Seven years of such devastating sorties by these denizens of the desert, brought Israel very low, and they importuned their God, Jehovah. In response an unnamed prophet appeared and rebuked them for their disobedience. Then an angel of Jehovah came to Gideon (fifth judge), who was threshing his wheat in a winepress to avoid the raiding Midianites, and said, " Jehovah is with thee, thou mighty man of valour " (6:12). Gideon protested his insignificance, but was prevailed upon to drive ahead. He tore down the altar of Baal, cut down the Asherah, and built an altar to Jehovah, and offered thereon burnt offerings, and the wood of the Asherah idol. When the devotees of Baal demanded Gideon's death, his father protested that if Baal be a god let him contend for himself (Jerubbaal).

At the conclusion of the harvests the Midianites, Amalek-ites and the children of the East (desert) joined their raid-ing bands east of the Jordan, crossed the river and encamped on the plain of Jezreel. Gideon's call for volunteer soldiers met an immediate response from Manasseh and the northern tribes, up to 32,000 men. The fearful and tremulous among them, 22,000, were sent home, and the remaining 10,000 were reduced by a device supposed to reveal fighting quali-ties, to a lone 300. A master strategist, Gideon in the night-time arranged his little band in three companies about the multitudes encamped like locusts in the valley below. At a given signal from their leader each man smashed his pitcher, blew his trumpet, and waved his torch, shouting, " the sword of Jehovah and of Gideon " (7:20). Imagining each torch was that of a leader of troops, the motley bands of raiders broke for safety and rushed pell-mell for the Jordan, and across it into the lands beyond. Gideon called for addi-tional pursuers, and did not stop until he had driven the raiders into the desert.

With his own sword he slew the two kings of the Midian-ites, and achieved a notable victory over the international brigands that for years had gleaned their land of crops, flocks and herds.

The completeness of the victory led the people to offer the rulership over them to Gideon as a kind of guaranty against any such invasions in the future. In his response he said to them, " Jehovah shall rule over you " (8:23). To pacify them he requested them to bring to him their gold nose-rings. Seventeen hundred shekels of gold (more than $1,000) were cast into a garment spread out at his feet. With these Gideon made an ephod and put it in Ophrah, his city, where " it became a snare unto Gideon and to his house " (8:27). Gideon thereafter lived a peaceful and quiet life, as far as polygamy would permit it, in his own house until his death at a good old age.

112. Abimelech, Son of Gideon (Judges 9). Israel, forgetful of their remarkable deliverance by the heroic Gideon from the Midianite scourge, again wantonly pursued the baalim and made Baal-berith, a foreign god, their god; " neither shewed they kindness to the house of Jerubbaal, who is Gideon " (8:35).

Gideon's regally polygamous life soon bore fruits in the conduct of his son Abimelech by a Shechemite woman. Attempting to establish an inheritable right to rule over the people as a successor to his father, Abimelech appealed to the Shechemites with his claim. He stated his case in such a way that they naturally, though not enthusiastically, decided in his favour and gave him a political fund of seventy pieces of silver. To carry out his plan he hired with the subsidy a band of gangsters who went with him to his father's house in Ophrah; and they there slew his seventy half-brothers on one stone,—not regarded in that day as more than the necessary precautions of a ruler (cf. the similar massacre of the seventy sons of Ahab, and the forty-two brothers of Ahaziah by Jehu in 2 Kings 10:1-11, 12-14).

Jotham, his youngest brother, only escaped the assassin's axe. He made his way to Shechem, where from the top of a rock he shouted to the curious crowd of Shechemites the earliest parable recorded in the Bible (9:7-20). Its keen cutting sarcasm drove home to the listeners the present truth and the future outcome of such a perfidious intrigue on the part of his barbaric half-brother. Having shot his arrow and hit the mark, he escaped and afterwards dwelt peacefully at Beer,—a safe distance from the despotic and dangerous Abimelech (sixth judge).

" Abimelech was prince (not king) over Israel three years " only (9:22). " The men of Shechem dealt treacherously with Abimelech " (9:23). The dragon's teeth which he had sown now produced a crop of vipers. The day of reckoning was already dawning. His nemesis was beginning to rise in all its pitilessness. Plots and counterplots dogged his steps and drove him to desperation. Finally, at the end of three years, not of rule, but of suppressing conspiracies, Abimelech ignominiously perished at the hands of a woman at Thebez who dropped a piece of millstone on his head while he was besieging the city. " They that take the sword shall perish with the sword " (Matt. 26:52).

113. The Ammonite Oppression (Judges 10:1–12:7). After the story of Abimelech we learn of two judges whose achievements, if they had any, are not recited. In the far north, in Issachar, appeared Tola (seventh judge), who came down and lived in the hill-country of Ephraim, as judge, twenty-three years. And then over in Gilead, Jair (eighth judge) judged Israel twenty-two years,—perhaps simultaneously with Tola.

Israel's treason against Jehovah now became ominous, for they served the baalim, the Ashtaroth, the gods of Syria, Sidon, Moab, Ammon and the Philistines. They seem not even to have feigned to worship Jehovah.

Again they were sold into the hands of their enemies, the children of Ammon, for eighteen years. Now Ammon dwelt on the eastern or desert boundaries of Gilead of the east-Jordanic territory. Their oppression covered all the allotments of Reuben, Gad and the half-tribe of Manasseh. Ammon's aggressiveness also carried them over the Jordan,. where they fought against Judah, Benjamin and Ephraim.

In their humiliation and despair the Israelites again supplicated Jehovah for relief. After recounting his many deliveries of them from their enemies, Jehovah says, " Go and cry unto the gods whom ye have chosen; let them save you in the time of your distress " (10:14). Instantly Israel became humbly penitent and put away their strange gods, and served Jehovah; and Jehovah was grieved at their misery.

Over in Gilead the Ammonites raised a great army, possibly to clean up and complete their supremacy over the

Israelites. These latter also assembled their fighting men at Mizpeh, east of the Jordan, within striking distance of Ammon; but they had no commander-in-chief. As soon as the Ammonites became aggressive, the Israelite chiefs in Gilead bethought themselves of Jephthah, a bastard son of Gilead, who, driven from home by his half-brothers, became a leader of outlaw freebooters in the land of Tob. They sent to him and offered him their leadership. He accepted, on condition that, if victorious, he should be their head. At first there was an interchange of messengers in which Ammon demanded the return to themselves of the land formerly ruled by Sihon, king of the Amorites, on the ground that it originally belonged to them. Jephthah recalled to them the necessity which compelled Israel to capture the territory, which she now proposed to hold. Ammon turned a deaf ear to all such unpalatable reminders, and forced Israel to take the defensive. A single verse (11:33) tells the gruesome story of his smiting of twenty cities and of the great slaughter of the Ammonites, and their full subjection to the children of Israel. One event saddened the joy of Jephthah. The fulfilment of a foolhardy vow made before the battle compelled him to sacrifice to Jehovah an only daughter,— an entirely probable act for a cruel outlaw of the desert border to carry out.

The signal victory of this border ruffian, Jephthah, over the Ammonites aroused the jealousy of the proud Ephraimites, who sharply resented his slight of neglecting to call for their aid. They even sent troops eastward over the Jordan to emphasize their complaint. Jephthah hurled back their charges and attacked them, and defeated them. His forces took the fords of the Jordan where the Ephraimites would cross to their western inheritances. When an Ephraimite came to cross the river, the guard said, " Are you an Ephraimite? " If he said, " Nay," the guard said, " Say now Shibboleth;" if he said, " Sibboleth," he was immediately cut down with a sword—resulting in the slaughter at the fords of the river at that time of " 42,000 " Ephraimites. A similar test might be adopted to-day to identify a German, if we should require him to say, " think," when he would say " tink," or " those," when he would say, " zose."

Jephthah (ninth judge) was a kind of military leader and guide for the east-Jordanic tribes for six years, though with a crude frontier kind of justice that was extremely primitive and unwritten.

114. The Philistine Oppression (Judges 12:8–16:3). Minor judges appeared west of the Jordan in three different centres before the date of the exploits of Samson. In Bethlehem, Ibzan (tenth judge), with thirty sons and as many daughters, judged Israel seven years. Elon (eleventh judge), in Zebulun, far to the north, dealt out justice ten years. Abdon (twelfth judge), an Ephraimite, with a spectacular posterity, judged Israel eight years.

On the rich alluvial plain in southwest Palestine, somewhere in the twelfth century B. C., sea-pirates, the Philistines, from the islands of the Mediterranean (probably Crete) landed and built up a colony. Their coherency and their strength made them a people to be reckoned with for the next 800 years. They built five strong cities which were ruled over by as many powerful lords. If you notice carefully you will see that Joshua conquered none of these cities (Joshua 13:3), and that some of them were allotted to Judah for his inheritance.

These unconquered Philistines could not resist the temptation to push up into the hill-country that formed their eastern boundary. Israel had so far forgotten Jehovah that he delivered them over to the doubtful mercies of these invaders.

The stories of Samson, the Danite, are a collection of weird hero-tales, loosely strung together, having to do with these Philistines. We find here no army, no battles, no national or tribal uprisings, but merely the freakish acts of one Hebrew, with traits similar to those of the Babylonian mythical hero, Gilgamesh.

Samson's birth was an answer to the piety and loyalty to Jehovah of his parents. He was to be a Nazirite, one who should avoid certain foods and drinks and never cut his hair. Living in Zorah, in close contact with the Philistines, Samson early fell under their spell, even though Jehovah blessed him in the camp of Dan.

Down in Timnah, Samson saw a Philistine damsel who fascinated him, and he begged his parents to get her for him for a wife, since it was the father's business to negotiate with a damsel's father for her hand. They protested, but to no purpose. Finally they went down with him to seal the bargain (perform the ceremony) at Timnah. On the first day of the wedding-feast, Samson, to enliven the occasion, proposed to his thirty Philistine companions a riddle, whose solution by the seventh day would earn for each of them a fine linen wrapper and a gala outfit, or vice versa. Facing almost certain defeat at the hands of Samson, they threatened to burn the bride and her father's house if she could not inveigle her lover into revealing the true answer to his riddle. Her continuous and persistent lachrymose importunity broke down Samson's resistance. On the seventh day they gave the correct answer and Samson lost. In his wrath he said, " If ye had not ploughed with my heifer, ye had not found out my riddle " (14:18).

Fighting mad against his Philistine companions, Samson went down to Ashkelon, killed thirty men, took their outfits of raiment and paid his forfeit to the hypocritical thirty. More than that, he left the wedding-feast in exasperation without claiming his wife, and went off home to his parents.

After a little time in the wheat harvest he went down to visit and claim his would-be bride. His prospective father-in-law interrupted him with the news that he had given her to " his friend " (best man!) after Samson had returned on the evening of the seventh day; and now requested Samson to take her sister, younger and fairer than she. Samson's anger, ingenuity, and skill came to his rescue; for he is said to have caught 300 jackals, tied their tails together, two and two, with a torch between each two, and let them loose in the Philistine grain fields;—thus he burnt not simply their standing grain, but that already put up into shocks. The Philistines, in their bitter resentment, burnt down the house of the Timnite, Samson's father-in-law, over his and his daughter's heads. Then they attacked Samson, who " smote them hip and thigh with a great slaughter " (15:8), and escaped and hid himself in a cave at the rock Etam.

Samson's exploits among the Philistines stirred them up to retaliate. Raiders again started up into the hill-country. Three thousand men of Judah went down to the rock Etam and implored Samson to sacrifice his person in the interest of the whole land,—to allow himself to be delivered over bound to the Philistines.

When the Judeans swore they would not kill him, Samson permitted them to bind him with two new ropes, and they brought him to Lehi, where they met the exultant shouting Philistines. At once, the spirit of Jehovah came upon him, and the ropes became like flax caught on fire, and fell off his hands. He grabbed the first thing he found, a fresh jaw-bone of an ass, strong and heavy. With it he slew a thousand men, Philistines. Look up Shamgar's exploits (3:31) and that of Shammah (2 Sam. 23:11). Lehi means " jawbone."

Samson had another adventure in Gaza, where the citizens closed the gates of the city at night, thinking to entrap him. In the middle of the night he went out, and, finding the gates shut, bolted and barred, he pulled them off, bar posts and all, and carried them to the top of a mountain above Hebron.

115. Samson and Delilah (Judges 16:4-31). Samson fell in love with another Philistine woman in the valley of Sorek, whose name was Delilah. The five lords of the Philistines (Joshua 13:3) had their eyes on Samson, and when this opportunity arose, offered Delilah, each of them, 1,100 pieces of silver, if she would ferret out the source of his great strength. At the same time she had liers-in-wait in an inner chamber, ready for any kind of police service she required.

Samson jollied her along by first naming new bowstrings which the Philistine lords furnished her. When she said, " the Philistines are upon thee, Samson " (16:9), he snapped them like tow touched by fire. New ropes went the same way. The locks of his hair woven into the web of a loom would seem to be effective; but at her signal to the liers-in-wait, Samson, though lying down, arose and carried away the pin of the beam and the web fastened to his hair.

His Philistine Niobe employed all the tricks of her class (14:16) to discover the secret of Samson's strength. Fool that he was, finally, tired out, he succumbed to her wiles,— " let the cat out of the bag." She put him to sleep on her lap, cut off the seven locks of his hair, and probably bound him, and gave the signal to the hiding Philistines. Samson thought to himself, " I will go out as at other times and shake myself free " (16:20), for he was not aware that his Nazirite pledge had been violated nor that Jehovah had left him.

The Philistines arrested him, bored out his eyes, led him down to Gaza (2 Kings 25:7), whose city gates he had carried away; put him in the prison, fastened him with bronze shackles; and made him grind at the handmill,—the work of women slaves.

After a time the lords of the Philistines held a great thanksgiving sacrifice and feast unto Dagon, their god, at Gaza, because he had delivered their enemy into their hand. The high officials and their ladies from the royal cities were present; and they were jubilant when they saw Samson, a captive and impotent in their power. At the height of their festivities, they called for the captive Hebrew, whose wit on many occasions had been keen and sharp, to furnish amusement for them. Samson, blind and dependent, was led by a prison servant to the court of the great building and placed on the platform between two columns at the top of

the steps, in plain view of all the crowd within the pillared
court and on the roof which slanted toward the court.
There Samson entertained those revellers, probably with
melodramatic and humourous sayings and actions. When
his rôle had been completed, in a perfectly natural manner,
he asked for the pillars of the house, that he might lean
against them. His hair having somewhat grown, though
unnoticed by his captors, Samson made one supreme appeal
to Jehovah for strength to avenge himself on the Philistines
" for one of his two eyes." Upon that he gave one mighty
push with his right hand and his left against the two columns between which he stood, saying, " let me die with the
Philistines." With a death-dealing crash, down came the
house, pillars, roof and all its occupants, upon the gala
assemblage of revellers below. So that " the dead that he
slew at his death were more than they that he slew in his
life " (16:30),—about 3,000 men and women,—a retalia-
tory tragedy.

Samson's brethren and kinsmen tenderly carried back his
body and buried it in the family burying-place between
Zorah and Eshtaol. Samson (thirteenth judge) had
" judged " Israel twenty years.

**116. Migration of the Danites and Religious De-
generacy** (Judges 17 and 18). Chapters 17–21 embody
two narratives supplementary to the book of Judges proper.
The syncretism of worship resulting from contact with the
Canaanites and their religion is finely illustrated by the
case of Micah and his mother (17). She had dedicated
1,100 pieces of silver to Jehovah to be made into " a graven
image and a molten image " (vs. 3). Micah set aside one
of his sons to be a priest to him in his " house of God."
Later a Levite chanced to pass that way and Micah consecrated him to be his priest in his own private sanctuary
containing the images which he had made.

In these same years the Danites, whose activity had been
so restricted by the unconquered Canaanites or their own
brethren, sent five men to spy out the land, to discover

where they might find a possible opening for another settlement. On their way, they visited this notable Micah and
his individual priest, with whom they took counsel. On
towards the north they pushed until they came to Laish, a
city quiet and secure, " after the manner of the Sidonians,"
living in an isolated part of the land, " where there is no
want of anything that is in the earth " (18:10).

On their return the spies' favourable report started a
campaign of Danites of 600 men, armed for war. In their
march northwards they stopped at the house of Micah, and
forcibly took from him his images, his personal priest, and
all the paraphernalia that went with the priestly services.
When Micah strongly protested against such high-handed
banditry, he was gently warned to hold his peace; and he
submissively turned back to his house.

The invading band of 600 Danites finally came to that
city Laish, reported on by the spies, made a surprise attack,
" smote them with the edge of the sword, and burnt the
city with fire " (18:27),—an unprovoked, savage piece of
primitive warfare. The distance of the city from Sidon,
with whom it seems to have had political affiliations, prevented any relief or aid in its disaster.

The Danites then rebuilt the city, and dwelt there, and
called it Dan, after the name of their ancestor. Here they
set up the image stolen from Micah, even though the house
of God was in Shiloh, and installed the priest they had
brought with them.

So significant became this site that in the future it was
named as the northern extremity of Palestine in the phrase
" from Dan to Beer-sheba." The modern ruin is Tell
el-Kadi, immediately by the most abundant and crystal-
clear source of the Jordan, a place up to the present (1928)
untouched by excavator's tools.

117. A Tribal Protest against Moral Degeneracy
(Judges 19–21). The insidious and slippery moral character of the Canaanites very early showed its true colours
in the social fabric of the mingling peoples. Strange to say,

this was first exposed to public gaze by a degraded and revolting crime at Gibeah of Benjamin. The wronged Levite sent a part of the ghastly dismembered body of his murdered concubine to each tribe of Israel. The abhorrence of the other tribes against Benjamin was instantaneous, and they rushed together before Gibeah to learn the facts from the Levite himself. He told his story with all its repellent details, and asked " advice and counsel." Unitedly Israel demanded of Benjamin the guilty criminals. This demand was thrown back into their faces, with an immediate mobilization of all their men of war, 26,700. Israel's great army asked counsel of God at Bethel. Acting on instructions, Israel gathered before Gibeah, the guilty city. On the first and second charges the mass army was driven back with heavy loss. But on the third day, by the tactics used at Ai, the Benjamites were caught between two armies and annihilated, except 600 men who fled to the rock Rimmon. The cities of Benjamin were wiped out with sword and fire, —a kind of public execution of a tribe which had tolerated and abetted the most revolting degeneracies of the Canaanites among whom they dwelt. For sentimental reasons the victors, who had pledged not to furnish wives for the 600 vestiges of the Benjamite army, relented and looked about for means of finding them wives without violating their pledges. Upon taking the roll of the tribes in the army, no one was found from Jabesh-gilead. That seemed to offer a way out. Twelve thousand of the best men of war were sent to smite such a self-centred, unpatriotic city. The violent and savage deed was carried out with all the horrors of that day,—the wiping out of the entire population except 400 virgins, who were brought back and turned over to 400 Benjamites. To provide for the other 200 the Israelites commanded them to attend an annual feast of Jehovah at Shiloh, and to hide themselves in the vineyards until the daughters of Shiloh came out to take part in the dances. Out from their hiding-places the Benjamites sprang, and caught each a damsel and carried her off to his inheritance, and she became his wife,—like a similar event in the history of Rome, the rape of the Sabine women.

Upon the completion of this task the Israelites returned each to his own estate, satisfied with the penalty meted out, though regretful for the well-nigh extinguished tribe.

118. A Migration and a Return (Ruth 1). In preceding sections we have encountered the sagging of Israel's morale, the storms of revolution against her oppressors, the break-down of her defenses against pagan religions, and her resiliency toward Jehovah when she struck the limits of her endurance. In the midst of such ground upheavals in her moral and religious life, there were many years of calm and quiet when man enjoyed the fruits of his own toil in peace and unafraid.

One of those beautiful oases in the wide stretch of the moral desert of Judges is pictured in the book of Ruth,—whatever may have been the date of its composition. As so often in the Old Testament, a famine opened the drama. Elimelech, his wife and two sons, migrated across to Moab to escape the hardships of a famine. The climate or the food or disease, wiped out all the male members of the family within the ten years of their sojourn in this foreign land. The sons had married Moabitish women, and left childless widows at their death. Naomi, Elimelech's widow, heard in Moab that Jehovah had restored prosperity to her native Bethlehem. Then she and her two daughters-in-law packed up and started for the land of Judah. At some point on the way, probably at the border, Naomi kissed the two and said, " Go, return each of you to her mother's house: Jehovah deal kindly with you, as ye have dealt with the dead and with me " (1:8). Then she kissed them again and they wept aloud and refused to return. After picturing the futility of their plan to go with her, she again entreated them to go back. Orpah finally weakened and returned, but Ruth resisted every entreaty, and clung to her mother-in-law, saying, " whither thou goest, I will go; and where thou lodgest, I will lodge; thy people shall be my people, and thy God my God " (1:16). Such devotion and determination could not be answered, and won the day.

Naomi and Ruth went on until they reached Bethlehem, in the barley harvest. The small town was all astir over Naomi's return without husband or sons; and many were the hours spent in reciting her sorrows of the last ten years in the land of Moab.

119. The Natural Course of Events (Ruth 2–4). Naomi came back to kinsfolk; her husband's family were prominent people in Bethlehem. Boaz was a farmer of high standing, and Ruth by permission of Naomi gleaned in his field after the reapers. Boaz's treatment of his reapers and their high respect for him attracted her attention. Boaz also took notice of her and gave her exceptional privileges, and this encouraged Naomi to thicken the plot, to weave the web of Ruth about her husband's kinsman Boaz. Their wits worked rapidly day and night. When Boaz and his servants remained all night at the threshing-floor to protect the grain, Ruth went unawares to the same spot and crept in softly and lay her down at the feet of Boaz. Startled by the presence of a stranger, he said, " Who art thou? " In reply she said, " Spread therefore thy skirt over thy hand-maid; for thou art a near kinsman " (3:9); in other words, " Take me as thy wife, for it is thy duty as a kinsman."

Boaz was so responsive to the request of Ruth that he said " Yes " on the spot, provided a nearer kinsman than he would not play the rôle. The next day Boaz went to the city gate, the headquarters for all business transactions, and sat down until the nearer kinsman arrived. Boaz selected ten men as a kind of redemption council before whom the question should be settled. Then he presented the case in full; the kinsman who should purchase the field of the deceased Elimelech should also include therewith Ruth, the Moabitess, to raise up the name of the dead upon his inheritance. The nearer kinsman balked at that provision, for it would mar his inheritance. And the redemption and Ruth fell to Boaz as the next in line.

The next step in the deal for the redemption of the inheritance was the formal transfer of the property to Boaz. In the presence of the elders of the city, assembled at the gate, the other kinsman took off his sandal and passed it over to Boaz, who said to the elders, " Ye are witnesses this day that I have bought all that was Elimelech's, and all that was Chilion's and Mahlon's, of the hand of Naomi. Moreover, Ruth, the Moabitess, the (former) wife of Mahlon, have I purchased to be my wife, to raise up the name of the dead. . . ." (4:9, 10).

Ruth the Moabitess later became an ancestress of David, of the line of kings of Judah and of our Lord (Matt. 1).

The purpose of this little book is, (1) to locate a charming domestic incident in the midst of the stormy age of the judges; (2) to present a bright and beautiful picture of one of the progenitors of the Messiah, the Saviour of the New Testament (4:18-22).

120. What About the Age of the Judges? Israel had been tested in the retort of Canaanite civilization. Only partially conquered, these natives had gone the full length in their spirit of resentment against the invaders. Where military strength could not avail, the Canaanites, by social contacts and local religious advice and counsel, achieved some marvellous results. Intermarriages, trading relations, common religious appeals for local baals, did much to put both peoples on the same level.

The inhuman, barbarous and brutal spirit of man in that age was common to Israelite and Canaanite. The blotting out of the entire life of any community by an enemy was a not unusual means of self-preservation, or of devotion to one's god. Pitiless treatment of captives and innocents was a characteristic of the age. Restrictions upon blood revenge such as were furnished by the cities of refuge were necessary if there should be any progress toward the administration of justice by courts of law.

The repeated calls upon Jehovah after long oppression and tyranny of the Canaanites and the other encroaching neighbours was evidence that the God who had led them through the wilderness was not entirely forgotten, even though his worship had been almost smothered by the multitudes of baals who flourished on every hill-top and under every green tree.

But their fading conception of Jehovah as an austere and jealous God was more and more apparent as they mingled with the Canaanites, not only socially but religiously. Symbols and rites used only for baal became, in Israel's mind, valid also for the worship of Jehovah. In other words, their religious service gradually became practically an amalgamation of the baals and Jehovah.

The judges seem to have held a little more closely to the real Mosaic service of their God, though some of them were not the models that the Hebrews could implicitly follow.

This is a period where we find in Canaan some little traces of writing, some isolated and scattered fragments, though written documents had been produced in Egypt and Babylonia for long centuries before this day. Only the exceptional scribe and genius had been able to put into words such notable and picturesque dramas as we find embodied in the fifth chapter of Judges. While the great nations of that and earlier ages had their distinguished writers, in these dark ages of Israel's history, the Hebrews groped about in the miasmic bogs and fogs of ignorance, superstition and necromancy. Added to these dead weights were the moral degeneracies that linked-up their everyday life with that of the Canaanites, whose practices made them the execration of all true worshippers of Jehovah of that and subsequent times.

Then the savage and barbarous character of warfare as carried on by all nations of that day seem to have controlled the Hebrews in their treatment of enemies, captives and victims. It dulled their finer sensibilities and quashed every tendency to justice, mercy, and kindness. A rapid survey of the book of Judges will recall to the reader so many inhuman, degenerate, cold-blooded assassinations and massacres that one almost wonders why such records were allowed to appear within the same collection with the Psalms and Isaiah.

The compiler's purpose was probably religious,—a warning to Israel for all the future against such wholesale apostasies from Jehovah.

NOTE ON FIG. 94, tailpiece below: Excavations in Palestine, especially in Gezer, have yielded many of the common tools of mankind. These were made of flint, bronze, or iron. They are sickles, axes, chisels, nails, needles, awls, knives of several shapes, and saws,—the one in our cut being supplied with a modern method of mounting. Before 1000 B. C. flint or bronze was the material used, but thereafter iron came into general use.

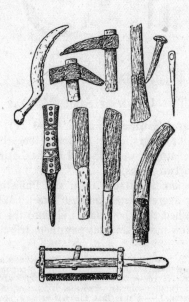

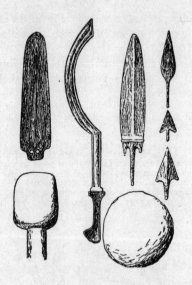

CHAPTER XIII

The Dawn of Samuel's Day

121. Eli and Samuel (1 Sam. 1:1–3:21). The books of Samuel, like Kings, were originally one, but for convenience of treatment were divided in the Latin Bible (the Vulgate) into two books.

Samson's sporadic attacks upon the Philistines had not checked their aggressiveness against Israel. Wherever possible they pushed their boundaries up into the hill-country, and made a few more Israelites pay them tribute.

NOTE ON FIG. 99, headpiece above: Macalister's finds are our source of information on these notable specimens of the weapons found in the débris of Gezer. Here we have from left to right above, a dagger, scimitar, sword (double-edged), arrowheads; below, a mace, and a sling ball (of stone),—of this last the writer saw scores about the diggings at Jericho.

Eli the priest (fourteenth judge) was judging Israel at Shiloh, the religious headquarters of all the Hebrews. Here he oversaw the sacrifices and offerings, and was counsellor to many who went up there to worship at the annual feasts. Among these worshippers were Elkanah and Hannah, the parents of Samuel, the lad who came in answer to Hannah's prayer. Reared in the precincts of the tabernacle and under the influence of Eli, he early learned to follow out the first teachings of Hannah, his mother.

Eli's own sons were morally Canaanite products appearing on corporate Israel. They disgraced both their father and the priesthood which they represented. It went so far that a " man of God " sharply censured them, and foretold the disaster that would surely befall the house of Eli, and that neither by sacrifice nor by offering could it ever be averted.

Samuel's faithfulness about the chores of the tabernacle and his care of Eli's needs, completely won over not only the affection of the old priest and judge, but of all the people who came up annually to worship at that centre. Though comparatively young, we are told that he received his prophetic call, and was recognized by Eli as the one whose message came direct from Jehovah; " And the word of Samuel came to all Israel " (4:1).

122. The Philistine Victory (1 Sam. 4:1–7:2). The Philistines became so aggressive that they forced Israel to meet them in battle at Aphek, presumably in the region of Mizpah, northwest of Jerusalem. Israel was defeated with a loss of about 4,000 men. To retrieve themselves they resorted to the device of bringing from Shiloh " the ark of the covenant of Jehovah," to go with them into battle. Its reception into Israel's camp was greeted " with a great shout so that the earth rang again " (4:5). The Philistines heard the noise and understood its meaning, and feared before the " gods that smote the Egyptians."

In the face of such odds the Philistines practically goaded themselves into battle by such provocative words as, " Be strong, and quit yourselves like men, O ye Philistines " (vs. 9). Into the battle they plunged, and Israel was smitten again, and lost 30,000 infantry; the ark of God was taken, and Eli's two sons, Hophni and Phinehas, of unsavoury fame, were slain.

The news of the terrific defeat of the Hebrews, the capture of the sacred symbol of God's presence, and the slaughter of Eli's two sons, were fatal to Eli, the ninety-eight-year-old judge of Israel at Shiloh. And Shiloh! What became of it? Subsequent hints and references seem to justify the conclusion that the Philistine invasion wholly laid waste this sacred city and destroyed its precious symbols of worship (Psa. 78:60-67; Jer. 7:12-14; 26:6, 9).

The victorious Philistines had taken as their prize captive " the ark of God." What should they do with it? Take it to Ashdod and present it to Dagon, their chief god, under whose auspices they went into battle. This they did. But the next morning Dagon had fallen from his pedestal on his face before the ark. The men of Ashdod set him up again in his place. The second morning they found him not only prostrate as on the previous day, but his hands and head were broken off on the threshold, and only his armless torso remained. In addition the people of Ashdod were smitten with an epidemic of boils. In their terror they called to the lords of the Philistines, who advised that the ark be taken to Gath. Its inception into Gath was accompanied by another outbreak of the same malady. And they sent it on to Ekron, to which the Ekronites protested, saying, " They have brought about the ark of the God of Israel to us, to slay us and our people " (5:10).

Then the lords of the Philistines were again requested to dispose of this fatal symbol of the God of Israel; because for seven months it had dispensed suffering and death to their people. On the advice of the priests and diviners it was resolved to send it back to Israel with appropriate trespass offerings to their god for the cessation of the plague. This plan was carried out with scrupulous accuracy until the

sacred symbol reached Beth-shemesh. Curiosity of the
Beth-shemites caused the death of seventy men (the 50,000
men is not connected with anything in the narrative; even
the conservative scholar Keil said it was an interpolation).
Upon the appeal of the Beth-shemites the men of Kirjath-
jearim went down and brought it to the hill of Abinadab,

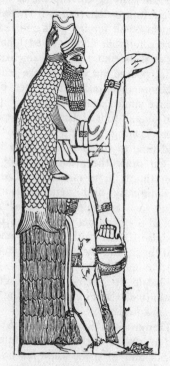

Fig. 21. Dagon, the Fish-god

One of the mythical figures whose activities are woven into the woof
of early Semitic life and worship. It represents a priest masked as
Ea, the god of the deep and of knowledge. In the daytime he mingled
with and taught men, and at night he disported in the sea. This
figure was first found in the palace of Ashurnatsirpal (884-860 B. C.)
in Nimrud-Calah.

who sanctified his son Eleazar as priest to keep it,— twenty years.

123. Samuel, the Leader (1 Sam. 7:3-17). The fatal consequences to the Philistines of the capture of the ark was merely a temporary check upon their daring incursions into the hill-country of the Hebrews. After the humiliating defeat of Israel accompanying the capture of the ark, Samuel conditions their future deliverance from the Philistines upon the banishment of all foreign gods and the Ashtaroth. They accepted the conditions and " served Jehovah only."

In a great national assembly at Mizpah, Samuel prayed for Israel; and they poured out water before Jehovah, as did the Canaanites before their gods, and fasted on that day, and said, " We have sinned against Jehovah " (7:6). And Samuel (fifteenth judge) judged Israel in Mizpah.

The Philistines, hearing of Israel's national gathering, thought it a good time to strike another blow at their perpetual enemy. On came the armed host to smite down Israel as at other times. The Israelites called to Samuel, and he prayed continually; and offered a young lamb as a burnt-offering, just as the Philistines were landing their attack. Jehovah also brought a great storm upon the attackers (cf. Joshua 10:10) with thunder and lightning, " and discomfited them; and they were smitten down before Israel " (vs. 10).

This decisive battle at Mizpah put an effective check upon the aggressions of the Philistines during the activity of Samuel as Israel's leader.

124. Israel Demands a King (1 Sam. 8). As judge, Samuel followed a circuit each year at stated times, at Bethel, and Gilgal, and Mizpah, while his own home was at Ramah. He appointed his two sons to sit as judges at Beer-sheba, down on the edge of the desert. But they accepted bribes and perverted justice, and became odious to the people. Other nations round about who were prosperous, even the Philistines, were led by kings (city-kings) whose authority was mandatory and final. The entire roll of judges who had dealt out justice through this period were neither uniformly good nor bad, in fact, some were quite mediocre in strength of character. Israel as a people now wished a more stabilized form of government and a more conspicuous person as head over them, like their neighbour peoples.

All the chief men of Israel met together and went as a delegation to confer with Samuel at Ramah. They were diplomatic and respectful yet painfully clear in their request that Samuel appoint for them a king to judge them. Of course, the old judge, the most powerful man in Israel, was displeased and grieved, that the conduct of his sons had precipitated the question. Jehovah pacified him by telling him that they were not rejecting him (Samuel), but their own God, Jehovah, and was told to listen to their demand. However, Samuel had the stern satisfaction of sketching the manner in which a king would treat them; even though he should oppress them and enslave them, their cry to Jehovah for relief would not be answered in the day when a king should rule over them.

Nevertheless, they insisted, that they might be like the neighbouring peoples. On Jehovah's command, Samuel was ordered to make them a king in place of Jehovah (8:7). And Samuel said to the delegation, " Go ye every man unto his city." The first story of Saul's choice (1 Sam. 9:1-10:16) is based on the command of Jehovah, and it was made privately; the second (10:17-27) was public and by lot. A theocracy such as that established by Moses and Joshua was now to be displaced by a monarchy,—a kind of electoral monarchy where the king should not be hereditary but chosen by some one, or by the people. This plan seemed to the converging tribes as their only salvation from the tyranny of such neighbouring peoples as the Philistines.

125. Samuel's Search for a King (1 Sam. 9). The romantic story of Saul's search for his father's lost asses is our introduction to the candidate for king. When it seemed doubtful whether they could find the asses, Saul's servant

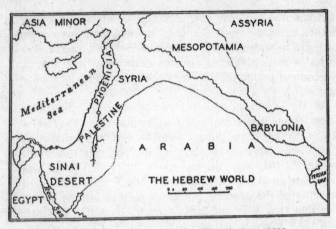

Map 6. Racial Map of the Hebrew World about 1000 B. C.

Egypt, Babylonia-Assyria, Asia Minor with Hittites and Aramæans, Phœnicia, and Arabia, were the great known lands and peoples about whom the Hebrews had heard.

suggested that they turn in at Ramah with their quarter-shekel of silver, and consult the " man of God," Samuel, " the seer." Samuel, having been forewarned of God, was ready to entertain Saul at a feast on the high place. After the feast and a brief interview they retire for the night. At early dawn Samuel called to Saul, " Up, that I may send thee away " (9:26). As they were passing out of the city Samuel took a vial of oil and poured it on the head of Saul, and kissed him,—as the President of France kisses an officer whom he decorates. And Samuel said, " Is it not that Jehovah hath anointed thee to be prince over his inheritance? " (10:1).

On that very day the anointed Saul met a band of prophets, who were under the guidance of Samuel, with their music and their prophesyings. The Spirit of Jehovah came mightily upon Saul, and he joined them with all his zeal He was lifted above his former self into a new realm of inspiration and thought.

To bring the kingship to a head, Samuel summoned Israel together to Jehovah at Mizpah. He reiterated some of Israel's past history and the part played in it by Jehovah, and accused them now of rejecting him and asking for a king to rule over them. This account specifies how the Israelites were arranged by tribes, and that a lot was cast for the tribe, the clan, the family and the individual. Saul was finally chosen, pulled out of his hiding-place, and set up before the people, head and shoulders above everyone else, a fine specimen of a royal form. Samuel said, " See ye him whom Jehovah hath chosen, that there is none like him among all the people? " (10:24). And all the people shouted, " Long live the king! "

Samuel again showed keen delight in specifying exactly how a king would treat them,—doubtless basing his statements on what he saw among the kings of that day; and to make sure that he would be vindicated in his judgment he wrote his words in a book and laid it up before Jehovah. This was the substance of his description: " He will take your sons and assign them for his own selfish purposes, for his chariots, to be his cavalrymen, and act as herald-runners before his chariots when on parade or diplomatic errands. He will appoint them captains over his army divisions and brigades; he will put them in charge of his agricultural enterprises, sowing, and reaping, and storing of grain. He will make them smiths to prepare implements of peace and instruments of war. He will take your daughters to be ' confectioners ' and cooks and bakers,—to manage the royal culinary department of service. He will appropriate the best of your fields, and your vineyards, and your olive-yards, for the royal household and its servants. He will tax you one-tenth of your crops, your seed, and your grapes for the use of his eunuchs and his other servants. He will commandeer your male and female servants and your choicest young men and your asses for his own work, and you shall be his servants."

Saul then went to his house to Gibeah, accompanied by a

retinue of warriors, though there were some who despised him and neglected their presents. But the greater part of the people were gratified that Jehovah had selected for them a king who should now be their security and guaranty for the future, against the incursions of any of their hostile neighbours, especially the Philistines.

NOTE ON FIG. 67, tailpiece below: The Egyptians had good reason to remember the Philistines. Ramses III (1198–1167 B. C.) repulsed their encroachments in the Delta, fought a great naval battle with them on the coast of Phœnicia, and for years effectively held them in check. Pottery and other remains found at Gezer and Lachish definitely locate them racially as Cretans, Greeks whose expansion effected the east and southeast coasts of the Mediterranean Sea. Their picturesque headdress with its coronet of feathers, secured by a strap under the chin, impressed the Egyptian artist. His long aquiline nose and dignified bearing, convey to us the temper of the peoples whose raids and dashes into the hills of Palestine were the dread of the Hebrews.

PERIOD V

THE MONARCHY

From Saul to Solomon

CHAPTER XIV

Saul's Tragical Career

126. Saul, the New King, Tested (1 Sam. 11). The presence of Saul in Gibeah gave the Israelites a sense of relief, for they greatly feared the encroachments of the

Note on Fig. 68, headpiece above: Ramses III in his defensive against these sea pirates from Crete, made large numbers of prisoners (note on Fig. 67). Note how securely their hands and arms were bound, in front of them, behind them, and over their heads. Powerful men as they were, they would be a menace even as prisoners, unless so manacled. This relief is found on the second pylon at Medinet Habu, Thebes, Egypt.

Philistines. But Saul's first call was to rescue the men of Jabesh-gilead from the distressing threats of Nahash the Ammonite, from the desert.

Saul's effective challenge sent to all the borders of Israel (11:7) worked like a charm; and troops rushed to his side in sufficient numbers to meet all requirements. Gathered together in the vicinity of Bezek, east of the Jordan, Saul arranged his armies into the famous three divisions (Judges 7:16; 9:43). By this strategy so often employed, they marched all night and came to the scattered camps of the Ammonites at the earliest dawn, striking them on three sides simultaneously. The effect was electric. The Ammonites, taken by surprise, scattered, ran and fled in all directions, completely defeated; and Jabesh-gilead, rescued, joined the enthusiastic admirers of the new king, Saul.

Samuel, to add strength to the new-king-sentiment, summoned the people to Gilgal (11:15) to renew the kingdom there. All the people went, and there made Saul king, offering sacrifices and peace offerings before Jehovah.

127. Samuel's Farewell Address (1 Sam. 12). Now that Saul had been anointed, chosen by lot, and confirmed by the people as king of Israel (whether as three reports of the same event, or three different occasions), Samuel stepped down from their leadership. But before he dropped all insignia of office he had a few plain words to say to them.

He resigned from his office because they now had a king, and because he himself was " old and greyheaded;" and he pathetically added, " behold, my sons are with you " (8:3, 5). Then he challenged them to impeach his past honesty in these words, " Whose ox have I ever taken? or whose ass have I ever taken? or whom have I ever defrauded? Whom have I oppressed? or of whose hand have I ever taken a bribe, to blind mine eyes? and I will restore it to you." And they unanimously testified to his absolute honesty and integrity as a man and a judge.

To emphasize the force of his position he gave them a retrospect of their past history, and how Jehovah had been their leader, merciful and kind, in spite of all their apostasies and double-dealing. He capped it off by coming back to their irresistible demand for a king. Their king they now have, but his permanence and value to them will depend entirely upon their faithfulness in following and obeying Jehovah their God. To confirm the truth of what he said, he called upon Jehovah to give an audible and visible evidence of his (Jehovah's) full agreement with Samuel's assertions. Then the thunder pealed and the rain poured, even though it was the time of the wheat harvest, a season when rain never fell.

So mightily were the people impressed by Samuel's words and character, and Jehovah's endorsement of him, that they broke out in an appeal for mercy and prayer. They even made a confession that their request for a king was evil. Samuel told them to fear not, but to follow closely Jehovah their God, and he would not forsake them. And still better, Samuel said, " Far be it from me that I should sin against Jehovah in ceasing to pray for you " (vs. 23; *cf.* Joshua 24).

128. Saul's Victory over the Philistines (1 Sam. 13 and 14). Chapters 13 and 14 have some repetitions and insertions that are confusing, but the real thread of the story seems plain. Saul's choice as king seems to have been requested to rescue Israel from the grip of the Philistines. Within two years after his election he chose 3,000 men for his army; but their pitiful lack of arms (13:19-22) seems to have been a handicap from the start. He divided his 3,000 men into three companies, of which he commanded 2,000 and Jonathan 1,000. Jonathan's valour and strategy gave the signal for the fight. He began by striking down the Philistine garrison in Geba. The contagion spread. Saul's trumpet rang through the hills, and Hebrews who had been fraternizing with the Philistines deserted them. Those who had been hiding in caves came out. And all joined in the pursuit and slaughter of the fleeing Philistines. So urgent

was the matter that Saul made a foolish oath to Jehovah
regarding anyone who should stop long enough to taste any
food. When his inquiry through a priest concerning pursuit through the night was met by silence, he suspected that
his oath had been violated. Upon investigation by lot, he
found that Jonathan had tasted a little honey to refresh
his spirit. Saul would have slain him, but the people
rescued him.

Another account tells us that at the end of a day of terrific slaughter the hungry people fell upon the spoil, the
cattle, sheep, and oxen, and ate them with the blood, until
Saul required that everyone should bring his animal to him
and drain its blood thoroughly before eating. Saul also
built his first altar to Jehovah at this place (14:31-35).

Thus ended this first great deliverance of Israel by Saul
from the invasions and incursions of the Philistines.

129. Saul's Clash with Samuel (1 Sam. 15).

As king
and military leader of Israel, Saul carried on wars with
Moab, Ammon, Edom, the kings of Zobah in the far north,
and ever and anon with the irrepressible Philistines.

Samuel brought a message from Jehovah to Saul to go
down to the edge of the desert and smite the Amalekites,
" man, woman, infant and suckling, ox and sheep, camel
and ass."

With an immense army mustered at Telaim, on the south
of Judah, he started on this campaign. At the city of
Amalek, which the author does not name, he began his
drive across the edge of the desert toward Shur before
Egypt. The population he wiped out, except King Agag,
whom he brought back as a trophy of victory. The best
of all kinds of cattle were also kept alive and driven back
as plunder.

The victorious army, with its booty and King Agag as a
show-prize, swept back on to the hills of Ephraim. Samuel, under divine guidance, met Saul, who greeted him with,
" Blessed be thou of Jehovah: I have performed the commandment of Jehovah " (15:13). With the keen sarcasm

of a strong man Samuel said, " What means all this bleating of sheep and lowing of cattle that I hear? " Saul had a ready answer, " They brought them from the Amalekites: for the people spared the best of the sheep and of the oxen, to sacrifice unto Jehovah thy God; and the rest we have utterly destroyed " (15:14, 15).

Then Samuel drew his cutlass and orally lashed Saul for his lack of fine moral distinctions, saying: " To obey is better than sacrifice, and to hearken than the fat of rams. For rebellion is as the sin of witchcraft, and stubbornness is as idolatry and teraphim. Because thou hast rejected the word of Jehovah, he hath also rejected thee from being king " (vss. 22, 23).

Saul understood, and pathetically confessed his sin against Jehovah; he deeply humiliated himself before Samuel and begged for mercy and recognition. Samuel finally relented, and " turned again after Saul." As if to seal his disapproval of Saul's act, Samuel ordered him to bring out Agag, the chief trophy of the Amalekite victory. With all the savageness required by the ban and the law (Lev. 27:28, 29), and characteristic of the age, Samuel hewed him into pieces. The fact that so noble a character as Samuel would adopt such a savage and cruel method of destroying a captive king, and also executed him with his own hands, bespeaks the almost total lack of any of the qualities of justice that we associate with the life of one who professes to worship God. In that day there was no inconsistency between piety toward God and the most brutal and inhuman treatment of one's enemies. Saul's wholesale massacre of the Amalekites was obedience and praiseworthy, but his saving the cattle and Agag was disobedience and condemnable. Then Samuel and Saul went, each to his own house, never to meet again. But Samuel's grief at the collapse of Saul clouded the old man's very life, until Jehovah mildly rebuked him, and let a ray of light in on his gloom. For he gave him the great honour of being selected to anoint a successor to the first King Saul, whose failure to carry out the orders of Jehovah were his impeachment.

NOTE ON FIG. 28, tailpiece below: The plain of Esdraelon is almost a right-angled triangle, with a twenty-mile base stretching from the north slope of the Carmel range to Mt. Gilboa—the apex being at Mt. Tabor. It lies 200–300 ft. above sea level, reaching its maximum near old Jezreel (*Zerīn*). It is drained by the Kishon, which flows north-westward to the sea. Its soil is exceeding rich, being volcanic in origin, from the age-long volcano on Little Hermon. Its population has been found usually on the edges, as the central area has been exposed to raids, and in winter the soil is marshy and quagmirish. This plain is the Armageddon of history, the battlefield of the nations.

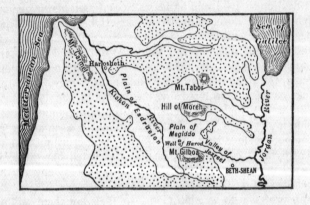

CHAPTER XV

DAVID'S PRE-REGAL CAREER

130. The Introduction of David (1 Sam. 16–20).
David is introduced to the reader of 1 Samuel in three
different narratives. In his first appearance he is the eighth
son of Jesse at Bethlehem, whom Samuel by divine direction anointed as Saul's successor on the throne of Israel
(16:1-13). In the next he was drafted into Saul's court as
a skilful player on a harp, to calm down the frenzied mental

NOTE ON FIG. 14, headpiece above: Beth-Shean (*Beisan*) lay near the
east end of the valley of Jezreel, about twelve miles south of the Sea
of Galilee and four miles from the Jordan. The University of Pennsylvania excavations show it to have been there earlier than 2000 B. C.
Fig. 73 shows that Ramses II held it in the thirteenth century B. C.
The early onsets of Israel did not conquer it, but later it was forced
to submit. Saul's and his sons' bodies were nailed to its walls by
their victors, the Philistines (1 Sam. 31:7 ff.). The Greeks called it
Scythopolis. In New Testament times it was the only city of the
Decapolis west of the Jordan.

attacks of King Saul (16:14-23). Thirdly, he was sent by his father down to the Israelite army, facing the Philistines, to inquire after the welfare of his three brothers; he came in the nick of time to slay the giant Goliath,—whose armour was Greek, and not Syrian—and thus defeat the army of the Philistines. This heroic deed won for him a place on the military staff of Saul.

However he may have first achieved distinction, the trend of the story is quite clear. David's popularity at court and among the people at large soured the milk of Saul's kindness. Bitter jealousy crowded out every kind thought of David; indeed, set traps for his life. Even Jonathan and Michal, children of Saul, intrigued to save him from the unwarranted attempts on his life by their father.

Jonathan, knit together with David in a covenant of friendship, planned, in the face of the wrath of his father, for David's safety. Saul's hatred of David led him to thrust a spear at his own son Jonathan, David's best friend at his father's court (20:33).

In David's various escapades from the javelin of Saul, none gave him a better sense of security than his flight to Ramah, to Samuel and his school of the prophets (19:20). Saul sent three successive sets of messengers to arrest David, but each fell under the spell of the prophets and did not return with the coveted prisoner. Exasperated at the failure of his messengers, Saul himself made the journey, and the Spirit of God overwhelmed him also, so that he, too, was powerless to take David.

Thereafter Jonathan and David had several secret conferences, where they signed, sealed and delivered their mutual friendship, and reluctantly decided that for safety's sake David would better get beyond the reach of Saul's wrath.

131. David's Outlaw Life (1 Sam. 21-24; 26). Saul's jealousy probably included the fact that David should be his successor on the throne of Israel. David, fully aware of the danger that kept trailing him, fled to Nob, to Abimelech the priest. There he secured the showbread for himself and his retinue of attendants. Likewise David asked for and received the sword of Goliath, which was kept there. He also saw there, to his dismay, one of Saul's alien servants, Doeg the Edomite.

For fear of Saul, David fled that day to King Achish of Gath. The Gittites recognized him, and this frightened him. Feigning madness, he saved his life, as anyone would in that day, from the hands of the vengeful Philistines, and fled back to the hills, and hid in the cave of Adullam. His brethren and all his father's house went to him there. This became also the rendezvous of every one that was in distress, every one in debt, every pessimist,—a renegade band of sympathizers,—400 of them.

Saul's detectives were so hot on David's trail that he fled to Mizpeh in Moab, where his plea to the king of Moab granted permission to David's parents to take refuge in the same fortress. Here " a prophet of God " appeared to David and ordered him back to the land of Judah; and he returned—to the forest of Hereth.

Saul's jealousy broke forth in reprimand of his servants who were sitting about him, for their remissness in not running down David. Doeg spoke up and said that while he was at Nob he saw David supplied with food and with the sword of Goliath by Abimelech, the priest at that place.

This gave Saul a new clue. At once he ordered Abimelech, and all his father's house, the priests that were in Nob, to report at Gibeah. They came and acknowledged the charges of Doeg, in part. When they began to take sides with David, Saul ordered his guard to fall upon and slay them. That guard stirred neither hand nor foot against the sacred officers of Jehovah. Then Saul turned to Doeg, the Edomite, who had no regard for Jehovah; and he pitilessly did the murderous deed, and cut down in cold blood eighty-five priests who wore " a linen ephod." He carried his atrocious slaughter even to Nob, where he wiped out everything that breathed (22:18, 19).

Report came to David that the Philistines were raiding Keilah, on the border. After a favourable response to his inquiry of Jehovah, David and his hardy warriors charged against them, defeating them, rescued the men of Keilah and drove back before them a great booty of cattle. Saul's ingratitude for David's defeat of the Philistines at this time was perfectly evident in his attempt to capture David within that walled town. God's warning put David and his faithful 600 far beyond Saul's reach, in the wilderness of Ziph, where Jonathan made him a visit and strengthened his heart and renewed their brotherly covenant.

The Ziphites volunteered to help Saul capture David, and they pursued him to the wilderness of Maon, and had just about surrounded him when a hurry-up-call came to Saul to return and head off a raid of the Philistines. That gave David a breathing spell, and he left that region and entered the rocky eastern strongholds of En-gedi, on the west shores of the Dead Sea.

As soon as Saul had repulsed the Philistines he mustered 3,000 chosen men to make a final dash to capture the outlaw. Down into the rough wilderness of En-gedi they plunged. Not as familiar with this inhospitable rocky region as the outlaw band, even his 3,000 men were often helpless in the face of 600 men dodging about, in, and over ravines, precipices, gorges, and caves.

At the end of a weary day of search Saul and his men entered a large cave at En-gedi, such an one as is to-day used for the safe-keeping of flocks at night. David's men had reached there first and were far within its deep recesses. After all had fallen asleep, David silently crept up to the sleeping King Saul and cut off the skirt of his robe. The next morning, after Saul and his men had gone out of the cave, and crossed the valley to the opposite side, David appeared at the mouth of the cave and called out, " My lord, the king " (24:8)! Then, in a few short, plain, direct words he showed Saul that his (David's) motive was pure, that the king's was vindictive and evil; and that he (David) had purposely spared the king's life when he could easily have slain him in the cave. Jehovah had been with him, and he would not lift up his hand against Jehovah's anointed. Saul was apparently penitent and deeply affected by the evident generosity of David, who had suffered so much on his account. Saul acknowledged that David would be his successor, and had presence of mind enough to put him under oath that he would not blot out his (Saul's) house after his death. After this formality had been sealed, " Saul went home; but David and his men gat them up unto the stronghold " (24:22), suspicious that Saul was not likely to keep such a pact after his diseased mind had seized the reins.

Not long after the episode in the cave and Saul's return home, the Ziphites appeared at Gibeah and reported that David was in hiding in the hill of Hachilah. Saul, wholly ignoring or forgetful of his experience at the cave of En-gedi, made another dash with his 3,000 troops (or was it part of the former campaign?) into the wilderness of Ziph. The encampment was in the valley, and the king and officers were within the barricade of wagons. David, and Abishai, brother of Joab, at night crept softly into the camp, and into the circle of wagons to the very place where lay Saul and his officers, dead in sleep. Abishai was eager to use Saul's spear, stuck in the ground at his head, to pin him to the ground, but David refused to allow it. The anointed of Jehovah he (David) would not slay, nor allow anyone under him to do it. Out of the camp unnoticed they escaped. Next morning, from the top of a nearby high mountain, David sharply reprimanded the guards; again mildly censured Saul for his pursuit of an innocent man. And also showed him that the king's life was voluntarily spared by the loyalty of himself. Saul again grovelled before David, and blessed him, and returned to his place.

132. Samuel's Last Days (1 Sam. 19:18-22). Samuel had established his home at Ramah in the early days (7:17). There he had built an altar of Jehovah. At the same place he had built up a school of the prophets over which he presided (19:20). To this same place came David as a refugee from the rage of Saul. Probably Samuel lived there a busy and quiet life during Saul's frantic pursuits of David. In Ramah Samuel died, mourned by all Israel, who assembled to bury him on his own place.

Samuel was, (1) a Levite; his grandson was Heman the singer (1 Chron. 6:33); (2) a judge, from Eli to the anointing of Saul; (3) a priest who officiated at sacrifices; (4) a prophet, who founded and presided over a school of the prophets (19:20); (5) a writer who prepared a history of his times (1 Sam. 10:25; 1 Chron. 29:29). His influence was referred to in later days (1 Chron. 11:3; 9:22; 26:28); he was compared with Moses (Jer. 15:1; Psa. 99:6; Heb. 11:32).

Samuel saw the concluding years of the period of the judges, and by his own hand anointed the first two kings of Israel; in other words, the end of the theocracy and the beginning of the monarchy. He was also a participant in the concluding worship at Shiloh, and in the new order of priests located at various places in the land. He also gave the entire prophet-movement an impetus by the bands of young prophets who lived under his influence and direction at Ramah. He saw the approaching dawn of peace and of a better spiritual day, even though the political chaos of Saul's régime was rather disheartening to Samuel's last days. The one bright hope was the character and spirit of David, the successor to Saul.

133. David and Nabal, the Carmelite (1 Sam. 25).

In the wilderness of Maon, southeast of Hebron, David and his 600 men found a reasonably safe hiding-place from the numerous spies of Saul's court. In this region one great shepherd was the dominating figure. With his 3,000 sheep and 1,000 goats he was often involved in quarrels with the border nomads of the desert. David and his own men made friends with Nabal's shepherds, in fact, on more than one occasion protected their flocks,—were a " wall " unto them—from the robber bands that drove in from the desert.

One day in the spring of the year David heard that Nabal had his sheep-shearing,—a time of large hospitality to neighbours and friends. He sent ten young men to greet the lord of the flocks at his shearing. The salutation was delivered in approved form; and then followed the perfectly legitimate request for the accustomed present on such occasions. Nabal sharply resented any such request from David, and the ten men turned on their heels and carried back to their master the hot words of the lord of the shearing.

David's rage expressed itself in this order, " Gird ye on every man his sword," and David also girded on his sword (25:13). With " blood in their eye " 400 men started for the sheep-shearing. Incidentally one of Nabal's servants had told Abigail, his wife, about the messengers of David and how her husband had railed at them; furthermore, this servant praised the conduct of David and his men while in the wilderness, and justified the request they had made of Nabal. Abigail, with a woman's intuition, realized the almost certain outcome of such an insult to the messengers of David, and made all speed to prepare an ample present for him, and sent it on asses down the mountain-side to forestall any possible reprisal on David's part for the insult he had suffered. Abigail followed on her beast. Fortunately they met the armed 400, led by David, at the foot of the plateau. Abigail, by her gracious manner, her humility and fine acknowledgment of the truth of the charges against her foolish husband, her intercession and her generous gift, appeased the anger of David and his men, and even won their admiration.

When Abigail returned home that evening she found her husband engaged in a feast, " like the feast of a king." He was so drunk that she said nothing to him about her adventure with David's raiders until the next morning. After the wine had left him, Abigail told him how near the precipice he had been the night before, how she had saved him and the entire family and plantation from extinction; and he collapsed, " dead as a stone." The stroke was so serious that in ten days he was dead, " smitten by Jehovah."

The report of his death came to David and he sent messengers at once to secure Abigail as a wife. Willingly and humbly she came to the man whose reputation and character had stirred her reverence and affection.

134. David among the Philistines (1 Sam., chaps. 27, 29 and 30). David had little confidence in the promises or oaths of Saul. He had been chased " like a partridge in the mountains," and thus far had escaped. But the future looked dark, for Saul was always on his trail. To be beyond the reach of such peril, he finally decided to risk himself in the hands of the Philistines, who were the enemies of Saul, his pursuer. In addition, such a move might put an end to Saul's pursuits of him.

With his 600 outlaws and their families, David migrated to King Achish of Gath, one of the five lords of the Philistines. After he became sure of his ground, he asked Achish to assign to him and his men a city to dwell in; and Achish gave him Ziklag, a former town of Judah (Joshua 15:31), and in the original list of Simeon (Joshua 19:5). David accepted the offer and occupied it.

Such a band of semi-professional raiders could not long resist the lure of their lives. In the south country on the edge of the desert, Egyptwards, they swept the horizon, and wiped out all the population, but saved all cattle and goods, which were brought back as legitimate plunder. Upon Achish's inquiry, David told him he had raided southern Judah,—Saul's country,—an evidence that David was an enemy of Saul. Achish was so taken with the valour and loyalty of David that he made him captain of his body-guard.

The clashes between the Israelites and Philistines were reaching an acute stage. Some of the Philistines had already penetrated to the valley of Jezreel, and encamped at Shunem. The lords of the Philistines marshalled their forces for a final stand against the Israelites. Achish took along David, his new ally, and his men, in the rear of his division of the army. But the princes of the Philistines objected, and David was sent back, with a most praiseworthy commendation by Achish, who had brought him along.

When David and his men, on their return, on the third day, had reached Ziklag, they found it a mass of smoking embers. The Amalekites had taken reprisals upon the raiders, who had laid waste a part of their territory. David was the focal point of the angry grief of his men. On inquiry through the priest, Jehovah ordered David to " pursue." Southwestward they drove on the trail of the raiders, and came to the wady Besor. Two hundred of David's men were too faint to go farther. The 400 went on, and found a fainted youth by the wayside. Having fed him and refreshed him, he, on condition that they would not kill him, led David's band to the encamped raiders. The attack was unexpected and the defeat and rout were complete. None escaped except 400 young men on swift camels. All the captive persons and goods, and an enormous booty were taken.

When the victors returned to the wady Besor with all the families and plunder, the renegades among the 400 wished to deprive the 200 of any share in the booty. David's fine sense of justice soon levelled that proposal by a decision that, " as his share is that goeth down to the battle, so shall his share be that tarrieth by the baggage: they shall share alike " (30:24). This set a precedent for Israel for all the future. When they had returned to Ziklag, David, in his goodness of heart, sent " of the spoil," presents to the elders of Judah and his friends, and to at least thirteen cities of southern Judah, where he and his men had been accustomed to haunt (30:26-31).

135. Saul's Last Stand and Death (1 Sam. 28 and 31; 1 Chron. 10). The Philistines, with whom David had gone part way as an ally and was sent back, massed their armies

on the plain of Esdraelon in the regions of Aphek and Shunem. Saul concentrated his forces within full view of Shunem on Mt. Gilboa. The former intrepid leader of the charge on Jabesh-gilead apparently had lost his nerve, for he trembled greatly. To relieve his anxiety he inquired of Jehovah as to the outcome of the battle just ahead. No answer was received either by dreams, the Urim or by prophets. What was he to do next? He could not inquire of a necromancer, as he had destroyed them out of the land.

In his desperation he appealed to his servants, who were supposed to have the inside track of the availables, to find for him a woman that had a familiar spirit that he might inquire of her. On ascertaining her whereabouts, Saul disguised himself and, with two trusted servants, crept across the valley past the Philistine guards under protection of the night, to the miserable little village En-dor, and found the woman. Suspicious that a trap was being laid for her, she wrested from the unknown inquirer an oath that she would not be guilty if she answered his request.

Thereupon, at Saul's request, she brought up Samuel, and when she saw him she cried " with a loud voice," in her fear, for she said, " Why hast thou deceived me? for thou art Saul " (28:12). The woman only, in her trance, saw the form of Samuel; and with her knowledge of the terror-stricken Saul, was able to put into words the dread message designed for him. With all its distressing detail the medium repeated to Saul the interview, and concluded with the heart-breaking message: " Jehovah will deliver Israel also with thee into the hand of the Philistines; and to-morrow shalt thou and thy sons be with me " (28:19) in Sheol,—the place of departed spirits.

Saul fainted dead away at that prediction, fully exhausted with fatigue and fear. The woman, when she again came to herself, pitied her king and prepared for him a refreshing meal, in the strength of which he sadly passed out under cover of darkness, back to his camp on Mt. Gilboa.

Early next morning the Philistines charged up Gilboa against the armies of Saul. A resolute and determined force could have held that position for days; but leaders who had lost the battle before it began, quailed at the first stroke, and the armies of Israel fled in defeat. The sons of Saul were slain, and the archers sorely pressed Saul himself. When he saw that his capture was certain he ordered his armour-bearer to thrust him through. Upon his refusal, Saul committed suicide by falling on the point of his own sword,—the armour-bearer following his example.

The next day the Philistines went over the battlefield to strip the slain and gather up the useful plunder. Among them they found Saul and his sons. They cut off Saul's head and sent it with his armour to Philistia as a trophy of victory; and they put his armour in the house of Ashtaroth, and his head in the house of Dagon their god (1 Chron. 10:10); and they fastened the bodies of Saul and his sons to the wall of Beth-shean.

When the men of Jabesh-gilead, whom Saul had saved in the beginning of his reign, heard how Saul and his sons had been slain and their bodies fastened to the walls of Beth-shean, all the valiant men arose and travelled all night, crossed the Jordan and took down the bodies of Saul and his sons from the walls of Beth-shean, and carried them to Jabesh, burnt them there, for fear of defilement, and buried their bones under the terebinth in Jabesh, and fasted seven days.

136. The Character of Saul. Saul was one of the enigmas of his day. Called from following the plow, his peasant ideas never entirely forsook him. His knowledge of what a king should be and do was limited. Immediately after his anointing by Samuel, he fell under the spell of the sons of the prophets, and seems to have become, for the time being, one of them (1 Sam. 10:10-12).

His sacred oaths were made in the name of Jehovah (1 Sam. 14:24, 34, 35), and he built an altar to Jehovah after his sweeping victory over the Philistines. And still more, he banished from the land the wizards and those that had familiar spirits (28:3, 9).

His rather mixed kind of religion is seen in the names he gave his three sons: Jonathan=gift of Jehovah; Melchishua=help of Moloch; Esh-baal=man of Baal. Another glimpse at the religious phases in his home is given by the presence in his daughter Michal's house of teraphim (19:13-16), household gods. His loose interpretation of the instructions given him by Samuel for the annihilation of the Amalekites reveals a defective sense of moral distinctions between obedience and disobedience, though he was penitent when the guilt of his action was pointed out to him.

He was a valiant, courageous, and generally successful soldier. During his reign he rescued Israel from the Ammonites on the east, the Amalekites on the south, and for nearly the whole time, the Philistines on the southwest. The Canaanites, too, kept under cover during that period.

As a king, he was the state. He had no cabinet or court officials like other kings. He seems to have passed upon all cases himself, to have controlled the army, the citizenry and the entire state. The loyalty of his officials must have been remarkable, as we have no intimation of an uprising among his inner circle. The magetism of his personality probably held them together.

The mental malady from which he suffered during his last years discoloured all his estimates and judgments of men, especially of David, his supposed rival in war and in peace. His slaughter of the eighty-five priests at Nob was one of the terrific results of his insane chase after David (22:11-18). His jealousy sat on the throne of his judgment to the end of his life, vitiating his sense of loyalty to promise and oath.

But in spite of these defects, Saul made a substantial gain for the Israelites. He united them under one command and gave them a sense of oneness, a national consciousness, and a new idea of their own strength, that served them well in subsequent years. His crude beginnings of a kingdom gave his successor a scaffolding, at least, by means of which he could erect the splendid structure which finally fell as an inheritance to Solomon.

137. Character of that Period. Samuel was the religious leaven of Saul's age. He seems to have trained the schools of the prophets (19:18-23) and to have put checks on the actions of Saul, as in the case of the Amalekite and Philistine wars. Since the destruction of the religious centre, Shiloh, priests were established at various centres through the land to serve the people religiously. Those at Nob whom Saul wiped out illustrate their service to the people of that time. David, in his outlaw life, even, called upon Jehovah through the priest and the ephod (23:6-13) to determine his next move for safety. But the people as a whole were far from the worship of Jehovah; the gods of Canaan and their religious rites were too deeply rooted to be extirpated by the loyalty of a few worshippers.

Politically, the period was anything but peaceful. Saul had held back a few of the border peoples, but the encroachments of the Philistines and their oppressions made the last days of Saul's career a nightmare. His mania to kill David and fear of reprisals by David, and his terror before Philistine aggressiveness, drove his unhinged mind to such desperation that finally, deserted by Jehovah, he resorted to a witch to forecast his future. Of course the Philistines won the final battle, and the entire land fell into their hands. They reckoned on David at Ziklag as their friend and ally,—in other words, the Philistines were masters of all Palestine.

Socially, the land was an amalgamation of the Canaanites and Israelites. Philistine overlordship affected their political and economic status only. It limited their use of iron for weapons of war, and imposed upon them taxes and tribute to the point of oppression. But common everyday homely customs that had grown up among the commingled old populations of the land were undisturbed by their new masters. Also, little did the Philistines care for the religions of their subjects.   Canaanite, Perizzite, Hivite, Moabite, Ammonite, Edomite might sacrifice to any god they chose so long as they paid the regular assessed tribute of these new Greco-Philistine rulers.   David's presence among them was in their favour; it added only to their strength and security for the future.

NOTE ON MAP 7, tailpiece below: After the drab age of the judges and the dawn of the kingdom under Saul, David created the high noon of Israel's military strength.   The quiescence of the great powers (noted in Map 6) gave him his opportunity, and he improved it.

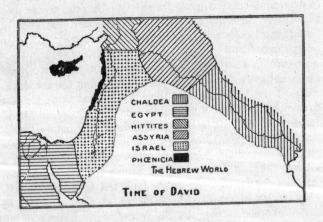

CHAPTER XVI

DAVID'S BRILLIANT REGAL CAREER

138. David Anointed King at Hebron (2 Sam. 1:1–2:7). David and his men had just returned from their reprisal raid upon the Amalekites (1 Sam. 30), when a man from the former camp of Saul, with the marks of great sorrow upon him, came to David. This man, an Amalekite, reported that he, at Saul's desperate request, slew him; and he brought his crown and bracelet to David, as his successor.

NOTE ON FIG. 48, headpiece above: When David decided to capture the fortress Jebus he faced great walls perched on high precipices, except on the north side. From these dizzy heights the Jebusites shouted contemptuously at David's helpless troops. But up through the water tunnel, led by Joab, a few valiant men captured the defenders and the fortress, and themselves stood on the twenty-foot thick wall here pictured, regarded by the Jebusites as impregnable (2 Sam. 5:6-9).

David and his men rent their clothes, and mourned and wept and fasted until even, for Saul and for Jonathan. Then David drastically rebuked the man for slaying Jehovah's anointed, and ordered him slain on the spot as a penalty for his crime.

In honour of his slain friends, David is said to have uttered a beautiful elegy found in the book of Jashar, and copied in this narrative of 2 Samuel (1:19-27):

> " Saul and Jonathan were lovely and pleasant in their lives,
> And in their death they were not divided:
> They were swifter than eagles,
> They were stronger than lions.
>
> .   .   .   .
>
> How are the mighty fallen in the midst of the battle!
> Jonathan is slain upon thy high places."

Upon inquiry from Jehovah, David is commanded by him to go up to Hebron. He removed his entire force of 600 men, with their households, to Hebron and its environs. When the men of Judah learned of his advent to this region, they joyfully came together and anointed David in Hebron king over Judah; of course, under the overlordship of the Philistines who ruled the country. At the same time David thanked the Gileadites for their kindness to the bones of Saul and his sons (1 Sam. 31: 11-13).

139. Saul's House at Mahanaim (2 Sam. 2:8–4:12). The living fragments of Saul's house after the fatal battle at Gilboa were taken by Abner, his captain, to Mahanaim, east of the Jordan. There Ish-bosheth (" man of shame "), Saul's son, was made king over all Israel, except Judah, which was under David. Both kings, as we understand it, were vassals of Philistia, to whom they paid tribute.

Beginnings of a civil war, well-pleasing to their Philistine overlords, arose. Abner, Saul's captain, centred his troops at the pool of Gibeon in Benjamin; and Joab, captain of David, went to the same pool. The battle was opened by an indecisive duel between twelve young men of each army.

Then the troops of Abner of Israel were beaten and driven back by the followers of David. In the pursuit of the northern army, Asahel, the youngest brother of Joab, David's captain, was slain by Abner, captain of the northern forces.

There was continual warfare between the house of Saul and the house of David,—David's becoming ever stronger and Saul's ever weaker. Abner, Saul's former captain, was easily the dominant figure in Israel. The so-called king, Ish-bosheth, made a serious charge against the conduct of Abner, and so incurred his ill-will that he took an oath that he would " transfer the kingdom from the house of Saul, and set up the throne of David over Israel and over Judah " (3:9, 10).

This break between Abner and his king forecast revolutionary changes in the dual government of the country. Abner sent messengers to David, asking for a league between them, to issue ultimately in the transfer of all Israel to him. David conditioned the consideration of such a proposition upon the return to him of Michal, Saul's daughter, his former wife. Michal, daughter of King Saul, was found and restored to David, an oriental symbol of his taking over the reign of Saul, his father-in-law.

Abner's next step in the project he had before him was to create public sentiment among the elders of Israel in favour of David as ruler over all Israel. This had to be done in a quiet, cautious manner, lest it leak out to the Philistine overlords, who would move to checkmate any such combination.

For secrecy and completeness' sake, Abner, with twenty men, slipped down to Hebron to see David personally. David gave them a royal reception with a feast. Abner volunteered to gather all Israel to David to make a covenant with him to rule over all that his heart desired. And Abner went away in peace.

The embassy from Israel has just left when Joab and a raiding troop came in with great spoil. Having learned that

Abner had been there, and gone away, Joab roughly re-proached David for having let him go. He said Abner was not sincere in his motive, but was really a spy. David kept silent, but Joab, without David's knowledge, sent fast messengers who overtook Abner and his embassy and brought them back. Joab, with Abishai's assent, met him, took him aside " to speak with him quietly," and, in revenge for the blood of Asahel, his brother, thrust him through with his sword at the gate of the city. When word of Joab's crime reached David, he declared his own innocence, and by an oath let it fall on the house of Joab; and prayed that in the same house there may always be one that has an issue, and one that is a leper,—two maladies that perpetually defile one; and that they may be so effeminate as to be unable to take up manly occupations. David commanded Joab and all the people to rend their clothes and gird on haircloth and mourn,—or employ the symbols of mourning for the dead leader of Israel. " And King David followed the bier " (3:31). David said, " As a man falleth before the children of iniquity, so didst thou fall;" " a prince and a great man is fallen this day in Israel " (3:38). " Jehovah reward the evil-doer according to his wickedness " (vs. 39).

When the report of the death of Abner reached Ish-bosheth, Saul's son, king of Israel at Mahanaim, his spirit swooned and he became impotent. There were two men about the court who had been captains of bands under Abner; but now that the swing of the kingdom was toward David, they, anticipating favours in the new merger, treach-erously slew Ish-bosheth and carried his head to David at Hebron. When the gruesome object was presented to him, David's good sense of justice, fairplay and loyalty, pointed the assassins to the fate of the messenger who reported that he had slain Saul in battle (2 Sam. 1:15). How much greater punishment did they deserve who had slain a right-eous man in his own house? And command was given his young men to dispatch them, cut off their hands and feet, and hang them up as a warning, beside the pool in Hebron.

But the head of Ish-bosheth, which they had brought, was buried in the grave of Abner, treacherously slain by Joab a short while before.

140. David King over All Israel (2 Sam. 5; 1 Chron. 14:8-17). The last barrier to the union of all Israel having been removed, all the tribes came to Hebron to David, to crown him their king. David made a covenant there before Jehovah; " and they anointed David king over Israel " (vs. 3). At this time he had already reigned over Judah seven and one-half years.

We note especially in both anointings at Hebron, that David was " chosen " king by the people in a democratic manner. He was no hereditary monarch, no self-proclaimed ruler, no upstart dictator, but was deliberately " chosen " because of merit—confirming the divine choice made under Samuel (1 Sam. 16:12, 13).

David's army had been brought up to the acme of efficiency under his intensive training (1 Chron. 11:10–12:40), so that he could now assume the aggressive in the further conquest of the land. The Philistines kept a close watch on the consolidation of these two little sub-kingdoms, with the purpose at the proper time of crushing any attempt at independence.

Judah had been the one prominent tribe in David's little kingdom; and now he assumes the supremacy in the union as over against Ephraim, who had gradually waned, until now of only minor importance. More or less jealousy was always evident in tribal life, but now Judah occupied the first place.

A report of the anointing of David by all Israel at Hebron and of the merger of the two little governments was doubtless wafted down to the Philistines. Fearful that their grip on the Israelites would be loosened, they sent an army up into the valley of Rephaim and seized Bethlehem. With strategic precaution, David withdrew to the cave of Adullam (1 Chron. 11:15, 16), twelve miles from Bethlehem, and inquired of Jehovah what he should do. When commanded to attack them, David made the charge and smote them and defeated them, and captured their idols which they had with them. Chagrined at their defeat, the Philistines, to retrieve themselves, immediately called out another army and marched up into the same valley. David's victory over these new troops was still more decisive, and he cleaned up the country from Geba to Gezer. In fact, it was the Philistines' Waterloo, and a blow to the sovereignty of the lords who had held sway since the defeat of Saul at Gilboa.

Hebron, David's capital while he was king of Judah, was too far from the centre of the country to be a real capital for the king of all Israel. In casting about for a more central location, he hit upon the old Canaanitish stronghold, Jebus, still unconquered by either of the tribes to which it had been assigned (Joshua 15:63; Judges 1:21).

141. Jerusalem the New Capital (2 Sam. 5:6-10; 1 Chron. 11:4-9). Jebus was an imposing citadel on a high hill with natural declivities on three sides, facing what were later called the Kidron, Hinnom and Tyropœon valleys. Underneath the citadel was a never-failing spring of fresh water. So impregnable was that citadel that it could be adequately protected by " the lame and blind," if the narrative can be properly so interpreted.

But David determined to capture it. By a device unknown to many, he uncovered the spring, the Virgin's fountain, and the first entrants went up through the water tunnel into the fortress, and took it by a unique piece of strategy. Contrary to the usual custom, the lives of the inhabitants were saved, and made citizens of the new centre. Others were brought in, and the entire fortress became known as Zion, the city of David, and later by its ancient name, Uru-salim, Jerusalem. The southeast corner of the whole Jerusalem area was that fortress, and on this part of the plateau between the surrounding hills David established his capital, and built his palace and his military defenses.

By the conquest of this centre David welded a link between the royal houses of Judah and Benjamin. Situated on an elevation protected by natural as well as artificial barriers, and difficult of approach for an enemy, it became a splendid centre from which to reach every part of the land. Jerusalem henceforth became the capital of the newly merged kingdom.

142. The Ark Brought to Jerusalem (2 Sam. 6; 1 Chron. 13 and 15). David's wide experience with the mixed peoples of Palestine convinced him that Israel could never endure without a strong centre for the worship of their God, Jehovah. Now that Jerusalem had been made the political capital, he must see to it that very soon in its development it should also become a centre of worship. Ever since the destruction of Shiloh, the ark had been stranded at Kirjath-jearim in Judah (1 Sam. 7:1-3), at the house of Abinadab.

David summoned all the chosen men of Israel, and the priests and the Levites, for publicity's sake, to bring the ark from the house of Abinadab up to Jerusalem. When all were ready, the priests, instead of carrying it as required by law, set it upon a new cart drawn by oxen. In front of the procession, David and all Israel played various musical instruments and sang " with all their might " in their joy at the transfer of this sacred symbol to the new capital.

But just as the jubilant procession reached the edge of the city, either because the road was rough or the oxen stumbled, or both, the ark seemed to sway as if it would fall to the ground, when Uzzah, one of the drivers, put out his hand to steady it, and dropped dead " before God." The joyous procession was brought to a sudden halt at such a stroke. And David . . . was aggrieved at such a sudden breach in the proceedings and said, " How shall the ark of Jehovah come unto me? " The sanctity of the symbol must be learned again, even at a costly lesson (Num. 4:15, 19, 20). David was unwilling to go further that day, and

ordered it carried into the nearby house of one of his faithful Philistine servants, Obed-Edom, of Gath.

Its presence in this house brought blessings upon it in
such abundance that at the end of three months, David gave
orders and the priests carried it into the city, accompanied
with sacrifices, dancing by David himself, and with a blare
of trumpets. It was set in its place, in the midst of the tent
that David had pitched for it. And there he offered special
burnt-offerings and peace offerings before Jehovah. And
at the close of the service he blessed the people in the name
of Jehovah of hosts, and handed out to everyone refresh-
ments of a substantial character that they might be able to
return to their homes.

As a side issue we should note the heartless attack made
upon David by his wife Michal, Saul's daughter,—that he
had danced before the ark in an unseemly manner in the
presence of the lookers-on. David's keen retort must have
cut to the quick and have closed the mouth of such an
unsympathetic companion.

David immediately went farther and prepared the Levites
to officiate and a choir of singers to take part in the services
at the ark (1 Chron. 16). In this array we find Asaph as
chief singer with an orchestra of musicians to accompany
them (cf. Psa. 105:1-15; 96: 1-13; 106:1, 47, 48). These
were the early and provisional arrangements made by
David, according to the Chronicler, for the worship in the
new capital.

143. David's Military Organization (2 Sam. 21:15-
22; 23:8-39; 1 Chron. 11:10-46; 20:4-8). Now that the
kingdom had become established in Jerusalem as its political
and religious capital, David must more than ever take stock
of his military strength. During his outlaw life and while
he was king over Judah he had drafted into his service the
best men he could find. Their choice was based upon some
distinguished service or heroic act in the army or for him.

The nucleus of his army consisted of a roll of valiant
heroes, mentioned both in 2 Samuel and 1 Chronicles,

though in rather a bewildering order. Of these, thirty men stood in a class by themselves, as capable of being captains or leaders of divisions of an army. At the head of this notable body stood Abishai, brother of Joab, commander-in-chief of all the troops. Abishai won his rank by slaying 300 with his own spear single-handed, and received honourable mention among David's three. Next to him was Benaiah, who dispatched two sons of Ariel the Moabite; he also went down into a pit and slew a lion in the winter snow; and, single-handed, with only a staff he wrested from him, slew a giant Egyptian with his own spear. These feats ranked him as the peer of any of the thirty, but not up to the first three.

David's real knights were his imperial three. They were enshrined by their daring and success in single-handed combats. Jashobeam had slain 800 (Chron. 300) at one time. Eleazar met and cleaned up a band of Philistines until his hand refused to let go the handle of his sword. The third was Shammah, whose valour led him to defend a lentil field against a foraging band of Philistines, with a great victory.

The writer, as an illustration of the daring of these men, described a nameless three of the thirty, as breaking through the Philistine lines to get David a drink of water from the well at Bethlehem. The king, however, poured it out as sacred before Jehovah, refusing to drink what represented the life-blood of his soldiers.

With such intrepid warriors and loyal troops as the nucleus of his army, David was prepared to meet his foes and undertake expansive measures when occasion arose. The military arm of his government was well organized and ready for immediate service.

144. David's Administrative Organization (2 Sam. 8:16-18; 20:23-26; 1 Chron. 27:33). The efficiency of David's government depended on the character of the men who constituted his cabinet, and the selection of the cabinet was in the hands of the king himself. Direct rule in the tribes or districts was carried on by the elders and other men of tribal standing, who were the intermediaries between the people and the central government at Jerusalem.

David himself was the chief justice of the kingdom and held court for all the people (2 Sam. 8:15), either personally or, occasionally, through a deputy or master in chancery. The king was also chief priest with oversight of all religious services.

The royal cabinet was made up of close counsellors of the king and the trusted heads of his departments: (1) The head of the army, Joab; (2) the state recorder or chronicler, Jehoshaphat; (3) the "king's friend," a personal counsellor and adviser; (4) the scribe or private secretary, Seraiah (or Sheva). Two priests were attached to the royal house, Ahimelech, David's companion in flight, and Zadok, who had the care of the ark of Jehovah; and Ira, the Jairite, who took charge of the king's own chapel. Benaiah was given the captaincy of the king's own body-guard of 600 men, who were responsible for the safety of David in all his many movements about his realm. At a later time, when captives were numerous and defenses were being enlarged and strengthened, the king added to his responsible heads Adoram as overseer of the *corvée,* the forced labour.

Significant is the fact that some of the best men in David's service were foreigners, non-Hebrews; as Ittai, of Gath, a Philistine (2 Sam. 15:19-22), Uriah, the Hittite, Zelek, the Ammonite, Ithmah, the Moabite, illustrating the loyalty which he inspired in all his followers and the confidence which he placed in his subordinates.

145. David's Foreign Conquests (2 Sam. 8; 1 Chron. 18). The fixing of David's capital at Jerusalem, the concentration of the kingdom of all Israel in this stronghold, seemed to challenge the enemy and half-enemy peoples on every side. The Philistines refused to lie down and quit; but made another drive at the new capital, Jerusalem, only to be defeated and driven back with the loss of Gath and its suburbs.

The Moabites, east of the Jordan and Dead Sea, measured their strength with Israel, and suffered a decimating penalty and became servants of David.

A king of the north, Hadadezer of Zobah, met a crushing defeat in which he lost to David 1,000 chariots, 1,700 cavalry and 20,000 infantry (Sam. and Chron. not in agreement). The Aramæans of Damascus went to their rescue, but lost 22,000 men and unnumbered amounts of gold and bronze. David garrisoned the conquered territory to keep it under control.

Toi, king of great Hamath, sent messengers to thank David for giving Hadadezer, his enemy, such an effective beating, and along with his thanks sent presents of gold, silver, and bronze,—all of which David carried back to Jerusalem to dedicate to Jehovah.

David also made a campaign against the Edomites in the valley of Salt and slew 18,000 men, and garrisoned the entire country. This victory gave David access to the headwaters of the Gulf of Akabah, which later played such a rôle in Solomon's reign. Presents and tribute he received also from Ammon and Amalek and all the smaller peoples on the borderlines of Israel.

146. David's Loyalty to His Oath (2 Sam. 9). David and Jonathan were the Damon and Pythias of the Hebrews. They had sworn to be true to each other for all time. And after David had trapped Saul in the cave at En-gedi, David swore to him that he would not cut off his seed after him (1 Sam. 24: 21, 22).

After the kingdom had become comfortably consolidated at Jerusalem, David could not blot out of his mind the events of his youth. He bethought himself of the narrow escapes he had experienced in the house of Saul, and how Jonathan not only protected him but more than once risked his own life to save him. When events were at their worst they had covenanted together to cover all the future (1 Sam. 20:14-17). All those kindnesses now protruded and called for extensions.

On inquiry from an old servant of the house of Saul

David learned that a crippled son of Jonathan, his covenant friend, Mephibosheth, was still alive. David sent for him, and requested him to be a perpetual guest at the king's table. He also restored to him all the real property of Saul, presumably at Gibeah, and commanded Saul's old servant, Ziba, and his family to work the land and produce crops thereon. Henceforth Mephibosheth, son of Jonathan, crippled in both his feet, lived in Jerusalem, and ate at the king's table.

147. War against Ammon and Aram (2 Sam. 10; 1 Chron. 19 and 20). When David heard of the death of Nahash, king of Ammon, he thoughtfully sent his condolence with messengers to his son Hanun. But Hanun's princes ridiculed the idea, and persuaded him that David's messengers were spies. They also induced Hanun to treat the men scandalously, cutting off one-half of their beards and one-half of their flowing robes, such as royal ambassadors always wore. So humiliated were these men that they sent back to David news of their disfigured plight, and he ordered them to stop at Jericho until their beards should be grown, and then return.

Now the Ammonites saw that they had made themselves offensive to David, and they sent messengers to hire Aramæans of Beth-rehob and of Zobah and Maacah and Tob, 33,000 men to defend them against a war which they had recklessly provoked. When David heard of the foreign mercenaries which Ammon had summoned, he sent Joab with his crack regiment over the Jordan toward the country of Ammon. The Aramæans set themselves in array out on the open plain, while the Ammonites were at the gate of their capital city, Rabbah. Joab took the best troops to meet the Aramæans, and Abishai led the remainder against the Ammonites. Joab's violent charge with his famed fighters shocked and pushed back and routed the Aramæans; the sight of their flight led the Ammonites to break and flee in every direction.

The Aramæans were not to be so quickly counted out. To

retrieve themselves, Hadadezer summoned another army,—
bringing some of the men from the other side of the
Euphrates River. When they were fully mustered under
Shobach, captain for Hadadezer, at Helam, David's army
met them and administered to them a defeat of such enormous proportions as to silence the Aramæans for the remaining years of David's reign. But the Ammonites were still
unconquered and continually menaced Israel on the east.
Joab campaigned into their country and laid siege to Rabbah when the writer breaks in with the story of David's sin.

NOTE ON FIG. 45, tailpiece below: The so-called "Holy Rock" is a
supreme object of reverence in the Holy City. Covered by the beautiful "Dome of the Rock" (erroneously called "Mosque of Omar"),
it is 58 ft. long by 44 ft. wide, and stands from 4 to 6½ ft. above the
pavement. The whole Rock is screened with traditions. David is
said to have purchased it for fifty shekels from Araunah (Ornan) the
Jebusite (2 Sam. 24:16-25), after the destroying angel withdrew from
the slaughter of Israel. David erected here an altar and offered
sacrifices thereon.

CHAPTER XVII

DAVID'S CLOSING TRAGEDIES

148. David's Grievous Sins (2 Sam. 11:1–12:31; not in Chron.). David had about reached the acme of his ambitions. His kingdom was fully organized and well established, and he could now enjoy the fruits of a successful and righteous career.

External foes had been practically silenced, but enemies of his moral character were still a menace. The luxuries

NOTE ON FIG. 59, headpiece above: Macalister reports that in the excavations of 1923-24 at Jerusalem, remains of a fortress tower were unearthed which have been partially identified as Millo (2 Sam. 5:9). When Solomon came to the throne he repaired the breaches made in the wall by David his father, and built up Millo. Hezekiah did the same in the face of the Assyrian threat. The picture facing us seems to answer the requirements of those passages.

of palace life, the softening of the hard moral muscle of his earlier years, and the maintenance of an oriental harem, led to the usual abuses found in such a court.

David himself became guilty of adultery and a plot to have one of his best officers, Uriah the Hittite, husband of Bath-sheba, slain in the army, that he might take her as his wife. He carried out his murderous scheme in cold blood. In an ordinary oriental court it would have been scarcely noticed. But here in Jerusalem, centre of Jehovah worship, with all his priests and pious background, the people were outraged and horrified at such procedure, even by a king who was thought to be responsible only to God for his acts.

To meet the situation squarely, Nathan the prophet, well-known to David for the temple episode (chap. 7), was sent around by Jehovah to see the king. The prophet presented to him ostensibly a case of the rich oppressing the poor, under the guise of a rich man with flocks and herds, who took and killed the pet lamb of a poor man to entertain a traveller-guest. David, as chief justice, was thoroughly wrought up over the case, and said, " As Jehovah liveth, the man that hath done this thing is worthy of death: and he shall restore the lamb fourfold, because he did this thing, and because he had no pity." And Nathan, looking David straight in the eye, said, " Thou art the man " (12:5-7).

What a thrust! And it caught David off guard, too. Without giving him a chance to reply, the prophet drove right ahead and recited how God had delivered him from the hand of Saul, anointed him king over all Israel, and turned over to him all the belongings of the royal house. He then indicted him for despising the word of Jehovah in killing Uriah with the sword of the Ammonites, and taking Uriah's wife as his own wife. As the climax of his message, Nathan, with true prophetic fire, gave God's message and said, " Now therefore the sword shall never depart from thy house, because thou hast despised me, and hast taken the wife of Uriah the Hittite to be thy wife." " Still other disgraces shall be added to your family as a result of your sin."

The thrust pierced David's conscience and brought him to, and he said to Nathan, " I have sinned against Jehovah " (*cf.* Psalm 51). To which Nathan gave assurance that Jehovah had put away his sin and would not slay him. But his example would be flouted by the enemies of Jehovah, and the child to be born would surely die.

David's real penitence and sorrow growing out of his sins tried him severely in the fatal illness and death of Bath-sheba's child. His hope, however, was couched in these words, " I shall go to him, but he will not return to me " (12:23). The birth of Solomon concludes this depressing tale of Israel's choice king.

The writer inserts a brief note here to the effect that David went out with an army and completely subdued the Ammonites, and made them to serve Israel with axes and saws, in timber work, and with harrows, farm work, and in the brick kiln,—all most accursed tasks for nomads and shepherds of the desert.

149. Sins in David's Household (2 Sam. 13 and 14). David's nine wives and eighteen children, mentioned in the Old Testament, furnished the background for misunder-standings, jealousies, and quarrels of first-class proportions. When we remember that several of his foreign wives were married for political reasons, and their children were only half-blooded Israelites, is it any wonder that the royal household became an incubator of factions, feuds and family rows? David's own example of lack of restraint, and self-indulgence in the latter part of his reign added nothing to the moral stability of his manifold family.

Amnon, his oldest son and first heir to the throne, was treacherously murdered at a banquet by his half-brother, Absalom, ostensibly in revenge for a wrong done his half-sister Tamar. A report that came to David was that Absa-lom had slain all the king's sons. After he had gone through the agonies of believing it, the truth finally reached him. But Absalom fled to his kinsfolk, the king of Geshur, and remained there three years.

David's love for Absalom was shown in his mourning for him during his long absence from court. Joab devised a plan whereby a wise woman of Tekoa presented to David a hypothetical case of threatened blood revenge for fratricide. David saw the application in his breach with Absalom, and allowed Joab to go to Geshur and bring back Absalom and his family to Jerusalem. Even then David refused to see him, and let him go to his own house. At the end of two years of such strained relations, Absalom forced an invitation to see his father David, who went through the form of greeting him,—a kind of cold though full recognition.

150. Absalom's Rebellion (2 Sam. 15:1-12). David's indifference and neglect had wounded the royal pride of Absalom. His two years of practical exile in Jerusalem before he saw David's face fostered his resentment and fed his secret ambition. Immediately after David had again recognized him he capitalized this event to his own advantage. As the next legal heir to the throne he prepared a chariot and horses and fifty men to run before him. This gave him a kind of prestige before the people wherever he drove.

The gate was the administrative, judicial, military, and social centre of every city. At this popular place the handsome, well-groomed young Absalom took his stand day after day, and met the people who came here from the tribes of Israel for advice and justice, with a suggestion that if he were judge each man would receive his just dues. By sympathetic expressions of interest in every one, " Absalom stole the hearts of the men of Israel " (15:6).

At the end of four years of such kindly proceedings at the gate, Absalom probably was well informed about the undercurrents of disaffection that were at work in all the tribes, and aware of his growing popularity as a possible successor on the throne. To give his next step royal approval, he asked the king's permission to go to Hebron to fulfil a vow which he had made while he was in Geshur. Of course, David said, " Go in peace."

A royal welcome awaited Absalom, for Hebron and the proud tribe of Judah had never quite forgiven David for removing the capital to Jerusalem. To make sure of the success of the event, Absalom had sent spies to all the tribes of Israel,—of course, only to his friends—saying, as soon as you hear the sound of the trumpet, shout, " Absalom is king in Hebron." Absalom took with him from Jerusalem 200 men who were quite innocent of the purpose of the journey. And he also called Ahithophel, David's counsellor, from Giloh, while he was offering sacrifices there. With the influx of many from the other tribes and the enthusiasm of Judah, the conspiracy grew strong and gained continually.

151. David's Flight (2 Sam. 15:13–16:14). The trumpet alarm reached David's ear in Jerusalem. His wide experience and narrow escapes in the past, prompted him to act quickly. His word went out to all his court and guard, " Arise, let us flee." Together they started,—strangely few in all. When David protested against the going with him of Ittai the Gittite (from Gath), a foreigner, Ittai asserted his loyalty with an oath in the name of Jehovah; after which David said, " Go and pass over." In their rush to get everything in motion, the two priests, Zadok and Abiathar, came out with the ark of Jehovah to accompany them. But David ordered it back with the priests in charge.

And all the country wept aloud at the humiliating exit of the king, the government, and the army, before the threatened attack and investment of the city by the rebel Absalom. The refugees crossed the valley of Kidron and climbed the slopes of Mt. Olives, including even David weeping with his head covered and barefoot,—all headed for the Jordan valley.

In their flight some one told David that his former counsellor, Ahithophel, grandfather(!) of Bath-sheba, had espoused the cause of Absalom. Knowing men as David did, he immediately sent back Hushai, his " friend," to feign

loyalty to Absalom,—and, of course, to become his counsellor to counteract the counsel of Ahithophel, a traitor to
David.   Important decisions of Absalom were to be dispatched through the lines to David by the two young men,
sons of the priests who also remained in the city.

After David had passed over Mt. Olives, Ziba, former
servant of Saul, brought him an abundance of supplies for
the journey. On inquiry after Mephibosheth, David learned
from Ziba that he had remained in Jerusalem to receive the
kingdom of Saul. David believed him, and there turned
over to Ziba all the property of Mephibosheth. A little
farther down the road, Shimei, of Saul's house, heaped
curses upon David as the one who had wrested the leadership of Israel from his father's house. Abishai, brother of
Joab, nephew of the king, stung by the insults thrown at
his lord, asked permission to go over and take off his head.
David said, " let him alone and let him curse; for Jehovah
hath bidden him " (16:11). Apparently, from the narrative, the few refugees gathered at the Jordan to await
further word from Jerusalem.

152. Absalom in Jerusalem (2 Sam. 16:15–17:23).
Probably with no resistance whatsoever, Absalom and his
retinue and all the people, the men of Israel, marched into
Jerusalem. He took over the city, the palace and so much
of the royal harem as was left behind. When Hushai appeared, Absalom hesitated to receive him. But his pro-
testations of loyalty were so strong that all objections were
brushed aside, and he was accepted. When the capital was
in Absalom's full possession he had other problems on hand.
Before the next move, he called into counsel Ahithophel.
In addition to giving advice, Ahithophel asked the privilege
of taking 12,000 chosen men to pursue David with all speed
that night. Before Absalom would consent to such rapid-fire
action he called for Hushai, to know what his counsel would
be. Hushai advised delay and, on what seemed to be perfectly valid reasons. He would gather an enormous army
from all Israel, overwhelm David's little troop, and pull

them into the river. Hushai's counsel won out, and he sent a secret dispatch to David. When Ahithophel saw that his own counsel was set aside, he went out and hanged himself.

153. Battle of Mahanaim (2 Sam. 17:24–18:32). On the basis of the dispatch from Hushai the refugees crossed the Jordan and hastened to Mahanaim, a well-known city in the east-Jordanic country. To this centre the Ammonites in loyalty brought great quantities of supplies and food for David and his suffering followers. At the same time Absalom with his army was crossing the Jordan in full pursuit. Over his army he had appointed Amasa, a first cousin of Joab (1 Chron. 2:16, 17), general of David's army.

David organized his little army, or what he had of one, into three divisions, under captains Joab, Abishai, his brother, and Ittai, the Philistine from Gath,—no numbers are given, for they must have been comparatively small. When they passed out through the gate of the city Mahanaim, to battle, David commanded each of them, " Deal gently for my sake with the young man, even with Absalom " (18:5).

The battle was joined in a forest near Mahanaim. And Absalom's army was wholly defeated, smitten down before David's men,—to the number of 20,000. The rocky wildness and jungles of the forest destroyed more than the sword. In the flight of Absalom's troops, so the story runs, the usurper's mule ran under a terebinth tree with low-hanging limbs; and his heavy locks became so entangled therein that the mule went on from under him and left him suspended in midair. When Joab learned of it, in spite of David's order, he went and thrust three darts through his heart. The rebel king having been slain, Joab blew his trumpet and the pursuit was checked. They took the body of Absalom and threw it into a deep pit in the forest and covered it with a great heap of stones.

When couriers brought the news to David it was delivered with true oriental comportment, leaving the saddest words for the last. Avoidance of telling just what happened by the first courier, left the real truth to the second, a dark-skinned Cushite, whose circumlocutions were less involved than those of the Israelite, so David soon perceived the outcome of the battle,—the death of Absalom.

154. David's Return to Jerusalem (2 Sam. 18:32–19:43). David's grief for his son Absalom smothered all the joys of victory. Where David should have welcomed the victorious troops after the battle, he was hiding himself in mourning in the apartments over the gate of the city. So serious was the effect of his despondent attitude that the returning warriors began to despair of the favour of the king, and were melting away. Joab, the strong self-willed commander-in-chief, observed the weakening of the discouraged victors as they came in from the battle. With cold-blooded bluntness Joab called David to time; and coolly rebuked him for his own selfish position and disregard of the interests of all the nation. The old king's weakness suddenly changed to sane action; and he sat in the gate to receive with gratitude the returning soldiers who came by before him.

Now that the rebellion of Absalom had been crushed, David seems to have pardoned the rebels, and to have looked for early efforts to restore himself to Jerusalem. The remissness of the people was distressing. The two priests at Jerusalem were appealed to, to stir up the elders of Judah who had enlisted their loyalty to the rebellion of Absalom. The northern tribes were at loggerheads, and no one seemed enthusiastic enough to take up the cause of the old kingdom. Judah was finally reconciled when David offered to place Amasa, the general of Absalom's army, over his own troops in place of the cold-blooded but efficient Joab who had so grieved and angered him by killing Abner and Absalom.

King David returned to the Jordan, and the Judeans went to Gilgal to welcome him over the river on his triumphal journey to Jerusalem. And Shimei, the Benjamite who so roundly cursed David on his flight, came with 1,000 men of Benjamin; and Ziba, Saul's servant, with his sons and servants, seems to have managed the convoy to bring over the king's household. Shimei was most profuse in his obeisance and in his insistence on the king's forgiveness, which was finally granted with an oath that he would spare his life. Then came Mephibosheth, the crippled son of Jonathan, in a filthy dishevelled condition, with a pathetic story of a different tenor from that told David by Ziba. To even up the case, David divided Saul's land fifty-fifty between Ziba and Mephibosheth, and the cripple still continued to eat at the king's table. Another character who accompanied the king to the Jordan to see him safely over was Barzillai the Gileadite, whose munificence David enjoyed at Mahanaim (17:27-29). David affectionately bade him good-bye, and brought Chimham, his servant, as Barzillai's representative to Jerusalem.

155. Sheba's Rebellion (2 Sam. 20:1-22). The majority of those who welcomed David back over the Jordan were men of Judah. The men of Israel were jealous and rebuked Judah with sharp words. They even resented the neglect of advising with them regarding the return of the king, " and the words of the men of Judah were fiercer than the words of the men of Israel " (19:43),—a kind of initial revolt on the part of Israel that simply needed a spark to touch off the magazine.

The requisite leader was ready at hand. Even before David had reached Jerusalem, Sheba, " a base fellow " of Benjamin, blew the trumpet, gave the signal, and Israel openly deserted David and rallied to the new command. As soon as David reached Jerusalem, to meet the uprising he ordered Amasa, the new general whom he had appointed in the place of Joab, to summon the troops of Judah within three days. Amasa failing to act promptly, David gave orders to Abishai, Joab's brother, to muster the army, the body-guard, and all the mighty men, to pursue the rebels. As they reached Gibeon, the deliberate Amasa caught up

with them.   Joab, the former generalissimo, was there, and
went up to Amasa ostensibly to greet him with a kiss.   At
the same moment he treacherously ran him through with his
sword,—Abner, Absalom, Amasa, all cut down by that unscrupulous, dastardly nephew of the king!   Joab at once
took his old position at the head of the army.   He and his
brother Abishai led in pursuit of the rebel troops of Israel
until they took refuge in Abel-beth-maacah, a city of
Naphtali, far in the north part of the country.   After laying
siege to the city and partially undermining the wall, the
besiegers agreed to desist on condition that the rebel Sheba
should be delivered over to them.   Soon the head of Sheba
was thrown over the wall, and Joab blew the trumpet; and
the army withdrew and returned to Jerusalem.

156. A Famine and Its Cause (2 Sam. 21:1-14).
Disasters seemed to follow David in rapid succession.   A
three-year drought and consequent famine sent David to
inquire of Jehovah.   He was told that Saul had disregarded
Joshua's oath to the Gibeonites (Joshua 9:15) and had
slain some of them.   Such a breach could be atoned for
only by a reprisal on Saul's house.   The Gibeonites demanded and David granted the lives of seven descendants
of Saul, sparing, however, to make good his own oath, the
life of Mephibosheth, son of Jonathan.   Then the drought
ceased and the rains fell as usual

This bloody reprisal shows us how primitive and crude
were the ideas of Jehovah that were current in Israel in
that day.

The maternal love of Rizpah in watching over the remains
of her two sons during all the summer months has no parallel in filial loyalty in the Old Testament.   David's deep
affection for the house of Saul is seen in his bringing back
from Jabesh-gilead the bones of Saul and Jonathan, and
their burial with the bones of the seven reprisal victims in
the ancestral tomb of Kish, the father of Saul, in Zela of
Benjamin.

157. A Plague and Its Results (2 Sam. 24; 1 Chron.

21). " The anger of Jehovah was kindled against Israel;" why, we do not know; and he stirred up David to number Israel. Chronicles says an adversary was guilty in inciting David to the act. At any rate, David, against the protests of Joab and the captains, took a census of all Israel from Dan to Beer-sheba, occupying nine months and twenty days. The count in 2 Samuel is given as 800,000 warriors and Judah 500,000. The Chronicles record gives 1,100,000, and Judah 470,000, leaving out Levi and Benjamin. No harmony of those figures is attempted.

This exhibit of David's desire to show his military strength greatly displeased Jehovah, and he smote Israel. The prophet Gad gave David his choice of one of three kinds of penalties to be visited upon Israel for his sin. Seven years of famine, three months of defeat before his foes, or three days' pestilence. David chose the pestilence, because in that case he said he would fall into the hand of Jehovah, who is merciful. So a pestilence fell upon the whole land and snuffed out the lives of 70,000 men. All such calamities sent upon Israel in that day were supposed to be sent by Jehovah as punishment for sin.

When the angel of death, with his drawn sword, hovered over, and was on the point of carrying out his command upon Jerusalem, Jehovah repented of what he had done,— even David himself saw the destroyer over the city, over the threshing-floor of Ornan the Jebusite. In penitence and sackcloth David pleaded the cause of the people, and was commanded to go build an altar to Jehovah. To secure full rights he purchased the threshing-floor, the oxen, the wood of the threshing instruments, the wheat; and he offered burnt-offerings, peace offerings, and meal offerings to Jehovah. And the angel sheathed his sword, and the pestilence was stayed.

This threshing-floor later became the site on which Solomon built his temple, and is probably to-day near the site of the Mosque of Omar, the Dome of the Rock (see p. 213).

158. David's Last Assemblage and Words (1 Chron.

28:1–29:30; 1 Kings 2:1-11). David's final address to all the hosts of Israel reviewed God's favour in all the past, and his promises for the future. He had wished to build a temple for Jehovah, but was prevented because he had shed much blood. God had revealed to him by the prophet that such a centre of worship would be erected by his son Solomon, who would be a man of peace. David, according to the Chronicler, had gathered together an immense quantity of materials for the temple (1 Chron. 22 and 28:11-21). He had likewise prepared a plan of the building and its chief equipment. Out of his own resources David had given freely large quantities of metals and other materials. As a climax he offered a prayer of praise and thanksgiving to God. The people then blessed God and offered sacrifices to him. As he had the right to do, David named Solomon as his successor on the throne.

For the moment we pass by the intrigues for the throne, and find the weak old king giving his last charge to Solomon. " Be a man and keep wholly the charge of Jehovah, and you will prosper in your ways. Take vengeance on the cold-blooded and heartless Joab, son of Zeruiah, who slew two army generals in times of peace. Be kind to the sons of Barzillai, who took care of me in Mahanaim beyond the Jordan; forget not the vile cursings of Shimei, who reviled me in my flight from Absalom."

And David died, having ruled forty years,—seven years in Hebron and thirty-three years in Jerusalem.

159. David's Character and Work. From the time of David's first appearance, his personality carried about it a kind of halo of attractiveness.

In his introduction to Saul he seems to have been a likable, companionable young man. The ease with which he captured Saul's family and court, and the men who stuck to him throughout his outlaw life, confirm us in believing in the gripping amiability of his person and character. Even the Philistines, as Achish, and many of his body-guard, were held to him by an affection that led them to go any lengths to please their leader. To his friends he was always loyal, and magnanimous to his foes. His cold, hard nephews, Joab and Abishai, in the face of even cutting rebukes, were always true to their royal kinsman. Only when David had become spoiled by the demoralizing life of the court did some of his long-time friends desert him for new thrills.

As a warrior David was a courageous antagonist. From his clash with Goliath to the last wars of his reign he was fearless, intrepid, and often savage as we regard it to-day. Examples of his brutal warfare are seen in (1) his slaughter of a hundred Philistines to pay Saul the dowry for Michal as a wife; (2) his slaying of all the male Edomites, condemned centuries afterwards by the prophets; (3) his terrific massacre of two-thirds of the captured Moabites in his wars against that eastern tribe.

On the other hand, his valour and bravery accomplished more for national Israel than any other leader. When he began his career, David found the tribes unorganized, disunited, and paying tribute to other peoples. By his steady, wise, and far-seeing methods he gradually won over Judah; and by patience, skill and diplomacy he brought Israel into the fold. Then he consolidated all the tribes with their capital at Jerusalem. Warfare against outlying peoples carried his realm to its farthest limits, almost to the Euphrates in the north, to the desert on the east, to the Gulf of Akabah and the river of Egypt on the south and southwest respectively. David really founded the Hebrew monarchy with all its oriental accessories.

As a leader and king, David possessed practically all the essential qualities. He knew men, and could measure their worth with amazing precision. His wild outlaw career was an unparalleled school of observation and experience. His later leaders grew up with him and were trained in all the essentials of success. With such a band of trusted and trusting aides and advisers, David organized his government and planned his campaigns. His own skill and wisdom shaped the administration of his regime, and directed the management of all the tribal relations and their co-operation with the central authority in Jerusalem. In spite of the apparent moral decline of David and his family at the last, the stability of the organization of the monarchy was practically unshaken.

As a king, David did not reach the sketch made by Samuel (1 Sam. 8:11-18) in his reply to Israel's request for a king. That picture was drawn on the model of Egyptian, Babylonian and Aramæan kings of about 1000 B. C., where the ruler was a despot and all his subjects were merely his personal servants. All property was available for the king's use, and everything produced on the fields, crops, flocks, and herds, was tithed with the royal exchequer and commissary department. But David's progress in that direction was marked and definite. His administrative and military departments, organized to the point of greatest efficiency, took over all local affairs of state and province, and the defense of tribal and national interests, respectively. To accomplish such results necessitated the drafting into public service of the best men of the realm, irrespective of any private interests. Behind the above the commissary department required the best and most effective service in providing food and its preparation for the armies of officers, labourers, and soldiers, who were dependent on the king's table. Though David did not reach Samuel's sketch, he took a long step toward the real position and power of the oriental monarch of his day.

As a religious character David offers us an enigma. From his anointing by Samuel to his fatal walk on the roof of his palace, David seems to have taken no important step without inquiring of Jehovah. His emotional zeal was so genuine, the depth of his piety so sincere, that campaigns, battles and deeds were gauged only by the oracle of Jehovah. Saul's person was sacred to him because he was the anointed of Jehovah. He early brought into Jerusalem the ark, placed it in a tent, and appointed Zadok and Abiathar priests to care for it. Nathan and Gad were his favourite prophets, who answered his beck and call, and gave him the orders of Jehovah. How extensive his organization of worship may have been, we do not know, since the Chronicler speaks of the one he recites as being designed for the temple,—for a much later date, of course.

David's idea of God was crude and primitive; his God was one whose reconciliation could be effected by the slaughter of innocent animals in sacrifice; by the murder of the seven descendants of Saul; by the wiping out of 70,000 Israelites by a pestilence. But that was the conception of the age, and David, of course, shared in it. His attractiveness to us is based on his loyalty to what he thought was right and true, and not his coarse and provincial conception of Israel's God.

David's skill as a musician first brought him to the attention of Saul. His talent as a poet linked therewith have given him a high place in the hymnology of the Old Testament. His earliest preserved poems are those in memory of Saul and Jonathan (2 Sam. 1:17 f.) and Abner (3:33, 34). Tradition has attributed to him the entire book of Psalms. But now we know better. Second Samuel 23, practically the same as Psalm 18, seems to paint for us, in exquisite form, poetical conceptions of David's day. How many other psalms were composed by him is merely a matter of conjecture, since the superscriptions were added at a date later than the time of composition. David's spirit of confidence in Jehovah breathes through many of the psalms of the first book of the Psalter.

David's weaknesses emerged after his settlement in Jerusalem, when plenty and luxury surrounded him and duties multiplied on his hands. His negligence in the training and guidance of his children, his poor example in self-restraint, the influence of his court environment on his family, and the gradual sagging of his own moral standards, were ominous forecasts for the future of the kingdom he established. But in spite of all these infirmities, David

shines out with a brilliancy in Hebrew history that is sur-
passed by none except Moses.

Note on Fig. 52, tailpiece below: The Kidron Valley is the long deep
valley running from north to south on the east side of Jerusalem. It
is 150 feet below the floor of the temple area at the present Geth-
semane, and 200 feet below at Job's well. On the east bank are found
the "Tomb of Absalom," "Tomb of Jehoshaphat," "Grotto of St.
James," and "Pyramid of Zacharias." On the west bank, a Moslem
cemetery, the "Virgin's Fountain," and the "Pool of Siloam." The
sixth camel in the picture covers the entrance to the Virgin's Fountain. It was named "Valley of Jehoshaphat" in the Christian era.

CHAPTER XVIII

SOLOMON'S STATESMANSHIP

160. Plots for the Succession (1 Kings 1). David's old age and helpless condition for ruling the kingdom engaged the thoughts of other members of the royal family. No policies had been adopted in Israel for a successor to the throne. Naturally, as in other kingdoms, the oldest

NOTE ON FIG. 17A, headpiece above: The most popular timber-tree for building palaces and temples in southwestern Asia and Egypt was the cedar of Lebanon. The wood is cream colour and of a beautiful grain, and almost indestructible. For finishing purposes it is unsurpassed. The kings of Babylonia, of Egypt, and of Israel secured it whenever possible for their court complexes. The Phœnicians used it for building ships, for pillars, and for roofs of their public buildings. To-day these noble trees are almost extinct.

son was thought to be the regular heir, though no one disputed the right of a ruler to name his successor. Since Absalom's death, Adonijah was the next in age of the sons of David. There probably had been some secret plotting by different persons in high authority looking toward David's successor on the throne.

Adonijah was the first to launch his plot. He had already prepared chariots and horsemen with heralds to run ahead of him; he had enlisted the support of the great Joab, generalissimo of the army, and of Abiathar the priest,—David being practically incapacitated through old age. They met together at En-rogel, the junction of the valleys of Hinnom and Kidron, below Jerusalem, where they sacrificed sheep, oxen, and fatlings. To this would-be coronation feast Adonijah had invited all his brothers except Solomon, and all the men of Judah, the king's servants, favourable to his succession. The narrative does not reveal the exact steps the *coup d'etat* was to take. But Nathan the prophet, Benaiah, chief of David's body-guard, and Solomon, were conspicuous for their absence.

In the meantime, the secret got out, and a counter-plot was immediately put into full action. Nathan the prophet intrigued with Bath-sheba, mother of Solomon, secured David's orders, the backing of Zadok the priest, and of Benaiah with the mighty men of David's body-guard. Solomon, the rival candidate for the throne, mounted the royal mule and rode in the midst of his royal backers, down to Gihon in the valley of Kidron, on the east side of Zion. There Zadok immediately anointed the young man with a horn of oil out of the sacred tent. And they blew a blast on the trumpets and all the people shouted, " Long live King Solomon." The royal procession filed back up into the city to the music of pipes and shoutings whose sounds " rent the earth," and Solomon sat on the throne of Israel.

The coronation feast of Adonijah was startled by the dramatic burst into their festivities of Jonathan, son of Abiathar, who gave a frantic recital of what had just taken place in the coronation caucus of Solomon. The guests of Adonijah hastily broke up the council, and each slipped out, and took to cover before anything worse should happen. But Adonijah sought the only safe refuge of a rival for the throne,—the horns of the altar, where he awaited Solomon's mercy and promise not to slay him. Adonijah finally came to Solomon and bowed before him in recognition of his kingship; and Solomon brusquely said, "Go to thy house" (1:53).

161. Playing Safe for the Future (1 Kings 2:12-46). Now that Solomon was seated on his father David's throne, an oriental throne, it was the part of prudence to see that his succession was not jeopardized by dangerous characters. Adonijah, his older brother, had been practically forgiven for doing the very thing he had a right to do; and he might have lived in peace all his days, if he had not seriously fallen in love with the Shunammite nurse who took care of his father in his last days. Not wishing personally to ask any favour of his younger brother Solomon, Adonijah requested Bath-sheba to ask Solomon to give him Abishag for a wife. In an oriental court, the harem of a king always became the legal possession of his successor. This fact Adonijah was supposed to have known, but may have thought in this case that he could get away with it.

At the mere suggestion of such a thing Solomon scented a deep-laid plot, backed by Abiathar and Joab, to carry out their original purpose of making Adonijah king. The young ruler flared up with rage, swore vengeance on Adonijah, and sent Benaiah, as his executioner, to slay him. Abiathar the priest was then and there expelled from his office, and ordered to Anathoth, the priests' town, as one worthy to die; but he would be spared now because under David he had helped carry the ark of Jehovah. This expulsion carried out the prophecy made regarding the house of Eli in Shiloh (1 Sam. 2:27-36).

All Jerusalem soon learned of the drastic steps taken by Solomon to make his throne safe. Joab, also having supported the rival candidate, Adonijah, now fled to the tent of Jehovah and took hold of the horns of the altar. On refusing to leave the sacred spot, Solomon vengefully gave orders, and Benaiah slew him right there in the sacred tent of Jehovah, nominally to clear his and his father's skirts of the cold-blooded murders which he had committed during his life, but really, to wipe out all partisans of a rival claimant to the throne. And this same bloody executioner was put in Joab's place as head of the army.

Shimei was next sent for by Solomon, was ordered to stay in Jerusalem, and not to leave it on penalty of death. Neglectful of the threat, Shimei pursued and brought back two of his runaway slaves. The king heard of it and sent around that same bloody executioner, who killed him.

Now that Adonijah, Abiathar, Joab and Shimei were out of the way—three of them murdered—Solomon's crown should have rested easy on his savage young head, for there seem to have been no others to endanger his right to the throne.

162. A Vision and a Choice (1 Kings 3:4-15). The records of Solomon's reign in Kings and Chronicles are loosely put together without chronological or logical order. Those in Kings rather magnify the glories of his reign until the last years, and give one a kind of desultory conception of the period. But by careful analysis we are able to construct a reasonable record of Solomon's career.

Early in his reign Solomon, and an assembly with him, went out of Jerusalem to the high place at Gibeon, about six miles to the northwest, to offer sacrifices there; for that was a notable high place, where there was some kind of a tabernacle, according to Chronicles. After a holocaust of animals had been slaughtered to implore Jehovah, Solomon went to his rest for the night. God appeared to him in a dream and said, " Ask what I shall give thee." Solomon's modest recognition of all that God had done for David's house, and that he had chosen him to follow his great father; and his request for an understanding heart to judge the people and to discriminate between good and evil, pleased Jehovah. And God said, " Because thou hast not asked long life nor riches nor the life of thine enemies, I will give thee an understanding heart to discern what is just. And more, I will give thee both riches and honour, so that there shall not be another king like thee all thy days. If thou shalt walk in my ways as did David thy father, I will lengthen thy days." When Solomon awoke he perceived that it was a dream. On going down to Jerusalem he stood before the ark of the covenant of Jehovah and offered up still more burnt-offerings, and gave a banquet to all his servants.

163. Solomon's Inherited Dominion. When Solomon took over the kingdom of David it embraced all the territory from the river Euphrates on the northeast to the land of the Philistines and the border of Egypt on the southwest, including also Damascus on the northeast, and the Gulf of Akabah on the southeast. It covered the greatest extent of country ever ruled over by an Israelitish king,— about 50,000 square miles,—a little less than the area of Illinois and a little more than New York state. Embraced within it there were besides Israelites, Philistines, Canaanites, Amorites, Moabites, Edomites, Ammonites and Aramæans,—a precarious mixture of tribes and peoples under one government. David had left none of them, except some Philistines and Aramæans, unconquered. More than that, he had practically unified them politically under his own sway and guidance.

Probably early in Solomon's reign two rebellions took place within this realm. A royal refugee from Edom to Egypt at the time of David's slaughter of the Edomites, returned and set up his Edomite kingdom again and remained quite undisturbed by Solomon. Up in Damascus Rezon, a refugee from Hadadezer of Zobah, organized a troop and took over the rule of Damascus and held it during all Solomon's reign. Solomon, however, enjoyed a reign of warless activity, and Israel dwelt safely, every man " under his vine and under his fig-tree " . . . " all the days of Solomon."

164. Solomon's Government. Solomon seems to have selected an adequate and more complete cabinet than had David his father. In this group of officials we find (1) a priest, Azariah, son of Zadok; (2) secretaries, Elihoreph and Ahijah; (3) a chronicler, or historian, Jehoshaphat; (4) generalissimo of the army, Benaiah; (5) priests, Zadok and Abiathar; (6) overseer over the twelve commissary officers, Azariah, son of Nathan the prophet; (7) chief-priest, and the " king's friend,"—counsellor, Zabud (son of Nathan the prophet); (8) court chamberlain, Abishar; (9) superintendent of slave service, Adoniram.

The entire country was divided into twelve administrative districts, nine west of the Jordan and three east of it; and over each district a commissary officer whose business it was to provide the king and the court with provisions for one month of each year. The provision for a single day was 337 bushels of fine flour, 674 bushels of meal, ten fat stall-fed oxen, twenty pastured oxen, 100 sheep, besides harts, gazelles, roebucks, and fatted fowl, as they could find them; also barley and straw for the animals in the government stables.

Solomon's army took on new dignity by the introduction of chariots and cavalry. He had, according to the records, 40,000 stalls of horses, and 12,000 cavalrymen, and 1,400 chariots. These were kept in Jerusalem or in his fortified cities, so distributed as to be readily available in time of need. In the desert beyond Damascus he built Tadmor, and many store-cities,—among them Hamath, Hazor, Megiddo, Gezer, Beth-horon the lower, and Baalath. These had walls, gates and bars, and were centres such as were

NOTE ON MAP 8, opposite. The Kingdoms of David and Solomon,— about 975-40 B. C.: David's legacy to Solomon was a well organized kingdom covering the full length of the promised land, from the river of Egypt (*Wady el-Arish*) to the great river, the River Euphrates.

befitting a realm like Solomon's. Transportation from place to place by chariots and cavalry required roads of a type unheard of in Israel's past.

165. Solomon's Foreign Relations. David had already cultivated the friendship of Hiram, king of Tyre, and had established commercial relations with the Phœnicians. Solomon's peace policy threw off their guard and greatly modified the attitude of the small tribes subdued by David and now embodied in Israel's realm.

The international policy of maintaining peace by marriage between members of royal houses had been in vogue among other nations for many centuries. Solomon's ambition as an oriental monarch led him early to adopt this expedient to promote peace within and about his realm. So he took in marriage the daughter of Pharaoh, king of Egypt, and women of the (royal houses of the) Moabites, Ammonites, Edomites, Sidonians and Hittites, and of how many more is not stated. Such foreign domestic alliances would seem to be a guaranty of peace abroad if not at home; making Jerusalem a kind of Hague conference between all those smaller peoples represented in the royal family.

The introduction of so many foreign women into Solomon's court internationalized Jerusalem and made it a cosmopolitan city. Each prominent foreigner who took up residence at the capital brought with him or her the customs, manners and religion of his or her homeland. So Jerusalem became a city of a pantheon, of many gods.

And still more it became a centre over which the quiet spirit of peace brooded during nearly the whole of Solomon's forty years' reign.

166. Solomon Builds the Temple. Early in his reign Solomon resolved to put into effect the promise of his father that he (Solomon) should build a temple in Jerusalem (2 Sam. 7:1-13). David had planned for it, and Jehovah had refused him the privilege of building it, for he had been "a man of war." Since the destruction of

Shiloh by the Philistines, the ark had dwelt in several temporary tenements.

The " tent of meeting," said to have been set up in the wilderness, was its first home; the houses of Abinadab and Obed-Edom its temporary abodes, until David with great joy brought it into his new capital, Jerusalem. According to tradition the temple was to be built on the site of the threshing-floor of Ornan the Jebusite, purchased by David (2 Sam. 24:17-25). To provide ample space for its foundations, the platform of the hill was extended 270 feet over arches. This terrace is said to have concealed reservoirs of water (cf. Psa. 46:1-5).

The plan of the temple to be built on that terrace seems to have been practically twice the size of the original tent of meeting,—not large, but exceeding rich and splendid in its appointments and finish (1 Kings 5-8; 2 Chron. 3-5). The specifications included 1) an outer and inner court; (a) the outer court contained, (1) the large bronze altar thirty feet square, and fifteen feet high; (2) the sea of bronze resting on twelve bronze oxen; (3) ten lavers or wash-basins for the operating priests; (4) possibly a grove of trees. 2) A porch or vestibule, on either side of which stood the decorative bronze pillars Jachin and Boaz, sixty feet high (Septuagint reading) (2 Chron. 3:4) at the entrance. 3) A holy place—the greater house (2 Chron. 3:5); (a) a ten-branched candlestick; (b) ten tables; (c) folding doors; and (d) an altar of incense. 4) The holy of holies (the oracle), in which were the cherubim and the ark of the covenant. On either side of these courts were the chambers for the priests, three stories high.

Since Solomon could find no builder in his realm who was capable of carrying out such an undertaking, he turned to Hiram of Tyre, whose skilled contractors and artisans had built David's house, and many famous Phœnician temples. Hiram made a contract to furnish Solomon cedar timber and skilled workmen for an annual delivery of a specified amount of food (1 Kings 5:11). Solomon furnished wood-

choppers to cut the cedars in Lebanon. These were floated
in rafts down the Mediterranean Sea to Joppa, where they
were broken up; and the timbers were dragged overland,
not by powerful motor trucks, but by sheer human strength,
to Jerusalem. The stone was dug out of the limestone quar-
ries nearby, cut and transported to the site of the temple
by slaves (non-Israelites), 80,000 stone-cutters and 70,000
common labourers whom Solomon put to work under 3,600
overhead slave-drivers, one driver to every forty slaves,—
a kind of premonition of the galley slaves of Rome. The
metals, gold, silver, bronze, and iron were, of course, all
imported, and in such quantities that, except the gold, they
were uncounted.

The Phœnician workmen superintended the entire building complex, and were so efficient that when the temple was
finished it became the " joy of all the earth." Its delicate
wood carvings, its choice vessels of gold, its artistic ensemble, made it a most fitting place in which to put the ark
of the covenant of Jehovah.

The purpose of this glorious dwelling of the Most High
was primarily to centralize and fix the worship of Jehovah
in Jerusalem; to symbolize the presence of Jehovah in
Israel; to be a focal point to which all the tribes would
migrate to worship at the same altar and shrine. It also
would be a sanctifying influence in the midst of the worldliness and spiritual declension of an oriental capital of

NOTE ON FIG. 92, opposite: Dr. Conrad Schick, after long years of
study, has produced this " lifelike " and convincing model of the great
temple. The upper left-hand corner is guarded by the fortress Millo.
Next below is the temple proper facing eastward, with a court of its
own enclosed by the three-storied priests' chambers. In front of the
arched entrance, facing the temple, was the priests' court. Outside
this quadrangle was the people's court, surrounded by Solomon's porch
and other royal buildings. At the lower left-hand corner was the
" House of the Forest of Lebanon." At the right adjoining the lower
right-hand corner of the great enclosure was the Judgment Hall.
Across on the other side below was the house of his Egyptian wife,
and part of the same group the harem and the king's apartments,—
an ensemble of buildings that magnified the glory of that oriental
monarch, Solomon.

Fig. 92. Schick's Reconstruction of Solomon's Temple

cosmopolitan character. And—it contributed no little to the pride of Solomon's glory.

167. Dedication of the Temple. Solomon, upon the completion of the temple, at the end of seven years, had all the sacred vessels and articles for use in worship brought in and put in their places. He summoned the heads of the tribes and princes of the fathers' houses to Jerusalem. With solemn procession the ark of the covenant was removed from the tent where David had put it, and was carried by the priests and placed in the holy of holies, beneath the cherubim,—all done with hecatombs of sacrifices by all the congregation. And a cloud filled all the house to screen the glory of Jehovah.

Solomon then blessed the assembled multitudes, and recited the history of the building that had materialized in the present house, and what he had contributed to bring it to its completed state. Standing before the altar of Jehovah, Solomon spread out his hands toward heaven and offered the prayer of dedication, one of the most comprehensive found in any religious literature. He prayed that Jehovah would hear and answer prayers (a) on the oath of ordeal, (b) under defeat, (c) for rain, (d) under several distressing calamities, (e) for the army, (f) in captivity. The conclusion appeals to the attentiveness and continued presence of God, that he might clothe his priests with salvation and his saints with goodness.

The final acts of dedication were the slaying of herds of oxen and flocks of sheep as sacrifices to Jehovah in the great court, accompanied by the music of instruments.

168. Solomon Builds the Palace Complex. The Phœnician contractors probably carried on both building projects simultaneously, until the temple was completed at the end of seven and one-half years. The construction of the palace complex occupied thirteen years.

The make-up of this palace group may be enumerated from the entrance to the hill from the city on the south. The first structure to be entered was the house of the forest of Lebanon, 150 feet long by 75 feet wide and 45 feet high; and named after the cedar pillars which stood in three rows of fifteen each, and supported the upper part of the house. This structure was an arsenal for the storage of arms above; and below it may have been used for assemblies.

The next building was also a pillared hall 75 x 45 feet, a kind of ante-room to the hall of judgment where the king received his high officers and foreign ambassadors and distinguished guests. His throne was a masterpiece of art, made of carved ivory and overlaid with gold, with a footstool of gold, approached by six steps, flanked on either side (as one ascended the steps) by six standing lions; "there was not the like made in any kingdom."

The king's own house came next and was constructed with the same materials and grandeur, and in size ample to comport with the royal dignity and the number of the royal inmates, whether they were the 700 wives and 300 concubines (1 Kings 11:3), or the sixty queens and the eighty concubines of the Song of Solomon (6:8), and the necessary servants. For the Egyptian wife alone Solomon built a residence attached to, or near the king's own house, with the splendour befitting an Egyptian king's daughter. And the royal palace was enclosed by a wall, partly within the wall that surrounded the temple and palace.

All these buildings made up the royal palace where Solomon lived, administered the affairs of state, and entertained his princes and guests.

The final dedicatory celebration was rounded off by a colossal banquet shared by all Israel from Hamath to the brook of Egypt,—the eighth day being a solemn assembly, after which the people returned to their homes.

169. Solomon's Commercial Relations and Revenues. Solomon's first commercial contract seems to have been made with King Hiram of Tyre for timber for his building projects already described. This treaty involved him in the annual payment of 225,000 bushels of wheat and 1,800 gallons of beaten olive oil. In addition to furnishing timber, Hiram's men helped cut stone, and his builders erected the entire group of buildings. How these building contracts were liquidated does not appear in the text. At least it looks as if Solomon must have run short of funds, for he turned over to Hiram "twenty cities" in Galilee, probably in lieu of debts to him. With these Hiram, in true oriental trade-affectation, was not pleased. But, as true evidence of his pleasure, immediately thereafter he seems to have made a loan to Solomon of sixty talents of gold.

Another contract was made with Egyptian traders (or was it the Mutsri of Asia Minor?), whereby horses and chariots were brought to Solomon, who served as a distributor to the Hittites and Aramæans at a good profit. This business may have been the means through which Solomon became acquainted with and married the daughter of the Pharaoh of Egypt, which had such significance politically in Israel's relations to that country.

But in many respects the most profitable commercial enterprise that Solomon engaged in was maritime trade, not on the Mediterranean Sea, controlled by the Phœnicians. But he built ships at Ezion-geber, of the Tarshish type, at the head of the Gulf of Akabah, down across the frontiers of Edom; and Hiram's experienced tars manned and sailed them on the Red Sea, the Indian Ocean, and even to Ophir (wherever that was), in three-year round-trips. The returned cargo of these vessels consisted of gold, as much as 420 talents (over $12,000,000) on one trip, algum or sandal-wood in great quantities, precious stones, silver, ivory, apes, and peacocks, partly to help meet the huge governmental budget, and partly to establish the magnificence of the royal court.

We should mention here also the store-cities, or warehouse centres, which the king had built up and equipped through the entire stretch of his realm (2 Chron. 8:4-6) for the maintenance of his standing army, and for meeting any urgent defensive necessities of the central government. It is also probable that Solomon did not neglect to exact

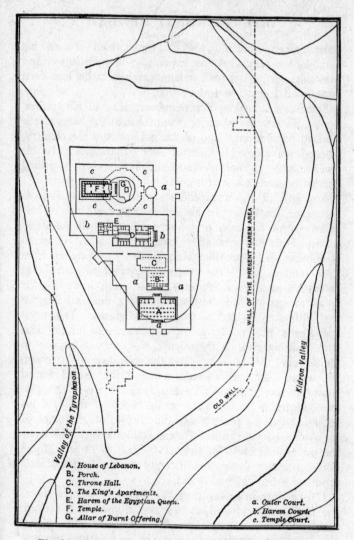

Within the figure:

c   *c*

F   G   *a*

c   *c*

b   E   *b*

D

a   C   *a*

B

A

a

WALL OF THE PRESENT HAREM AREA

Kidron Valley

OLD WALL

Valley of the Tyropœon

A. House of Lebanon.
B. Porch.
C. Throne Hall.
D. The King's Apartments.
E. Harem of the Egyptian Queen.
F. Temple.
G. Altar of Burnt Offering.

a. Outer Court.
b. Harem Court.
c. Temple Court.

Fig. 91. Stade's Plan of Solomon's Complex of Buildings

Professor Stade (died Dec. 7, 1906) made a careful and elaborate study of Solomon's structures. This plan is self-explanatory and differs somewhat from that of Schick pictured above. Note especially the lines of the valleys that surround the area.

tariff money from all the caravans which crossed his dominions in any direction, especially between Egypt and Mesopotamia and Arabia, where caravan trade had been established from time immemorial.

Solomon's annual gold revenue, exclusive of his traders' profits, his merchants' traffic, the tribute of the kings of the "mixed populations," and of the governors of the country, reached the incredible sum of over $20,000,000. In his revenue silver is not reckoned, neither is there anything put in the same class with gold.

But with all of his stupendous revenues, most of it from commerce, the budget of his government could not be balanced except by taxes and forced labour which painfully burdened his subjects. The later appeal of all Israel to Rehoboam, Solomon's son and successor, for relief from their burdens is all the evidence required to prove that Solomon's royal establishments, while magnificent in their appointments and administration, were a financial incubus that ultimately helped to wreck his kingdom. This royal spendthrift could not have reached the acme of his ambition if he had not rivalled the oriental monarchs of his day in his revenues, his buildings, and the splendour of his court. To secure such magnificence required the use of forced labour, of slaves, and of all available man-power. This also carried with it his disregard of the rights of many of his subjects, and the positive egoistic and selfish character of his so-called royal claims. He can fulfil almost to the letter the outline sketched by Samuel (1 Sam. 8:11-18) of the king for whom Israel so insistently asked,—a despot and tyrant of a true oriental brand.

170. Solomon's Reputed Wisdom. Solomon's ancestral heritage would lead us to expect him to be a shrewd, far-sighted, keen-witted man, with more than ordinary personality. His advantages as head of an inherited peaceful kingdom contributed greatly to the mental processes which add to the knowledge and wisdom of men.

The Old Testament writers are at least faithful to the

reputation of their great monarch when they attribute to him a good part of the book of Proverbs, the Song of Solomon, and Ecclesiastes. The superscriptions give him two psalms (72, 127); and tradition assigns to him the apocryphal "Wisdom of Solomon," and "Ecclesiasticus."

The writer of 1 Kings (4:29-34) was an enthusiastic admirer who placed him above all the wise men of the East, some of whom he mentions by name. Solomon's observation and knowledge covered animal and plant life as he saw them in that day. His practical wisdom was radiant in his dealings with people, whom he seems to have fathomed with a peculiar insight, as in the decision rendered to the mothers who were quarrelling over a living child.

Being chief justice of his realm, Solomon decided all cases of dispute that came up for decision. His innate knowledge of men, and his understanding of the import of questions that would baffle ordinary judges gave him an advantage rarely possessed. How far proverbial good sense is embodied in our Proverbs is only a conjecture. But he must have had far more than the insight and wisdom of ordinary kings, else his reputation would not have been wafted even to the land Sheba. It is also true that his fame probably included the magnificence of his palatial court and surroundings, which would also seem to be outgrowths of his wisdom. Solomon's personality so overshadowed everyone in his court and entourage, even the prophets, priests, and government officers, that he stood practically alone in the minds of the recorders and historians of that and subsequent days. This fact would also add to his fame wherever it was carried.

The queen of Sheba came from southern Arabia to see this paragon of wisdom, and to test him with hard questions; and she says that the half had not been told her about his "wisdom and prosperity." More still, "there came of all peoples to hear the wisdom of Solomon, from all the kings (kinglets) of the earth [Hebrew says, "land"] who had heard of his wisdom."

While listening to the applause of the writers of that day, we must hold our judgment in suspense until we shall have taken an inventory of the results as they appear at the close of his life, and of the national status of subsequent centuries.

NOTE ON FIG. 54, tailpiece below: The princes of the Lebanon forests are cutting cedar trees for the great king Seti I of the nineteenth dynasty of Egypt (1313–1292 B. C.). Like other royalty, Solomon for instance, Egyptian rulers used this valuable timber in constructing their palaces and temples. The denseness of the growth and slenderness of the trunks are in sharp contrast with what we know of the few existing cedars of Lebanon to-day, and of the cut above (17A).

CHAPTER XIX

SOLOMON'S FATAL WEAKNESS

171. Solomon's Court Life. We have already referred to the foreign wives whom Solomon introduced into the royal family at Jerusalem. Each one of them was an individual alien who brought with her her own national religious, social, and mental peculiarities. These Solomon, in all his wisdom, could not ignore. In fact, he was under obligation not only to recognize them, but also to provide for them the necessary facilities for enjoying their own national rites, customs, and practices. After furnishing a home for a foreign wife, the king next saw that her religious requirements were met, generally by the setting up of an idol where said wife wished, either in her house, in a separate shrine, or elsewhere.

NOTE ON FIG. 85, headpiece above: Solomon's venture in mercantile marine was inspired by Phœnician and Egyptian activity on the sea. Five hundred years before Solomon's day Queen Hatshepsut sent her fleet to Punt, tropical east Africa, to bring back its products. Here the sailors are loading gold, ivory, skins, incense, sycamores, live leopards, a giraffe, with many plants and fruits unknown in Egypt. A record of this expedition was carved on the wall of the queen's funerary chapel at Deir el-Bahri, at the base of the mountain containing the tombs of the kings,—opposite old Thebes.

However pure Solomon's worship of Jehovah may have been at the beginning of his reign, probably as good as the best of the nation, efforts to pacify and please his wives gradually took all the edge off the earlier sharp distinction between Israel's God and the procession of court divinities of his wives. The God of Moses and Samuel finally became confused in thought with those foreign gods whose rites were a disgrace, a defilement, and an outrage to the moral sense of the faithful worshippers of Jehovah.

What shall we say as to the wisdom of Solomon in this phase of his life? Instead of strengthening the bulwarks of the God of the Hebrews, Solomon undermined the walls and endangered the entire stronghold. But did he not build the temple? Certainly, but at the same time he undermined it by conceding to his wives the practical equality of their gods to his own national Jehovah.

172. Solomon's Old Age and Death. Even if Solomon's moral and religious character had been staunch and unsullied at the beginning of his career, the increasing luxuries and dissipations of his court life weakened his resistance, and broke down his opposition to the claims and requirements of the gods of his foreign wives.

Polygamy brought in the foreign women, the foreign women brought in their idols, the idols commanded some attention and deference even on the part of the king. As Solomon grew older, his wives so influenced him that he neglected Jehovah and went "after Ashtoreth, the goddess of the Sidonians, and after Milcom, the abomination of the Ammonites." He also built a high place for Chemosh, the abomination of Moab, on Mt. Olives.

This toleration led to esteem, and finally to a kind of reverence that seems to discount in large part the real wisdom of a man who would plunge headlong into the maintenance and promotion of such a flood-tide of paganism.

So serious became his neglect of his own God that Jehovah said to him, " I will surely rend the kingdom from thee,

but not during thy days, out of respect for David thy
father; and thy son shall have only two tribes, and that
simply for David's sake, not for anything that thou art or
hast done." Such an arraignment must have given pause
to a king who had been the centre of admiration and reverence for nearly forty years.

Another untoward event, and the first we find near the
end of his life, was the insubordination of Jeroboam, an
Ephraimite labour-leader that reconstructed the fortress
Millo. Ahijah, the prophet, whom the writer of Kings
does not mention as ever having spoken to Solomon, though
doubtless he had, met and encouraged Jeroboam by tearing
his own new robe into twelve strips and handing ten of
them to the labour-leader as a symbol of the ten tribes that
he should rule. He also gave him specifically the reasons
why such a rent should be made in Solomon's realm
(1 Kings 11:29-33). A report of the interview and the
prophecy reached Solomon's ears; and Jeroboam fled for
his life to Shishak, king of Egypt, where he remained until
he heard of the death of his king, which took place in his
own palace in Jerusalem. And he was buried " in the city
of David his father," leaving behind a long line of worthy
and doubtful honours.

173. Solomon's Career and Contribution. David's
kingdom fell into Solomon's lap full-orbed. Israel as a
united realm was an accomplished fact. And more than
that, it ruled over peoples who for centuries had been
thorns in the sides of the Hebrews. Practically all this large
territory was enjoying the fruits of peace and prosperity.
But the capital, Jerusalem, was little more than a great
stronghold. Solomon, by long and patient planning and
work, made it one of the most beautiful and attractive of
the smaller royal cities of the world of about 950 B. C. Its
architecture, its artistic designs and decorations, its utility
as a centre of worship, its royal residence, were the marvels
of that day. These accomplishments occupied most of the
time of the first half of his reign of forty years, in which he

was extravagantly wasteful of public funds, and merciless in his galling exactions of taxes and service.

The expansion of his commercial activities on land and on sea, the revenues of his trading companies, and the taxes of his dependencies,—all contributed towards the maintenance of his elaborate and brilliant oriental court. But the last half of his reign was full of the enjoyments of a wide and extensive cultivation of friendship with foreign peoples.

To insure continued peace among all his dependent peoples, and foreign powers, Solomon, according to the mode of the day, married princesses of the royal families of many of these lands,—how many we cannot determine—and incorporated them into his own capital family. This act of oriental diplomacy, however much political significance it had at first, was Solomon's greatest contribution to the wrecking of both his political and religious dominions. Autocrat and despot though he was, he failed to stand up against the swell of the pagan tide that finally drove him on the rocks.

Solomon's active and practical mind contributed some permanent nuggets to the wisdom of the ages. Parts of Proverbs probably display some of the pithy remarks that he made or wrote down for the benefit of his contemporaries. He took an interest also in the cultivation of the knowledge of nature and of music.

Though there were prophets in his day, as Nathan and Ahijah, there is not a single reference to his contact with one of them during all his forty years' reign. Whether they were overawed or ignored by him, or forced into the background, or simply omitted by the historian, we do not know. He probably let them alone, and they allowed such a self-willed monarch as Solomon to go his own way unmolested.

In spite of the defects of Solomon's character and reign already noted, subsequent Jewish history looks back to the period of David and Solomon as the golden age, where

Hebrew national life reached the acme of its glory. Solomon's age was more splendid but less substantial than that of his greater father. Such despotism as Solomon established bore within it the very seeds of its decay. And the power that crushed the liberty and freedom of the people soon lost its grip on the sceptre of state, resulting in the violent rupture of his realm, as Ahijah had foretold.

NOTE ON FIG. 84, tailpiece below: When Sennacherib swept into Phœnicia (701 B. C.) the Phœnicians fled in native boats, of which this is one, to the island of Cyprus. For several centuries B. C., especially from the twelfth to the seventh, they were some of the craft that cut through the Mediterranean Sea and its neighbouring waters.

PERIOD VI

DUAL MONARCHIES

From the Disruption of the Kingdom to the Fall of Samaria (931–722 B. C.)

CHAPTER XX

RIVAL KINGDOMS AT SWORDS' POINTS

174. The Monarchy Torn Asunder (1 Kings 12:1-19; 2 Chron. 10). The groanings and mutterings of Israel under the burden of taxes and forced labour during the later years of Solomon's reign were portentous of the future.

NOTE ON FIG. 86, headpiece above: Shishak, first king of the 22nd dynasty, was an interpreter of the times. When he saw the split-up of the empire of Solomon into two rival kingdoms, he seized his opportunity to make a swift and successful raid into their territories, and returned loaded with precious booty (1 Kings 14:25, 26).

When he died there must have been few regrets among the people of the country, who were forced to sustain his elaborate royal establishments.

To make sure of his succession to the throne, Solomon's son, Rehoboam, by an Ammonite wife of the royal harem, was crowned king by his close friends at Jerusalem. The ten tribes ominously went to Shechem. Obviously, secret word of Solomon's death had been carried to the refugee Jeroboam in Egypt, and he had returned to his home. When Rehoboam appeared at Shechem for confirmation of his coronation, Jeroboam and his friends held up the proceedings until they could have a declaration of policy by the would-be king. They requested a promise of lighter taxes and burdens before they would consent to approve of Rehoboam as their king. That was too much of a demand to be decided offhand; and Rehoboam dismissed the assembly for three days,—after which he would answer them.

He first turned for advice to the old men who had lived close to Solomon. They had seen the storm brewing; and fearful of its break, they warned him to be conciliatory and serviceable if he would be their king forever. Not hospitable to such advice, he next turned to the " young " men with whom he had lived during the forty-one years of his court life. These " young " middle-aged men, whose days had been spent in the pleasures and luxuries of the royal palace, advised an opposite policy.

Rehoboam was wise enough to " stall " for time, and to ask counsel, but too much of a fool to adopt sound advice. At the end of the three days he appeared before the assembly and, in the spirit and voice of a despot, answered: " My father loaded you with a heavy yoke, I will make it still heavier: my father chastised you with whips, I will chastise you with scorpions."

The reaction was electric. The assembly instantly recoiled from such a threat and policy, and shouted in the face of the tyrant, " What portion have we in David?

Neither have we inheritance in the son of Jesse: to your tents, O Israel: now see to thine own house, David." Apparently obtuse to the real import of such a defiant spirit, Rehoboam sent Adoram, the officer in charge of labourers, to his usual task of setting the people to work. Even Adoram's appearance was a challenge, and the people rose up and vengefully stoned him to death. Rehoboam's fright led him to flee for safety to Jerusalem.

And all the people of Israel called Jeroboam and " elected " him in Shechem king over the ten tribes of Israel,—leaving Rehoboam's crown to cover Judah and Benjamin only.

175. Causes and Some Results of the Disruption. Israel's conceptions of liberty and freedom were inherited from their nomadic past. Tribal jealousies, especially between Judah and Ephraim, were always lurking just in the background. The old animosities between the kingdoms of Saul and of David had never succumbed. The ten tribes under Saul's son, Ish-bosheth, never forgot their identity. Solomon's grievous burdens of taxes and service wore out Israel's spirit of endurance. His weak-kneed reverence for the idols of his foreign wives disgusted the loyal worshippers of Jehovah (1 Kings 11:29-33). These were cumulative causes of the break.

Immediate and direct reasons for the split were (1) Ahijah the prophet's encouragement to Jeroboam the Ephraimite, to push his revolt to a finish; (2) the outrageous policy proclaimed at Shechem by Rehoboam, the court-spoiled heir to the throne of Solomon.

The inevitable took place. Solomon's realm was torn asunder from top to bottom. The ten tribes elected their own king, unrelated to any royal house. Their southern

NOTE ON MAP 9, opposite. The Kingdoms of Israel and Judah— 931-722 B. C.: Solomon's kingdom had almost reached the breaking point before his death. Merely the straw of Rehoboam's tyranny finished it. The shrunken limits of both kingdoms included little if any more than the territory assigned to the tribes of Israel (See Map 5).

boundary cut across the backbone of the country, east to west, about ten miles north of Jerusalem. They had more than three-quarters of the old kingdom, with all its best pastures and plains. They had seashore and mountain, and the trade-routes between the Euphrates and the Southwest. The greater part of the population was theirs, including many of the peoples who were subject to Solomon.

Judah and Benjamin held less than one-fourth of the Solomonic area, and that the poorest of the land. But it had the capital with its strong fortifications, its palace, and especially the central Levites who were worshippers of Jehovah. While politically at a disadvantage, the religious significance of Jerusalem was all in favour of Judah.

In union there was strength, but in division there was danger. Civil strife meant jeopardy in the presence of enemies, and ultimately subjection and submission to outside powers.

176. Rehoboam's Suicidal Policy (1 Kings 12:21-24; 2 Chron. 11 and 12). When Rehoboam found that the northern kingdom was a fact, he mustered a tremendous army to bring it to his feet. But the prophet Shemaiah vetoed such a move. Nevertheless, Rehoboam's hostile attitude never changed, for " there was war between Rehoboam and Jeroboam all the days of his life " (1 Kings 15:6). However, if such wars were waged openly we have no records of them.

Great foreign powers had not appeared in Palestine for more than a century, largely due to their inability to enter on far-reaching campaigns. But after Rehoboam had begun to feel reasonably secure, Shishak (Sheshonk I), first king of the twenty-second dynasty of Egypt, following the example of many of his great predecessors, invaded southwestern Asia. Let us not forget that Jeroboam, Rehoboam's rival, had been a refugee in Shishak's court before Solomon's death. Was Jeroboam the instigator of the attack made by Shishak against his enemy Rehoboam? If so, we should not expect Shishak to invade Jeroboam's realm. But in the list of 156 towns and cities taken by him, noted on the walls of the temple of Karnak, more than one-third are identified as having been located in Jeroboam's realm, such as Beth-shean and Penuel.

Now Shishak's capture and looting of Jerusalem left Rehoboam financially a wreck. The treasures of the temple, of the palace, and the golden shields of the house of the forest of Lebanon,—all were carried away as plunder to Egypt. What Shishak found with Jeroboam was not worth recording, for the northern kingdom had no treasures.

Rehoboam's religious zeal took shape in the promotion of the cults which Solomon had adopted in his dotage. No memorable acts are attributed to his reign of seventeen years. When he died he was buried in the royal tombs in the city of David. Abijam (Abijah in Chronicles), his son, succeeded him.

177. Jeroboam's Experiment (1 Kings 12:25-33). When Rehoboam defeated his own prospects of being king over all Israel, Jeroboam was ready for the crisis, as we have seen, and became ruler over the ten tribes. He had no ready-made capital, no cabinet, no temple nor army. He began at the bottom. Shechem, an ancient sacred place, he made his first capital, and fittingly built it up.

But the most serious problem that faced him was politico-religious. The sacred temple in Jerusalem, with all its appointments and service, was a powerful attraction to all worshippers of Jehovah in whatever part of the land they lived. To allow them to make pilgrimages to worship at that shrine would mean ultimately their adhesion to the kingdom of Judah, and the elimination of the kingdom of Israel. After taking counsel, Jeroboam made " two calves " (probably miniature bulls) of gold; and set up one in Bethel, about ten miles north of Jerusalem, and the other in Dan, in the far north part of the land,—two ancient sacred centres of worship. Jeroboam's proclamation to the people was, " It is too much for you to go up to Jerusalem: behold thy gods, O Israel, which brought thee up out of the land of Egypt" (12:28). The high places were housed, and priests from "among the people," not Levites, were consecrated to do service there, and at the two great shrines. A feast in the eighth month on its fifteenth day was proclaimed as a counter to the day of atonement in Judah;—also a counter to the diverse gods in Jerusalem introduced by Solomon's household.

Jeroboam's policy seems to have been to unify and strengthen his hold on the ten tribes. His attempt to divert their worship from the shrine in Jerusalem to the "calves" at Bethel and Dan was a political success; that is, it held the tribes together under the king, and turned the worship of the northern kingdom into what became almost a state religion, wherein they worshipped their ancestral gods in the primitive way. In fact, Jeroboam's policy divorced Israel from Jerusalem for at least a half-century.

Jeroboam's zeal for such worship and his sacrifices before the shrines were vehemently rebuked by the prophets. He was accused of casting Jehovah behind his back, and of doing worse than anyone before him in making other gods and molten images. And, worse than all, because of these things, his house should be short-lived and soon swept away "till it all be gone."

Politically, Jeroboam was a strong ruler. For twenty-two years he held the reins of the northern kingdom with a firm grasp. But religiously he was the symbol of obliquity for all the succeeding kings of Israel. When he died he was succeeded by his son Nadab.

178. Judah's Good King Asa (1 Kings 15:1-8, 9-24). Rehoboam's son, Abijam, is characterized as having "walked in all the sins of his father, which he had done before him,"—a doubtful honour and record. The Chronicler attributes to him an extraordinary battle with Jeroboam in which he (Abijam) was vanquished. At the end of three years he slept with his fathers, and Asa, his son, reigned in his stead.

Asa was a grandson of Absalom (1 Kings 15:10), but

with a bent for the right. He began to clean house by
expelling the Sodomites and taking down all the idols set up
by his predecessors. His idolatrous mother, Maacah, he
removed from being queen-mother, and burnt her idol,
Asherah, down by the brook Kidron. He bade Israel seek
Jehovah, and put into the temple newly dedicated vessels.
His zeal for Jehovah attracted to him many from Ephraim,
Manasseh, and Simeon, and from all Israel, when they saw
that Jehovah was with him.

The Chronicler waxes eloquent over the fortified cities
built in Judah, and over Asa's standing army of 580,000
men ready for any emergency. Possibly in imitation of
Shishak's earlier campaign, Zerah the Ethiopian swept into
the land with 1,000,000 men and 300 chariots. He penetrated as far as Mareshah, near Beit Jibrin. Asa, with his
great force and the favour of Jehovah, completely routed,
defeated and destroyed them. This battle is not mentioned
in Kings. Zerah is identified with Osorkon I (by H. R. Hall,
Camb. Anc. Hist., III, p. 261) of the twenty-second dynasty, a contemporary of Asa. (Zerah, as a name, is found
in South Arabian inscriptions.) Asa, however, was victor,
and the invader was subdued.

About the sixteenth year of Asa, Baasha, king of Israel,
began to strengthen his southern frontier fortifications at
Ramah, five miles north of Jerusalem, to prevent any famil-
iarities between his people and those of King Asa. So
formidable were those barricades that Asa became alarmed.
Following a customary but dangerous strategy, he took all
the silver and gold of the treasuries of the temple and
palace and sent them to Benhadad, the Aramæan king of
Damascus, saying, " Let there be a league between me and
thee; . . . lo, I have sent unto thee a present of silver and
gold; go, break thy league with Baasha, king of Israel."
Benhadad fell for the money. Faithful to this new ally, he
sent an army against Baasha's realm, against the cities of
Naphtali, far to the north. Asa's strategy was successful.
Baasha called off his fort-builders, to drive off Benhadad's

raiders in the north. Asa then summoned his best masons, carpenters and burden-bearers, tore down Baasha's defences, and with the timbers and stone built up the bulwarks of Geba (between Ramah and Jerusalem) and Mizpah, for his own protection.

Asa's reign of forty-one years, in the main, pleased the prophets, who kept a close watch on him, until he bribed Benhadad to break his treaty with Baasha. The Chronicler tells us that Azariah the prophet rebuked him for abandoning Jehovah; and that Hanani the seer called him to time for neglecting to appeal to Jehovah instead of buying off Benhadad of Damascus. At this Asa became angry and put him in the stocks. When Asa became old he suffered greatly with gout, and is charged by the Chronicler with not calling on Jehovah, but on the physicians. Asa's reasonably successful reign, politically left Judah in fair shape for his successor.

179. Reigns of Sword and Fire in Israel (1 Kings 15:25–16:28; 2 Chron. 16:1-6). Ahijah's prophecy to Jeroboam's wife sped swiftly to its goal. Nadab, son of Jeroboam, in the second year of his reign was assassinated by Baasha of Issachar at a siege of Gibbethon in the land of the Philistines.

Baasha, probably an army officer, made Tirzah his capital. He carried out the policies of Jeroboam, " who made Israel to sin," and wiped out all the house of Jeroboam. His clash with Asa of Judah and with Benhadad of Damascus put him between two fires, and prevented him from doing much harm to either during the twenty-four years of his reign. Jehu, the son of Hanani, a prophet, doomed him and his house to a worse fate than he had dealt out to the house of Jeroboam. Baasha died a natural death, was buried in Tirzah, and was succeeded by his son, Elah. This scion of court life, in the second year of his reign, was carousing at an affair at the house of Arza, his court chamberlain, in Tirzah. The drinking bout was suddenly brought to an end by the assassination of Elah by Zimri, captain of half of the royal chariotry. True to the desperate tactics of such usurpations, this third dynasty ruler, to secure his tenure of the throne, slew every member of the house of Baasha.

Down in Philistia the army of Israel was again besieging Gibbethon. At the report of the death of Elah, the army made their captain, Omri, king over Israel; and he and his troops set out for the capital, Tirzah, and laid siege to it. When Zimri saw his case was hopeless, he took refuge in the royal palace and burned it over his own head, having had the thrilling joy of being king but seven days.

Omri's troubles were not over. A faction of Israel followed Tibni, to make him king. After four years of party struggles, of which we have no details, Omri won out, with Tibni's death,—whether natural or violent the text leaves us in ignorance.

This unbridled period of the northern kingdom saw at least four violent deaths on or near the throne: Nadab, son of Jeroboam, end of dynasty one; Elah, son of Baasha, end of dynasty two; Zimri, a suicide, end of dynasty three; Tibni, would-be successor of Zimri,—truly reigns of sword and fire.

180. Omri as King and Statesman (1 Kings 16:16-28). The writer of the book of Kings disposes of Omri with short shrift. His only credit in twelve years seems to have been the change of the capital from Tirzah to the newly purchased hill Samaria.

But the real ability and energy of Omri are confirmed by contemporary history. The Moabite Stone, discovered east of the Jordan in 1868, records his re-conquest of Moab, and its retention for forty years. The annual tribute collected by the northern kingdom is recorded in 2 Kings (3:4). With Syria he had many sanguinary clashes, some of them disastrous to his country (1 Kings 20:34). Up along the prosperous Phœnician coast, Omri, according to tradition, had made satisfactory treaties, commercial and domestic, involving his son Ahab.

Omri's reputation for power and far-reaching influence stretched as far as Assyria, for the land of Israel was designated later for a century and a half, by the Assyrian historians, as the " land of Omri," or the " land of the house of Omri." Even Jehu, of the next following dynasty, is called by Shalmaneser III, " Son of Omri."

These contemporary witnesses, added to the wisdom of his choice of a new capital for Israel, place Omri, the founder of the fourth and the only real dynasty of the northern kingdom, alongside Jeroboam II in the forefront of the kings of Israel. Religiously, he scored in the same column with Jeroboam, the son of Nebat, who made Israel to sin. His successor was his son Ahab.

181. Ahab's Early Career (1 Kings 16:29-34). Omri's alliance with Ethbaal (or Ithobaal), priest-king of Astarte, who through bloodshed had become king of Sidon, was secured by Ahab's marriage with his daughter Jezebel. And Jezebel was an ardent worshipper of Melkarth, the Phœnician Baal. Into Israel she brought her religion with all its ritual and intolerance, its prophets and its persecutions. The prophets of Jehovah were destroyed by her, except 100 who had been hidden and fed by fifty in a cave by Obadiah, Ahab's court chamberlain.

The exact order of events during Ahab's reign cannot be settled; but obviously Jezebel's religious aggressiveness came very early, before Ahab met his international problems.

Rivalry between Jezebel's type of Baalism and Jehovah worship became violent. Jezebel's imperious commanding personality drove all Jehovah worshippers as far as possible to cover, and let loose her own religious promoters and principles throughout Ahab's realm. Ahab himself built altars and temples to Jezebel's liking in Samaria and elsewhere,— almost turned over the machinery of government to her will.

182. Elijah and the Prophets of Baal (1 Kings 17:1– 19:21). When Ahab had consolidated the kingdom of his father, and had helped Jezebel to inaugurate her new brand of religion in Israel, a rough, uncouth man of the desert, clad with sheepskin, suddenly faced him for the first time, and foretold a three-year drought, and then as quickly disappeared. As the story goes, this desert man wandered to the brook Cherith and then to Phœnicia, for three years. At Jehovah's word, near the end of the famine, Elijah again appeared to Obadiah and then to Ahab. Ahab's salute was thrown back into his own face by Elijah, who commanded him to bring together to Mount Carmel 450 prophets of Baal and 400 of Asherah, who were guests at Jezebel's table. He (Elijah) alone would represent the God of Israel. This would be a test of the power of the respective divinities of the two parties. Ahab regarded that as a fair proposition and yielded.

The 450 prophets of Baal presented themselves for Jezebel's Baal, and Elijah himself alone represented Jehovah. At Elijah's request they first prepared their offering, then called all day in desperation and dismay for Baal to send lightning to consume it, but in vain. Then Elijah prepared his sacrifice on the repaired altar of Jehovah, called on his God, and fire came down and consumed the entire offering, the altar, and the water about it. The victory was sudden and decisive: Jehovah routed all the rain-causing Baals of Jezebel. With feverish enthusiasm the people took the 450 prophets of Baal down into the valley, to the brook Kishon on the north of Carmel, and slew them there (cf. Deut. 13:5; 18:20).

Was Ahab present at that test? Anyhow, as soon as the Baal-prophets were dispatched, Elijah said to Ahab, as if he were there, " Get thee up, eat and drink; for there is the sound of abundance of rain." Ahab mounted his chariot and rode back that eighteen miles to Jezreel, with the desert man Elijah running before him. Jezebel's alert ears soon caught word of that recoil against her faith. Fearless and unscrupulous, she swore vengeance on Elijah within twenty-four hours. Elijah, fearful lest she should wipe out Jehovah's cause, fled southward to Beer-sheba and then on into the desert. There God met him, fed and encouraged

Fig. 60. The Moabite Stone

Found at Dibon east of the Jordan in 1868, this stone, fitted together from broken bits, is now in the Louvre, Paris. It was written at the order of Mesha king of Moab about 850 B. C., in the Phœnician characters of that day. It was set up to celebrate Mesha's deliverance from the yoke of Israel (2 Kings 3:4-27). Mesha was a contemporary of Ahab.

him, and sent him back northwards to find Elisha, who should do great things for the future of Israel. Elisha was taken from the plow, and symbolically consecrated to be his follower in the fight for Jehovah against Baalism. Jehu and Hazael were to receive their commissions at a later time.

183. Elijah and Naboth's Vineyard (1 Kings 21). Among the other nations of that day the king was a despot, absolute in authority. Solomon practically reached that acme of power, and Ahab had imbibed that notion. But when he requested of Naboth his adjoining vineyard for a vegetable garden, the peasant owner refused, and protested that he could not thus give away his family inheritance. Ahab was so irritated that he had a fit of melancholia. When Jezebel discovered the reason for his sulks, she rebuked him and then immediately relieved him by her resourcefulness. Brought up with the idea of the inherent right of kings, she sent letters stamped with the king's seal to the chief men of Jezreel to arrest Naboth on the charge of blasphemy and treason, and to hire two false witnesses to testify against him and his sons. The despicable plan was carried out, and the victims were brutally stoned to death as a judicial execution of the state (2 Kings 9:26). Jezebel then triumphantly told Ahab to take possession of the vineyard he had requested.

As Ahab was looking over the ground to decide how he would use it to suit his purpose, lo! Elijah walked in, unheralded. Ahab, startled at the spectre-like appearance, said, " Hast thou found me, O mine enemy? " Elijah said, " I have found thee." Then he roasted him with hot words, accusing him of violating the laws of Jehovah, and warning him that his house would be wiped out as had those of Jeroboam and Baasha, and that his family would be unburied in city and country; that where the dogs had licked the blood of Naboth, there they should lick his blood.

Ahab was caught, convicted, and condemned to a speedy extinction. He was so overwhelmed by the sentence that he broke down, rent his garments in sorrow, and slipped out quietly. When Elijah saw his penitence, he so far modified the sentence as to postpone its fulfilment until after his day.

184. Ahab's Foreign Relations (1 Kings 20 and 22). Since Omri's treaty with the Phœnicians, and Ahab's marriage to Princess Jezebel, relations with those rich commercial cities on the coast had been most friendly. Exchange of goods had been mutually advantageous. And Ahab had paid an annual tribute to Benhadad of Damascus. Syria was not satisfied with so small a share of Ahab's prosperity, and sent an army with thirty-two kings to Samaria to hold up Ahab. He refused to comply with any such brigand-demand. On the advice of a prophet, Ahab chose 232 choice young princes from the provinces as leaders, and by strategy, while Benhadad and his thirty-two royal allies were drunk at noontime in their tents, made a sudden attack in which each prince slew his man; and the Syrians fled pell-mell, on horses and afoot, defeated with great slaughter.

The Syrians who escaped charged their defeat to the Israelitish gods, who, they said, were gods of the hills. Next year the Syrians came again with an army of the same size, but with thirty-two captains instead of kings, to fight Israel on the plains. This time they encamped at Aphek east of the Jordan. Israel's army before them was like " two little flocks of kids;" but the Syrians filled the country.

" A man of God " spoke to Ahab words of encouragement. After the armies had faced each other for seven days, they joined battle and Israel slew untold numbers of the Syrians. The rest escaped into Aphek,—even Benhadad their king. On his unconditional surrender, Ahab gave Benhadad surprising quarter and made a covenant with him, by which Benhadad agreed to restore the cities which his father had taken from Israel, and to allow Israel to establish bazaars in Damascus such as his father had had in Samaria. Then Ahab set his prisoner free.

One of the sons of the prophets disguised himself, and presented to Ahab a typical case of a man whose charge

Fig. 80. A Portrait of Shalmaneser III (860-825 B. C.)

This was the first Assyrian king to touch the Hebrew nation in Palestine. Ahab fighting with the allies against him at Karkar in 854 B. C., and Jehu's submission (Fig. 81) were premonitions of what should be expected in the future from the Romans of southwestern Asia. This portrait came from Nimrud-Calah near Nineveh.

escaped while he was not attending to his business. Ahab's decision fitted his own case exactly, and the prophet severely arraigned him for letting his prisoner go. But Ahab was a wiser statesman than the " son of a prophet."

If Ahab had slain Benhadad and taken over Damascus, he would have reduced the principal bulwark between the oncoming forces of Assyria and his own domain, Israel. Ahab seems to have known that Shalmaneser III was on his way westward, and that he would soon cross the Euphrates and strike at Syria. In 854 B. C. a league of western powers was summoned to meet the army of Shalmaneser III at Karkar in North Syria, near the river Orontes. Shalmaneser's own record of the battle names among his twelve (or thirteen) allied enemies, " Ahab of Israel," with 2,000 chariots and 10,000 infantry, the third largest ally in the coalition, and Hadad-idri (Benhadad) of Damascus, with 1,200 chariots, 1,200 cavalry and 20,000 infantry. Ahab's wide knowledge of the powers of southwestern Asia led him to decide not to destroy Benhadad, and not even to levy on him a humiliating payment of reparations for his gratuitous invasion of his territory.

While Shalmaneser III claims an overwhelming victory in the battle of Karkar, the outcome is not evident from subsequent events. It would seem from the Assyrian account to have been little more than a draw. For the moment at least, it had forced an alliance between Israel and Syria for defense against a dangerous common enemy.

185. Beginnings of Jehoshaphat of Judah (1 Kings 15:24; 2 Chron. 17). Good Asa of Judah was succeeded by his son Jehoshaphat, a worthy and more able ruler than his father. His loyalty to Jehovah and his broad interest in the welfare of the people of his realm gave him large influence at home and abroad. The Chronicler has given us a fulsome report of his removal of high places, and of his zeal in sending out princes, priests, and Levites to teach the law of Jehovah throughout the cities of the land. He is also given the honour of having built up and garrisoned the fortified cities of Judah and Ephraim, and of having completely organized the army,—increasing its quota to 1,160,000 men under a competent staff of officers.

But in all these records, not a word is mentioned about any of the old hostility between the kingdoms of Judah and Israel. Ahab's good sense and Jehoshaphat's good religion seem to have let that Martian giant starve to death. Every sign points to an understanding, to an *entente cordiale* between the two kings. This pact was securely tied up by the marriage of Jehoshaphat's son, Jehoram, the crown prince, to Athaliah, daughter of Ahab, king of Israel. The marital bond, tied between Israel and Phœnicia by Ahab's diplomatic adoption of Jezebel as his wife, had given the northern kingdom a powerful commercial alliance with the naval masters of the Mediterranean Sea. Now, the marital alliance of the two royal houses of Judah and Israel meant the beginning of an economic, social, and commercial pact, that forecast the formation of friendly relations in all that meant prosperity between these two powers. This new treaty also carried with it as a side-issue, definite diplomatic, if not full commercial, advantages as touching all the allies of the northern kingdom, including, of course, the favoured nation policy of the powerful Phœnician traders of Tyre and Sidon. When the religious problem is mentioned the entire question takes on new significance, that permeates down through the succeeding reigns of Judah and Israel.

The northern kingdom, from the beginning of Jeroboam's reign, adopted a policy of countering the religion of Jehovah, as centred in the temple at Jerusalem, by promulgating the ancestral worship of the majority of the people, in setting up the golden calves. Now Ahab had married Jezebel, who brought into Israel Phœnician Baal worship with all its dread accompaniments. This new cultus she soon incorporated into the state as the authorized religion. On the other hand, Jehoshaphat, king of Judah, represented the better side of Jehovah worship and promoted it by his own living and example. But when his son Jehoram married

Athaliah, daughter of Ahab, a new problem faced the kingdom of Judah. Would Jehoram abide by the faith and worship of his father, or would he fall for the Baalism of his wife? Such a marital alliance forecast an ominous future for the house of Judah.

NOTE ON FIG. 88, tailpiece below: The Hebrews themselves left us no portraits. To the Egyptians and Assyrians we are debtors for what we know of their physiognomy. For 270 years no Egyptian ruler had dared to invade Palestine. In 926 B. C. Shishak raided the land, and afterwards recorded at Karnak 156 cities and towns that he had captured, each on an elliptical form surmounted by a human head and shoulders. The artist gives these three as representatives of the faces of Hebrews. This relief is in the museum at Berlin.

CHAPTER XXI

ENTENTE CORDIALE BETWEEN JUDAH AND ISRAEL

186. Jehoshaphat's Relations with Ahab (1 Kings 22; 2 Chron. 18). Three years after the famous battle of Karkar, Jehoshaphat was invited to a royal banquet by King Ahab in Samaria, his capital. Benhadad of Syria, who, at Aphek, with a rope around his neck, had been so ready to restore all the Israelitish cities to Ahab, now, at the end of three years had not turned over Ramoth-gilead. When Ahab asked Jehoshaphat to join him in re-taking it by force of arms, Jehoshaphat replied, " I am as thou art, my people as thy people, my horses as thy horses." No better terms could be used to describe an offensive and defensive alliance between the two kingdoms of Israel and Judah.

Before starting on such a hazardous campaign, Jehoshaphat made an inquiry of the prophets about the possible outcome. Strange episode it was! At any rate, the kings and their troops crossed the Jordan and headed for

NOTE ON FIG. 8, headpiece above: These two Aramæans, especially the first on the left, has a strong face. The second was from Yaunamu in the north, and resembles a nomad. The Judean on the right is one of the Shishak faces. All represent captives taken by Egyptian raids up through Palestine. The Judean dates from the early days of the dual kingdom.

Ramoth-gilead. Ahab disguised himself to hide his identity. The Syrians had been instructed by Benhadad to slay Israel's king at all hazards. Seeing Jehoshaphat in royal regalia, the expert archers drove for him to shoot him; but fortunately his outcry notified them that he was not Ahab, and they passed him by. But a common archer took a random shot into the *mêlée* and his arrow struck between the joints of Ahab's armour. The king, mortally wounded, was held up in his chariot to encourage his troops. But at sundown he died, and the troops, defeated in their purpose, dispersed to their homes: and Jehoshaphat returned to Jerusalem.

Ahab was taken back and buried in Samaria, as a partial fulfilment of Elijah's prophecy against him and his house. He was politically a shrewd ruler, but religiously a Jezebelite.

187. Reign of Ahab's Sons, Ahaziah and Jehoram (1 Kings 22:40–2 Kings 1:18; 3:1-27). Ahab was succeeded by Ahaziah, his son. Israel's ally, Jehoshaphat of Judah, and the new king of Israel formed a partnership, and built a commercial fleet of ships of Tarshish at Eziongeber at the Gulf of Akabah to sail to Ophir for gold. But the storms beat down on the headwaters of that gulf and smashed them on the rocks.

Moab, who had been paying tribute to Israel for forty years, rebelled and struck for freedom. But Ahaziah was not equal to a campaign to reduce them. Soon in the second year of his reign he had a serious accident from which he died.

Jehoram succeeded his brother Ahaziah on Israel's throne. His first task was all ready for him. Moab's plentiful annual tribute (2 Kings 3:4) had ceased, and it left a big deficit in the annual budget of Israel. He invited Jehoshaphat, king of Judah, and the king of Edom, to join him in this war of subjection. Together they swept over the hills and valleys down around the south end of the Dead Sea, to drive a wedge between the Moabites and the Edomites in the far south. At a crisis in the journey Jehoshaphat asked for a prophet of Jehovah, and Elisha was found to be present. By the playing of a minstrel Elisha solved their riddle,—resolved their difficulty.

The king of Syria,—an Elisha story goes—tried repeatedly to entrap the king of Israel; but the prophet as often gave warning not to encamp at a certain place. Finally a Syrian raiding band at night surrounded Dothan and trapped Elisha. Next morning, the prophet prayed and a dense blindness seized the entire host; and then he led them to King Jehoram in Samaria. The king wished to slay them, but Elisha forbade it. Rather, Elisha gave them a great feast and sent them on their way to their master.

Benhadad, king of Syria, could not longer resist the temptation to invade prosperous Israel. With a vast army he besieged Samaria (2 Kings 6:24–7:20). The siege was so effective that famine began to consume the population. Elisha's presence rebuked Jehoram's profanity and foretold abundant deliverance. Four lepers, not allowed within any city walls, made the discovery that the Syrians had fled at a suspected noise of a great host of supposed Hittites and Egyptians. So precipitately did they make their escape that they left their camp intact, even their horses tied and their treasures all in place. Word having reached the city, the entire population rushed out and gorged themselves with the abundance of food and booty of untold value, and the city was tremendously relieved.

188. Jehoshaphat's Foreign Relations (1 Kings 22; 2 Chron. 19:1–20:37).

When Jehoshaphat returned from the battle of Ramoth-gilead (§186), Jehu, son of Hanani, the prophet, reproved him for his unholy alliance. On the

NOTE ON FIG. 2, opposite: The identification at Samaria of these as the foundations of Ahab's palace is practically certain. They are well built of trimmed stone, probably by Phœnician masons, for Solomon was obliged to find his artificers among that people, and Ahab would have had less trouble in that direction. This building was 160 ft. square, divided into rooms about open courts. Additions were also made of immense proportions.

Fig. 2. Foundations of Ahab's Palace

other hand, Jehoshaphat seems to have been popular with the border peoples, who brought him presents and tribute in great abundance (2 Chron. 17:11). However, the Chronicler reports that a coalition of southeastern peoples, Moab, Ammon and Edom, swept around the lower end of the Dead Sea, and on up into Judah,—headed for Jerusalem. Jehoshaphat was alarmingly frightened. He called an assembly of Judah, and sought help of Jehovah by a long and retrospective prayer. After a favourable reply through Jahaziel the prophet, Judah, Cromwell-like, advanced into battle at the music of song. When Jehoshaphat reached the camp of the enemy, he found that they had fallen out and had cut each other to pieces,—leaving the whole landscape strewn with the bodies of the slain,—a victory without a stroke. For three days Jehoshaphat and his army gathered an immense booty from the dead bodies, and carried it back to Jerusalem, praising Jehovah for their multiple blessings.

While Jehoshaphat was risking his life in battles, he appointed Jehoram, his son, regent in the eighteenth year of his reign, and gave his other six sons gifts, gold, silver, and fortified cities. But in the twenty-fifth year of his reign Jehoshaphat died, and was buried in the city of David. Thus passed on one of the best kings of the kingdom of Judah,—able, righteous, peaceful, far-sighted and popular in his day.

189. Oral Prophets and Prophecy since Solomon. The prophets were either silent or muzzled, or both, during Solomon's reign; for the Chronicler refers for further information about Solomon to the "words of Nathan the prophet, the prophecy of Ahijah the Shilonite, and the visions of Iddo the seer, concerning Jeroboam the son of Nebat" (2 Chron. 9:29). They must have been within range of the capital, even though they are not mentioned by the historians.

Samuel's schools of the "sons of the prophets" (1 Sam. 19:20) had certainly been well attended and productive of large good. The first prophet who dared to speak near the end of Solomon's reign was *Ahijah* the Shilonite, whose attitude toward Solomon was transparently clear when he supported by word and deed the revolt of Jeroboam against the king. His subsequent relations to Jeroboam were close and vital (1 Kings 12:15; 14:2-18; 15:29). *Iddo* was another silent prophet who prepared and left a history (now lost) both of Rehoboam of Judah and of Jeroboam of Israel. *Shemaiah* vetoed Rehoboam's move to force Israel back into submission (1 Kings 12:22-24). *Azariah* warned Asa to be humble and loyal to Jehovah (2 Chron. 15:1-8), while *Hanani* the seer rebuked him for appealing to Benhadad of Damascus rather than to Jehovah (2 Chron. 16:7-10) for help against Baasha. *Jehu, son of Hanani*, condemned Baasha for having slain Nadab (1 Kings 16:1-5, 7, 12) to get his crown; and reprimanded Jehoshaphat for having gone with Ahab to the battle of Ramoth-gilead (2 Chron. 19:2, 3; 20:34). *Micaiah* was the one faithful prophet out of 400 who foretold to Ahab and Jehoshaphat the doubtful outcome of the battle at Ramoth-gilead (1 Kings 22:8-28). *Eliezer* rebuked Jehoshaphat for associating with so wicked a king. Several prophets and men of God are mentioned in line of duty whose names are not given (1 Kings 13:1, 11; 20:13, 22; 2 Chron. 25:7, 15).

But the most striking prophetic characters of this period were *Elijah* and *Elisha*, about whom many marvellous stories were handed down. They came " to the kingdom for such a time as this." When the kingdom of Israel was sinking into the slough of Phœnician Baalism, an ordinary prophet would have been ignored or slain. When the royal house fostered and promoted the baldest kind of immoralities and infamies, nothing short of prophetic thunderbolts would be noticed. Like a meteor from the sky, Elijah appeared to Ahab at some crisis, and then as suddenly vanished. His blow was aimed at the head of the monster from Phœnicia. He was the champion of Jehovah against idolatry, injustice, and disloyalty. He was an individualist, a desert-man, a hermit, an uncompromising prophet of Jehovah, the God of Israel, and his words were like swift arrows discharged from the bow of a skilful archer.

After six years of training under Elijah, Elisha took up the mantle of his master. He lived with men, was approachable, companionable, a man among men,—quite different from his master. He associated with kings, princes and prophets; and was especially at home in the schools of the prophets at Bethel, Gilgal, and Jericho. His influence was far-reaching and potent in the interest of right and humanity, and in loyalty to Jehovah.

190. King Jehoram of Judah (2 Kings 8:16-24; 2 Chron. 21:1-20). Jehoram had been made regent in the eighteenth year of his father's twenty-five years' reign. As soon as it seemed safe, after the death of his father, Jehoshaphat, he massacred all his six brothers and any other possible rival for the throne (2 Chron. 21:1-4). His wife, Athaliah, being a daughter of Ahab, he fell for the religion of Jezebel and forgot his good father Jehoshaphat and Jehovah, the God of Israel.

Edom on the southeast rebelled against his yoke. In his campaign against them, he and his forces were surrounded, but cut their way out by night, and escaped without reducing the rebels to submission. Libnah also refused to pay him tribute.

Elijah is reported to have sent a letter to the king, denouncing him for not following in the way of either Jehoshaphat or of Asa, but for trailing after the kings of Israel, and for slaying his brethren who were better than he. Yea, more, a terrific incurable disease would smite him.

A raid of Philistines and Arabians [i. e., Edomites] came to the backbone of the country and carried off great substance, including even all King Jehoram's sons except the youngest. After two years of painful suffering and horrible disease he died unmourned. The people burned no incense at his death, and he was not buried in the royal tombs,—an ignominious passing after only eight years reign.

191. Ahaziah King of Judah (2 Kings 8:24-29; 9:16-28; 2 Chron. 22:1-9). Ahaziah was the grandson of Ahab, and the son of Athaliah and Jehoram of doubtful fame. Young as he was (twenty-two years), he was chosen king of Judah by the inhabitants of Jerusalem, for raiders had carried off all his older brothers. He, too, followed the counsel of his wicked mother, to walk in all the ways of the house of Ahab. As a family affair, he went with Jehoram of Israel, his uncle, to fight Hazael of Syria at Ramoth-gilead. Jehoram was wounded in battle and came back to Jezreel to be treated for his wounds. Ahaziah returned to Jerusalem, but later made a trip down to Jezreel to see how his uncle fared.

192. Elisha Coaching the Prophets. Neither Ahaziah of Judah nor Jehoram of Israel was aware of the deep-seated hatred of Phœnician Baalism that was burning in the bosoms of all the prophets of Jehovah. Elisha, who had donned the mantle and spirit of Elijah, was the chief moving spirit in all that activity. He worked through the schools of the sons of the prophets at Gilgal, Bethel, and Jericho, which Elijah and he together had fostered (2 Kings 2:2-6). On his return from Elijah's translation, he dropped in to confer with the fifty sons of the prophets at Jericho; then he went on up to another school at Bethel, and on the way was mocked by smart young rowdies of the village, only to be avenged by two savage she-bears. Thence he passed on to Mount Carmel, a headquarters of the worship of Jehovah, and again returned to Samaria to be in touch with Jehoram, king of Israel. His activities for the help of the sons of the prophets and others were frequent and numerous. He multiplied the failing oil of the widow of a son of a prophet; raised the Shunammite's son from the dead; cured the poisonous pottage at the Gilgal school of the prophets; multiplied food to meet the needs of a multitude (2 Kings 4); and restored the lost axe-head of a son of a prophet at Jericho who was enlarging one of their dwellings (2 Kings 6:1-7). These are a few of the many mysterious stories woven about Elisha's career.

Elisha's work touching political and national affairs laid secure foundations for the perpetuation of the worship of the true God. In Jehoram of Israel's campaign against Moab, Elisha had forecast to Jehoshaphat the solution for the scarcity of water. When Naaman, the Syrian general, applied for a cure of his leprosy, Elisha met his request (2 Kings 5). The king of Israel was saved " not once nor twice " from the Syrian army by the counsel of Elisha (2 Kings 6:8-10). His fame was well-known abroad, especially in Syria (2 Kings 6:12). Thinking they could catch a man who foretold things, the Syrians surrounded him in Dothan; he blinded, then feasted his captives and sent them home (2 Kings 6:13-23). When the Syrians nearly starved out Samaria, Elisha forecast the plenty that would be theirs; then the enemy took fright at a noise and fled, leaving a full camp of plunder (2 Kings 6:24—7:20). Elisha's influence restored the Shunammite's property (2 Kings 8:1-6). Elisha's errand at Damascus resulted in the murder of Benhadad by Hazael, who became his successor on the throne (2 Kings 8:7-15). Jehoram of Israel and Ahaziah of Judah met the Syrians at Ramoth-gilead. Elisha returned from the battle and, fulfilling one of the injunctions given Elijah in the wilderness (1 Kings 19:17), sent one of the sons of the prophets to anoint Jehu king over Israel (2 Kings 9:1-10). This was the climax of Elisha's fight against Phœnician Baalism, as seen in its results.

Elisha's final act during his sickness was his prophecy to Joash, king of Israel, regarding his future clashes with Syria, in which Syria would finally win (2 Kings 13:14-19). Elisha's activity began before the reign of Jehu and continued forty-five years after that revolution. His personality must have been peculiarly attractive, as he seems to have been accepted in the courts of both Israel and of Syria.

His knowledge of men and his skill in speaking the right

word at the right time made him an influence for righteousness wherever he went. His effective training of men for prophetic duties in a dissolute and waning kingdom was his best contribution to the final overthrow of Baalism in Israel and Judah. These men, distributed at several strategic points, were ready for any revolution which would oust from office the shameless house of Ahab, and its hangers-on. Fully acquainted with Jehu and his desperateness, he seems to have understood that his coronation would mean the elimination of the house of Ahab from the throne of Israel, —a long-sought-for, and devoutly-wished-for, object of his life-work.

NOTE ON FIG. 95, tailpiece below: Tyre was the defiant little island city about one-third of a mile off the shore of Phœnicia. Its origin is covered by the mists of the ages. Its superb location, its choice little harbours, and its smug self-confidence, in the face of the great powers, gave it a place all its own. Not until Alexander bridged the chasm between it and the shore was it wholly subdued, humiliated and started on the downward road to obliteration.

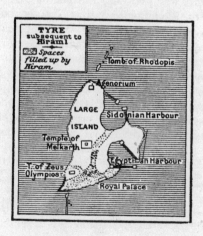

CHAPTER XXII

PHŒNICIAN BAALISM CHECKED

193. Jehu, Executioner for Jehovah and More
(2 Kings 8:25–10:17; 2 Chron. 22:7-9). When Jehoram
of Israel and Ahaziah of Judah (§191) returned from the
battle of Ramoth-gilead, they left the army holding the city
against the Syrians.

In the meantime, Elisha, probably at Jericho and fully
aware of what was going on, sent one of the "sons of the
prophets" to Ramoth-gilead to strike the hour for the
revolution. When he arrived he was recognized as one of
his order. Apparently the staff officers were holding a council. He summoned Jehu into a house, and poured a vial of
oil on his head, and said, "Thus saith Jehovah, the God of
Israel, I have anointed thee king over the people of Jehovah, even over Israel" (strong language!). And the sweeping commission he gave Jehu was enough to stir the bad
blood in any army officer of that day. This was the order:

NOTE ON FIG. 70, headpiece above: This gruesome picture of a pile
of heads at the city gates was found on the bronze plates of the gates
of Balawat, put there by Shalmaneser III. The same horrid spectacle
was seen at Jezreel, ordered by Jehu after his slaughter of seventy of
Ahab's kinsfolk at Samaria. "Lay ye them in two heaps at the entrance of the gate until the morning" (2 Kings 10:8), said Jehu,
that exterminator of Ahab's house.

" Thou shalt smite the house of Ahab thy master, that I may avenge the blood of my servants the prophets, and the blood of all the servants of Jehovah at the hand of Jezebel. For the whole house of Ahab shall perish. . . . I will make the house of Ahab like the house of Jeroboam the son of Nebat, and like the house of Baasha the son of Ahijah. And the dogs shall eat Jezebel in the portion of Jezreel, and there shall be none to bury her. And he opened the door and fled " (9:1-10).

The " mad fellow " was gone. When Jehu's fellow-officers learned the truth, they made a temporary dais, blew the trumpet and shouted, " Jehu is king! "

Like the able officer Jehu was, he commanded that no one should leave the city to tell it in Jezreel before his arrival. With a chariot fully equipped, protected by a few mounted guards, he was off and soon faded away in the distance, to cover the thirty miles to Jezreel.

The alert watchman on the tower of Jezreel was on the lookout to catch any report from the battlefield. Far down near the Jordan River he spied a company heading up the valley toward Jezreel. He reported to his master, King Jehoram, who was entertaining his nephew Ahaziah of Judah. The king sent two successive horsemen to inquire as to the purpose of the delegation. Neither one came back. The watchman suspected from the furious speed with which they approached Jezreel that it was Jehu, the well-known captain of the chariots.

Jehoram, fearful of the news from the front, ordered his chariot; and he and his nephew went out, each in his own chariot. In the field of Naboth they met Jehu. The answer to Jehoram's question struck terror into his heart and he shouted, " Treachery, O Ahaziah," and they turned to flee. But Jehu shot an arrow through Jehoram's heart, and ordered his body cast into the field of Naboth, where Elijah had condemned Ahab for the death of Naboth and his sons. Ahaziah fled, but was pursued and smitten. He died at Megiddo, and his body was taken to Jerusalem.

Jehu then entered Jezreel and went to the royal palace. Jezebel had been told of the *coup,* and scented her fate. Decorated and beautified as a queen-mother should be, fearlessly she put her head out of an upper story window and called out to Jehu, whom she knew all too well, and said, " Thou Zimri, thy master's murderer! " He made no reply. But at his command three eunuchs pitched her headlong to the street, and Jehu drove his chariot over her lifeless form. Then he went in to dine. When through his meal he sent to have her given the burial due a king's daughter, but the prophecy of the " son of a prophet " to him had been fulfilled by the dogs of Jezreel (2 Kings 9:10).

Instead of going to the capital, Samaria, at once, Jehu sent letters to the leading men of the city, ironically requesting them to put on the throne the best of Ahab's seventy sons, and then to defend him with all their military strength. Knowing Jehu of old and what he had done at Jezreel, they cowered, and promised to stand by him and do what he should command. That was simple enough; if they were for him, they would send to him the heads of the seventy descendants of Ahab. Next day the heads were duly delivered in baskets; and they piled them at the gate of the city, as was often done in Assyria, until morning, as a warning to the populace that he was master and the fulfiller of Jehovah's word to Elijah (2 Kings 10:10). To clean up Jezreel, he wiped out every kinsman, every great man, every familiar friend, every priest of the house of Ahab,—thus stepping entirely outside the authorization of his commission.

He must needs make a personal visit to Samaria ere his commission could be fulfilled. On his way he met forty-two princes of Judah coming down to visit their royal kinsfolk in Israel. By Jehu's command they were dispatched at a shearing-house on the highway to Samaria.

Jehu also met Jehonadab, son of Rechab, the unique originator of that abstemious clan of nomads faithful to Jehovah (*cf.* Jer. 35:6-19). Related to the Kenites (of

Moses' kin) and with Judean and Palestinian connections (1 Chron. 2), he sympathized with Jehu's reforms. Being assured of his co-operation, Jehu said, " Come with me, and see my zeal for Jehovah;" at which he was made to ride with Jehu in his royal chariot. Upon arrival at Samaria Jehu slaughtered, as at Jezreel, every one connected with, or friendly to, the house of Ahab, thus obliterating all possibility of rivals for the throne which he had so murderously and brutally seized.

194. Jehu's Blow at Baalism (2 Kings 10:18-28). Jehu had already cut down the priests of Ahab at Jezreel and Samaria. Baalism came next. Feigning enthusiasm in, and devotion to, Baal, he proclaimed a solemn assembly in the Samaria temple which Ahab had built for Jezebel. All prophets, priests, and worshippers should be there, subject to a death penalty for absence. Care was taken that no Jehovah worshipper was present. Jehu, too, and poor old abstemious Jehonadab were on hand. All were dressed in their finest vestments. When the sacrifices and burnt-offerings were at their concluding stage, by pre-arrangement eighty swordsmen were given the signal, and they rushed in, and in cold blood cut down the entire assembly. They broke down the pillars of Baal, and wrecked the entire temple; " thus Jehu destroyed Baal out of Israel " (vs. 28).

195. Athaliah on the Throne of Judah (2 Kings 11:1-3; 2 Chron. 22:10-12). Though Jehu could have rightfully claimed the throne of Judah, he does not seem to have attempted it. When Athaliah, however, heard that Jehu had smitten all the house of her father Ahab, including her own son Ahaziah, she was furious, but equal to the emergency. Good oriental that she was, she, as queen-mother, seized the throne of Judah and put to the sword all the royal heirs she could find in Jerusalem. She ruled in her majesty six years, a kind of vengeful protest to Jehu's counter-rule in Israel. Under her sway Tyrian Baal worship was promoted and Judah was submissive. In her murderous slaughter of the seed royal, she had overlooked a little one—

year-old grandson. His aunt, Jehosheba, wife of Jehoiada, a high-priest of Jehovah, had rescued him and his nurse, and had hidden them during all the years since the *coup d'etat* of Athaliah.

196. Jehu's Overworked Commission (2 Kings 10:29-32). Jehu was commissioned by the prophet who anointed him, to blot out the house of Ahab. This he did, as he supposed, quite completely, but he did not stop there. He instituted and carried out a horrible massacre which included Ahab's nobles, friends, and even priests. Then, to put a climax to the bloody orgy, he treacherously slew an untold number of Baal worshippers in their own temple. "Zeal for Jehovah!" Indeed! Jezebel put him where he belonged,—with Zimri who, unprovoked, had treacherously cut down Elah (1 Kings 16:8-10).

While Jehu did good service in exterminating the house of Ahab, he left his commission far in the rear, and savagely committed unpardonable crimes against Israel and the cause of righteousness. Even the later prophets could not keep silence over such infamy. Hosea had properly weighed his deeds when he said, "I will avenge the blood of Jezreel upon the house of Jehu" (1:4). If it was "zeal for Jehovah," why did he not destroy the golden calves at Bethel and Dan? This might have been too tame a procedure for his bloody spirit. Or did he think of those calves as symbols of Jehovah?

Such blood-letting horrors could bring about no true reformation. On the other hand, the reaction and rebound of such excesses would be disastrous to the future prosperity of the nation, especially in a spiritual and moral sense.

197. Reaction in Judah (2 Kings 11:4-12; 2 Chron. 23:1-21). As long as Athaliah sat on the throne of Judah, the house of Ahab was not obliterated. The little royal heir had now reached a recognized coronation age,— seven years. Jehoiada, the high-priest, was in full control of the temple worship of Jehovah; his wife was in charge of

Fig. 79. The Black Obelisk of Shalmaneser III

was the first great discovery made by Layard in the mound Nimrud-
Calah. It is black basaltic rock, set up by Shalmaneser III in his
palace at Nimrud before 825 B. C. It carries five registers reaching
around the shaft, picturing five caravans or trains of five different
nationalities bringing their tribute to their Assyrian lord, with inscriptions interspersed describing this tribute.

the hidden seven-year-old lad. Before making any revolutionary move, Jehoiada ascertained how secure he was with the soldiery. To win their favour and confidence he quietly took them into the temple and showed them the royal prince; and they, at the same time, entered into a covenant of loyalty.

Jehoiada worked out all the details of the proposed coronation and submitted them to the council of officers. When the plan was approved, the time was set for a Sabbath day at the hour of the changing of the guards, when all the companies were available on the temple-grounds. The lone remaining scion of the Davidic line was brought out, stood on a platform surrounded by guards. He was anointed, the crown put upon his head and " the testimony " in his hands; and all the crowd clapped their hands, and shouted, " Long live the king! "

Queen Athaliah, in the royal palace not far away, heard the joyful shouts of the crowd, and the blare of trumpets, and started for the house of Jehovah. The soldiers barred her entrance, but she went near enough to see the young king, at whose sight she rent her clothes and shouted, " Treason! Treason! " But she was forced back between the lines until she reached the royal palace, where she was slain.

The covenant was then renewed in triplicate, between Jehovah and the king, between the king and the people, and between Jehovah and the people. With all this tremendous impetus turned toward Jehovah's cause, the people of the

NOTE ON FIG. 81, opposite: These four sections form one continuous procession of Hebrews. The first represents the Hebrew king Jehu humbly doing obeisance to the great Shalmaneser III with his two attendants. Behind Jehu are also two armed Assyrian officers to see that the Hebrew king is sufficiently humble. Over the submissive Jehu are the symbols of Ashur and Ishtar, gods of Assyria. On the next panel comes a bewhiskered Hebrew officer guarded from behind by an armed Assyrian officer; then follow thirteen Hebrews carrying the tribute named as silver, gold, bowls of gold, chalices of gold, cups of gold, pitchers of gold, lead, a royal sceptre, and staves. Note their cast of countenance, their whiskers, their stooped shoulders, their unique clothing—of course the creation of the Assyrian artist.

Fig. 81. The Panels of Hebrews Bringing Tribute (842 B. C.)

land rushed to the house of Baal, wrecked it, smashed his altars and images, and slew Mattan the priest by the altar. (There is some ground for believing that he was Athaliah's cousin.)

Then the high officers and guards formally transferred the new king from the temple to the royal palace, and set him on the throne of Judah. Thus culminated the revolution which was a kind of twin movement to Jehu's uprising six years earlier in Israel, though Judah was in reality a vassal of Israel under Jehu.

198. Jehu's Political Decline (2 Kings 10:32-36). At the very moment when Jehu was carrying on his wholesale murders (in 842 B. C.), Shalmaneser III appeared in the northeast. Jehu's savage revolution was a kind of boomerang. His slaughter of Jezebel and all her house must have bitterly estranged the Phœnicians, who had been close friends of Israel. All friendship from that quarter was killed. Jehu was not on any too friendly terms with Hazael of Damascus, nor could he expect anything but hatred from Athaliah of Judah. He had ruthlessly slain the old statesmen and officers of the Omri dynasty. In fact, he had no one whom he could summon to his aid against the oncoming Assyrian. His only recourse, therefore, was to make the best terms he could.

The Old Testament does not mention this culminating crisis, but the Black Obelisk of Shalmaneser fills the gap, not only by a narrative, but by a series of four registers, which picture " Jehu, son of Omri " prostrate on his face before the great Assyrian monarch; and behind their humble king Assyrian officers, an elder, and thirteen servants loaded with valuable presents for their new lord from the East. Such tribute was probably paid to Assyria annually during Jehu's reign.

Hazael of Damascus met Assyria, but was defeated, and retreated within his own capital. Near the close of Jehu's peaceful reign (after his murderous beginning) of twenty-eight years, Hazael of Syria overran all the east-Jordanic country of Israel, and savagely reduced it to serfdom,—Israelites and Moabites.

Jehu, strange to say, finally died a natural death, and was buried in Samaria, which he had made run red with blood; and Jehoahaz, his son, became king.

199. Jehoiada and King Jehoash of Judah (2 Kings 11:21–12:21; 2 Chron. 24). The high-priest, Jehoiada, uncle of the seven-year-old king of Judah, was in fact the ruler. The priests had put Jehoash on the throne, and the priesthood seems to have dominated the government. A plan for the repairing of the temple miscarried because for sixteen years the priests had appropriated the contributed money for their own purposes. That order was now entirely reversed. A new collection box was installed at the entrance of the temple; and the repairs went on apace with amazing success. The priests, too, were amply supplied.

Jehoiada kept his hand on the rudder during all the first half of Jehoash's reign and the kingdom prospered. But when the grand old high-priest died (at 130 years of age), the suppressed party of princes appealed to the king and won their plea. They and the king overturned the priestly government, forsook Jehovah, the God of their fathers, and served the Asherim and the idols. Prophets sent to them made no impression. Then Zechariah, son of the late high-priest, publicly called them to time; and they stoned him to death in the very court of the house of Jehovah. As he died under the rain of stones he said, " Jehovah look upon it, and require it " (2 Chron. 24:22).

The ambitious Hazael of Syria, who had taken over the control of the east-Jordanic country, tried his fortunes west of the river. He swept down to the Mediterranean coast, took Gath and then made straight for Jerusalem. Jehoash, who had not yet tried his mettle in any battle, was so frightened that he bought off the Syrian by emptying the gold of the temple and palace treasuries into his coffers; and Hazael withdrew, of course.

Jehoash's religious relapse, in the later years of his reign, angered and embittered the close friends of his earlier years, especially for his ingratitude toward the son of the high-priest, and for permitting him to be stoned in the very temple court itself. His own servants finally killed him on his own bed, after he had been king forty years. He was not even buried in the tombs of the kings; and Amaziah, his son, succeeded him on the throne.

200. Jehu's Posterity on the Throne of Israel (2 Kings 13:1–14:1, 8-16; 2 Chron. 25:17-24). Jehoahaz, son of Jehu, came to the throne in the twenty-third year of Jehoash of Judah. His record fully tallied with that of Jeroboam, son of Nebat. His realm seems to have been entirely at the mercy of Hazael of Syria, who allowed him a mere fragment of an army,—50 cavalry, 10 chariots, and 10,000 infantry. His seventeen years of reign, practically under the beck and nod of Syria, left no increment of value.

His son Jehoash inherited a realm groaning under the burdens of Hazael. But this Syrian ruler soon died, and his son Benhadad took up the reins of government. From the first he was under the necessity of meeting enemies from the north. Adad-nirari III (805–782 B. C.) of Assyria, now well established on his throne, plunged his army into this western country about 797 B. C. Among the lands and cities which he specifies in his inscriptions as having been subdued by him, though not mentioned in the Old Testament, were Tyre, Sidon, "land of Omri" (Israel), Edom, Philistia (first contemporaneous mention as a political entity), to the sea of the setting sun (Mediterranean). No mention is made of Judah. Was it pro-Assyrian, or under Israel? Having isolated Damascus, he came back and besieged it, and forced the payment of a tremendous indemnity,—in fact, so large that Damascus henceforth gave Israel

NOTE ON MAP 10, on opposite page. Western Asia about 800 B. C.: Another check-up on the great powers shows Egypt about holding her own; Assyria master of Mesopotamia and west to the Mediterranean Sea; the Aramæans and Hittites crowded back into Asia Minor; and the Phœnicians in control of the commercial marine of the Great Sea.

little trouble. After Adad-nirari had withdrawn to the East, out of the way, Jehoash, now quite sure of his ground, defeated Syria in three successive battles (2 Kings 13:18, 19) and restored to his realm cities that Hazael had seized (2 Kings 13:25). So powerful did he feel that he scornfully met the proud challenge of King Amaziah of Judah, scored against him, took him captive, broke down about 600 feet of the north wall of Jerusalem, plundered the temple and palace treasuries, and took a pledge of him, binding it with hostages. Judah seems by this record to have been held in bondage to Israel, while both were probably tributaries to Assyria. But Israel was at least free from Syria and independent of Judah. On Jehoash's death the kingdom fell to his son Jeroboam II.

201. Amaziah of Judah (2 Kings 14:1-22; 2 Chron. 25). Amaziah, son of Jehoash of Judah, began his rule by killing the murderers of his father, though he saved their children. His conquest of the Edomites puffed up his pride, and led him to the hazard of a clash with Jehoash of Israel, already described (§200). This disaster did not improve the friendly relations between the two kingdoms, nor settle their difficulties. Amaziah's crass worship of the gods of Edom stirred up such a popular revulsion of feeling against him that he fled from Jerusalem to Lachish (Tell el-Hesy), thirty-five miles southwest of Jerusalem, where he, too, was murdered. His body was brought back to the capital and buried with his fathers.

202. Jeroboam II of Israel (2 Kings 13:13; 14:16, 23-29; 15:1). Jeroboam II, the fourth king of the line of Jehu, came to the throne at an auspicious moment. Though politically the most successful of all the nineteen kings of Israel, he is little more than mentioned by the historians. Adad-nirari III of Assyria was so busily occupied in Armenia and other parts of the East, that his western provinces gradually slipped away from him; and his successors were not equal to a campaign of conquest west of the Euphrates River. Thus Jeroboam had a fair field for conquest before him; and he seized his opportunity and extended Israel's border from the "approach to Hamath" in the far north, to the sea of the Arabah (Dead Sea) on the east side of the Jordan,—as forecast by Jonah the prophet, son of Amittai of Gath-hepher (2 Kings 14:25). He was the real deliverer and saviour of Israel in their distress, and practically restored to them all the former territory of the Davidic domain, except that of Judah. He brought great military and commercial prosperity to his country, and again put her on the map during the forty-one years of his reign.

With Uzziah, his contemporary, on the throne of Judah, the two kingdoms, apparently in working harmony, reached the zenith of their power and prosperity for the first time since the brilliant reign of Solomon,—due chiefly to the inactivity of Assyria. The inflow of revenues and the ease of living brought with them luxuries and laxness of conduct. Lack of moral restraint, and disregard for the rights of others, filled the land with violations of all the laws of man and God. Jeroboam's religious career never left the groove made by the first Jeroboam, the son of Nebat.

At the end of forty-one years of political and economic success, Jeroboam died, succeeded by his son Zechariah, the fifth member of the house of Jehu. He " did as his fathers had done," and in six short months was assassinated by a conspirator, Shallum, who sat on his bloody throne. Thus ends the dynasty of Jehu (2 Kings 10:30), some of whose kings were brilliant, far-sighted, but unscrupulous, imperious, and defiant of all principles of right.

203. Uzziah (Azariah) of Judah (2 Kings 14:21, 22; 15:1-7; 2 Chron. 26). While Jeroboam II was in the midst of his conquests and glory in Israel, the people of Judah crowned the sixteen-year-old son of Amaziah. The Chronicler records the most that we learn of his long reign. From the first he displayed notable ability as a practical ruler and monarch. He reorganized the government, built up the army, strengthened the fortifications, defenses, artillery, and the walls of Jerusalem. He conquered the Philistines, the Ammonites toward Egypt, and the Arabians (Edomites) in Gur-baal; he built Elath on the gulf of Akabah, and his fame went abroad among all peoples. On the peace side, he promoted agriculture and encouraged animal husbandry; built store-cities in the wilderness, and increased the water-supply of the country by digging many cisterns.

Such development of home resources and extension of political power immensely increased his revenues and rapidly made Judah wealthy and prosperous, at the same time that Israel was enjoying the incomes and resources of the reign of Jeroboam II.

As long as Uzziah conducted his service of God in accordance with the words of Zechariah the prophet, he prospered. But when he was strong he became haughty and high-handed against Jehovah. In this spirit he went into the temple to burn incense on the altar of incense,—a thing lawful only for the priests. Fourscore priests protested against such desecration. Simultaneously with his rising anger, leprosy broke out on his forehead; and he was driven from the temple, and forced henceforth to live in an infirmary apart from the people. This painful episode occurred, as near as we can estimate, about the thirty-sixth year of his reign.

Josephus states that when Uzziah reached the climax of his desecration of the priests' office, an earthquake split the roof of the temple; and through the crack thus made the rays of the sun poured down and struck the desecrater, making him leprous.

To meet this emergency, Jotham, his son, was made regent, in reality king, to administer the affairs of government.

Right here chronologers of earlier days were switched from the proper track. If Uzziah had ruled thirty-six or seven years when he was forced by his leprosy to leave his office, he should be credited with only that many years of rule. But the historian adds to that number the remaining years of his life passed in a leper's house, thus giving him fifty-two years, even though Jotham's reign overlapped those leprous years. The overlappings must always be taken account of in summarizing the reigns of the kings of Israel and Judah (see Chronology, pages 438 ff.).

NOTE ON FIG. 83, tailpiece below: This peculiar shaped seal found at Megiddo has over the lion " Shema " ('hear'), and beneath him " servant of Jeroboam." Whether this was one of the two kings of Israel named Jeroboam we do not know. He was at least a prominent character to possess such a symbol of office.

CHAPTER XXIII

FATAL RESULTS OF PROSPERITY

204. The Real History of these Times. The economic prosperity of the two kingdoms under Jeroboam II in Israel and Uzziah in Judah was a notable fact, even in the brief records we possess. But the social, moral and religious aspects of their reigns receive scant notice by the historians. The significance of the great wealth of a few, and the extreme poverty of the many, find slight explanation in those records.

But we have a source of reliable and unequivocal information on this very period, written down by those who were contemporaries and eye-witnesses. They are the earliest writing prophets. Amos and Hosea, whose works

NOTE ON FIG. 93, headpiece above: Tiglath-pileser III in his chariot. The Hebrew kingdoms had about eighty years of comparative peace (825–745 B. C.) before this great monarch swept into the Westland. His regal policy of deportation of rebellious enemies, and importation of foreign peoples, and of autonomous provincial government, revolutionized the former colonial methods of Assyria. This one monarch mentions in his inscriptions Menahem, Pekah, and Hoshea, kings of Israel, Ahaz, king of Judah, and Rezin, king of Damascus.

pulsate with the life of the times, and breathe the atmosphere of the age.

205. Amos, Prophet to Israel (Book of Amos). Amos was a layman of Judah, a shepherd and fruit-grower of Tekoa, and he spoke two years before an earthquake, possibly the one mentioned in Zechariah (14:5), about 750 B. C. He had doubtless travelled somewhat, and understood the national and international questions of the day as they touched the Hebrews. His outdoor life and observations of men and events, gave him a keen sense of God's presence and of his own duty.

The people of northern Israel had assembled at Bethel to observe one of the annual feasts in the presence of the golden calf. Without warning, Amos, having gone about thirty miles northwards from his Judean home, suddenly appeared among the happy worshippers and spoke to them a message of caution and counsel. Not being a professional prophet, his words pulsated with earnestness and strength, and possessed the flavour of a native countryman, thus attracting immediate attention.

In a brief analysis of the message of his book, we find three divisions. An introduction (chaps. 1 and 2) arraigns Gaza, Tyre, Edom, Ammon, Moab, and Judah for having violated the ordinary universally recognized laws of humanity. They were guilty of slave-dealing, of barbarities in warfare, of disregarding their oath. All Israel doubtless shouted " Amen." But before the sound died away, Amos said, " And you, too, Israel, are guilty of the same sins and will suffer the same punishments."

Three sermons or addresses follow (chaps. 3–6), each beginning with " Hear ye this word." Amos cites his authority for speaking; then formally charges the government at Samaria with gross perversions of justice, grinding down of the poor, self-indulgence and drunkenness, hollow mockery in the name of religion; and forecast punishment for the hypocrites and indifferent, tempered with a constant appeal to them to turn to Jehovah as the real God of Israel.

Five enigmatical visions forecast certain punishment (chaps. 7–9), at the hands of a national invader, unnamed, but certainly the Assyrian (5:27; 6:7, 14). He also predicted a restoration and joyful future after the punishment.

A detailed study of this first written prophetic book reveals a drab background of the social and religious conditions in the northern kingdom, where wealth, luxury, oppression, and injustice were commonplaces, where religion was mere form, and righteousness a sham. Amos called a halt by declaring Jehovah to be a universal God of right and justice who demands the same of his people.

Amos was a true leader of a long line of writing prophets in Israel.

206. Hosea, Prophet of Israel (Book of Hosea). Hosea followed soon on the preaching of Amos to Israel. Reared within the environs of Jeroboam II's dominion, he must have been saturated with all the customs and habits of Israel. Unfortunate in his marriage relations, he seems to have taken this misfortune as one of the lessons of life. The personal experiences of Hosea with that wife dissolve into a metaphoric description of the relation of Jehovah to Israel, as husband to wife. God also attempts to restore his people, says Hosea, under the figure of himself buying back his faithless companion. Israel had treated Jehovah precisely as Gomer had treated Hosea; still his love had not died out, nor his affection perished.

Sad, sad pictures of the moral breakdown of Israel fill the next eleven chapters. Consecution of thought is scarcely to be found in the book. "Each verse is a whole in itself, like one heavy toll in a funeral knell" (Pusey). Some of the sharpest counts in the arraignment are: the violation of all pledges and covenants, and of the ten commandments; the perfidy and hypocrisy of the priests who have no respect for law, and are even robbers (4:6; 6:9); wine, drunkenness, adultery, and loss of understanding are everywhere; lies, perjury, deceit, intrigue have permeated all business life; the king, princes, nobles, and the wealthy are given to heavy drinking and debauchery (7:5); life and property are not safe; religion, though plentiful in form, is merely the old Baalism of the Canaanite.

The climax of all is, that these degeneracies have so weakened the national morale that the nation will soon fall a victim to the great powers, Egypt and Assyria (7:8-16). They will then carry them into captivity, as a punishment for their rejection of Jehovah and their apostasies to the gods of other nations. After all this chastisement and suffering, penitence will restore some of them to the favour of their former God.

Hosea's eleven chapters of indictments have interspersed here and there the love of God as his prevailing attribute. Punishment for sin is inevitable, but behind it all there is a loving God ready to forgive each penitent. Amos emphasized the justice and righteousness of God, while Hosea's God abounds in love for Israel for his own sake.

207. Anarchy in Israel (2 Kings 15:8-31, 37; 16:5). The forebodings of the prophets found their subsoil in the life and character of the kingdom of Israel. They knew that lack of moral stability and disregard of all law and right would end in destruction. No sooner was the house of Jehu blotted out than anarchy occupied the throne, and the dagger was the symbol of the immediate future.

Shallum, who assassinated Zechariah, the last of Jehu's house, after one-month's reign, was himself cut down in cold blood by Menahem in Samaria. Tiglath-pileser III had already reduced northern Syria and the Phœnician coast (743-740), and had taken over and organized the governments of all these countries. In 738 he says in his own records: " Nineteen districts of the city of Hamath, together with the towns in their environs, situated on the shore of the sea of the setting sun (Mediterranean) . . . I restored to the territory of the land of Assyria; my officers as governors I placed over them."

In that same year, he started south to gather in other lands and peoples. Menahem, who, by assassination. had usurped the throne of Israel several years earlier, took steps to protect himself. Having no allies and no capable army, the historian, in 2 Kings 15:19, 20, tells us how he saved his country:

" There came against the land Pul (Babylonian name) the king of Assyria; and Menahem gave Pul 1,000 talents of silver, that his hand might be with him to confirm the kingdom in his hand. And Menahem exacted the money of Israel, even of all the mighty men of wealth, of each fifty shekels of silver, to give to the king of Assyria. So the king of Assyria turned back, and stayed not there in the land."

Almost $2,000,000 of silver handed over by Menahem as an indemnity to the Assyrian monarch to let him alone, and all of it collected from the well-to-do and rich of Israel,— nearly 60,000 of them.

Tiglath-pileser gives in his annals, among many others, the names of these tributary kings: Rezon of Damascus, Menahem of Samaria, Hiram of Tyre, Panammu of Sam'al —lately brought to light at Sinjerli. With untold booty and pledges of submission from Syria, Phœnicia, and northern Israel, the monarch returned to Nineveh to prosecute other campaigns in Media and the East.

At the end of ten years' rule, Menahem died; and his son, Pekahiah, sat on the throne. When anarchy proclaimed its sway in Israel in 750 B. C., Pekah probably set up an independent government east of the Jordan, and maintained it for about fifteen years. After Tiglath-pileser III withdrew with his plunder, in 738, Pekah regarded it safe to cross the Jordan westward with fifty Gileadites, to try his mettle as a warrior. Finding Pekahiah the king ready to accept him as leader of his troops, he seemed to be in a fair way to carry out his ambitions. Within a year, and perhaps less, Pekah and his conspirators slew Pekahiah in the palace at Samaria and seized the reins of government.

208. Reign of Jotham of Judah (2 Kings 15:32-38;

2 Chron. 27). When Uzziah (Azariah) was smitten with leprosy and forced to live in an infirmary, his son Jotham was made regent, and continued to be such until the death of Uzziah, in 736 B. C. His record is approved by the historian. The Chronicler credits him with having built castles and towers in the tops of the mountains, and of having subjugated Ammon, from whom he collected an annual tribute of large proportions. His might, the historian tells us, was the outgrowth of ordering his ways before Jehovah his God. One year after the death of his father, he was gathered unto his fathers; and Ahaz, his son, formally took the throne.

209. Reign of Ahaz of Judah (2 Kings 16:1-20; 17:13-19; 2 Chron. 28; Isaiah 7:1-20). Ahaz had been prince regent for some years (since about 742 B. C.) when Jotham died, and in 734 B. C. he became absolute king. This twenty-eight-year-old ruler longed to be himself and to live his own kind of life; so he threw overboard all the teachings of his fathers and the prophets. He adopted the religion of the kings of Israel and outside nations as well, including even child-sacrifice. He robbed and closed up the house of Jehovah, sacrificed and burnt incense in high places on the hills and under every green tree. He put pagan altars in every corner of Jerusalem, and stooped to the abominations of the Canaanites,—whose depravity words cannot express.

About the beginning of Ahaz's reign, Pekah of Israel and Rezin of Damascus formed an alliance to ward off a new invasion by Tiglath-pileser. Apparently Ahaz had refused to join such a league; for both Syria and Israel overran northern Judah, defeated its armies, carried off captives without number, and attempted to force the surrender of Jerusalem. Ahaz, in a panicky spirit, appealed in desperation to the invincible Tiglath-pileser, just appearing over the horizon. Such practical rejection of their proposal angered the two allies, and they harried the entire upper country of Judah, and then rushed north to prepare to meet

the Assyrian monarch. In the meantime, the Edomites had
re-taken the port of Elath on the gulf of Akabah, and
sorely beaten southern Judah. The Philistines re-took
(2 Chron. 28:17) the cities which Amaziah had made
tributary to Judah. In fact, Ahaz was already reaping the
harvest of his own individuality and stubbornness. To in-
duce Tiglath-pileser to rescue him, he sent messengers
northwards with (1) his abject submission, " I am thy servant and thy son: come up and save me out of the hand of
the king of Syria and . . . Israel;" and, most important of
all, (2) the gold and silver that was found in the temple
and palace at Jerusalem, as a present,—the *sine qua non*
for help.

Isaiah the prophet kept his eye on Ahaz, but with futile
results. Meeting him outside Jerusalem (7:1-17), the
prophet advised him not to fear those " two tails of smoking firebrands " from the north, Rezin and Pekah, but to
put his faith in Jehovah. What cared Ahaz for Jehovah?
He wouldn't even ask a sign of him.

But in the face of the sneering response of the timorous
Ahaz, Isaiah proclaimed a coming sign: " a young woman
shall bear a son and call his name Immanuel " (" God with
us "). Before the child shall grow up the lands whose two
kings are now threatening Judah shall be desolate, and later
their inhabitants shall be carried off to Assyria.

The fact is, Ahaz had already sent his messengers with
gold and silver to the Assyrian monarch, to rescue him from
those two firebrands. Tiglath-pileser ravaged the Phœnician
coast and swept over into upper Galilee, the territory of
Israel, and as far south as the Carmel range; and then over
and down through the trans-Jordanic country, gathering up
thousands of captives to take back home. Damascus was
soon isolated. Its turn came next; and he made short work
of it. He slew Rezin, its king, and carried its population
captive to Kir (732 B. C.). He set up his throne in
Damascus, and to him came the petty kings like Ahaz,
who submitted without a blow. Ahaz played the game of

submission, prostrated himself before Tiglath-pileser,—true to the sycophant that he was. Indeed, he saw a new altar in Damascus and sent a sketch of it to his priest in Jerusalem, who made a replica of it. On Ahaz's return, he removed the large altar of Jehovah and set in its place this new Damascus altar, and ordered the regular morning and evening sacrifices to be offered thereon.

Tiglath-pileser's annual tribute required of Ahaz became so burdensome to his reduced territory and income that he was obliged to take the bronze of the lavers and of the oxen that supported the brazen sea in the court of the temple, and turn them over as part payment to Assyria. Such great and good prophets as Isaiah and Micah were powerless in the face of the avalanche of paganism that Ahaz brought down upon Judah and Jerusalem. They could only watch and wait for better days. Finally, in 727, Ahaz also slept— blessed sleep!—with his fathers.

210. Last Kings of Israel (2 Kings 15:30; 17:1-6). Tiglath-pileser's sub-province, Samaria, was afflicted with anarchy. However it happened, Pekah, the enemy of Assyria, was put out of the way ("killed," says 2 Kings 15:30) by Hoshea, probably by the orders of Tiglath-pileser,—with the promise that he could have his throne. Hoshea kept up the reputation of Jeroboam, the son of Nebat, religiously, and within a few years heard a siren call from Egypt for rebellion against Assyria. Tiglath-pileser finally died, in 727; and Hoshea, tired of turning over to Nineveh an annual tribute of about $300,000 in gold and about $2,000,000 in silver, looked about for relief. Egypt, which had attended strictly to its own business since Shishak had invaded Palestine in Rehoboam's reign, was now ready to coquette with Hoshea. Upon the promises of So, an Egyptian officer in the northeastern Delta, Hoshea withheld his usual annual tribute to Nineveh. The new Assyrian king promptly came westward and swooped down on the little kingdom, routed its army, captured the last king of northern Israel and put him in prison,—where, we do not know. More than this, he went at once to Samaria, the capital city, but found it barred against him. So he settled down for a long and stubborn siege,

211. Beginnings of Hezekiah of Judah (2 Kings 18:1-8; 2 Chron. 29–31). " In the third year of Hoshea " (728 B. C.) Hezekiah began as regent with his father Ahaz; and in 727 became king. His first steps were sharp reactions against the entire religious policy of his father. He did right as David had done right; he removed the high places, broke down the pillars, cut down the Asherah and chopped up the brazen serpent that Moses had made. He opened the doors of the temple which Ahaz had shut, rounded up the priests and Levites and commanded them to sanctify themselves; cleaned out the house of Jehovah and sanctified it; offered solemn sacrifices with the music of David and Asaph; offered burnt-offerings,—priests and Levites officiating. There was great rejoicing among the better class of people that Jehovah was again honoured and worshipped in the temple.

The Chronicler amplifies the preceding reforms and carries them much farther. The revival of all the services of Jehovah was one of the objects of the new king's reforms. After taking counsel, Hezekiah set out to re-establish the observance of the passover. But finding that it could not be done in the first month, he appointed it for the second month. Letters were sent from Dan to Beer-sheba, inviting the faithful to the observance. Responses came from Asher, Zebulun, and Manasseh. Some of those from Ephraim, Manasseh, Issachar, and Zebulun, though not purified according to the exact requirements of the law, ate the passover; for King Hezekiah had prayed, " The good Jehovah pardon every one that setteth his heart to seek God, Jehovah, the God of his fathers, though he be not cleansed according to the purification of the sanctuary " (2 Chron. 30:18, 19). So inspiring and refreshing was this feast, that it was observed over another seven days,—fourteen days in all,—Hezekiah and the princes supplying the necessary animals for the sacrifices and feasting. Upon the conclusion of this fortnight of celebration, all Israel who were present went out to the cities of Judah, Benjamin, Ephraim,

Fig. 74. Sargon II, Captor of Samaria

Sargon II's name is found only once in the Old Testament (Isaiah 20:1). But in Assyria he ruled with a master-hand 722–705 B. C. One of the first acts of his reign was the capture of Samaria, capital of the kingdom of Israel, and the dispersion of 27,290 of its population throughout the Assyrian domains. He retained the capital, and imported other nationalities to repopulate and strengthen it.

and Manasseh, and desecrated and destroyed all the symbols and high places of idol worship,—thus taking a long step toward a restoration of the worship of Jehovah, in contrast with the awful degradations of Ahaz.

212. The Fall of Samaria, 722 B. C. (2 Kings 17:5, 6; 18:9-11). We left Samaria (in §210) beleaguered by the Assyrian king, Shalmaneser V. While the army was still trying out its starvation siege, the Assyrian monarch died; and Sargon II, a usurper, took the throne. The Kings record seems to imply that the king of Assyria who began the siege, captured the city (18:9-11). But that credit is now due his successor, Sargon II. Sargon's own records of this event are specific:

" In the beginning of my reign, in my first year (Dec., 722 B. C.) Samaria I besieged, I captured. Twenty-seven thousand two hundred and ninety persons of its inhabitants I took captive; fifty chariots for my royal equipment I chose; I made it (Samaria) greater than it had been before; people of the lands (I had conquered, I settled there. I appointed my governor over them). Tribute, taxes, I imposed upon them as upon Assyrians."

This record fills out that in 2 Kings, in that it gives explicitly the name of the conqueror, and the number of captives. But it omits, while the Kings account gives, the names of the places to which the captives were taken,—" in Halah, and on the Habor, the river of Gozan, and in the cities of the Medes " (2 Kings 18:11).

The reasons given in Kings for the fall of Samaria are religious. Israel had rejected Jehovah, and served other gods; had built up the high places; set up obelisks and Asherim; disregarded and ignored the warnings of seer and prophet; worshipped the host of heaven; and even burnt their children in the fire to pagan divinities. The immediate cause, however, was the violation of the oath of fealty of King Hoshea to Assyria, and his rebellious intrigues with Egypt.

The fall of Samaria meant the utter collapse of the kingdom of Israel, the wiping out of the ten tribes as a political unit. Their territory was made a part of the Assyrian empire. The captive ten tribes distributed in their separate distant localities were probably soon amalgamated with, or absorbed by the peoples where they were slaves. The finding in these days of the so-called lost ten tribes of Israel is a mere figment of the imagination, and not worthy of the serious effort of any real scholar.

NOTE ON MAP 11, tailpiece below: Intrigues with Egypt and the Philistines for a coalition against Nineveh brought Hezekiah to his knees (in 701 B. C.). Assyria was the controlling world power, with Egypt anxiously looking on.

JUDAH
ASSYRIA
EGYPT

THE HEBREW WORLD

TIME OF HEZEKIAH, 700 B.C.

PERIOD VII

PROPHETS PREACHING

From the Fall of Samaria to the Fall of Jerusalem
(722–586 B. C.)

CHAPTER XXIV

ISAIAH AND HEZEKIAH

213. The Samaritans (2 Kings 17:24-41). Tiglath-pileser III had established the policy of transporting populations from one country to another to prevent uprisings

NOTE ON FIG. 58, headpiece above: Merodach-baladan was an ambitious leader among the Chaldeans who lived about the head of the Persian Gulf, in the latter half of the eighth century B. C. He stirred up trouble for two great Assyrian kings by seizing the throne of Babylon in their absence, and holding it (721–710; 703–02, ¾ of a year), until driven back to his swamps (*cf.* 2 Kings 20:12–15; Isa. 39). In this picture he is making a grant of land to one of his officers.

and revolutions. Consequently Sargon II imported "men from Babylon, and from Cuthah, and from Avva, and from Hamath and Sepharvaim, and placed them in the cities of Samaria instead of the children of Israel." These men also brought with them their gods; "Babylon made Succoth-benoth; the men of Cuth made Nergal; the men of Hamath made Ashima; and the Avvites made Nibhaz and Tartak; and the Sepharvites burnt their children in the fire to Adrammelech and Anammelech, the gods of Sepharvaim."

Sargon also names in his records other peoples than those named in the Old Testament which he imported and placed in Samaria about 715 B. C. "The tribes of the Tamud, Ibadid, Marsiman, Khayapa, distant Arabs, who inhabit the desert, who recognize no overlord, who had paid tribute to no king, I smote in the service of Ashur, my lord, the remaining inhabitants I carried away and settled them in Samaria,"—an importation of new desert blood to build up a decadent civilization.

When the partially depopulated territory was overrun by dangerous wild animals, the Israelites who were left in the land appealed to Assyria for help against such ravages by Jehovah. And a priest of the God of the land (of Bethel) was sent back from among the captives to teach the people the law of the God of the land,—a sure indication of their belief in their God as local in character. But what would take place among such a conglomeration of nationalities? Naturally they soon formed social units, spoke a common language and possessed a syncretistic religion. The report in Kings tells us in a word what took place. "So these (amalgamated) nations feared Jehovah, and served their graven images; their children likewise, and their children's children, as did their fathers, so do they until this day" (17:41),—in the time of the exile when Kings was compiled.

These conglomerate peoples were the basis of the later Samaritans, who gave Nehemiah so much trouble when he was rebuilding the walls of Jerusalem. After the reforms of Ezra and Nehemiah, a Jew (Manasseh!) expelled from

Jerusalem is said to have established the worship of Jehovah on Mt. Gerizim, where the Pentateuch was adopted as their Bible,—later called the Samaritan Pentateuch,—with many variations from the Hebrew. In the time of Christ they were a people quite beneath the notice of a Jew, with whom the Jews had no dealings. In the town of Nablous (Shechem), there are to-day about 100 so-called Samaritans, who claim that they have a manuscript copy of the Pentateuch written by Moses himself. They seem to eke out a pathetic existence through the charity of friends and tourists.

214. The Prophet Isaiah. Isaiah the prophet came upon the stage of action about the time of the death of Uzziah (736 b. c.), king of Judah. The short reign of Jotham after his father's death wrought no perceptible changes in the character of his kingdom. But the coronation of Ahaz was the signal for a reversal of all the best policies of Judah's earlier kings. Ahaz installed and promoted worse forms of paganism than were ever known in the northern kingdom. Isaiah, with all his reserve and dignity, must have suffered in heart and soul to see the horrible desecrations and debauches of that royal degenerate. Isaiah lived in Jerusalem, and was a helpless witness of the ravages made upon the worship and temple of Jehovah.

His words of admonition were disdained, ignored or scorned. No prophet ever had a better opportunity for studying the adverse conditions of his times; the evil influence of king upon people; the significance and power of a monarch on the throne. On the other hand, the prophet must have had his faithful friends, true worshippers of Jehovah who kept in close touch with each other, and who fostered and extended true worship among the young and among the reactionaries against the drag-down of the royal monarch. When Ahaz died, Isaiah had his opportunity, and used it with all his energy and skill. The twenty-five-year-old Hezekiah, who became king in his father's place, was ready to accept the prophet's counsel. The closeness of their relationship seems to point to a long earlier friendship, probably reaching back to the boyhood of the king.

The evil reign of Ahaz had so inoculated the common people with the virus of paganism, that Isaiah was forced to use every legitimate expedient to counteract the spread of the disease. Hezekiah's reforms, Isaiah's and Micah's preaching and living among the people, and political issues, all were used as antidotes.

Isaiah's knowledge of the moral and religious conditions of the day, of the real demands of Jehovah made upon the people, of the certainty of punishment by invasion and exile, gave him a message that not only smote the consciences of the then thoughtful Israelites, but have been models of insight and comprehensiveness for all reformers since his day.

Standing as he did, close to the reigning King Hezekiah, he occupied a large place in the political issues of the state, and moulded many of its policies at home and abroad.

215. The Prophet Micah. Micah, a contemporary of Isaiah, was reared in a village, Moresheth-gath, down on the edge of Philistia. His life and sympathies were with the simple country-folk, as over against the sophisticated artificial life of the city. His conceptions of the moral and religious life of his times were keen and discriminating. He saw on the political horizon the threatening approach of the armies of the Mesopotamian valley. It meant to him the rod of Jehovah's anger, to chastise the rebellious Israelites who had deliberately wrecked their loyalty to their own God for the alluring divinities of other nations.

Like the faithful Amos, he vigorously arraigned those who had openly and wickedly done that thing. With some resemblances to Isaiah, he gives us also the pith of all the Mosaic laws in that model definition of religious duty (6:8):

" What doth Jehovah require of thee, but to do justly, and to love kindness, and to walk humbly with thy God? "

Though a " Minor " prophet, his sermons were major in every sense of the word.

216. Hezekiah and Sargon II. It seems plausible that Hezekiah began to carry out some of his religious reforms in the earlier years of his reign; for the people, especially the prophets and worshippers of Jehovah, naturally rebounded from the vicious, pagan debauch of Ahaz, back to the religious order of Uzziah, Jehoshaphat, and David.

We have no hint as to any political move that he may have made at that time. Doubtless he meekly submitted to the tribute to Assyria which Ahaz his father had fastened on Judah. Sargon's capture of Samaria, and his 720 B. C. campaign to suppress the rebels of the Westland,—ending in the battle of Raphia against the Egyptians down on the border of Egypt,—left Hezekiah undisturbed in his peaceful capital.

During the next few years Hezekiah solidified his kingdom by building cities, fortresses and walled towns. He built up trade and agriculture, and erected storehouses for the preservation of surplus products. In addition, he improved the water supply of Jerusalem by cutting a tunnel from the Virgin's spring under the east side of the city of David, through solid rock 1758 feet long, to the so-called pool of Siloam, within the walls of the lower part of the city. This splendid piece of engineering deprived any possible enemy of the use of the spring, and secured it for the city itself. The so-called Siloam inscription, found at the Siloam-pool-end of the tunnel, gives a vivid description of the happy meeting of the two sets of diggers from opposite directions when they met in the middle of the tunnel under the hill (see Fig. 89, p. 313).

Hezekiah doubtless took these precautions with the expectation that sometime in the near future, he would sorely need such a necessity.

Sometime about 712–711, while Sargon was busy elsewhere, Egypt's new Ethiopian king, Shabaka (712–700 B. C.) cast longing eyes toward Asia. To aid in achieving his purpose, he induced the cities of Philistia to join a league against Assyria. Sargon's own records tell us that

" Philistia, Judah, Edom, Moab, who had paid tribute and gifts to Ashur, my lord, planned rebellion and evil against me; they brought gifts of friendship to Pharaoh, king of Egypt, 'a prince who could not save them,' and endeavoured to form with him an alliance."

Sargon's name occurs but once in the Old Testament, and that is in Isaiah 20:1, which reads as follows: " In the year that Tartan came unto Ashdod, when Sargon the king of Assyria sent him, and he fought against Ashdod and took it." This was the short, swift and effective campaign that swooped down upon the rebellious Philistine centre Ashdod, crushed it, and carried off its inhabitants as captives. The Egyptian king at least gave up Azuri, king of Ashdod, whom he held as a captive, to Assyria, and caused no further trouble for some years. There is no evidence that the other neighbouring states were punished or even disturbed by this punitive expedition of Sargon.

217. Hezekiah's Sickness. The exact order of the political events of this period is not certain. Since we have the beginning of Hezekiah's reign at 727, it seems reasonable to locate this sickness at about 712, the date of Sargon's Ashdod campaign. At least it was before Sennacherib's invasion, for (1) the treasury was still full (Isa. 39:2, 6 contrasted with 2 Kings 18:14-16); (2) deliverance from Assyria was still in the future (Isa. 38:6); (3) Hezekiah refers to no deliverance in his psalm of thanksgiving,— hardly possible if it were past; (4) Sennacherib began to reign 705 B. C. Hezekiah was attacked by an inflammatory cutaneous disease which was so painful that he nearly died. This fell upon him like a rebuke or a punishment, to urge him to better works, to bring him to himself and to his God (Isa. 38:17). He was so distressed that he sent for Isaiah, who told him that he would die. After humiliating himself in prayer, the prophet was told by Jehovah to go to him and tell him his life would be extended fifteen years. Then he gave command, and they put a poultice of figs on the inflamed part, and a cure followed.

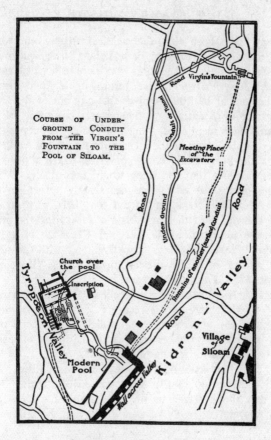

Fig. 89. The Siloam Tunnel

At first sight this is a confusing plan. Find the Virgin's fountain near the upper right-hand corner. The dotted lines running down to the old pool are the old surface drain. But Hezekiah, fearful of a siege by the Assyrian army (2 Kings 20:20), and a possible lack of water, decided to cut a conduit under the hill of Zion to the pool of Siloam within the walls.

Excavators began work at both ends and finally met in the middle. The channel is 1,758 feet long and six feet high,—a notable piece of engineering for that day. Note carefully the winding direction of the conduit, and its emptying into the pool of Siloam within the walls, out of reach of the enemy. The Siloam inscription found at the mouth of the channel is pictured and translated in MOT, pp. 326–27.

It may have been that the sickness struck him while Sargon was either threatening or punishing those southwestern Philistine rebels. As soon as they were sufficiently chastised, the Assyrian would give Jerusalem its due. Isaiah assured him that he would deliver this city out of the hand of the king of Assyria, and defend it. No name of an Assyrian king is mentioned, though on the above supposition Sargon would have been the ruler referred to.

Hezekiah, like all his contemporaries, asked a sign as advance evidence that the thing would take place. When given his choice, he asked that the shadow return on the dial of Ahaz's ten steps, and it did so. This, with all our meagre knowledge of their processes of measuring the progress of the sun, is a riddle. Second Kings 20:11 reads, "shadow;" Isaiah 38:8 says, "shadow . . . with the sun." Was it refraction, optical illusion, or an eclipse (there was one Sept. 13, 713 B. C.)?

Isaiah 38:10-20 presents a marvellous "psalm of thanksgiving" of Hezekiah for his recovery from going down to the gates of the underworld; acknowledging the good purpose of his sickness, and resolving in all the future to render praise to Jehovah for saving his life.

218. The Embassy of Merodach-baladan (about 710 B. C.) (2 Kings 20:12-19; 2 Chron. 32:31; Isaiah 39). When this throne-seizer in southern Babylonia saw that Sargon was getting ready to attack Babylon, he sent mes-

NOTE ON FIG. 75, opposite: About twelve miles north of Nineveh, the royal grounds of Sargon II covered somewhat more than one square mile, the whole surrounded by a wall, whose angles are set to the points of the compass. Near the middle of the northwest side of this wall, mostly inside, but partly outside, was built (710–706) on a raised platform 46 ft. high, this splendid palace, covering about twenty-five acres. Its proportions were immense, and its appointments the acme of convenience. The courts and rooms were wainscoated with sculptured alabaster slabs, and the entrances guarded with sculptured colossi, human-headed bulls of alabaster. The main entrance was from inside the grounds, by steps for pedestrians, and by ramps for charioteers. On the top was the sacred ziggurat on which the shrine of the patron deity was worshipped. This palace was discovered in 1842 by M. Botta, French consul at Mosul, and excavated by the French government.

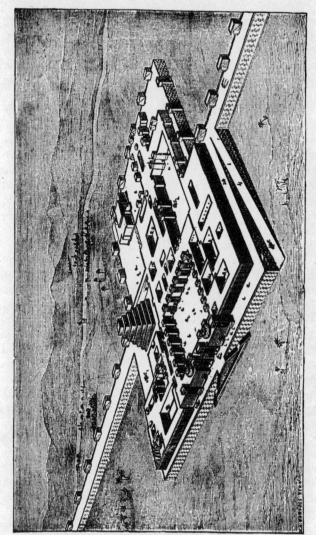

Fig. 75.   Reconstruction of Sargon's Palace at Khorsabad

sengers to Jerusalem,—nominally to congratulate Hezekiah on his recovery from his sickness, and inquire about the dial; but really to effect a political league, and to spy out Hezekiah's resources as a member thereof. The Chronicler says, " God left him to try him that he might know all that was in his heart " (2 Chron. 32:31).

Hezekiah gave the ambassadors a royal reception, became quite confidential, and proudly showed them all his equipment and treasures. Isaiah was close at hand and promptly rebuked the pride of Hezekiah, and told him all these treasures would be carried to Babylon and his posterity would be slaves in its palaces. In humility Hezekiah recognized God's right, and requested that it should not take place in his day. The embassy returned with inside information about Judah and Jerusalem, and what they could contribute to such a coalition as Merodach-baladan tried to form.

But before the alliance could ripen, Sargon dropped down on Merodach-baladan at Babylon (709 B. C.), defeated him, and drove him back into the swamps about the Persian Gulf, whence he had come.

219. Hezekiah's Revolt against Assyria (2 Kings 18:7). Ever since Sargon defeated the Egyptian army at Raphia in 720, and crushed Ashdod about 712, Egypt had been quietly fomenting rebellion against Assyria among the small peoples of the southwest. Even in Jerusalem there was an Egyptian party busily at work to tie up Judah in such a coalition. Hezekiah at first, and Isaiah constantly, opposed any such combine.

The prophet had tried to restrain Hezekiah from yielding to the alluring propositions of the Egyptians, by strong words (Isa. 30 and 31), and then by walking the streets of Jerusalem three years in the scant kilt of a captive, as a picture of what would happen to Judah if they should rebel against Assyrian sovereignty (Isa. 20:2-6).

In 705 B. C. Sargon lost his life in a campaign against a small people east of Nineveh. Sennacherib, his son, succeeded him. Merodach-baladan rushed up from the swamps and again seized Babylon. Sennacherib turned his first attention to reducing to submission all the would-be rebels about Nineveh and in Babylonia.

Fig. 78. Sennacherib at the Head of His Army

The royal chariot at this period had two wheels, drawn by two or more horses, or mules as here, and carried the king, the driver and an attendant, all standing on the car platform. Behind on foot is the royal body-guard, equipped with coats of mail and army boots, and the captain with a spear and dagger. When actual battle began this dress parade form was laid aside.

During those four years, Hezekiah's loyalty to Assyria weakened; and in 702 he cut off his payment of large tribute to Nineveh, simultaneously with joining in the general uprising against Assyria. Sidon in Phœnicia, and Ashkelon and Ekron in Philistia followed suit. The anti-Assyrian rebellion was contagious, and claimed all this southwestern country except Padi, king of Ekron, who refused to rebel against his overlord. His own people seized him and turned him over to Hezekiah, who imprisoned him in Jerusalem. In the meantime, the frantic popular enthusiasm of the city ran into all kinds of excesses, in the very face of disaster that Isaiah had held up before them (Isa. 22). Blind to all such threats, the populace plunged into a riot of revelry and joy over the release from the shackles of Assyria.

220. Sennacherib on the Horizon (2 Kings 18:13-16). The various layers of Old Testament records, and the order of the events of Sennacherib's campaign of 701 B. C., have not been by any means agreed upon among scholars; but the general sweep of events, and the outcome are in no doubt. A critical estimate of those accounts would require more space than we can spare for this event.

When Sennacherib had completed his suppression of the rebels in the East, he turned his armies toward the Mediterranean. He first swept across North Syria and struck Sidon, whose king, Luli, had fled over the sea to the isle of Cyprus; other Phœnician cities fell prostrate at his feet, and Tuba'al, the Sidonian, was made governor over them for Assyria. Tyre is unmentioned,—probably because it was inaccessible and unconquered. Thence Sennacherib pushed down the coast. One after another the cities collapsed before him, until he reached Lachish, which required a prolonged siege with modern siege-works,—pictured on the walls of Sennacherib's palace. While he was here, detachments of his army devastated the surrounding country,—capturing fortresses and taking captives by the thousands. At the same time several small rebel states, as Edom, Moab, Ashdod, rendered submission. Hezekiah, fully aware of the danger threatening Jerusalem, also sent messengers to Lachish to buy off the Assyrian. In humility he said, " I have offended; return from me: that which thou puttest on me will I bear."

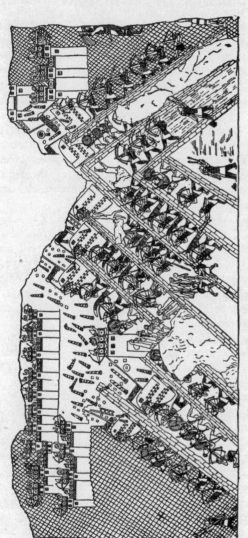

Fig. 53. The Storming of Lachish by Sennacherib's Army

Lachish was the first city in Palestine to defy Sennacherib's demands. This vigorous charge against its battlemented strength, carved on the walls of the king's palace at Nineveh, bespeaks the victory already in sight (2 Kings 18:14, 17; 19:8). Battering-rams, archers, slingers, all in action. The enemies are hurling torches upon the wooden rams which are kept wet by streams of water poured over their exposed surfaces. The surrendering women and children are coming out of a side gate with their effects, and rebel leaders are impaled on stakes. The victory was complete, and Lachish destroyed.

The biblical narrative puts the payment of an indemnity immediately following Hezekiah's submission, while Sennacherib's record places it at the end of his account after he had returned to Nineveh. Hezekiah was put to it to raise the required metal. But by emptying the treasuries of the temple and the royal palace, and by stripping off the gold plating of the doors and doorposts of the house of Jehovah, he turned over to Sennacherib thirty talents of gold and three hundred talents of silver, equal to about $1,500,000, by actual computation. The Assyrian greed, not satisfied with such a splendid cash payment, decided to demand the surrender of a city whose resources could turn out such a mass of valuable metal.

221. The Assyrians before Jerusalem (2 Kings 18:17–19:7; 2 Chron. 32:9-15; Isaiah 36:2–37:7). Sennacherib sent three of his officers, Tartan, Rabsaris, and Rabshakeh, "with a great army" from Lachish, where a determined siege was in progress, to Jerusalem. When they approached the city and saw its fortified location and high walls, they decided to make a gesture of an attack, and demand its surrender.

They called for Hezekiah, and he sent out three envoys. Apparently they stood some distance from the Assyrian officers, who gave them a message for Hezekiah. The shrewd Assyrian spokesman ridiculed their confidence in Egypt, "a staff of a cracked reed; whereon if a man lean, it will go into his hand, and pierce it." How could Jehovah rescue a king who had taken away his altars and high places? To prove their weakness, his master would furnish 2,000 horses if Jerusalem would furnish riders for them. "We have come at Jehovah's request to destroy you."

The envoys appealed in vain to Rabshakeh to speak to them not in Hebrew but in Aramaic, so that the listeners on the wall could not understand. Louder than before, and in Hebrew, he railed at the pretense of Hezekiah to save the city. "If they would surrender he would take them to a land like their own with plenty of the choicest food and

drink. Yea, more than that, had any of the gods of the
nations saved their countries out of the hand of the king
of Assyria? Can Jehovah deliver Jerusalem out of my
hand?"

The people on the wall, who had heard all the loud

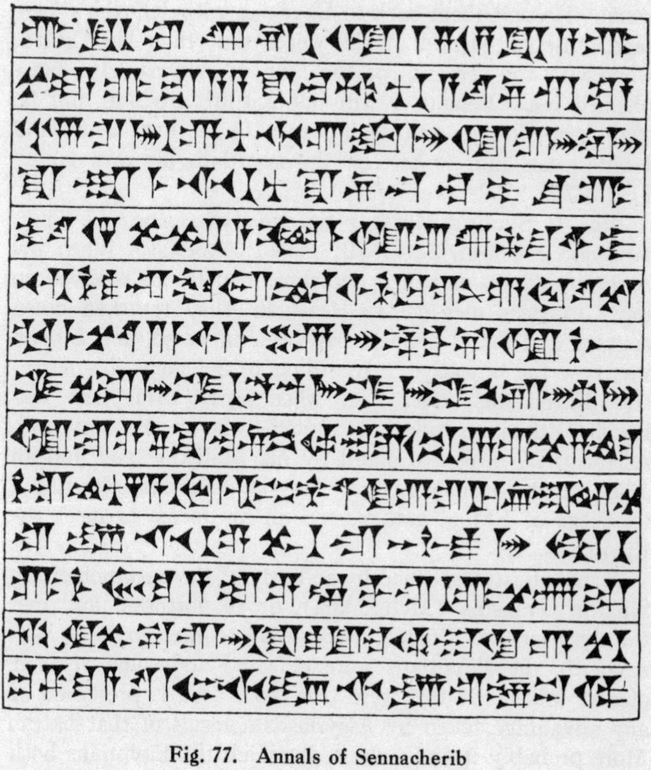

Fig. 77. Annals of Sennacherib

This excerpt from one of the inscriptions of that monarch recites the
name of Hezekiah (last five signs in the first line read: *Ha-za-ki-a-u*),
king of Judah (727-698 B. C.), whose disloyalty to his oath of allegiance had been one cause of the Assyrian's campaign into the Westland. Of course, Sennacherib's record gives his side of the case, and
as usual leaves out the unfavourable and disastrous results of his
expedition.

harangue of Rabshakeh to the envoys, kept still. And the envoys returned through the gate of the city, rent their clothes, and went in to the king with their desperate report. Hezekiah's sorrow gave vent to itself by his rending of his own garments. He sent Eliakim and Shebna to Isaiah the prophet, with their doleful message. Isaiah's real turn had come. He sent them back to Hezekiah with Jehovah's message, " Be not afraid of the words that thou hast heard, wherewith the servants of the king of Assyria have blasphemed me. Behold, I will put a spirit in him, and he shall hear tidings, and shall return to his own land; and I will cause him to fall by the sword in his own land " (19:6, 7).

222. A Second Bluster before Jerusalem (2 Kings 19:8-34; 2 Chron. 32:17-20; Isaiah 37:8-35). When the Assyrian officers and their detachment of troops received no reply to their message to Hezekiah, they returned down country and found Lachish had been captured, and Libnah was now the objective. According to Sennacherib's narrative, Ekron was under siege when report came that Tirhakah, Ethiopian ruler of Egypt, was on his way into Asia with an army to stand by his Philistine and Judean allies in the league against Assyria. Sennacherib raised the siege of Ekron, and massed all his forces to meet the Egyptians.

Tirhakah, strengthened by an army of the governor of the Sinaitic peninsula (Melukhkha), drove northeast and met the Assyrians at Eltekeh. According to the report of Sennacherib, the Egyptians were defeated and some of their officers taken. If this were true, no record is preserved of any advantage taken by Assyria as a result of that battle. More probably it was a draw, in which the Egyptians both fulfilled their loyalty to the league and put an effectual check on Sennacherib's ambition to invade Egypt at this time.

It appears from the Old Testament that as soon as the report came to Sennacherib that the Egyptian army was moving toward Philistia, he sent other messengers with a letter to Hezekiah, who was still safe behind his walls in Jerusalem. This letter recited the futility of trusting in Jehovah to save them, since no god had saved any city which Assyria had attacked. "What has become of the king of Hamath, and of Arpad, and of Sepharvaim? All gone."

Hezekiah received the letter, went up to the house of Jehovah, spread it before Jehovah, poured out his half-belief in the statements of the letter, and agonized in prayer for the deliverance of his city from the hands of the fearful devastators.

Isaiah, cognizant of the fright of the king, himself carried the message of Jehovah to Hezekiah. The insolence and arrogance of Assyria shall be countered by the God who knows his downsitting and his uprising. He guides the nations as he will. "I will put my hook in thy nose, and my bridle in thy lips, and I will turn thee back by the way by which thou camest" (2 Kings 19:28).

Furthermore, Isaiah assured Hezekiah that Jerusalem would not be besieged, nor a mound cast up against it, nor an arrow shot there,—but that the city would be defended for his servant David's sake. Somewhere, probably during this period when Sennacherib had taken Ekron, on demand Hezekiah had surrendered Padi, the Philistine king loyal to Assyria, whom his fellow-citizens had turned over to the Judean king for imprisonment.

223. Sennacherib's Disaster (2 Kings 19:35, 36; Isaiah 37:36, 37). Sennacherib reduced the rebel cities of Philistia to subjection, gathering in multitudes of captives, wiping out some centres and reorganizing others, so as to crush the possibility of another revolt. Hezekiah was " shut up like a bird in a cage " in his capital, but was not besieged, captured, nor destroyed, even after two rather insolent attempts to force a diplomatic surrender. Jerusalem was too well fortified and too far off to one side of the rebellious centres to allow a long, weary siege to be staged against it. Indeed, the gods of Assyria had not prevailed over Jehovah, God of the Hebrews (cf. 2 Kings 19:10-12, 17 f.).

The second set of messengers must have withdrawn from the city without inflicting anything more than a salutary scare upon Hezekiah and the pro-Egyptians in Jerusalem.

The mass of the army was encamped in Philistia, where its many rebellious centres were located. All at once, by the biblical record (Isaiah 37:36): "The angel of Jehovah went forth, and smote in the camp of the Assyrians 185,000; and when men arose early in the morning, behold, these were all dead bodies." This tremendous onslaught seems to be confirmed by another Isaianic item (17:14): "At eventide behold, terror; and before the morning they are not. This is the portion of them that despoil us and the lot of them that rob us." Read Byron's, "The Assyrian came down like a wolf on the fold," etc.

How is such a fatal stroke to be explained? Of all the various theories proposed, the most plausible seems to be that it was a terrific outbreak of pestilence such as has not infrequently occurred on this part of the coastal plains of the Mediterranean Sea.

Sennacherib's inscriptions are, of course, silent about any defeat or disaster in the southwest. His records jump from Philistia to Nineveh with no information regarding any return movement. He mentions the princesses and ladies of the royal palace, male and female musicians, and the tribute that Hezekiah sent to him to Nineveh, which is the same in amount that the Bible narrative (2 Kings 18:14) locates at the beginning of the Assyrian campaign. Could this have been the same tribute sent the next year? Or, was it a literary smoke-screen of the Assyrian historian to hide some disaster in southwestern Asia? Or, has there been some confusion of this campaign with another against some other rebellious subjects?

Curious, though true it is, that Sennacherib never came to the Westland again, during the next twenty years of his life, preferring to confine his campaigns to more profitable territory and less dangerous(!) areas.

The biblical record concludes with this statement—" as he was worshipping in the house of Nisroch (Nusku), his god, Adrammelech and Sharezer smote him with the sword; and they escaped into the land of Ararat. And Esarhaddon, his son, reigned in his stead " (2 Kings 19:37).

224. Isaiah, the Statesman Prophet. Isaiah (*cf.* §214) lived in the midst of great national movements. He saw the rolling-in of Assyrian armies from the northeast, and the break-down of the opposition of Israel and Judah. He heard the fall and crash of the northern kingdom before the same invincible forces from Nineveh. As a prophet he was powerless to defend the victims. When subtle suggestions came to Hezekiah to join a unified revolt against the power on the Tigris, Isaiah was at his elbow. When the uneasy semi-rebellious Philistine cities secretly visited Jerusalem to take the temperature of the spirit of freedom and liberty, the wise prophet had his hand on the pulse of the population. Neither was he passive during these demonstrations. His known character and loyalty to Jehovah had a profound influence on the most thoughtful of the officials and people. Egypt's propaganda among all these southwestern kingdoms was persistent and potent. Isaiah fought like a hero in defiance of any rebellion against powerful Assyria in favour of Egypt with its smooth and slippery promises. Isaiah's appeal to the right was not as strong as that to the futility of any course they wished to pursue. But with all the artifices of language and rhetoric, he cautioned, warned, and threatened any breach of loyalty to their oath,—be it to Jehovah or to man-made treaties. An oath in the name of Jehovah had the same sanctity as his worship, and its violation was a blow at a divine covenant.

Isaiah's conception of Jehovah was that he was majestic and holy; that faith in him was essential to right service and prosperity; that Zion was inviolable; and that a remnant would be saved after the inevitable punishment which would come upon Israel; that ultimately there would be established a divine kingdom.

Isaiah's life and character was an embodiment of all these principles. By them he stood at all times, and emphasized them by word and deed; he really saved Judah from going down the same slopes as Israel, to an immediate and calamitous captivity and utter destruction. Isaiah stands out as the greatest prophetic character in the Old Testament, consecrated, sincere, firm, and always dependable for his good sense and sane counsel and guidance in the ways of Jehovah, the God of Israel. His counsel and advice to the kings of Judah received their vindication in all subsequent events.

225. How Matters Stood at 700 B. C. Hezekiah was king of Judah, though severely shorn in extent of territory, and his land badly devastated by the Assyrian army. He was paying a heavy tribute to Nineveh, smarting under his humiliation, and was now simply one of the little puppet kings of this western district of Sennacherib.

Isaiah and Micah were the strong pillars of loyalty to Jehovah worship, using their powers to rebuke and call down the sinners and criminals of their day, who were all too reckless and impudent in their disobedience of known law. The words of these prophets openly condemn priests and judges for their hypocritical attitude toward worship and the devotees who trusted them. Close to this degradation were the pagan idols which were still revered by those reared under the horrors of the reign of Ahaz.

One of the distressing social conditions of the times was the great gap between the rich and the poor. Oppression of the poor by the rich carried with it all the evils of cheating, stealing, lying, enactment of crooked laws, and slavery. Simultaneously there grew up an abnormal greed, lack of mercy, small common respect, and indifference bordering on indignity and even hatred.

Wealth was the easy road to luxuries in eating and drinking. These evils gripped more than the wealthy. Isaiah gives a sad picture of the priest and prophet that " reel with wine, stagger with strong drink; . . . they are swallowed up with wine, they stagger with strong drink; they err in vision, they stumble in judgment " (Isa. 28:7). Drunkenness obliterated social distinctions, put all on the same level of disgrace and sottishness, and dragged down the poor deeper into the morass of misery.

Oh, no, all were not this bad, else Isaiah and Micah had lived in vain! There were a few whose sturdy righteousness shone out through all the land, and were set as lights on a hill for all who chose to follow their example.

NOTE ON FIG. 65A, next page: Nineveh was the capital and royal residence city during the last seventy-five years of the life of Assyria (700–626 B. C.). Sennacherib was the first Assyrian king to build his palace in that centre. He fortified and beautified the city, and built fourteen gates through its walls; and later added one more, —each with a name. In addition to his magnificent palace near the Quay gate he built an inner wall of dressed stone, and an armory for housing war material. At that time the Tigris ran close along outside the wall as seen in our plan, while now its bed is quite a distance westward therefrom.

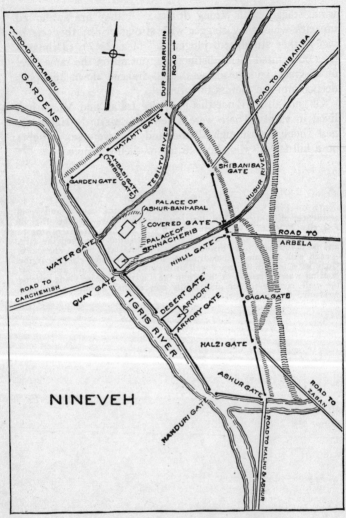

Fig. 65A. Plan of Nineveh in Sennacherib's Day

(See page 327)

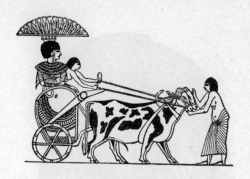

CHAPTER XXV

THE RECOIL AGAINST JEHOVAH WORSHIP

226. Reaction against the Prophets (2 Kings 21; 2 Chron. 33). Hezekiah's reign had been a kind of suppression of the generation of idolaters who had grown up under the tutelage of Ahaz. These devotees of pagan cults had not been entirely extinguished, but were quietly biding their time. The death of the pious old king, the old age of Isaiah and probably of Micah, and the accession to the throne of the impressionable twelve-year-old Manasseh, gave them their opportunity. The rebound toward paganism was instant. They installed in public places Baal and Astarte worship, as had Ahab of Israel; the service of the host of heaven and the Assyrian astral cults, in the courts of the house of Jehovah (2 Kings 21:3); and Moloch worship, where children were burned in the fire to that god. They also brought back augury, enchantments, wizards, and familiar spirits;—in fact, they indulged in every available kind of worship except that of Jehovah.

NOTE ON FIG. 65B, headpiece above: We have a unique outfit for travel. Here a countrywoman of Tirhakah, a Nubian princess, is touring down to Egypt in a chariot drawn by oxen. This figure is found in Lepsius' *Denkmaeler* with some modifications, and presents a feature quite foreign to Egyptian usage, but interesting as coming from their southern frontier.

Fig. 27. Portrait of Esarhaddon

This beautiful portrait of the son of Sennacherib was found in the ruins of Sam'al by von Luschan. The king holds in his right hand a libation vase, and in his left a sceptre and two leashes which are fastened to hooks in the lips of Baal king of Tyre, the larger figure, and the smaller Tirhakah (2 Kings 19:9) the Ethiopian king of Egypt (688–663 B. C.). Note the symbols of gods just in front of, and over his face. This statue was set up in Sam'al (Sinjerli) in 670 B. C.

More than that, they persecuted and destroyed the prophets of Jehovah, as Josephus tells us. Even 2 Kings (21:16) says " Manasseh shed innocent blood very much, till he had filled Jerusalem from one end to another; besides his sin wherewith he made Judah to sin." Tradition tells us that Isaiah was caught in this onslaught of paganism and was " sawn asunder " in a tree (cf. Heb. 11:37). The entire people seem to have gone over to devotion to foreign gods, thus dragging down both young and old with orgies never seen before or after the long years of Manasseh's reign.

227. Assyria's Stranglehold on Palestine. Hezekiah's headstrong treatment of Isaiah's warnings against breaking his oath to Assyria, resulted in his leaving to his son, Manasseh, just a little dependency of the Ninevite monarch. Annual tribute to Nineveh he paid for the price of his stubbornness. After Sennacherib was slain in Nineveh in 681 B. C., the same annual tax was doubtless sent to Esarhaddon (681–668 B. C.), son and successor on the throne. We find the name " Manasseh of Judah " in a long list of his puppet tribute-payers of the Westland. Esarhaddon had only partially dissolved his troubles with rebels in the valley of Babylonia, when his ambitions saw on the horizon in the far west Asia Minor, Phœnicia, Egypt, and Arabia. In 678 B. C. he started westward, and soon reduced Phœnicia—which was in league with Cyprus and Cilicia— except the defiant little island and city Tyre. Rebellious Sidon he seems to have pitilessly and barbarously crushed, if he tells the truth, for its intrigues with Syria and Egypt; and he received tribute from all the small kings thereabouts. He later made a treaty with Baal, king of Tyre, who violated it by forming an alliance with Tirhakah of Egypt. His humiliation of these two kings is symbolized on the Sinjerli monument, where they are standing before him with thongs through their lips (cf. 2 Kings 19:28, seen in Fig. 27, above). Esarhaddon's close touch with the Phœnician cities is vividly pictured in his own records. He next marched southward unimpeded, until he reached the Arabian desert, where he spent two years in reducing the population about the Gulf of Akabah and the Sinaitic peninsula. Thence into Egypt he drove, according to the Babylonian Chronicle, in 675 and again in 671 B. C. In the first campaign, he met the Ethiopian and other troops of Tirhakah at Eltekeh, and forced them back in defeat. In the second campaign, Memphis, the capital, was taken; and as a warning his troops looted and destroyed that venerable Egyptian centre. Tirhakah, however, had made good his escape to Napata in Ethiopia; and all Egypt, up to Thebes, surrendered to the powerful Esarhaddon, who was the first Assyrian king to make Egypt a province of the throne of Nineveh. Within the twelve years of his reign, Esarhaddon had reached the desired goal of a long line of earlier Assyrian monarchs.

Ashurbanipal (Osnappar of Ezra 4:10), the son, was successor of Esarhaddon in 668 B. C. The new king had, as his first task, to put down the ever-present rebel Tirhakah, who had again come down from Ethiopia into control of Egypt. In 667 B. C. he defeated this Ethiopian king and the Egyptian army; and Tirhakah again took refuge at Napata.

The Assyrian king commandeered a Phœnician fleet which had sailed up the Nile to Memphis. Upon it he embarked with his army, and sailed in forty days up to Thebes, which received the conqueror without a blow. He re-appointed Esarhaddon's officers over the city and departed, leaving Thebes unhurt. With troops garrisoned in the main Egyptian cities, Ashurbanipal withdrew from the country and returned to Nineveh.

The malcontents in Nubia, Thebes, and the Delta, soon got their heads together to plan the ousting of the Assyrian officers and garrisons. With almost unheard of patience, Ashurbanipal dealt with the rebels who were sent to him to Nineveh. But revolt, treachery and independence were in the air. Nothing remained but to make a punitive campaign. In 663 B. C. Ashurbanipal swept westward and southwestward into Egypt. The rebel leader, Tandamane, fled from Memphis to Thebes. Pursued to that city, he fled to Kipkip (of Nubia). This time Ashurbanipal let loose all the fierce dogs of war on beautiful Thebes. The city was subjected to unrestricted looting and plunder, to sword, fire and rapine: " I let my weapons rage and showed my might," says the devastator. " Silver, gold, precious stones, all the possessions of his palace, vari-coloured clothing, linen, great horses, men and women servants," etc., were some of the hoards of trophies and plunder which were carried back to Nineveh.

The prophet Nahum (3:8-10) sensed the terrible disaster that had overtaken that strong city (No Amon) of old Egypt. In fact, Thebes was never rebuilt, and practically remained a ruin as it is to-day.

Psamtik I of Egypt became the Assyrian underlord from the sea to Syene—Assuan, the first cataract—who sent his tribute to Nineveh annually. About 651 B. C., the garrisons in the Delta were withdrawn, or possibly driven out (says Herodotus) by Lydian mercenaries. This date synchronizes with Ashurbanipal's trouble with his brother in Babylonia. At best or at worst, Assyria left Egypt never to return. While the dates are not exactly fixed, the general order of events is known. Somewhere about 648 B. C., according to the Chronicler, Ashurbanipal, for some unknown reason, but possibly Manasseh's sympathy with Shamash-shum-ukin, and all other western rebels against Nineveh, carried the king of Judah captive to Babylon. Upon his penitence and sworn loyalty to Ashurbanipal, as he had done with Necho of Egypt so he did with Manasseh, and returned him to his throne. How much of a rôle Judah played in a military way against any possible encroachment from Egypt, we do not know. Nevertheless, he stood in the way of Egypt's advance into Syria.

Both Esarhaddon and Ashurbanipal probably carried away large numbers of Jewish captives, for they both imported colonists into Palestine (Ezra 4:2, 10) to fill up the country.

228. Kings Manasseh and Amon (2 Kings 21; 2 Chron. 33). Manasseh's half-century of pagan propaganda ceased at his captivity, according to the Chronicler, which is not at all incredible. On his return, he embraced Jehovah as his God, thrust out the foreign gods which he had installed in the sacred precincts, built up the altar of Jehovah and offered sacrifices thereon. His religious activity carried along with it certain military precautions, such as the strengthening of the outer wall of the city of David and building it up to a great height. The fortified cities of Judah were manned with efficient officers, against any possible invasion from Egypt or elsewhere.

With all his energetic attempt at the extirpation of the paganism which he had promoted during the fifty years of his reign, he could not banish two generations of idolaters which he had reared and fostered. He was doubtless accused of being feeble-minded and vacillating when he right-about-faced on his views of worship.

Upon the death of Manasseh, whose rule outstretched all other kings of Israel or Judah, Amon, his twenty-two-year-old son, reigned in his stead. (" Amon " is the name of an Egyptian deity.) This new king, trained in his earlier years to serve the pagan gods of his father, still followed the same road, vying with Manasseh's earlier years. So outraged were his own servants at his conduct, that the very next year they slew him in his own palace. Vengeance on these killers was taken by " the people of the land," who put on the throne Josiah, his eight-year-old son (*cf.* the case of Jehoash, §199).

229. World Events as Josiah Began to Reign. The Assyrian empire which had conquered all southwestern Asia and Egypt was now on the defensive. Babylon, that had intermittently fought for independence had " her foot in the door " against Assyria. Scythia, in the far northeast, was spilling over into Asia Minor and would soon run down the coastal cities toward Egypt. Josiah's little realm was on the outskirts of the waning power of Nineveh. Egypt was turning her longing eyes toward Asia, where she could render military aid against the upstarts at Babylon.

In fact, the entire Near East was groping in the darkness, and dreaming of the outcome of the far-reaching national and international problems that were facing them.

In this period, the prophets occupied a large place in Judah's history,—if not in their lives at that time. Jeremiah, Zephaniah, Nahum, and later, Ezekiel checked up on the life of their times, and have given us a social, political and religious picture of what they saw.

NOTE ON FIG. 10, tailpiece below: Ashurbanipal was the sportsman monarch of Assyria. His chief delight seems to have been lion-hunting. This royal two-wheeled chariot carried four persons, the king, in this instance an archer, a driver, and two attendant lion-fighters armed with spears. The steeds rush ahead at full speed, while the monarch and his attendants shoot or spear the attacking beasts. A dead lioness has fallen behind the chariot while her mate springs at the fighters only to be speared by the aides.

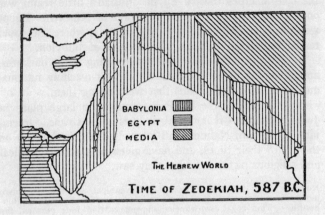

BABYLONIA

EGYPT

MEDIA

THE HEBREW WORLD

TIME OF ZEDEKIAH, 587 B.C.

CHAPTER XXVI

THE TRAGEDIES OF JOSIAH AND HIS SONS

230. Beginning of Josiah's Reign (2 Kings 22:1-7; 2 Chron. 34:1-13). A healthy reaction against the excesses of the idolatrous reigns of Manasseh and Amon began with the coronation of Josiah. Fortunately, the eight-year-old lad had been trained by faithful worshippers of Jehovah and was under their guidance. The regency was also administered by the same loyal parties. When Josiah was twenty-six years of age, he instituted a thorough repair of the temple which had fallen into decay. (The Chronicler credits him with the removal of idolatrous symbols at an earlier age.) Shaphan, the scribe, gave Hilkiah, the priest, and his staff explicit orders about the use of the money col-

NOTE ON MAP 12, headpiece above: Within one generation the world's seat of power passed from Assyria to Babylon. With Egypt on the southwest, Media on the northeast, Babylon was master of the so-called fertile crescent,—from the Persian Gulf northwest to the Mediterranean Sea and down the coast to the borders of Egypt.

lected for the restoration of the house. In the clearing-out process, Hilkiah found a roll of a book in some recess in the house of Jehovah. This was turned over to Shaphan, the scribe, who read it, and took it to the king, before whom he also read it. So distressed was Josiah at its predictions that he rent his clothes. At once he sent an embassy with the scroll to visit Huldah, the prophetess, to ascertain whether its threats regarding the destruction of Jerusalem would be carried out. Her reply was instant and affirmative, with the reasons therefor. But the humility of the king would defer such a disaster until after his days.

Josiah was so agitated over the warnings and threats of the book, and over present moral and religious conditions, that he summoned a general assembly of the priests, the prophets, and the people both small and great. " And he read in their ears all the words of the book of the covenant which was found in the house of Jehovah " (2 Kings 23:2). In the presence of all the assembly, the king covenanted with Jehovah to carry out all the requirements of the book, and the people " stood to the covenant."

231. Josiah's Drastic Reforms (2 Kings 22:8–23:30; 2 Chron. 34:14–35:27). In the year 626 B. C., Jeremiah began his activity as a prophet, picturing (chaps. 2–6) with wonderful realism the enemy from the north, presumably the Scythians (635–625 B. C.). In 621 B. C., " The book of the law," probably Deuteronomy, was discovered in the débris of the long-neglected temple. Jeremiah may have been one of the right-hand supporters of Josiah in the general assembly, where the covenant of faithfulness was made, but we are ignorant on that point.

The enthusiasm was so sincere and deep-seated that, when the assembly broke up, the priests and people went out to enforce the law and began a regular " clean up " of the pagan symbols of worship. Out of the very temple of Jehovah itself they dragged the Asherah, the vessels of Baal, and the host of heaven, and burned them in the valley of Kidron, and polluted their ashes by scattering them over graves. Graven and molten images of all kinds, sun images, bronze horses and chariots of the sun, were all ground to powder.

Even the places of worship, the high places throughout the land, Tophet, the sodomite centres, the altars of Ahaz on housetops, those of Manasseh in the house of Jehovah, the Solomonic high places, and those of Jeroboam the son of Nebat at Bethel, and others in Samaria, Simeon, and Naphtali, were not only pulled down but desecrated and destroyed.

And, most drastic of all, the idolatrous priests in Jerusalem and throughout the land, were slain and even sacrificed on their own altars, to defile them against any further use.

All this reported summary obliteration of paganism was followed by a national, not a family, observance of the passover; more general, more piously observed than any since the time of the judges. With a king zealous for the true God, the priests and the people spared no pains to magnify the occasion with great holocausts of animals in sacrifice and devotion to Jehovah. As a sequel to this festal occasion, the people cleansed the land of necromancers, soothsayers and witches, in accordance with the law now in their hands.

The thoroughness and permanency of these drastic reforms was somewhat discounted by the subsequent life of Judah and her kings. We should keep in mind the fact that Josiah did not destroy or obliterate the common people in whose hearts many of the gods and other symbols were revered and worshipped.

232. The Prophet Zephaniah. About the time of the death of Ashurbanipal (626 B. C.), king of Assyria, Zephaniah spoke his burning words. On behalf of Judah and Jerusalem, Jehovah will punish all iniquity, even the stalking pride of Assyria. Judah's own idolatry and sin would not escape his wrath. The northerners, guests at his banquet, would meet their fate. Only a few penitents, meek and humble, would be saved. Zephaniah fought the social and religious sins of his day, with a fine sense of real moral values. The book winds up with hope for the penitence and conversion of pagans, and joy for the once exiled peoples.

233. Jeremiah the Prophet. Jeremiah had a call in 626 B. C. which he could not ignore. Josiah had been on the throne about twelve or thirteen years. The Scythian hordes presumably were already on the horizon of Judah. Jeremiah's chapters 2–6 seem to see those rough-riders from the north with all their barbarous customs bearing down on southwestern Asia. Incidentally he took the lid off the corruptions and sins of Judah and revealed the cause of the invasion.

The remainder of the book is not arranged chronologically, but is considerably confused in its order. Before attempting to make any historical use of it, the reader should put it into a reasonable time-order.

The character of the messages and the numerous citations, locate all that follows chaps. 1–6 as later than 621 B. C. The laws and ethical codes of Deuteronomy penetrate and colour all the succeeding narratives of the book, both in style and in language. Jeremiah seems to be thoroughly saturated with the spirit and thought of " the book of the law."

Another notable characteristic of the book is its abundance of biographical material. We know more about Jeremiah's personality and character than that of any other prophet. His life was lived in the midst of national and international upheavals, where nation clashed with nation and empires rose and fell.

He was a living protest against the current of Judah's life and trend. He stood adamantine against the apostasy and deceit of his people, against the treachery and faithlessness of his generation. He warned against divine judgment that would certainly overtake and overwhelm his corrupt and sinful people.

234. Shifting Empires. While Josiah was feasting on

the fruits of peace, and Judah was fair and prosperous, the great nations of the earth were fighting for their " place in the sun." Assyria was tottering to her fall, and Egypt was stretching out to her a helping hand. Babylon was rising

Fig. 64. A Brick of Nebuchadrezzar

Most interesting is it that we have a genuine brick not only of the greatest builder in Babylonia, but of the captor and custodian of the Hebrew exiles. His building activity made Babylon famous. The bricks in his walls carried this significant stamp—" Nebuchadrezzar, king of Babylon, supporter of Esagila and Ezida, exalted first-born son of Nabopolassar, king of Babylon."

up in her strength, and Media in the mountains to the northeast was cheering her on. Babylon in the south and the Medes in the north, joined forces to slay the fierce lion of Nahum, the city Nineveh, capital of Assyria.

Egypt diplomatically took sides with Assyria, against the rising Babylon. In 616 she had an army in Syria to encourage Assyria. But in 612 B. C., the forces of Cyaxares the Mede, and the Babylonians under Nabopolassar, surrounded, besieged, captured, and destroyed Nineveh the far-famed, cruel capital of Assyria. Part of the Assyrian army that escaped, fled to Harran in Western Mesopotamia, and made it a temporary capital.

A new king of Egypt, Necho (in 609 B. C.) attracted by the prospects in western Asia, started for Carchemish on the Euphrates to join forces with Assyria against the united Babylonians and Medes. As he was crossing Palestine at the pass of Megiddo, without even stopping to secure its submission, Josiah, in spite of the protests of Necho's peace envoys, marched against him.

Why did Josiah attack him? Was the Judean king favouring Babylonia, as Manasseh had favoured Shamash-shum-ukin, the rebel brother of Ashurbanipal, when the latter carried Manasseh captive to Babylon? How many political parties there were in Jerusalem at this time, we do not know. It may be that when it seemed certain that Assyria would crumble, Josiah favoured that nation nearest him and most powerful of all, viz., Babylon. Or, did Josiah hope in the break-up of Assyria that his kingdom would secure its independence of any outside ruler? At any rate, the best-loved king of Judah, against protest, met the Egyptian archers, who shot him through and killed him. Josiah's body was taken back to Jerusalem where, with genuine sorrow and lamentation, even by Jeremiah, whose praises were not profuse (22:15 ff.), he was buried.

" The people " put Shallum, a younger son of Josiah and his Libnah wife, on the throne,—possibly because of his antipathy to Egypt,—and changed his name to Jehoahaz. Necho had hurried northwards to secure Syria, and made his headquarters in Riblah. For some reason, probably political, at the end of three months he summoned Jehoahaz, the people-appointed king of Judah, to appear before him.

One contact was enough to test the loyalty of the young man. Necho bound him with fetters and sent him to Egypt, whence he never returned (Jer. 22:10). And he put on the throne his older brother, Eliakim (" God establishes "), and changed his name to Jehoiakim (" Jehovah establishes "), thus distinguishing him as king of the people whose God was Jehovah. Evidently he had shown his submissive attitude toward Egypt, and was ready to pay the indemnity which his deposed brother had refused to meet,— about $230,000, exacted from the people of the land as a regular annual tribute. This was a heavy tax on the little realm of Judah. But Jehoiakim's ambition for a palace and court of royal proportions led him to add to the burdens of the already oppressed people. Then Jeremiah's keen sense of right spoke out:

" Woe unto him that buildeth his house by unrighteousness, and his chambers by injustice; that useth his neighbour's service without wages, and giveth him not his hire; that saith, I will build me a wide house and spacious chambers, and cutteth him out windows; and it is ceiled with cedar, and painted with vermilion. Shalt thou reign, because thou strivest to excel in cedar? . . . thine eyes and thy heart are not but for thy covetousness, and for shedding innocent blood, and for oppression, and for violence, to do it " (Jer. 22:13-15).

The gist of this arraignment was that Jehoiakim had built his royal buildings by forced labour, and that he had persecuted and slain innocent persons. Jeremiah's arrest and threatened execution, because he had warned the king and people against trusting in the inviolability of Jerusalem, brought out the fact that a prophet, Uriah, for a similar prophecy, had been forced to flee for his life, and to Egypt he went. But he was pursued, brought back, and slain by the sword of this same Jehoiakim, and " his dead body cast into the graves of the common people " (Jer. 26:20-23).

Jeremiah was already on the same road as Uriah, but the elders of the land came to his aid and rescued him from the bloody gang led by the king.

Necho's presence in the north, and his coalition with the remnant of the Assyrian army at Harran, promised much. But at the great battle of Carchemish (in 605 B. C.), the Chaldeans (Babylonians) under Nebuchadrezzar, son of Nabopolassar the king, were overwhelmingly victorious; and Necho's ambitions in Asia vanished as he was forced to an inglorious retreat and escape to the land of the Nile. The battle of Carchemish fixed the fate of southwestern Asia for nearly a century. All Assyria, Syria and Palestine fell at the feet of the Chaldeans. Nabopolassar having died about the time of the battle of Carchemish, Nebuchadrezzar II returned to Babylon and became the ruler of all those lands (604–561 B. C.).

235. Jehoiakim's Perfidy (2 Kings 23:37–24:6; 2 Chron. 36:5-8). Jehoiakim was put on the throne by Necho of Egypt in 608 B. C. The battle of Carchemish defeated and forced him back to his homeland in 605. Jehoiakim now fell under the suzerainty of the victor of Carchemish, Nebuchadrezzar II. To switch his loyalty so suddenly to a new lord must have aggravated the headstrong youth. Indeed, Jeremiah, chap. 46, adds to the far-reaching effect of the defeat of Necho at Carchemish, by specifying how the vengeance of the day of Jehovah will daze Egypt and Judah for their apostasy. Somewhere about 604 B. C. Jehovah revealed, and Jeremiah dictated to Baruch, his amanuensis, prophecies against Israel, against Judah, and against all the nations. These Jehudi read to Jehoiakim the king, who slashed the scroll with his knife and vengefully threw it into a fire burning before him. Jeremiah again dictated the destroyed prophecies, and " many like words " (36:32) to fill up the gap thus made by the wanton act of the king.

Judah was now free to grow in her own way under the rule of Babylon. Doubtless there were factions as always with differing foreign policies. Some still favoured Egypt, their nearest strong neighbour, while the majority, of course, spoke for Babylon. Finally, at the end of three years, Egyptian influence became so regnant that Jehoiakim cut off his tribute to his new sovereign Nebuchadrezzar. As a punishment, 2 Kings says, Jehovah sent against him guerilla bands of Chaldeans, Aramæans, Moabites, and Ammonites to despoil his land. They overran the country and drove the peasants into the cities. The Septuagint (2 Chron. 35:6) leads us to infer that they had to withdraw from the spoliation of Jehovah's heritage (cf. Jer. 12:7, 17). These marauding bands may have forced the abstemious Rechabites to take refuge within the city walls, where they seem to have been in Jer. 35, when their loyalty was contrasted with the vacillating policy of Judah.

The political situation did not improve, and Nebuchadrezzar dispatched an adequate army to bring Jehoiakim and Judah to terms. In the subsequent siege of the rebel city, the records are not clear as to the fate of Jehoiakim. The Chronicler says that Nebuchadrezzar " bound him in fetters to carry him to Babylon " (2 Chron. 36:6), but does not say that he took him there. Jeremiah (22:19) says, " he shall be buried with the burial of an ass, drawn and cast forth beyond the gates of Jerusalem;" also (36:30) " his dead body shall be cast out in the day to the heat, and in the night to the frost." In other words, Jehoiakim probably was slain in the fighting about the walls during the siege, and was left unburied on the surface of the ground, as would any insignificant animal.

236. Jehoiachin and the First Captivity (2 Kings 24:8-16; 25:27-30; 2 Chron. 36:9, 10; Jer. 22:20-30; chap. 13). Jehoiachin (Coniah), an eighteen-year-old son of Jehoiakim, succeeded him as king of Judah. Three months were enough to try him out. His defiant attitude toward his father's sovereign ruler drew the fire of the Chaldean army, and again it besieged the city. Wise enough to see that resistance was vain, Jehoiachin capitulated, says Josephus (*Antiq.*, x, 7, 1; *Wars*, vi, 2, 1), on condition that the city should be left intact. Then the king, his mother, wives and the royal family, came out to their conquerors. The Chaldeans also took all the princes, the mighty men of valour, even 10,000 captives, and all the craftsmen and the smiths, and led away all of them captive to Babylon (597 B. C.). Among the great men in the list was the prophet Ezekiel. In violation of their promise (in Josephus) they emptied the coffers of the temple and the royal palace, and carried away the golden vessels of Solomon that they found in the temple of Jehovah, to Babylon.

Jeremiah was outspoken in his condemnation of such disloyalty and treason. He called the king a " despised broken vessel," who shall never have a successor on the throne of David (22:28, 30).

Carried to Babylon, Jehoïachin was imprisoned for thirty-seven years, or until the close of the marvellous reign of Nebuchadrezzar II.

237. Zedekiah, Last King of Judah (2 Kings 24:17–25:7; 2 Chron. 36:10-16; Jer. 27–29; 50; 51; 21:1–22:9; 24; 37; 34; 30–33). Mattaniah (" gift of Jah "), full brother of Jehoahaz, with his name changed to Zedekiah (" righteousness of Jah "), was put on the throne in place of his ignominious nephew. He took the usual oath of allegiance to Nebuchadrezzar. But what a motley mob he had to rule! The best and noblest men of the kingdom had been carried off to Babylon, and he, a twenty-one-year-old lad, was chosen to manage those who were not thought valuable enough to carry away. Though himself of royal blood, he was obliged to man his offices with men of the common sort, ignorant, of course, of the policies of government and the problems of state that faced a king in such a country as Palestine. What could a young man, practically alone so far as sane advisers were concerned, do in such a position? Jeremiah was there, but he was unpopular with the idolatrous mob, and hence *persona non grata* with the king and court, though influential in certain ways (Jer. 38:14-28).

Zedekiah's loyalty to Babylon was unquestioned until he gave a favourable reception to envoys from the kings of Edom, Moab, Ammon, Tyre and Sidon (Jer. 27:1-11), whose visit was an appeal to him to join a coalition against Babylon. This royal attention to the young king stimulated his pride, and gave the false prophets a needed persuasive power when they predicted an early release from the yoke of Babylon (as Hananiah, chap. 28). Jeremiah delivered a telling counter (27:12–28:17) to all such unauthorized messages. He also sent a letter to the restless exiles in Babylonia, urging them to settle down and cultivate the land and make permanent homes for themselves, for the time will be long (chap. 29).

Rumour of all these agitations against Babylon must have reached Nebuchadrezzar; for Zedekiah made a trip to Babylon in the fourth year of his reign, to right himself with his sovereign lord. His attendant, Seraiah, chief chamberlain, is said to have taken with him and to have read to some audience Jeremiah's prophecy concerning Babylon, and then to have tied a stone to it and sunken it in the Euphrates (51:59-64). Zedekiah's assertions of loyalty allowed him to return and resume his throne.

Jeremiah's letter to the exiles, and the trip of Zedekiah to the royal court, put a quietus for the time being on the suspicions of Babylon. But the little kingdom of Judah was not in sound health. Its social and religious inheritance was honey-combed with excesses of all kinds. The moral law was violated as a matter of course. A man's word and his oath were strangers to each other. There was no sabbath observance, nor proper service in the temple. Pagan gods and cults flourished in the courts of the house of Jehovah, which even Ezekiel in Babylon saw in a vision and recorded for us in his book (chap. 8). Jeremiah was as frank and outspoken as safety to his life would warrant.

But a new king came to the throne of Egypt, Hophra

(Apries), in 589 B. C. By this time the pro-Egyptian party in Jerusalem got the ear of the king, and he sent " ambassadors into Egypt that they might give him horses and much people " (Ezek. 17:15). An alliance was probably made, as Hophra would be only too willing to join any league against the powerful Babylonian empire. Of course, Zedekiah's next move would be refusal to pay his annual tribute to Babylon. This was done, with the result that the Chaldean army started westward to counter Egypt's intrigues. At some fork of the roads in the trans-Jordanic territory,

Fig. 42. A Sphinx of Hophra (Apries)

In Egypt the sphinx is often a portrait of a king, the lion's body symbolizing the ruler's power. Apries of the twenty-sixth dynasty, was the Hophra (588–569 B. C.) of the Old Testament. He was the coconspirator with Tyre and the Ammonites against the Chaldean Nebuchadrezzar at Babylon. Zedekiah of Judah joined this rebellion and so brought on the siege and destruction of Jerusalem in 588-586 B. C. and the great captivity in Babylonia.

Nebuchadrezzar resorted to divination to see whether he should first strike Rabbah of Ammon or Jerusalem (Ezek. 21:20-22); and the lot fell for Judah and Jerusalem.

238. The Siege of Jerusalem (Jer. 25:8-38; 21:1–22:9; 24; 37; 34; 32–33; 2 Kings 25:1, 2). As the Chaldean army swept down into Judah, it reduced to submission almost all its small cities and towns. Jerusalem was next invested, in the ninth year, the tenth month and the eleventh

Fig. 55. Terra-cotta Model of a Sheep's Liver

This peculiar object is inscribed with omens and magical formulæ. The omens on this model are divided into compartments, prepared for instruction in divination methods in the temple schools. This was found near Baghdad. One of the " close-up " uses of such methods in the Old Testament is attributed to Nebuchadrezzar in Ezek. 21:21—" For the king of Babylon stood at the parting of the way, at the head of the two ways, to use divination: he shook the arrows to and fro, he consulted the teraphim, he looked into the liver." And finally made his charge against Jerusalem.

day, of Nebuchadrezzar's reign. Disloyalty to man and God had brought it on; consequently there would be no averting the certain disaster that had come down like an ominous storm from the north. Isaiah had foretold it to

Hezekiah (2 Kings 20:17); the prophets had forewarned Manasseh (2 Kings 21:10-16) that Jerusalem would not escape; Huldah had predicted its certain downfall (2 Kings 22:16, 17); and Jeremiah had spelled it out to Jehoiakim (Jer. 25:9-11), and now pointed it out to Zedekiah before his very eyes (34:22). Jeremiah advised immediate surrender, but was ignored by Zedekiah, who leaned on the strength of his defences and the help of his Egyptian ally.

As soon as the siege was well under way, the king covenanted with the people to let all Hebrew slaves go free,— either to reduce the number of mouths to be fed, or to win the favour of the prophets and of Jehovah himself (Deut. 15:12-15). Not long after this emancipation agreement went into effect, report came that an oncoming Egyptian army was on the southwestern horizon of the land. Jehovah was thought to come to their relief! The Chaldean army, however, was forced to raise the siege, and to manœuvre to meet and check Hophra's army. Jerusalem, in the meantime, broke into the wildest anticipations of relief. But Jeremiah was on hand to chill any such hope, by a prediction that the Chaldeans would surely return and finish their siege (37:1-10). This warning hurt Jeremiah's standing, for the people wholly ignored it, disregarded their oath to Zedekiah, and hence to God, by seizing the slaves they had set free.

While attempting to pass out of the gate of the city to visit his home-town, Anathoth, Jeremiah was arrested as a deserter, was beaten and imprisoned in the house of the secretary, Jonathan (37:15). In the meantime, the Egyptian army was defeated (Ezek. 30:20 ff.); and the Chaldeans returned and renewed the siege of Jerusalem more vigorously than ever.

Jeremiah sharply arraigned the slave-owners who had violated their oath in seizing the freed slaves. He declared that because they had not proclaimed permanent liberty, every man to his brother and every man to his neighbour, Jehovah would proclaim unto them a liberty " to the sword, to the pestilence and to the famine " (34:17); they would all be delivered to their enemies, and they would burn this city with fire. With such a statement as a background, he urged the populace to surrender and save their lives. Such

Fig. 16. A King Blinding the Eyes of a Prisoner

While Nebuchadrezzar showed forbearance toward the rebellious Hebrews, his patience wore so thin that it snapped at Zedekiah's second revolt. Jerusalem was besieged, captured, and razed to the ground, and the defiant rebel king subjected to the agonies of seeing his own sons slain before him, and then all the earth became dark to him, and he was carried in fetters to Babylon to reflect on his own follies in all the past.

a policy declared openly in the invested city, paralyzed the morale of the defence; and the prophet was arrested and let down into a cistern, into the miry sediment at the bottom (38:1-6). From this exposure he nearly died, but was finally pulled out by a sympathetic Ethiopian slave and his helpers. He was still a prisoner, however, in the court of the guard, where he was fed with the other prisoners of the city.

Zedekiah had about reached the end of his rope, when again he sent for Jeremiah, to inquire of him. The prophet, however, extracted a secret promise from the king that he would not put him to death, nor turn him over to others who were seeking his life. Jeremiah then let loose his reserves on Zedekiah. He advised him to capitulate to the Chaldeans, and save his life and the city from destruction. Zedekiah professed fear that the Hebrews who had deserted would " mock " him. Jeremiah, with the sharpest language, cut away every excuse he mustered, and pictured the awful disaster that should befall himself, the inhabitants and the city. With not a word to say in self-defense, Zedekiah requested Jeremiah, for his life, to keep this interview strictly confidential (38:24-27). And he did.

239. Downfall and Destruction of Jerusalem (2 Kings 25:3-12; 2 Chron. 36:17-21; Jer. 39:2-18). Many of the people had probably taken Jeremiah's advice, had quietly slipped out of the city under cover of night to escape the sharp tooth of famine and to save their own lives. The desperation of the king and his princes is reflected in their later interviews with the prophet. The certainty of the end, with every thud of battering-rams against the walls, was cumulative. In the eleventh year, fourth month and ninth day (about July, 586 B. C.), a breach was made in the north wall (Jer. 39:2), through which the Chaldeans rushed in. The king, his family and body-guard, made good their escape by night out of the lower part of the city, and struck for the Jordan,—thinking to cross over to the highlands of Gilead, and there set up their government, as had Ishbosheth (2 Sam. 2:8 ff.), and possibly David (2 Sam. 17:24-29); or, to reach Rabbah of Ammon, which was also rebelling against the Chaldeans (Ezek. 21:20-22). But the enemy was too quick for them, and overtook them in the plains of Jericho, and led them north to Riblah on the Orontes River, headquarters of Nebuchadrezzar. There

Zedekiah saw the king of Babylon with his own eyes, saw his own sons killed;—after which he was blinded, and was carried a prisoner to Babylon, which he never did see (Ezek. 12:13). This third son of Josiah fared no better than his older brothers,—each tragically winding up an ignominious career (cf. Ezek. 19).

To wipe out any possibility of a new rebellion of Jerusalem, seventy-three outstanding citizens were taken to Riblah and slain in the presence of the king of Babylon (Jer. 52:24-27). The inhabitants of Jerusalem were then taken captive, and formally brought before officials at Ramah to determine the grade of punishment to be meted out to each before they should start on their long march to Babylonia. The prophet Jeremiah also was found bound among the captives. He was quickly recognized as a long-heralded friend of the Chaldeans, and was given his choice, either to go to Babylon or to remain in his homeland. He chose to remain with the poor Jews in Palestine.

In about one month after the surrender of the city, Nebuchadrezzar issued his orders for its systematic plundering and destruction. The Chaldean army looted it of everything valuable, from the bronze metal in the palaces to the sacred vessels in the house of Jehovah. Then they set fire to the royal palace, the temple of Jehovah, all the public buildings and many private dwellings. They pried over the walls and fortifications to prevent another similar revolt in this former strong centre of wealth and power. They carried into captivity somewhere about 25,000 persons, mostly inhabitants of Jerusalem; but for their own protection and the good of the land, the Chaldeans left the poorest people on the soil, whose part in any uprising would be minor and negligible (2 Kings 25:12).

Here endeth the kingdom of Judah, the city of David, the Jewish nation as a separate entity, the temple-centre of Jehovah worship, and a specified land as the home of the chosen people Israel. But Jeremiah's prophecies not only pictured the calamities that overtook the rebellious, but saw also the gleams of a brighter day; when out of its ashes and out of its ruins there would rise a new age, when Israel would come to herself and again follow and worship the true God.

NOTE ON FIG. 25, tailpiece below: The thoroughness with which the Assyrian and Babylonian armies razed their captured cities was the tragedy of ancient warfare. Nebuchadrezzar's final capture of Jerusalem (586 B. C.) was simply the first step to its destruction. Plunder, burning and demolition of the walls and battlements followed in regular succession. With picks, axes, and bars they rarely left one stone remain on another. In the meantime the victors piled up their loot and feasted on the abundance of their finds.

PERIOD VIII

THE EXILES

*From the Fall of Jerusalem to the Fall of Babylon
(586–538 B. C.)*

CHAPTER XXVII

PROPHETS IN THE EXILE

240. A Jewish Babylonian Colony (2 Kings 25:22-26; Jer. 40–44; Ezek. 36). The policy of leaving the Jewish peasants on the soil shows that Nebuchadrezzar was conciliatory toward the innocent poor population of the former kingdom of Judah; and to protect them he appointed

NOTE ON FIG. 65; headpiece above: No portrait of Nebuchadrezzar has been found among his records. This cameo was certainly prepared under Greek auspices, at a very much later date, but its inscription is good Babylonian, and easily legible as the name of that greatest ruler in the Neo-Babylonian empire. It reads: "To Marduk, his lord, Nebuchadrezzar king of Babylon, for his life has given (devoted) this."

Gedaliah, whose father was a friend of Jeremiah in the days of Josiah (Jer. 40:1-6), as governor,—even before the liberation of Jeremiah. This was a wise choice of ·a native, rather than a Chaldean. Gedaliah made Mizpah (*Nebi-Samwîl*) his capital city, a high point about six miles northwest of Jerusalem. Jeremiah was his counsellor; and Gedaliah wisely advised the guerilla bands and scattered fragments of the Judean army, still at large, to swear loyalty to the Chaldeans. Refugees returned from other countries round about, as Moab and Edom, and at Gedaliah's encouragement settled down and cultivated the soil. This was apparently an attempt to re-establish on their homeland, under the surveillance of Babylon, a unified, industrious, agricultural Jewish colony.

Better times flourished for a while. But ambition and intrigue mixed in improper proportions forecast disaster. Claimants to royal blood appeared way over in the country of Ammon. They told their secret to Baalis, king of that people, who was only too ready to aid in his own interests in some plot to dispose of the upstart Gedaliah west of the Jordan. Gedaliah was warned of that intrigue, but generously discounted its danger. Johanan, an officer of Gedaliah, sought permission to slay the plotter, lest the little community established around the governor at Mizpah should be broken up and scattered. But the amiable Gedaliah not only refused to believe it, but told Johanan that he lied about Ishmael's intentions.

On the third day of the seventh month (581 B. C.), Ishmael and his co-conspirators, armed to the teeth, came to Mizpah and murdered Governor Gedaliah and all the Jews and Chaldeans that were with him. Two days later, these same assassins treacherously slaughtered seventy men from Shechem, Shiloh, and Samaria. Not able longer to conceal their atrocities at Mizpah, the assassins attempted to carry off the " king's daughters and all the people that remained in Mizpah with Gedaliah;" but Johanan, the chief officer, was hot on their trail, and rescued all the victims;—only

Ishmael and eight of his accomplices escaping to their Ammonite asylum.

This awful disaster gave the little colony a severe case of heart-attack. Nebuchadrezzar certainly could not overlook the slaughter in cold blood of Chaldean soldiers. Indeed, it seemed to the colonists that their future was doomed, and the only safety from the vengeance of the Chaldeans was flight to Egypt. Jeremiah's advice and prophecies were against any such refuge, but the leaders took the old prophet and Baruch, his scribe, with them, and a considerable company of Jews, to Tahpanhes, a border town in Egypt where foreigners were a common sight. But Jeremiah could not be silenced. Even here he told his fellow-refugees and other Jews that they would not escape Nebuchadrezzar, for he would pitch his tent before Pharaoh's palace in that very town. He was disheartened to see how thoughtlessly the Jews in Egypt turned Jehovah out of their hearts for the gods of Egypt. Even the " queen of heaven " (Astarte) sat on the throne of their affections, and was the chief concern of their worship. Jeremiah's last sad utterances and sharp censures were aimed at the apostasies which the Jewish refugees and exiles in Egypt had accepted and adopted.

Jeremiah was last heard of in Egypt. Tradition has reported him either as stoned to death by his own people in that land, or as carried off to Babylon, where he disappeared from history.

241. Jeremiah in the Decline and Fall of Judah. The chief figure in the last half-century of the kingdom of Judah's existence was Jeremiah. As prophet, patriot and statesman, he stood head and shoulders above every man in that epoch. With unerring aim he hit the target with his messages of God and right. With unswerving will-power he stood by the policy of faith in, and faithfulness toward, all oaths made with man or God. With a prophetic vision of national and international questions, he was a wise friend and counsellor of kings and potentates.

Behind and beneath all stability and prosperity, he saw

religion linked with high standards of morality and integrity. Fighting against laxness and weakness, he pointed out the value of constancy and strength. Unpopular and persecuted though he was, his God-given sense of duty and precaution for his own safety carried him through all the crises and disasters of the final years of the kingdom of Judah. The deprivations of his private life, without home or family, and the head-winds which he encountered in all his public career, made his life from beginning to end a series of martyrdoms. No great prophet ever embodied in his character more elements of self-sacrifice and service under the same cross-fire of public opinion.

Retrospectively, Jeremiah's person and importance in the age he served shine out brighter and fairer with each new ray of contemporaneous light. His zeal for the true God, and his hatred of pagan idols and other symbols of apostate worship, are the two hemispheres of a well-rounded godlike character.

242. Ezekiel, Prophet to the Exiles (Ezek. 1–24). Ezekiel was carried away with Jehoiachin by the Chaldeans in 597 B. C., in the first captivity. He had grown up in Jerusalem as a priest and had become familiar with the service at the temple of Jehovah, and of course, saw everything with the eye of a priest. His location in exile was with the Jews on the river Chebar, where, in 591 B. C., he received his vision and call to prophesy (1:1–3:21) and to lead his people in their thought and worship. He was a meditative and quiet figure, a student, and man of the people. He was well posted in the events of his day, and in the problems that faced his own fellow-exiles. He was familiar with the past history of the Jews, and with the writings of those who had preserved it. With all this background, he uttered and probably wrote the first twenty-four chapters,—first half of his book,—before the fall of Jerusalem. He taught by example, by symbolism, by parable; some of his lessons were acted out by himself in the presence of a wondering audience. But his preaching was to individuals, privately, or by written word. He tackled many of the same problems as Jeremiah, his contemporary, though neither of them ever recognized or acknowledged in his book the words or the existence of the other.

243. The Exile in Retrospect. Warnings, threats and predictions had portrayed the exile in Babylonia, from Isaiah down to Jeremiah. We can name only a few cases. (1) When Hezekiah had displayed his resources to the envoys of Merodach-baladan of Babylon, Isaiah told him definitely that all his stores of valuables would be carried to Babylon, and his sons would be menial servants in the palace of the king of Babylon (2 Kings 20:17, 18). (2) Micah pictured the " daughter of Zion " as going to Babylon (4:10). (3) Jeremiah forewarned the vacillating Zedekiah of his capture and deportation to Babylon (34:2, 3), where his people would serve the king of Babylon seventy years (25:11).

The captivities which recruited Jews for the Babylonian exile are rather confusing in their reported numbers. The writer of Daniel (1:1, 2) gives the impression that the four " children of Israel " in the court of the king of Babylon were carried away in the third year of Jehoiakim, —to such a captivity at that time no other reference is found.

In the seventh year of Nebuchadrezzar (597 B. C.) he carried off 3,023 persons (Jer. 52:28). The narrative in 2 Kings (24:10-16) names the round number 10,000 carried to Babylon with the young king, Jehoiachin. After the fall of Jerusalem, neither the Kings record (25:11) nor Jeremiah (39:8-10) names any special number of captives; but the supplementary section of Jeremiah (52:29) gives 832 persons. Five years after the fall of Jerusalem, in his twenty-third year, Nebuchadrezzar carried away 745 persons,—possibly a kind of aftermath of the confusion following the killing of Governor Gedaliah. As an indication of the mechanical character of this supplemental record, the compiler properly totalled the whole as 4,600,—leaving entirely out of account the 10,000 mentioned in 2 Kings (24:14).

Various methods have been devised to harmonize these irregularities; but for the present, the most that we can say is that usually such numbers are those of heads of families, —non-dependents. Such a method of calculation, based on the genuineness of each of the numbers given in these instances, would place the number of persons who went into the Babylonian exile at the different periods (597–581 B. C.) as somewhere in the neighbourhood of 50,000 persons.

244. The New Babylonian (Chaldean) Empire. The original home of the Chaldeans was on the shores of the Persian Gulf. For more than a century they had intermittently seized the throne of Babylon, and held it until driven back to their swamps in the south. But when the Assyrian empire began to wane, these sea-peoples saw their chance. In 625 B. C., under the leadership of Nabopolassar, they again seized the capital city of Babylonia and became independent. At the fall of Nineveh, in 612 B. C., and of Carchemish, in 605 B. C., they became the masters of the Tigris-Euphrates basin and of all the territory west to the Mediterranean Sea. This was practically the compass of the Neo-Babylonian Empire when the Jews were carried into captivity, 597–581 B. C.

After Nebuchadrezzar had effectually disposed of the Jewish nation, in 586 B. C., by their captivity following the destruction of Jerusalem, he turned next to Tyre. At the end of thirteen years' siege (586–573 B. C.), whose details are not known (Ezek. 29:18), that proud city succumbed and became with all the surrounding district his subjects. Babylonian contract tablets written in Tyre itself give us positive evidence thereof.

245. The Exiles at Home. A careful reading of the narratives that describe the different captivities brings out the fact that the best of the population only was regarded as worth leading away as captives. The wealthy, the political leaders, and the skilled artisans were transplanted into the home country of their new lord.

The Tigris-Euphrates valley is one of the richest agricultural regions of the world. The two great rivers furnished an abundance of water for an extensive irrigation system that supplied water both for the crops and for the cities, and also for an adequate net-work of canals for transportation of persons and products between the cities which dotted this notable valley. The so-called river Chebar (*Kabaru*), mentioned so often in Ezekiel, was one of those navigable canals between Babylon and the city of Nippur, so extensively excavated by the University of Pennsylvania. Down into this rich valley were led the Jewish captives, and settled on soil that yielded many fold larger crops than the rocky hills of Palestine. With their families and religious organization practically intact, they should have been content. But false prophets harangued them, and agitators berated them, saying that in two years more they would go back to their beloved homeland. Jeremiah (chap. 29) sent them a letter advising them to be content and settle down, cultivate the soil, build up families, and seek the peace of the city whither they were carried captive, for there would be no return until the completion of the seventy years.

The monarch of Babylonia, during about the first half of the seventy years of the exile, was Nebuchadrezzer (604–561 B. c.); and his generous attitude toward the exiles was a large element in their increasing contentment in this rich land. The exiles apparently were permitted to live in groups at certain places distributed among the native population, such as at Tel-melah (" hill of salt "), Tel-harsha (" hill of forest "), Cherub, Addan and Immer (Neh. 7:61). Some of these may have been villages built on knolls, safe above the inundations which sometimes covered the flat lands. From such centres they went out by day to work on their fields and returned at night. Whether they paid the government taxes, or worked by relays on royal undertakings, we do not know. They must have satisfied the government, otherwise they would not have been permitted the freedom of worship and trade which they enjoyed.

246. The Exiles, their Social and Religious Status.
The social standing of the exiles probably depended in the first instance on their former attitude toward the Chaldean government. For example, the captured Hebrew king, Jehoiachin, was thrust into a Babylonian prison where he spent thirty-seven years. On the other hand, Daniel (1:19-21) probably gives a true picture of the favour at court with which some of the brightest Jewish youths were received and treated. Between these two extremes are to be found the great body of the exiles. Jeremiah's letter (chap. 29) to the restless captives implies that they had among themselves every facility for contentment and prosperity if they really settled down and carried on the normal activities of life. Some of them suffered; and, under their enforced absence from Jerusalem, seem to be recorded in such exilic utterances as " O thou afflicted, tossed with tempest, and not comforted " (Isa. 54:11). The earlier Hebrew organization, with its elders as heads of communities, seems to have been everywhere prevalent, especially during Ezekiel's activity and under the reign of Nebuchadrezzar (Ezek. 8:1; 14:1-4; 20:1). These tribal and family relations were maintained apparently without any local restraint by the government.

The exiles carried with them into Babylonia many of the beliefs and practices which Jeremiah and other prophets had so severely condemned (Ezek. 20:30-39). False prophets were also active and persistent in keeping the Jews in a ferment about their future. How far they may have also gone in adopting Babylonian divinities we do not know. But their former tendency to take up with every new form of worship, would lead us to expect a considerable lapse in that direction.

But the presence, among these away-from-home Jews, of such a character as Ezekiel, modest though he was, must have put a check on the excesses of the careless, helped the wavering to stand firm in their trust in Jehovah, and inspired the faithful to do larger service in behalf of the integrity and right-living of their fellow-exiles.

The everyday lives of such men as Ezekiel and other contemporary prophets, and later of Zerubbabel and Joshua, and later still, of Ezra and Nehemiah, were to the exiles wholesome and shining examples of righteous living. It was just such men as these who preserved the nucleus of the true worship, brought about the returns from exile, and restored true religion at Jerusalem.

247. The New Big World of the Jews. From the tiny little province of Judah, the captives were carried down into the great Babylonian empire. From a merely local, provincial view of state affairs, they were now face to face with an imperial government at work. The chief officials, who had existed in imagination only, were now flesh-and-blood men. The great system of irrigation, of water-transportation, of municipal expansion, opened their eyes. The tremendous city of Babylon grew before them to be the real centre of the political and cultural world. Its temples, palaces, and defiant walls stood out in all their glory before the end of Nebuchadrezzar's reign. In utter amazement and expansion of ideas, the Jews' conception of government and authority stretched to proportions never before imagined. Great armies and royal pageants gave them an idea of the magnitude of a full-fledged empire, which controlled the destinies of hundreds of thousands of the human race. The provisions made for the welfare of all the people were on a scale that staggered their thought. And some of them began to act and to think in terms of a big world.

The opportunities for commerce and for piling up wealth appealed to their cupidity. The advantages of living in great cities, and of enjoying the cultural facilities of its schools and entertainments, soon captured some of their keenest minds. In fact, the lure of all these new mines of wealth gripped some of the exiles so firmly that they soon forgot the poor little stony hills of Judah. They were almost another people before the seventy years rolled around, when they were given the privilege of returning to the ruins of their former beloved Jerusalem.

248. Ezekiel, and the Religious Gain of the Jews. Ezekiel was the star figure of the exile. He was the quiet pastor, the unassuming guide and counsellor of the Jews. He stood as guard against the encroachments of the subtle paganism of the Babylonians. He stood as sponsor for the faith of the Jews in their God, Jehovah. He recognized the necessity for Judah's punishment, denounced the misleading prophets of falsehood, and warned the remnant in Judea that they must not look for an early release from the yoke of Babylon. He taught the exiles that they were not suffering for the sins of others, but that each one was personally responsible for his own evil deeds (chap. 18).

More than that, he gave them heart by promising a time when they would be restored to their former homeland with renewed spirits and a new faith in Jehovah.

Ezekiel was so intimately bound up with the religious life of the exiles that he may be credited in part with their new conception of Jehovah their God. While they were in Palestine, Jehovah was regarded as their local, provincial God (2 Kings 5:17), limited in his power and influence to their homeland (2 Kings 17:25-28). Now that they were carried off into a faraway land, they were taught that he was with them if they were true to him; in other words, he was more than a local God, he was the God of the Jews, wherever they were. This new conception was commensurate with that of their larger thought of the physical and political world. With Ezekiel's and other prophetic teachings under these Babylonian skies, Jehovah gradually became the God not simply of the Jews, but of the nations associated with them, and then of all mankind. Their early national divinity had now acquired international significance, in short, had become the God of all the earth.

This new world-view of their God sank into the hearts of

the most thoughtful of the exiles. Under Ezekiel's instruction, they realized their duty so to act as to exemplify the highest standards of religious living in the presence of the debasing forms of paganism that flourished in Babylonia. Of course, only a precious nucleus of the masses of exiles in Babylonia reached these lofty conceptions. But these are the faithful few who kept alive and propagated the true faith, that later gave to us the purified and spiritual Judaism which prevailed in the pre-Christian centuries.

249. Ezekiel's Ideal Temple and State (Ezekiel 40–48). The temple of Jehovah in Jerusalem had been destroyed by the Chaldean army in 586 B. C. Its elaborate ritual service, including sacrifices, had gone down at the same time. The exiles who missed them, had to content themselves with the merest fragments of the sacred service, perhaps with nothing more than a reading out of some of the sacred books rescued at that time. Gradually, such faithful souls as Ezekiel and his helpers did what they could to supply the spiritual needs of these sorrowing exiles. Elders and heads of the fathers' houses, priests and Levites, singers and poets,—all contributed to fill up the vacancy made by the absence of the facilities for worship wiped out in 586 B. C.

So indelibly was affection for the destroyed temple and its services stamped on the hearts of the pious exiles during Ezekiel's activity (591–570 B. C.), that the prophet made a new venture. His conception of Israel's real needs and how they could be met, shaped themselves in his mind as an ideal temple and state (chapters 40–48). The boldness of the plan, and its comprehensiveness, challenged the thought of the ripest religious teachers of later days.

Ezekiel gives specifications for the details of a temple to be built on the old site. It was more than a temple. It carried with it a body of land, the whole to be devoted to the promotion of holy living. The temple and the civil state were to be separated. The officials of the temple were independent of civil authority, and carried out an exact specified ritual. The sanctity of the sacred courts barred the people and the civil ruler from any intrusion therein. This inaugurated a new and more strictly official and ritualistic worship. The ordinary worshipper would merely look on while the proper officer carried out the new and exclusive forms. This method prevented the familiar religious freedom of earlier days (1 Sam. 2:12-17; 9:12-14; Deut. 12:13, 14, 27), wherein desecration and personal punishment resulted (2 Chron. 26:16-21). Former minor priests in small places would become Levites in the new temple, while the priesthood proper would consist only of the family of Zadok (Ezek. 44:10-16).

Ezekiel laid down principles that guided the adjusters of the Levitical code. Out of his strict rules grew up the later Judaism that had such a large influence in the religion of the later pre-Christian centuries. His dreams were, however, too ideal for any full realization, either in the immediately succeeding centuries, or in the Herodian temple, though the strict ritualistic forms took deep root.

250. Some Literary Products of the Exile. The entire book of Ezekiel was most probably spoken, and written down, in the empire of Babylon by the prophet himself. Scribes and annalists were also among the exiles, who credibly took with them to Babylonia what manuscripts they saved from the wreckage of Jerusalem. How many and what other prophets and writers there may have been among them we have no means of knowing. Babylonian writers and writings must have been a stimulus to the trained and educated Jews of that period,—so much so that the Jews gathered up and put into permanent historical form the rolls of Hebrew annals which they had in their possession. They were now far enough away from the actual events to appreciate their religious and moral value for the history of their people. It is now generally thought that these careful religious men put their final touches on Judges, Samuel, and Kings while they were exiled in that strange land. These stories, royal annals, and snatches of poetry were so interwoven as to teach Israel the real lessons of her past. Their present exilic condition was shown by their records to be the result of forgetting Jehovah and bowing down to strange gods. The book of Deuteronomy which was found in the temple in Josiah's day (621 B. C.) had a profound influence on the compilation of the books of Kings, as the style, the phrases, and the seriousness of the effort deeply impress the reader.

Another piece of exilic compilation was the gathering into final form of the scattered groups of laws and ordinances touching temple worship. These were mainly earlier laws which were now put in shape for use in ceremony, ordinance, and worship, and are found in Leviticus 17–26, sometimes called the " holiness code."

251. Chaldean Kings after Nebuchadrezzar. Nebuchadrezzar died (561 B. C.) after a brilliant reign of forty-three years of marvellous prosperity. His son and successor, Evil-merodach (*Amel-Marduk*), opened the prison doors to Jehoiachin, former king of Judah, who had been confined for thirty-seven years, and promoted him above all the other rebellious kings kept at Babylon (2 Kings 25:27-30). After about three years of reign, the dissipated Evil-merodach was murdered by his brother-in-law, Neriglissar (Nergal-sharezer), who was probably one of the staff officers at the fall of Jerusalem (Jer. 39:3, 13). Neriglissar's successful reign ended in 556 B. C., when his infant son, Labashi-Marduk, nominally became king. In nine months he was deposed by the priestly party, who put on the throne Nabonidus (*Nabu-na'id*) (556–538 B. C.), a Babylonian of priestly descent.

By his own claims he had been a successful officer in the army of Babylon, and for that reason " Marduk promoted him to sovereignty over the nation." He was an enthusiastic antiquarian, and a devotee of some special gods. For example, he built elaborate temples in Ur and Harran to the god Sin. His reign saw some unrest in the West, where, however, he maintained loyalty well through his seventeen years of reign. So devoted was he to pious religious activities, that the actual administration of his kingdom seems sometime during his career to have been turned over to his son Belshazzar, who plays such a rôle in the book of Daniel, and is called " king " in chapter 5.

NOTE ON FIG. 50, tailpiece below: When Sennacherib had stormed and captured Lachish, he sitting on a throne, received the humiliated captives, and assigned each to his fate. Multiply this face by thousands you have the physiognomy and numbers of the exiles who were the wards of Nebuchadrezzar and his successors in the Babylonian valley between 586 and 538 B. C.

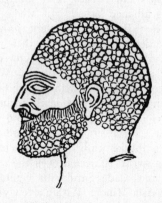

CHAPTER XXVIII

RESCUE FOR THE EXILES

252. The Rise of Cyrus. Nebuchadrezzar's remarkable reign owed its peaceful character largely to an alliance made between himself, Cyaxares of Media, and Alyattes of Lydia. Soon after his death, and during the reign of Nabonidus, this alliance lapsed. In Media, Astyages succeeded Cyaxares. In a northwestern province of Elam called Anshan, a dependency of Media, there appeared above the horizon, in 559 B. C., a new character of royal blood, Cyrus by name, about thirty years of age. Within ten years he became king of all Media, with his capital at Ecbatana, in the Zagros mountains. His domain included all Persia, the north Babylonian valley, Armenia and Asia Minor to the Halys River. His liberal policy toward all his subjects enlisted them enthusiastically under his banner. Across western Asia he swept, subjected even the reputed wealthy King Crœsus, and made Sardis his capital, as his own headquarters in Asia Minor. Within a few years he reduced all the Greek provinces, to the Ægean Sea, thus making him king from the river Indus in the East, to the Greek Sea in the West.

With all that territory under his sway, he had practically

NOTE ON FIG. 20A, headpiece above: This reproduces the text of Cyrus' own inscription, giving his name and only one part of his title, the most important one at this juncture of the history—king of the newly captured metropolis of the world, Babylon.

isolated the chief city of southwestern Asia,—the Chaldean capital, Babylon.

253. Events Focussing Deliverance (Isaiah 13:1–14:23; 21:9, 10; 41:1-7; 42:1-4; 44:28; 45:1-7, etc.). Some prophet or prophets among the exiles saw in the trend of national events the approaching end of the exile; and also saw the leader who should be the " shepherd " and " anointed of Jehovah." Cyrus is named twice in Isaiah (44:28 and 45:1) as the chosen of Jehovah. The overthrow of Babylon had been forecast in Isaiah (13:1–14:23) and Jeremiah (25:12; 28:4, 11; chaps. 50 and 51), as a time when the exiles would be free to return to their ancestral home to serve Jehovah on consecrated sites and soil.

The book of Daniel points back to this epoch, when the entire royal house was put to the test of its efficiency and endurance. However confused the writer may have been in his chronology and racial relations, he doubtless gives a reliable picture of the superstitious hauntings that trailed every public officer in those days.

NOTE ON FIG. 20B, tailpiece below: To make Cyrus' title more comprehensive, he here announces himself king of all Babylonia, under the terms Shumer (South) and Akkad (North) Babylonia (from his cylinder inscription).

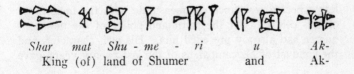

Shar	mat	Shu - me - ri	u	Ak-
King	(of)	land of Shumer	and	Ak-

ka - di - i
kad

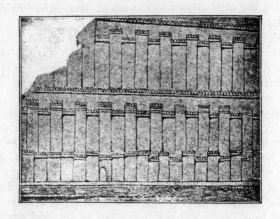

PERIOD IX

THE RETURNS

From Zerubbabel to Nehemiah (538–432 B. C.)

CHAPTER XXIX

Cyrus and the Returned Exiles

254. The Fall of Babylon (538 B. C.). Turning his army toward Babylon, the greatest prize of all, Cyrus doubtless expected resistance commensurate with the importance of this centre. But the spirit and policy of the new conquerer had already preceded him. His own character, and the conduct of his campaigns of the last twenty years, gave

NOTE ON FIG. 13, headpiece above: The last king of Assyria, Ashurbanipal, decorated the walls of his palace at Nineveh with this representation of the walls of Babylon, which he faced when he put down his rebellious brother, Shamash-shum-ukin, about 647 B. C. Note that they appear to have a treble row of battlements exactly as Diodorus Siculus says they were built by the great queen Semiramis.

Fig. 20. A Portrait of Cyrus

A Persian artist has left us a portrait of the first Aryan conqueror of Babylonia. It was set up about 538 B. C. at Cyrus' royal residence at Pasargadæ (Murghab), Persia, after he had taken over the rule of Babylon, including the exiled Jews. His features are those of an Aryan, and the four wings in imitation of the cherubim of Babylonia-Assyria. The crown is Egyptianized.

Cyrus a reputation as a ruler that opened to him the gates
of the enemy. This proved to be literally true in the case
of Babylon. The records of both the reigning king of
Babylon, Nabonidus himself, and of Cyrus' own cylinder,
tell us that the priests of Babylon,—already often offended
by the neglect of their gods by the reigning king,—opened
the gates of that impregnable stronghold and welcomed such
a deliverer and ruler.

Where, when and how the regent Belshazzar was dispatched the inscriptions do not tell us, though the report in
Daniel finds him slain at a royal banquet. But we are informed that King Nabonidus was taken prisoner and
carried away.

Thus Cyrus and his army fell heirs to all the remaining
territory, peoples, and cities of southwestern Asia, without
another stroke.

All that territory now quietly passed from the reign of a
Semitic ruler over to Aryan domination. Really, Semitic
sovereignty had held sway more or less continuously over
all this part of Asia since the days of Hammurabi (2081
B. C.). And for the next thousand years the Aryans kept
it in their grasp.

255. The Policy of Cyrus. Compared with the former
rulers of Babylonia, Cyrus stood alone. He was a master-
mind among men. His skill in controlling them was almost
uncanny. His friendliness, discretion, wisdom, magnanim-
ity, frankness and valour gave him almost magical power
over friend and foe. In addition, he was not only tolerant
of every religious belief, but himself treated them all with
reverent regard, though the Persian god Ahuramazda was
his own true god. In Babylon he revered the god Marduk
and repaired his shrine. Freedom to worship each his own
god, as he chose, gave Cyrus a grip on the various religious
worshippers in all his broad realm.

Babylonia had become rich and powerful through the
scores of thousands of captives and slaves whom Nebuchadrezzar and other rulers had brought in to preserve peace

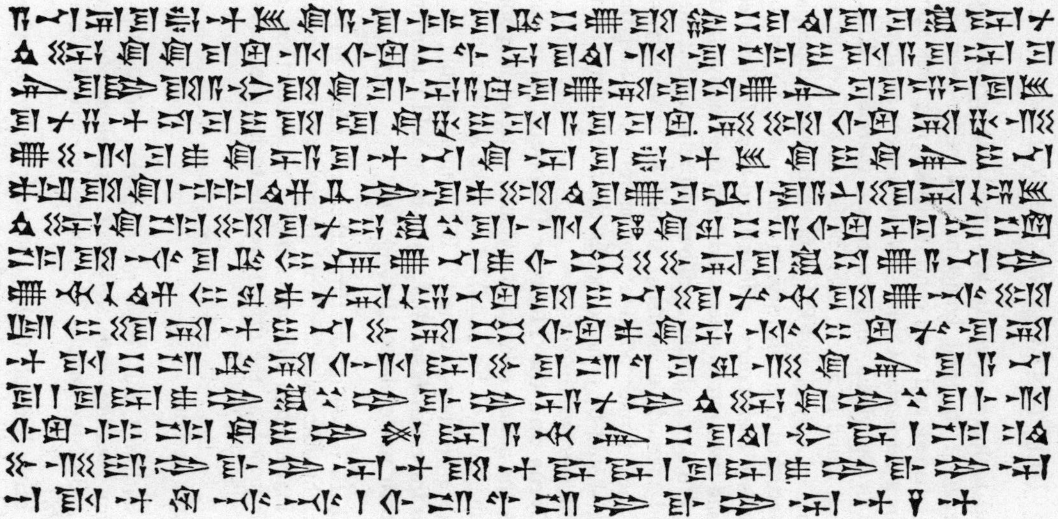

Fig. 19. Cyrus Describes the Capture of Babylon

Cyrus has left us his own record of the fall of Babylon, preserved in the best cuneiform script of that day. He also embodies in the same record his own genealogy, as of noble stock. He claims that he was the man of destiny among those of his day. This inscription covers lines 15–22 of the so-called Cyrus cylinder.

abroad and to increase wealth at home. Many thousands of these exiles from their homeland had never been contented or satisfied, and were continually keeping their communities in a ferment. Cyrus saw the restless aggregation of nations in Babylonia, and the reason therefor. With a daring often found in a new ruler, he issued a novel decree. Where kings of Assyria and Babylonia had deported peoples and often crushed their identity, to bring peace, Cyrus now wholly reversed their policy. He ordered that all those peoples who had been forcibly deported from their native lands, and desired to do so, should be allowed to return; that their deities and methods of worship should be graciously restored to their former position and prominence; and that everything should be done to better their condition and to soothe their sorrows.

256. Cyrus and the Hebrew Prophets. Now that Cyrus was the actual ruler of Babylonia, with all its population in the palm of his hand, let us take a glance at the words of the Hebrew prophets. His coming should be a comfort to the exiles (Isa. 40:1, 2), who should return and build up their waste places (Isa. 44:26).

" Who hath raised up one from the east, whom he hath called in righteousness to his foot? he giveth nations before him, and maketh him rule over kings; he giveth them as dust to his sword, as the driven stubble to his bow " (Isa. 41:2).

And again we find:

" That saith of Cyrus, He is my shepherd, and shall perform all my pleasure, even saying of Jerusalem, She shall be built; and of the temple, Thy foundation shall be laid " (Isa. 44:28).

" Thus saith Jehovah to his anointed, to Cyrus, whose right hand I have holden, to subdue nations before him, and I will loose the loins of kings: to open the doors before him, and the gates shall not be shut. . . . For Jacob my servant's sake, and Israel my chosen, I have called thee by thy name:

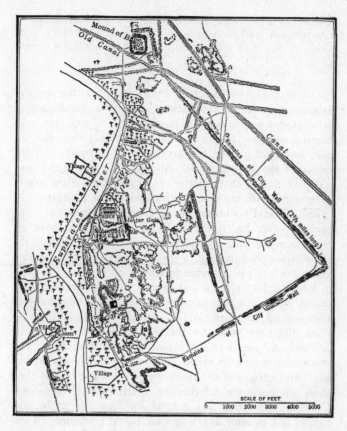

Fig. 12. Plan of Babylon

Babylon was the chief city of Babylonia for long centuries. It stood on both sides of the Euphrates, though mostly on the east. Here Koldewey, the German excavator, uncovered (1899–1913) the Ishtar gate, the procession street, and parts of several palaces and temples. The entire compass of the city was not over twelve miles, less than one-quarter of what Herodotus makes it. The walls probably enclosed parks and pleasure-grounds. Irrigating canals blessed all the landscape.

I have surnamed thee, though thou hast not known me. I am Jehovah, and there is none else: besides me there is no God. I will gird thee, though thou hast not known me" (Isa. 45:1, 4, 5).

Our prophet here names Cyrus specifically as the agent of Jehovah to conquer the nations; not as a worshipper of Jehovah but for his servant Jacob's sake. Cyrus may have heard from some friendly messenger in Babylonia just the part he would play in the overthrow of Babylon, and the rescue of the Jews in exile. At least, the part that Cyrus did play during that quarter-century in the Asiatic world harmonizes with the characterizations of the prophet.

257. The Proclamation of Cyrus (Ezra 1–6). The general policy laid down by Cyrus (§255) must have allowed many deported peoples to return to their homelands. His distinct proclamation to the Jews was issued in the first year (538 B. C.) of his reign as king of all Persia. The copy in Ezra (1:2-4) gives a few only of the specifications contained in the original document. Subsequent references in Ezra (3:2-7; 5:13-16; 6:1-5) reveal the elaborate provisions that were made for the rebuilding of the temple of Jehovah and the re-establishment of worship therein. The proclamation covered exiled Jews in any part of his dominion. And citizens of the realm were also authorized, if they chose, to assist the pilgrims to return to their homeland. Cyrus' proclamation was not wholly unselfish, as he was careful not to omit anything that would contribute to the rapid reclamation of the sparsely occupied Westland, near the border of Egypt, and that would be a possible buffer to any campaign originating with Egypt.

When that proclamation was sounded throughout the empire, it naturally stirred the hearts of the old exiles, the youngest of whom were not less than fifty years old. In addition to these, a new generation and a half had grown up on Babylonian soil, many of whom knew little and cared less about those faroff rocky hillsides of Palestine.

Babylonia was a rich agricultural country, where little work brought large rewards. Trading was attractive and prosperous in and about the great cities. Travel was easy on both water and land, and lent itself to the fancies of pleasure-seekers.

Doubtless many had married Babylonian wives, and *vice versa,* and were held by ties of family to the adopted land of their exile. Most of them had forgotten the worship of Jehovah amid the glories of the temple and ritual of Marduk, the god of Babylon. Prophets, priests, feasts and prayers could not pry them loose from the free, unrestrained life of the Babylonians.

The few religiously patriotic Jews were so scarce that they were called " the remnant,"—the faithful ones who preserved the true worship of their God and became the channel through whom, in later days, some of the truths of Christianity emerged.

258. The Return under Zerubbabel. About 537 B. C., those Jews who responded to the proclamation of Cyrus and could prove their genealogical descent, began their march of eight hundred miles from Babylonia to Jerusalem. They were under the charge of Joshua, the priest, of the house of Zadok, and Zerubbabel, prince of the house of David, and Shesh-bazzar, who was the custodian, on the march, of the sacred vessels of the temple which Nebuchadrezzar had carried to Babylon.

The whole number of returning persons is recited presumably in Ezra (2:64-67), though manuscripts by no means agree; and some suggest that this organized body refers to those who were in the homeland at a later date (Neh. 7:66-69). The Ezra record above mentioned specifies 42,360 Jews, who owned and brought with them 7,337 slaves,—200 of them singers. Four out of twenty-four courses of priests returned,—about 4,000 persons; and seventy-four Levites. Of animals they are said to have had 736 horses, 245 mules, 435 camels and 6,120 asses. Tradition says that this immense caravan was accompanied by a bodyguard of 1,000 cavalry, and that they were four months on the way.

The inspiration which led these pilgrims to take this long, dangerous journey was, (1) the religious impulse, the desire to worship Jehovah on the site of the ancient temple; (2) national pride,—a desire to return to the land of their fathers (though Abraham had migrated from Ur of the Chaldees in lower Babylonia); (3) the local attraction of the far-famed Jerusalem.

But how could such an army of persons subsist through a long journey, and at the end of that journey, until they could be self-supporting in a new country? They were aided by gifts from those who were so minded (Ezra 1:6), and grants by Cyrus the king. He also commanded his provincial heads in the Westland to contribute to their support. The wealthy Jews back in Babylon in a loyalty *in absentia*, also did much to support their own nationals, even though they thought they had gone on a visionary journey and errand to the barren hills of Palestine.

259. Palestine during the Babylonian Exile. The native population of Judah had gone through some radical changes since the captivity of 586 B. C. The territory of Palestine had been left so sparsely occupied that neighbouring peoples gradually flowed in,—peoples who had no love for the native Jewish peasants. Edom always had an envious spirit toward Judah. Ammon absorbed the east of the Jordan (Jer. 49:1), and with Moab, looked down on defeated Judah (Zeph. 2:8). Even the Philistines were no longer their friends (Ezek. 25:15). Ezekiel was well aware of what was taking place when he said (36:3-5):

" Because, even because they have made you desolate and swallowed you up on every side, that ye might be a possession unto the residue of the nations, and ye are taken up in the lips of talkers, and the evil report of the people; therefore, ye mountains of Israel, hear the word of the Lord Jehovah. . . . Surely in the fire of my jealousy have I spoken against the residue of the nations, and against all

Edom, that have appointed my land unto themselves for a possession with the joy of all their heart, with despite of soul, to cast it out for a prey."

Tyre had a selfish interest in Judah, as reflected in Ezekiel (26:2):

" Because that Tyre hath said against Jerusalem, Aha! she is broken that was the gate of the peoples; she is turned unto me; I shall be replenished, now that she is laid waste."

The Israelites always regarded the land as their own possession (Ezek. 11:15), and hence the influx of other peoples was an unwarranted intrusion. The Edomites and other related peoples pushed northward into and through the former abode of Judah toward Jerusalem, so that they seem to be enumerated with the tribe of Judah by the Chronicler (1 Chron. 2:55; 4:42). It may be that pressure from the desert, the later Nabatæans, crowded the surplus population of Edom northwards into the roomy hills of Palestine.

The commingling of the native peasant population with these rougher immigrant peoples of other clans and of the desert, gives us a social and religious status quite inferior to that of the former kingdoms of Israel. Their leaders are not named, but could scarcely have been more than " judges." Jerusalem being in ruins, one city-centre was Mizpah, which had already quivered with tragedy. There were also Bethel, to which a priest of the true God had been brought back (2 Kings 17:28), and Shechem, Shiloh, and Samaria (Jer. 41:5). The conglomerate population of the peoples imported by the Assyrian kings, called Samaritans (2 Kings 17:24; Ezra 4:2, 10), were prominent in the affairs of the land and desired to remain so.

260. Arrival in the Old Homeland. Palestine was now under Persian rule. It was sparsely occupied by the Jews and descendants of the Jews who were too worthless to be carried away in any captivity; and by a mixed population. Into this territory came the long caravan from Babylonia. The returning exiles soon distributed themselves in their ancestral towns, villages, and about Jerusalem.

Those who went up to see the ruins of the holy city were made up of sad-faced exiles, who may have been children about its streets; and have attended worship at Solomon's temple; and of the younger generation which now for the first time saw the masses of débris of the sacred city about which they had heard so much down in Babylonia.

Henceforth the order of events in Ezra, Nehemiah and Esdras is uncertain, and its re-arrangement a dilemma to the ordinary reader. We shall pass by the critical questions as too complicated for this treatment, and follow what seems to be one method at least of regarding the returned exiles in Palestine.

In wandering about the scattered walls and shattered buildings, the old people with tearful eyes crept over the temple court until they reached the original rock of the threshing-floor of Ornan the Jebusite (2 Sam. 24:25), upon which David had offered sacrifices to Jehovah.

To this place the children of Israel gathered as one man; and under the lead of Joshua, repaired the altar in its place, and offered thereon burnt-offerings unto Jehovah morning and evening. The returned orders of priests were installed, regular sacrifices established, and now after a half-century of silence a new relation inaugurated between Jehovah and his faithful worshippers. In addition Ezra (3:4-6) states that the regular feasts were kept, and full service rendered to their God.

261. Beginnings of the Second Temple. Ezra (3:7) states that the returned exiles engaged masons, carpenters, and other workmen, to inaugurate and push the work of building the temple by securing Phœnicians to cut and transport by sea to Joppa cedar timber of Lebanon.

In the second year of their return to their land, the foundations of the temple were laid with great rejoicings, blare of trumpets, and the singing of thanks to Jehovah. But the old men who had seen the first house, wept with a loud voice at the significant contrast between the two.

The foundations had no sooner been laid than an appeal came from the people of the land,—the mixed population already described (§259), " the adversaries of Judah and Benjamin " (Ezra 4:1) who wished to have a share in the new building program. Why not? They were not entirely foreigners, but partly Jewish in descent. Zerubbabel promptly replied, " Ye have nothing to do with us in building a house unto our God; but we ourselves together will build unto Jehovah, the God of Israel, as king Cyrus, the king of Persia, hath commanded us " (Ezra 4:3).

It may be that Zerubbabel and his counsellors remembered that idolatry,—faithlessness toward Jehovah—had been one of the chief causes of the downfall of Judah. To associate with the devotees of the mingled crude worship of the people of the land (2 Kings 17:41) at the very beginning of their construction of the new temple would defile the true worship.

Whether such a refusal were wise or not, it ruptured the friendly relations between the returned exiles and the settled population. With better organization between themselves and their other neighbours, the petitioners set in motion intrigues which obstructed and finally estopped the building program for sixteen years.

262. The Persian Empire's Sway. These were momentous years in the history of the world. Cyrus had closed the last nine years of a brilliant reign, and died in 529 B. C. His son, Cambyses (529–522 B. C.) stretched the boundaries of his father's kingdom to include Egypt (in 525 B. C.). But his reckless, unstatesmanlike treatment of the Egyptians sowed the seeds of dissension and rebellion,— not simply in the Nile lands, but wherever he ruled. His suicide, in 522 B. C., left the kingdom helpless. When Darius was chosen in 521, he found the realm a cyclone of uprisings. To stabilize his claim to the throne, he married Atossa, the daughter of Cyrus. Even with this domestic alliance, he was compelled to fight nine powerful rebels in nineteen battles within the first two years. Fortunately, he was victorious in every case, and the kingdom became firmly established under his rule.

263. The Temple Completed (Ezra 4:7–6:15). Since the hold-up of the building project of the temple, the Jews had spent their time and energy in improving their own conditions. They cultivated the soil, built themselves fine residences, established trade routes and stations, and became thrifty citizens of the land. It may be that some quiet work on the temple had been carried on during these years (Ezra 5:16b); if so, it had made slow progress, and was far from finished.

When the political upheaval in the Persian capital took place (522-21 B. C.), there was a general palpitation of heart throughout the realm; and changes were many and significant. In the second year of Darius (520 B. C.), a simple, quiet, unassuming prophet, Haggai, with a divine urge, prodded the consciences of Zerubbabel and Joshua to drive ahead and finish the temple begun sixteen years before. A young prophet, Zechariah, joined his elder and spoke with telling effect. Jehovah had been angry, but had now returned to his city (Zech. 1:14 f.; 2:1-5 ff.). The work began to go forward. The former antagonists and (or) suspicious Persian officers asked the reason why, to which they replied that Cyrus had given permission and the work had gone along ever since.

Though the Aramaic letters in Ezra are in considerable confusion on the order of events, it seems not unreasonable to present the matter in the following order. Appeal was made by the officer (Tattenai, or Persian, Ushtani) to Darius to search the records and ascertain whether Cyrus had actually decreed the building of the house of God in Jerusalem. Darius ordered a search to be made; and the decree of Cyrus was found in Ecbatana. The edict was re-enacted, and the Persian governor ordered, " hands off! " to all objectors; and more, he gave orders to put at the disposal of the Jews the " king's goods, even of the tribute beyond the River, expenses be given with all diligence unto these men, that they be not hindered." The governor was ordered to supply their needs in animals and other necessities for the temple service (Ezra 6:8-10).

The Persian governor obeyed, and " the elders of the Jews builded and prospered, through the prophesying of Haggai the prophet and Zechariah the son of Iddo. And they builded and finished it . . . on the third day of the month Adar . . . in the sixth year of the reign of Darius (516 B. C.) the king " (Ezra 6:14, 15). The dedication of this house of God with joy took place at once under the supervision of the priests and Levites. Holocausts of sacrifices were made, and the priests and Levites were formally assigned their specified parts in the regular services inaugurated on that day. How far the Jews expected this to be the consummation of their messianic hopes is purely a matter of conjecture. Prophetic hints are too vague to form the basis of any assertion. It is significant, however, that the narrative of the dedication nowhere mentions Zerubbabel, who was of the house of David. He falls out of sight never to appear again. In fact, the land was henceforth ruled by a Persian officer.

264. The Second Temple in Israel's Life. The vacancy of seventy years between the destruction of Solomon's temple (586 B. C.) and the dedication of this second temple (516 B. C.) was a nightmare in the history of the faithful few. In that period they had lived on reminiscences of the old and anticipations of the new house of Jehovah.

Their firm belief in the centralization of worship at Jerusalem had been shattered. Doubtless there had been built in Babylonia temporary shrines or sanctuaries for worship. We know specifically that the Jews at Elephantine, the island in the Nile at the foot of the first cataract in Egypt, had a temple of Yahu as their centre of worship, in this same period. It served the same purpose for this colony that the temple in Jerusalem did now for the newly organized community under Persian rule.

But the name Jerusalem had a peculiar significance to Jews in any part of the world, however negligent they were of real worship of, or devotion to, Jehovah. It suggested the city of their Hebrew fathers, where David ruled and Solomon spoke his words of wisdom. Though most of them, as to-day, were not willing to pull up and return to Palestine, they were quite ready to show their loyalty to their sentimental ideas by contributing gifts to the pilgrims who risked everything to go, and to the feasts they celebrated. Indeed, there grew up a custom among the Jews of making an annual visit to Jerusalem from long distances, to celebrate the chief feasts and to aid in the maintenance of the priesthood, and in the building up of a body of law that formed the backbone of Judaism. The new temple helped to unify all the loyal Jews of the world.

NOTE ON FIG. 22, tailpiece below: A seal cylinder representing Darius king of Persia on a lion hunt, under the protection of his god Ahuramazda, whose symbol hovers above him. The horses are leaping over a dead lioness, while the king is shooting at her furious mate. The inscription is in the three languages of the Behistun Rock—Persian, Susian and Babylonian—and reads: "I am Darius the great king."

CHAPTER XXX

The Judean Colony in the Fifth Century b. c.

265. Persia in the Fifth Century, b. c. The world ruler of the century was Persia. Darius (521–485 b. c.), who helped the Jews finish and dedicate their house of worship, was a wise, benevolent, and ambitious king, able and ready to aid all his willing subjects. His foreign conquests made him master from the Punjab in India to the borders of Thessaly in Europe (though defeated at Marathon in 490 b. c.), and from the Caucasus to Ethiopia in upper Egypt. So successful was he in the organization of his

---

Note on Fig. 23, headpiece above: Darius, son of Hystaspes, was without a peer among Persian kings. His magnanimous treatment of his loyal peoples, his far-flung postal service, his governmental provisions for the benefit of local provinces, and his far-sighted plans for future expansion, gave him a place in the forefront of the kings of ancient days.

realm, that he gave Persia a system of government that made her a flourishing empire for nearly two hundred years.

At his death, in 485 B. C., Darius was succeeded by the son of Atossa, daughter of Cyrus, an appointee of Darius himself, who adopted as his royal name, Xerxes. This new ruler, in full accord with his father's plans, made long and elaborate preparations for punishing Greece. After most spectacular marches, and crossing of the Hellespont, his reputed invincible armies were held up at Thermopylæ, defeated at Salamis, and nearly annihilated at Platæa (479 B. C.). Thereafter, Persia severely let alone the Greeks of Greece to dwell in peace and freedom in their own little realm, including the islands of the Ægean. The last years of Xerxes were drowned in the luxuries and profligacies of his seraglio, where the affairs of state were neglected and forgotten. He was finally assassinated by the captain of his guard and his chamberlain, who put on the throne the royal heir, Artaxerxes, son of Xerxes.

Artaxerxes I (464–424 B. C.) Longimanus ("Longhand") was a ruler with good intentions, but weak in character. His long reign of forty years was a continuous fight against local rebels in all parts of his realm. Megabyzus, satrap of Syria, was over the Jewish colony, whose government he left largely to the high-priest at the temple in Jerusalem.

Artaxerxes is remembered in the Old Testament mainly because of his relations with Nehemiah's return,—and possibly that of Ezra, for he is several times mentioned in the annals of that book. In 424, the "Longhand" king died; and after two assassinations, was succeeded by Darius Nothus (424–405), who ruled nineteen years, fighting against head winds during the entire period.

266. Queen Esther (Esther 1–10). This delightfully written romance, whenever and by whomsoever composed, has its plot laid in Susa (Shushan) in the reign of Ahasuerus (Xerxes). The excavations of the French at Susa since 1878, have uncovered marvellous remains that archæologists have connected with this queen during the Persian domination of that city. The highly dramatic character of the book has associated it in many minds with the best fiction of the late Greek or Maccabæan age. In the light of the Susian excavations, we may study the manners, customs and laws reflected in the book, touching what little we know of Persia in the period of her greatest prosperity.

The drama opens with a six-months' feast given by King Ahasuerus in the third year (483 B. C.) of his reign. From " India to Ethiopia " princes and nobles came in relays,

Fig. 29. Restoration of Esther's Palace So-called

One of the astounding results of French excavations at Susa was the disclosure of the remains of " Shushan the Palace." In this palace of Xerxes (485–465 B. C.), covering two and one-half acres, was found the throne-room, decorated with thirty-six fluted columns sixty-seven feet high, and supporting a flat roof ceiled beneath with cedar of Lebanon. The capitals of the columns were the heads and shoulders of oxen, back to back. The cornice and friezes of the interior were decorated with coloured glazed brick set in the forms of rosettes, soldiers, lions, and other decorative patterns. Queen Esther is thought to have presided here during her sovereignty in Persia.

covering the entire six months, to indulge in the luxuries of the royal board, to inspect the appointments of the imperial court, and to felicitate the king on his munificence and favours towards his subjects. The main purpose of these feasts was probably to counsel with his wisest men regarding another campaign against the Greeks. At the conclusion of these feasts, it was decided to outfit another expedition. In a great seven-day feast given the citizens of Susa, Xerxes became so befuddled with excessive drinking that, contrary to all custom, he ordered his chamberlains to bring in and exhibit to his drunken guests the beauty of his queen Vashti. The queen flatly refused, and the king, by advice of counsel, deposed her from her office, leaving a vacancy in the royal family.

For the next four years, Xerxes was actively engaged in the tremendous overland and sea expeditions against the hated Greeks, who had burned Sardis and otherwise defied the power of Persia. After the disastrous outcome of the entire enterprise at Platæa, in 479 B. C., the defeated monarch returned to his capital, humiliated and dishonoured in the eyes of his realm.

The remaining events in the book of Esther are placed after that defeat. True to his character depicted in Persian history, Xerxes may have drowned his humiliation in the luxuries and voluptuousness of his palace. Esther's presentation to him met with immediate favour and she was made queen in place of the deposed Vashti, and was decorated with the royal crown. This promotion was celebrated by "a great feast unto all his princes and his servants; and he made a release to the provinces, and gave gifts according to the bounty of the king" (2:18).

In dramatically rapid succession, we have the power and decree of Haman for the execution of the Jews, the elevation and promotion of Mordecai, the hanging of Haman, and the rescue of the Jews.

The French discovered the die such as were cast in determining the lot, and the palatial surroundings that seem to be a perfect background for the entire story. While the book of Esther contains nowhere the name of God, it seems to have at least three purposes standing out clear and plain. First, it reveals the wide distribution, the numbers and the power of the Jews in the Persian empire; again, it shows the goodness of God in preserving the Jews from their enemies; finally, it describes the origin and significance of the feast of Purim.

267. Return of Ezra (457 B. C.). Troublesome problems meet the Bible student when he takes up the study of Ezra and Nehemiah. The compiler of the Chronicles and of Ezra-Nehemiah thought that he was giving us the proper chronological order of the two patriots, though some scholars to-day reverse the order of their migration to Jerusalem.

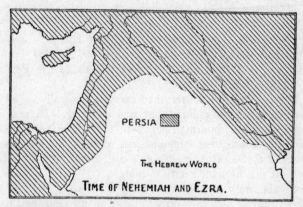

PERSIA

THE HEBREW WORLD

TIME OF NEHEMIAH AND EZRA.

Map 13. The World of Ezra's and Nehemiah's Day (about 440 B. C.) Within a few short years the sovereignty of Babylon passed over into the hands of Persia, who held the reins of all the world except Greece. The Jews were its citizens and their conduct gave them high positions of trust. From Persepolis to Jerusalem Nehemiah never left the domain of Artaxerxes.

The critical questions are too complicated for discussion here, and we shall regard the two reformers contemporaries, as did the Chronicler, with a possibility of error.

" In the seventh year of Artaxerxes " (457 B. C.), Ezra, as priest and scribe, determined to go up to Jerusalem " to teach in Israel statutes and ordinances " (Ezra 7:10). The Persian king gave him a generous grant and decree, especially designed to further the worship of Jehovah at the temple. In exercising his authority among the Jews, Ezra's word was absolute: " And whosoever will not do the law of thy God, and the law of the king, let judgment be executed upon him with all diligence, whether it be unto death, or to banishment, or to confiscation of goods, or to imprisonment " (Ezra 7:26). After he had secured the necessary passports and commission, he assembled those who were willing to return with him at the river Ahava, and they observed a fast. Twelve men were " set apart " to transport an enormous quantity of silver, gold, and vessels of precious metal to Jerusalem, to beautify and decorate the house of Jehovah (7:27; 8:24-30).

After about four months of travel they reached the holy city, had the precious metal certified to, offered burnt-offerings, and presented their commissions to the Persian governor of that region.

Ezra, as head of the returned caravan, naturally heard of everything in the colony that was irregular. Laxness in public worship, intermarriage with the native populations and the consequent abominations current among them, shocked the faithful priest and scribe, who rent his clothes and sat dumbfounded until evening.

As the story is told, at evening Ezra arose, fell on his knees, spread out his hands to Jehovah his God, and confessed the enormity of the sins of the people in mingling with their pagan neighbours. He pleaded their cause and besought God to forgive this remnant that stood before him.

Ezra's genuine earnestness and strong appeal drew a crowd of men, women and children in their sympathy for the old priest and leader. Some of the prominent ones confessed their wrongdoing. This culminated in the priests, Levites, and all Israel taking an oath that they would put away all the foreign wives and their children, " according to the counsel of the Lord " (Ezra 10:3). The penalty for neglect of anyone to carry out that order would be the forfeiture of all his substance. By a special court of domestic relations, every case was examined; and at the end of two months, the sessions of the court were closed,—leaving us a list of those who at the demand of Ezra were divorced from

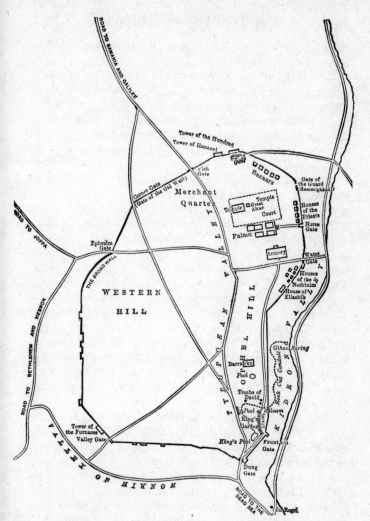

Fig. 47. Plan of Jerusalem in Nehemiah's Day

Distinguish carefully between the dark-faced wall line, and the light-faced roads about and through the city. Note also the two valleys, Kidron and Hinnom, and their relation to the city walls. The Tyropœon valley road follows the old depression of that valley through the lower part of the city. The remaining points are sufficiently plain on the plan.

their foreign wives,—a rather heartless procedure according to our idea of marriage.

268. Returns of Nehemiah (in 444 B. C.) (Nehemiah 1 and 2). Nehemiah, though a Jew, had " broken into " the court of Persia, as an attendant of King Artaxerxes I at Susa. He must have been a forceful character and a sincere man to have reached the responsible position of cupbearer. Hanani, his brother, brought to him pilgrims from Jerusalem, who told him a sad story of the defenseless condition of the city so sacred to his fathers. The story so worked on the sympathetic and patriotic feelings of Nehemiah, that when he next appeared before the king his sad countenance aroused the king's interest. Learning the cause of it all, and the desire of Nehemiah to return to Jerusalem, Artaxerxes gave him leave of absence and the required passports and commissions to present to the officials in the Westland. He had authority also to secure timber from the royal forest, and to build the walls of Jerusalem. A royal cavalry escort accompanied him and his small party over the 1,000-mile journey from Susa to Jerusalem.

Three days after he reached the ruined holy city, he made a night inspection of its broken down walls and fortifications. Word soon reached curious neighbours on every side, Samaritans, Ammonites, Arabians and Philistines, that the walls of that old city were to be rebuilt.

269. Nehemiah's Leadership (Nehemiah 3:1–7:5). This new governor of the city thoroughly organized the people at hand, assigning to each group under one head a section of the wall. We should remember that the thrown-down stone were at hand for rebuilding, and probably that each had been formerly marked for its location in the wall. Of course, the old foundations were in place where they followed the old wall-line, and it may be that in some places several tiers of stone were still on the foundations,—either never levelled down, or partially built by Ezra or some other patriot.

At any rate, Nehemiah so organized the people of the city

that the walls rose rapidly on all sides. Then Sanballat, an under officer of Persia, aroused by the zeal of Nehemiah, sent raiders against Jerusalem to unsettle and terrify the workers on the wall. To counter this method of attack, Nehemiah armed the builders on the wall, stationed armed citizens at exposed points, and had the entire works guarded day and night against a surprise assault. A trumpeter was likewise always ready to summon the armed forces to any single point of defense against the enemy. Nehemiah, with almost sleepless activity, oversaw the entire undertaking. Fifty-two days of such driving haste brought the work to a safe completion, at least beyond the reach of the enemy.

Sanballat had used all the devices he knew to entrap Nehemiah. He had summoned him four different times to a conference outside the city, with the purpose of assassinating him. He had threatened to bring charges of treason against him before the Persian king for building up the defenses of a former rebellious city. But Nehemiah knew his ground, stuck strictly to business, and let the noisy enemy shout to his heart's content.

The administration of the city was reorganized for defense, under Hanani, his brother, as local governor. The city was filled up with Jews from country places, and was made a defensible and habitable place after a long stretch of semi-ruin and exposure to attack.

270. Religious and Economic Reforms (Nehemiah 8–13). We can scarcely determine from the text how long Nehemiah remained in Jerusalem on this first visit. At the end he made his brother governor over the re-walled city and gave certain instructions to be carried out.

During the building of the walls, the poorer colonists raised " a great cry " against their brethren the Jews (Neh. 5:1). For these poor people had gone into the city to help restore the walls. To sustain themselves during this stretch of two months they had borrowed money, had mortgaged their fields, vineyards, and houses to the rich Jews, who took advantage of their absence and foreclosed their claims

Some had even made slaves of their children, that they might have bread.

This outcry touched Nehemiah, and he summoned the nobles and deputies to a conference. He appealed to their kinship, their sense of common fairness, the patriotic undertaking they were engaged in, and their obligations to obey the law of their God. He likewise pointed out that he himself was giving all his time as governor, and was supporting a company of the Jews at his own private expense.

They had nothing to say, but to cancel the debts of the poor, quitclaim their fields and houses, and stand by the decree of the governor.

Somewhere about this period, Ezra the scribe, already famous for his activity as interpreter of the law, read aloud to men, women and children out of the law in the open square of the city. To make certain that they understood it, interpreters put the message into the language of the common people. The text mentions Nehemiah the governor as one of those present, together with the Levites. All these quieted down the sad and unhappy populace, and inspired them to celebrate that day as a holy and happy time.

On the next day, Ezra and the heads of the fathers' houses celebrated the feast of booths as it had not been observed since the days of Joshua, son of Nun. Each day throughout the entire seven, they heard some part of the law read in their hearing.

Violation of the sabbath seems to have been general both by buyer and seller, by Jews and by outsiders. Nehemiah rebuked both, ordered out the Tyrian fishmongers, and commanded the gates of the city to be closed at sundown (Friday night) and to remain closed over the sabbath. If violators camped outside the city walls on the sabbath, they would be arrested.

He restored the temple-tax of one-third of a shekel for maintenance of the service.

Mixed marriages were the next evil he attacked. The law forbidding marriage with foreigners had been pushed aside with impunity. Nehemiah saw that persistence therein would obliterate the distinction between paganism and Judaism, and would ultimately mean the defeat of the true faith of the fathers.

To rid the Jews of this evil, Nehemiah seems to have lost his temper, for he says, " I contended with them and cursed them, and smote certain of them, and plucked off their hair, and made them swear by God " that they would not do that wickedness against God by marrying foreign women (Neh. 13:25-27).

He also expelled all foreign men from the precincts of the temple, that the worship of the true God should not be defiled. Just what reforms were carried out before Nehemiah returned to Artaxerxes (Neh. 2:6), and what he undertook on his second visit in 432 B. C., it is not possible definitely to determine. It may be that the conditions described in chapter 13 were those which he found on the second visit, and which stirred him to the drastic action he took against foreign marriages and all their racial alliances. His prime purpose was to maintain the purity of the Jews as a people, and the sanctity of the religion of the prophets of Israel.

271. Contributions of Ezra and Nehemiah to Judaism. The confusion in the literary make-up of the books of Ezra and Nehemiah detracts little from the sturdy religious and economic values of their characters. Ezra apparently was a greater man than the records declare. His contribution was religious and literary. He endeavoured to purify the service of God, to restore the priestly and ritualistic in the temple, to familiarize the people with the law in all its requirements. He is credited with having collected the Old Testament books that appeared before his day, into a kind of canon of sacred writings. It may be that he was one of the first after Ezekiel, to have helped in the establishment of the Jewish synagogue that played such a rôle in subsequent Judaism. As priest and scribe, he took a double part in the development of the priestly activities of the post-exilic period. Though he disapproved of foreign marriages, and forbade it in Israel, his antagonism was priestly and religious rather than social and political. With all his dramatic inferiority to Nehemiah, Ezra has a distinct and fixed place in the history of the beginnings of Judaism in the fifth century B. C.

Nehemiah is one of the most fascinating and romantic characters of the Old Testament. After long years of experience at the most brilliant imperial court of his day, he voluntarily undertook a hard task. He found a weak, disheartened colony of Jews, who were non-plussed by the political and religious conditions of their times.

Nehemiah boldly faced the problem, commanded all his resources, swept every difficulty aside, reorganized and built up the disheartened colony into a self-respecting and independent Persian colony under the governorship of Hanani, his brother. His reforms were such as would promote the patriotism of the Jews and distinguish them religiously from the paganism that crowded them on every side. His financial independence gave him large influence with the wealthy Jews of the land. His generosity towards the poor, stimulated a more liberal attitude of the rich toward their less fortunate brothers. His active, deep interest in the welfare of his nation, served as an example, during all subsequent history, of devotion to the cause of Jewish nationalism.

272. Malachi, the Prophet (Malachi). Malachi (" my messenger ") is a rough sketch of religious and social situations that seem to fit the times of Nehemiah. The temple had been built for some time. Civil conditions were about the same as those described in Nehemiah. The impious priests are roundly scored for their perversion of sacrifice; they offered the lame, decrepit, and the diseased, whereas the Lord required the perfect only (1:13, 14). The Jews were also marrying pagan women in preference to their own people,—indeed, after divorcing the wives of their youth.

" Will a man rob God? Yet ye rob me " (3:8). In

tithes and offerings the colonists had neglected their religious duties. Their neglect likewise crippled the temple service, and forced the priests to abandon their regular duties. The services that were carried out were formal, lifeless, and a mockery.

All this desecration and hypocrisy will be tested by the " messenger of the covenant " who will be a refiner's fire to see whether they are dross or silver or gold. He " will be a swift witness against . . . those that oppress the hireling in his wages, the widow, and the fatherless, and that turn aside the sojourner from his right, and fear not me, saith Jehovah of hosts " (3:5).

On the other hand, if the whole tithe is paid, blessings uncounted will pour out upon the giver until he has no more room to put them. This conversational, forcible, direct little book aimed to correct the evils of the Jewish colony current about Nehemiah's time, and to picture the possibilities in store for the obedient. They who were able to go through the refiner's fire would experience the joys of seeing Elijah the prophet as a forerunner of the day of Jehovah in the distant future,—apparently a glance toward the appearance of a Messiah.

The writer of this book had been saddened with a sorrowful sense of the terrific disgrace that the lax lives and loose religious deeds had brought upon the reputation of the Jewish colonists. It had degraded them in the eyes of their neighbours, and made the cause of Jehovah an offense and a stench among the pagans about them. Our writer speaks plainly and frankly when he points out the immediate causes of the semi-disasters that were on their trail and threatened to overwhelm them. On the other hand, if they should fill out his prescription and turn from their self-willed and obstinate ways, God's favour would shine on their pathway. The inevitable tests of all acts and service will find them pure metal. The last verses of this Malachi focalize the attention of the reader upon the future,—a new future for the pious and faithful Jews of that rather doubtful and uncertain age. In that new day, there will be a truer service, a better ruler, and joys that have haunted the lives and dreams of all the faithful worshippers of Israel's God. The best characters and rulers of the Old Testament were their models in word and in symbol.

NOTE ON FIG. 66, tailpiece below: Persian royal guards elaborately caparisoned, probably for dress parade, though fully equipped, with spear, bow and quiver full of arrows. They form part of the friezes on the palace of Darius at Susa, and were made of multi-coloured glazed bricks, a beautiful decorative method adopted by Assyrians, Babylonians and Persians. The animal friezes on the Ishtar gates and processional avenues of Babylon were built with the same technique.

PERIOD X

JUDAISM EXPANDING

CHAPTER XXXI

Diverse Interests

273. The Jewish Colony in Egypt. By the close of the fifth century B. C., Jews were scattered to all parts of the civilized world. They had migrated, had been taken as cap-

Note on Fig. 26, headpiece above: Elephantine is a small tropical island in the Nile just at the foot of the first cataract. A colony of Jews had settled there, either as immigrants or as mercenaries, long years before Cyrus captured Babylon or Nebuchadrezzar wiped out Jerusalem. These seventeen lines of a letter written by them to Bagoas, governor of Jerusalem, and to Sanballat of Samaria tells how jealous Egyptian priests and Persian officials conspired and destroyed the temple of Yahu (Jehovah). After three years' mourning they appealed to the above named officials for a permit to rebuild, and won their case. The Aramaic script you see in this letter is practically Phœnician, and substantially the same as that in which the Old Testament was written.

tives by Assyria and Babylonia, and had been sold as slaves by the Philistines (Amos 1:6), by the Edomites (Amos 1:9), and probably by the Phœnicians who carried them to the various Mediterranean countries. Some of them reached Egypt either as captives, merchants, or mercenaries. Jeremiah found a community of them in the Delta in 586 B. C.

But the most startling story of a Jewish colony, was that found on papyri discovered from 1895 to 1905 on the island of Elephantine in the Nile, at the foot of the first cataract,— opposite Assuan in upper Egypt. Out of ruins on the south end of the island were dug up ostraca and several rolls of dried papyri, covered with writing in the Aramaic language. The documents were the first Aramaic papyri ever found in such quantities. As a rule they were plainly written and with exact dates. They were composed 494 to 400 B. C. in this far western colony of the Persian empire, during the period when Ezra and Nehemiah were reorganizing and fortifying the colony at Jerusalem.

But one of the startling things we learn in these papyri is that, within a century after Jeremiah's words (chap. 44), there was a Jewish colony on this island that owned land, built houses, engaged in commercial transactions as merchants, were money-lenders, bankers, and citizens of the Persian empire. They also brought their religion with them, for they had built a temple to Yahu (Jehovah) as the name should be read,—the shorter form appearing many times in proper names in the Old Testament. This temple stood on King's Avenue on the island.

These Jews were tolerant of the Egyptian gods, and some of them may have worshipped them. We find a Jew named Hosea, son of Peti-Khnum ("gift of Khnum"). Some of them took their oaths by Egyptian deities rather than by *Yahu,* the God of their temple. This colony was subject to the laws of the Persian empire. They had their own "tribunal" for strictly colonial questions, but their rules for business and social life were Persian. Behind all contracts, wills, deeds, instruments of sale, and transfers, lies Babylonian law. Women held property as men, and by will disposed of it in the same way. Divorce was allowable for man or woman, but neither was valid except when granted in a public assembly.

The cosmopolitan character of this Jewish colony at Elephantine (its short name was *Jeb*) is revealed in the number of nationalities that are found in their business documents. Aside from Jewish names as witnesses on these legal papers, we discover nationals from every corner of the Persian empire. Of these we find Persians, Babylonians, Aramæans, Arabs, Berbers, and Egyptians. The double dating of each document, in Egyptian and Aramaic, is most helpful in studying the chronological systems then in vogue.

Of all the long list of papyri found, the most interesting is the letter sent to Bagoas the governor of Jerusalem after Cambyses of Persia had invaded Egypt in 525 B. C., wherein is mentioned the fact that the local Persian governor had destroyed the Jewish temple of Yahu. The first appeal to the governor of Jerusalem, three years earlier, had been ignored. This second appeal was made to the governors both of Jerusalem and of Samaria, for the rebuilding of the temple; and it is answered by a note from the governor of Jerusalem, which orders said temple to be rebuilt on its former site, " and meat-offering and incense let them offer upon this altar just as it was formerly done."

The date of this letter was 407 B. C., the seventeenth year of Darius Nothus (II), at which time the temple had lain in ruins three years. A real temple to the God of Israel in Egypt! Isaiah's prophecy implied as much (19:19-22).

Though far from the holy city and its sacred memories, these Jewish colonists, however they may have reached that place, contained a remnant of faithful worshippers of Jehovah whose character and lives were a leavening influence for the worship of Israel's God.

274. Persia's Last Century. The Persian rulers in general had been far superior to their predecessors, in character, policies and administration. They had been more liberal toward their subjects, and more helpful to the Jews. Since Nehemiah's reconstruction and reorganization of Jerusalem and the temple service, and his economic and social reforms, Persia had maintained a generous attitude toward this colony. In fact, these Jews largely managed their own local affairs under the governor of Jerusalem, who was accountable to the satrap of Damascus,—one of the twenty chief officers of the empire who were answerable for their official conduct to the king. The Jews, in their fealty to Persia, were required to pay their regular taxes, to supply recruits for the standing army, and to be true to their oath of allegiance.

The political situation was calm and favourable to the colony until the accession of Artaxerxes III (358-338 B. C.). He was antipodal in character to his predecessors. Tyrannical, despotic, and cruel, he aroused resentment, opposition, and rebellion. Egypt and the east Mediterranean seacoast openly rebelled. For ten years his armies struggled with the western uprisings before they were crushed. Whether the Jewish colony was involved we are not certain, though some of them were taken captive to Babylonia. Josephus is authority for the statement that Bagoas, a Persian general, became so angry because Johanan had assassinated his own brother in the temple, to secure for himself the high priesthood, that he defiled the sacred building and for ten years heavily taxed the daily sacrifice (Jos., *Antiq.*, xi, 7). The last king of Persia redeemed the good name of the earlier rulers of that world empire. Alexander the Great next appears on the horizon of world figures.

275. The Priests in the Jewish Colony. At the reorganization of the temple service, the priest was the most important functionary. His superior officer was the Jewish governor of Judea, who became virtually the high-priest after the dedication of the second temple,—and this office and authority became hereditary, as head of the Jewish colony in Palestine. The high-priest became the apex of the priestly pyramid, which was organized down to the ground.

In this class, including the Levites, we find most of the officials of the colony. To their support the merchants, bankers, peasants and all the other Jews theoretically contributed the tithe of their produce, the first-born of their cattle, or the same value in money. Certain specified portions of animals killed for food, of the wool of sheep-shearing, of meal-, of sin-, and of trespass-offerings, belonged to the priesthood. Other perquisites of many kinds helped to swell their exchequer, and they became rich and independent. Such results inspired men who were less fortunate, to inaugurate questionable methods, and even to bribe and assassinate their way into the high-priest's office.

276. The Scribes and their Work. A class of men under this name appeared during the monarchy of Israel, when each king had his " scribe " (or secretary) as, " Shebna the scribe," one of the envoys of Hezekiah sent out to confer with the officers of Sennacherib's army outside Jerusalem. The scribe, however, in exilic and post-exilic times was a transcriber, a compiler (or editor), and became especially an interpreter of the law. At first they were priests such as Ezra, who were experts in the knowledge and exposition of legal statutes.

Since the priests were limited in their powers, by written law, they were obliged to recognize the rights of other citizens, and themselves to submit to the general codes binding on all the Jews. The scribe's office was gradually being entered by others than priests; until down in the Greek period, and later, the scribe outranked the priest in his knowledge and influence, in the understanding of the written and traditional laws. He was the selecter and preserver of the books of the canon. He left quantities of notes, critical, historical, and religious, as well as editorial remarks of immense value, though anonymity was his regular practice.

277. The Samaritan Community. Nehemiah's drastic treatment of those Jews who had married alien women and refused to divorce them, led to far-reaching results (Neh. 13:28). Sanballat's son-in-law was expelled from Jerusalem, and led away with him many influential Jews, priests and laymen, who were parties to the same indiscretion. Josephus tells us (*Antiq.*, xi, 7, 8) that this son-in-law was Manasseh, grandson of Eliashib, and brother of the high-priest; and that he, with-the encouragement and financial support of Sanballat, founded the Samaritan sect, and temple on Mt. Gerizim, somewhere about 400 B. C.

This new religious body now had its own rival temple with all its own ritual service. It also adopted as its scriptures the Pentateuch only, probably because that was the only portion of the Old Testament writings which was generally regarded at that time by the Jews as authentic, and canonical.

This Samaritan community was only partially Jewish, as we have seen (§213), and hence quite liberal in its interpretation and execution of the requirements of the law. With their own temple, official priests, and regular services, they exercised a liberalizing influence on all the surrounding peoples as over against the narrow Judaism centred at Jerusalem. In fact, each community looked askance at, and regarded itself superior to, the other. This attitude of each toward the other increased in intensity until it became bitter and scornful.

In the time of Christ, a Jew regarded a Samaritan as an alien, a foreigner, one to be avoided. So that when Jesus sent out the twelve he said, " enter not into any city of the Samaritans " (Matt. 10:5), perhaps to avoid the inevitable clash of the two parties. If a Jew wished to travel from Galilee to Judea, he would even go over the Jordan and down the other side of it, rather than cross the country of the Samaritans. When Jews met Samaritans either on a highway or in their villages, sharp words, insulting remarks, or (and) even bloodshed might follow (Luke 9:52-54). The animosity existent between them is well illustrated in the Jews' cutting words to Jesus (John 8:48), " Say we not well that thou art a Samaritan, and hast a demon? "—also in the request of James and John that they be permitted to call down fire from heaven to consume the Samaritans because they rejected Jesus (Luke 9:54).

Jesus, however, met that problem face to face. In the parable of the good Samaritan he publicly censured any such attitude and spirit on the part of the Jews, leading us to infer that the so-called hostility of the Samaritans may be exaggerated, since all our information on that point comes from Jewish sources.

Descendants of these same Samaritans, to the number of about 100, are still living in Nablous (ancient Shechem)—an age-long village between Mts. Ebal and Gerizim. With their little synagogue and so-called ancient copy of the Pentateuch, and their annual passover observance on Mt. Gerizim, they are the last remnant of an ancient régime that has persisted through more than 2,000 years of checkered history.

278. Two Divergent Trends. The narrow, exclusive religious attitude of the Jewish colony in Judea was countered almost diametrically by the semi-liberal Samaritan community at Shechem. Neither was right in its attitude towards the other, towards mankind in general, nor in their religious conceptions and their relation to the nations of the world. The Jewish colony nurtured its own distinctive rites and institutions, irrespective of its neighbours and mixed races. The Samaritans, being in the main a conglomerate people, naturally imbibed and fostered fragments and principles of many religions,—thus liberalizing and enlarging their ideas of religion and worship. However, beyond a certain point they seem not to have gone, as they had enough Jews among them and Jewish blood in their veins to hold them within bounds.

279. Jewish Exclusiveness Rebuked (Jonah). The harsh restrictions of Ezra and Nehemiah against Jewish marriages with alien women may have been racially and religiously a good move. But it led to the growth of an aloofness and an exclusiveness that permeated their entire life. It gave them a self-satisfied and complacent thought of themselves, not only as superior to others, but also as having no responsibility whatever toward those outside their own pale of living.

Though the exiles in Babylonia had been broadened and liberalized in their ideas of their relations to outside nations, those who had returned and had settled down in Palestine seem to have developed precisely the opposite tendency. There were, however, a few characters who realized the largeness and expansiveness of the religion of Jehovah, and its adaptability to the needs of all nations.

There are books in the canon which strike directly at that forbidding attitude of heart and mind; and, on good grounds, their composition may be placed in this period of Jewish complacency. The book of Ruth is a good example of a foreign woman who adopted and worshipped the God of Israel. She married Boaz at Bethlehem, through whom she became the grandmother of David, king of Israel,—a Moabitess espousing Israel's God, marrying a Hebrew, and becoming a lineal ancestor of the house of David and the entire roll of kings of Judah.

But the most caustic arraignment of Jewish exclusiveness, religiously, is found in the story of Jonah the prophet. Jonah lived in the reign of Jeroboam II (2 Kings 14:25). But this story is really a parable of a later date, by an unknown author, to teach a specific lesson. Multitudes of questions vanish as soon as we see the real purpose of the book. When directed by Jehovah to go to Nineveh, the great city of Assyria, " to cry against it " because of its wickedness, Jonah recoiled from the order and decided to take a trip to Tarshish, in the opposite direction,—in fact, toward the western end of the Mediterranean Sea. He embarked regularly on a liner which sailed from Joppa for Tarshish. Apparently on the first day out, Jehovah " hurled " a great wind on the sea, and a furious storm broke loose and the ship wellnigh foundered. So alarmed were the sailors that each man cried to his god to save them.

After throwing overboard the cargo to lighten the vessel, they finally bethought themselves of that Hebrew passenger down in the hold of the ship, who had told them that he was fleeing from the presence of Jehovah (1:10). So dormant was his self-complacent conscience that he slept soundly even in the raging storm. At the appeal of the captain he arose and came up on deck, but his prayer to Jehovah was in vain. The storm still roared. To fix the blame for it, lots were cast; and the lot fell upon Jonah. The miscreant confessed his sin against Jehovah; and after all other expedients failed, they took him at his word and pitched him into the raging sea. The storm at once died down; and the sailors feared Jehovah, and offered sacrifices and made vows.

But Jonah! Jehovah had prepared "a great fish" to swallow him, and after three days to vomit him out on the dry land. When he received his second order to go to Nineveh to preach against it, he neither fled in the opposite direction nor protested against the command, but simply went and preached; "Yet forty days, and Nineveh shall be overthrown" (3:4). At this dire announcement, the Ninevites almost en masse repented in sackcloth and ashes, and the city was reprieved.

Jonah was highly displeased that God had not wiped out the hated foreigners as he himself had announced. This is the very result he had anticipated before he left home. His flight toward Tarshish was made to prevent any such repentance and consequent deliverance. Jonah's knowledge of Jehovah's mercy and lovingkindness told him that Nineveh would be spared. His anger was caused because his preaching had been the agency that brought about their repentance and their salvation. He was so angry that he wished he were dead. Jehovah said to him, "Doest thou well to be angry?" This gentle reproof went to its mark; for Jonah made no reply, but went out of the city, made himself a booth, and sat down to nurse his disappointment and sullenness. Next we have the episode of the gourd, in which Jonah was again angry because a worm had killed it and the sirocco had beaten upon his unprotected head. Jehovah asked him if his anger was justified, since he had nothing to do with the appearance or disappearance of the gourd. His reply showed up his wilful, refractory temper. He was angry (4:1) because Nineveh was *not* destroyed, with its half million population; and now he was angry because Jehovah had destroyed the gourd (4:9), for whose appearance he had nothing to do.

Jehovah then took Jonah severely to task and gave him an unanswerable lesson. Jonah had pity on the gourd when it withered and died, and should not he (Jehovah) have pity on Nineveh, that great city? He had sent Jonah to warn it, and it had repented; and, true to his character, he forgave it, as he had spoken through Jeremiah (18:7, 8), " At what instant I shall speak concerning a nation, and concerning a kingdom, to pluck up and to break down and to destroy it; if that nation, concerning which I have spoken, turn from their evil, I will repent of the evil I thought to do unto them." Besides the penitent grown-ups, there were 120,000 innocent little children too small to distinguish between right hand and left, and also " much cattle."

Nineveh's reputation as a commercial and political world-centre must have grasped the attention of every listener to, or reader of, Jonah's story. Even though destroyed in 612 B. C., Nineveh's fame, like that of Thebes in Egypt (Nah. 3:8), had gone to the ends of civilization. Its materialism and worldliness made its repentance in sackcloth and ashes the wonder and astonishment of every Jew. Jonah's character stands out in greatest contrast to that of the attitude of the broad-minded and liberalized Jew of that day. His rebukes by Jehovah should be withering and paralyzing to any such attitude as he displayed in the face of the deliverance of that great repentant city.

Thus endeth the book and the conclusive answer to the narrow, prejudiced and intolerant Jews of whom Jonah was a prevalent type. It teaches that God's love is " wider than the measure of man's mind," that it reaches out to all men, even to the enemies of his chosen people, whom he is ready to forgive and bless if they will only forsake their evil ways and follow him.

NOTE ON FIG. 98, tailpiece below: Naval warfare was quite in vogue in Phœnicia's heyday. This is one of a fleet of war galleys of the masters of the Mediterranean Sea. The prong on the prow of the boat was used for ramming the enemy ship. The rowers were usually on two decks, and the officers and guests occupied the "hurricane deck." Such craft made the Phœnicians a pre-eminent sea power for about six or seven centuries (1100–600 B. C.).

CHAPTER XXXII

ETHICAL AND SPIRITUAL LITERATURE

280. The Poetry in the Old Testament. Every race of peoples has a kind of innate love of poetry. Its balanced rhyme and rhythm seem to answer to the regular tramp, tramp, tramp of their walk and the time-keeping beats of their hearts.

As soon as we begin to read the Old Testament Revised Version, we fall upon snatches of poetically printed verses, dropped into the midst of long stretches of prose, as in Genesis (4:19-23); Numbers 21 (:14, 15); 24 (:3-9); 2 Samuel 1 (:19-27). Then we find entire books printed in verse form as the Psalms, Proverbs, Song of Solomon, and most of Job.

But when we try to read these lines as English poetry, we discover that they have neither rhyme nor metre. Their

NOTE ON FIG. 62, headpiece above: Assyrians were lovers of music, especially in connection with processions of any kind. When a victorious army returned, or a notable personage arrived, a band of harpers, sometimes accompanied by human cymbals, the clapping of hands, met them and celebrated the occasion with instrumental music.

poetic character is not due to any delightful balancing of sounds of metrical beats. The principle that underlies Hebrew poetry is a certain parallelism of thought, and rhythm of sense. This kind of poetry often far outstrips in genuine thought mere jingling rhymes and mechanical metres.

As in other languages, we find in Hebrew a graduation of poetry, from poetical prose and prosaic poetry to the most exquisite balancings of idea and thought. Only a few samples can be cited here to illustrate the chief characteristics.

Parallelism of thought is the chief feature that strikes every careful reader of Hebrew verse. Of such parallels we have several varieties: (a) Synonymous parallelism—in which two lines, either successive or separated by one or more lines, present almost synonymous thoughts; as,

> " O Jehovah, rebuke me not in thy wrath;
> Neither chasten me in thy hot displeasure.
>
> Lord, all my desire is before thee;
> And my groaning is not hid from thee."
>
> (Psa. 38:1, 9.)

> " O come, let us sing unto Jehovah;
> Let us make a joyful noise to the rock of our salvation.
>
> Let us come before his presence with thanksgiving;
> Let us make a joyful noise unto him with psalms."
>
> (Psa. 95:1, 2.)

(b) Antithetic parallelism—where the thoughts are set over against each other:

> " A good man shall obtain favour of Jehovah;
> But a man of wicked devices will he condemn.
>
> A worthy woman is the crown of her husband;
> But she that maketh ashamed is as rottenness in his bones."
>
> (Prov. 12:2, 4.)

> "*A soft answer turneth away wrath;*
> *But a grievous word stirreth up anger.*
>
> *The tongue of the wise uttereth knowledge aright;*
> *But the mouth of fools poureth out folly.*"
>
> (Prov. 15:1, 2.)

(c) Progressive parallelism, though scarcely a parallelism, is where the second line simply adds something to the first; as,

> "*Bow down thine ear, O Jehovah, and answer me;*
> *For I am poor and needy.*
>
> *For thou art great, and doest wondrous things;*
> *Thou art God alone.*"
>
> (Psa. 86:1, 10.)

> "*They that go down to the sea in ships,*
> *That do business in great waters;*
> *These see the works of Jehovah,*
> *And his wonders in the deep.*"
>
> (Psa. 107:23, 24.)

(d) Synthetic parallelism introduces a new thought not mentioned or implied in the first line, rounding out the entire idea; as,

> "*Seest thou a man wise in his own conceit?*
> *There is more hope of a fool than of him.*
>
> *The sluggard is wiser in his own conceit*
> *Than seven men that can render a reason.*"
>
> (Prov. 26:12, 16.)

(e) Comparative parallelism presents the exact relation of the lines; as,

> "*As the hart panteth after the waterbrooks,*
> *So panteth my soul after thee, O God.*"
>
> (Psa. 42:1.)

> "*As vinegar to the teeth, and as smoke to the eyes,*
> *So is the sluggard to them that send him.*"
>
> (Prov. 10:26.)

> " *As a ring of gold in a swine's snout,*
> *So is a fair woman that is without discretion.*"
> (Prov. 11:22.)

Hebrew poetic license allowed several modifications of these parallelisms as given above, but all of them emphasize the sense rather than the form of the verse. Parallelism sometimes extended to as many as fourteen lines.

Hebrew poets also constructed several kinds of mechanistic verse, as alliterative, alphabetic, acrostic, responsive.

Measures were by beat or accent, and were usually of three beats or trimeters, four beats, tetrameters, pentameters, or hexameters. Most of the Psalms, Proverbs and alphabetical poems are in the simple trimeter form.

The content of Hebrew poetry is as varied as its poets. Taking the books and snatches of poetry found throughout the Old Testament, we discover personal odes, war songs, ballads, national hymns, triumphal songs, and poems of joy. In the Psalms we have temple verse, warm expressions of the depth of the inner life, of confession and appeal for forgiveness, of enmity, of hate, of revenge, and other attitudes of heart and soul. But permeating it all there was a religious spirit, however subtle it may have been. Every phase of the religious life found expression in its simple form, thus contributing to it the element that gave it a universal appeal to mankind.

Hebrew poetry was prevailingly of four kinds: (a) lyric, the oldest and most popular, found everywhere in the historical and prophetic books, and especially in the Psalter. (b) Didactic or gnomic, is that found in the wisdom literature, Proverbs, Ecclesiastes and a few psalms. We should designate these as ethical rather than religious. Warmth of feeling is wholly lacking, as they are pre-eminently intellectual in spirit (Judges 9:8-15). (c) Semi-dramatic, is a kind of form that is not yet agreed on. Such may be seen in Job, though action is found only in the prologue and epilogue. The Song of Solomon also fails to measure up to the standards of drama. (d) Elegy is seen in a few places, as Lamentations and some minor passages among the prophets.

281. The Psalms and Israel's Spiritual Life. The emotional and sentimental side of Israel's life had often expressed itself, during long centuries, in Hebrew verse or poetry. Its spiritual emotions, desires, and longings, began to emerge in set terms and conspicuous thought in the time of David. Not, however, until the exile and the second temple did the volume of this literary form swell to commanding proportions. The exilic psalms give us an insight into some of the distresses and sorrows of the faithful who were deprived of the presence of the temple, and of the solacing effect of Jehovah's answers to their cries (Psa. 120). The second temple and its inspiration for the returned exiles, produced a class of psalms that ring with joy and glow with warmth in the hallowed presence of Jehovah. When the cry of the prophet was dying down, psalmody was flourishing in full bloom (Psa. 107). The pilgrims that gathered annually to celebrate the passover in the holy city, cheered each other on the way by those charming pilgrim psalms (120–134). Doubtless they had much to do with the spirit and devotion not only of the faithful who lived in Palestine, but of those scattered to the ends of the civilized world, who made that annual pilgrimage to the shrines of Jehovah.

These psalms, too, must have had their liberalizing influence on the colony as touching their obligations religiously toward alien peoples, though the leavening process was carried on in a chilly atmosphere and through a long era.

282. Music in Israel's Worship. We know little of song in the worship in Solomon's temple. It seems also from hints here and there that in this period musical instruments accompanied much of the lyric poetry when used in song. The presence of such prominent singers as Heman, Asaph and Ethan—all Levites (1 Chron. 15:17)— is some evidence in David's day that singing may have been one of the popular accompaniments of the temple service.

The second temple (516 B. C.) is the one place where we first learn about any general use of music.

When the exiles returned from Babylon, in the fifth century B. C., Nehemiah's annals tell us that there were " 245 singing men and singing women " (7:67). Along with this singing there must have been musical instruments, as there have always been in all the past. The musical notations in the superscriptions of the psalms convince us that the recital of those particular psalms in the second temple, and later, was regularly accompanied with such instruments. Deep emotion and profound feeling were intensified by the instruments which accompanied the choruses and choirs of singers.

The variety of instruments named in the Old Testament includes the usual three classes found in every first-class orchestra to-day; viz., string, wind and percussion. The precise form and sound of the Old Testament instruments is not yet certain. They cannot be determined by those Persian and Greek instruments mentioned in Daniel, since these were probably never used in the temple worship at Jerusalem.

283. The Wise Men of Israel. The Old Testament contains a kind of poetic literature that is attributed to wise men or sages, and is popularly called " wisdom literature." The first use of the term, " the wise," is seen at scattered intervals in pre-exilic times. The first mentionings are " a wise woman " of Tekoa, whom Joab employed in persuading David to invite Absalom back to Jerusalem (2 Sam. 14:2); and " a wise woman " who saved the city of Abel, and gave it a reputation because of her counsel (2 Sam. 20:16, 18). Solomon's wisdom was superior to all the wise men of his day, to those of the East and to those of Egypt. Mention is made especially of Ethan the Ezrahite, and Heman, and Calcol, and Darda, sons of Mahol (1 Kings 4:30, 31).

It is thought that there were probably schools of wisdom, where men studied the practical every-day problems of life and the best method of stating solutions to them in short, snappy maxims or proverbs. The presence in the Old Testament of parables (2 Sam. 12:1-6) or riddles (Judges 14:14) in a set form, helped to stabilize the form of the sayings of the wise, such as we find in the book of Proverbs. It is thought that the chief aims of the wisdom schools may be found stated in Proverbs 1:2-6.

The counsellors of the people anciently appeared at the gate of the city, where they discussed individual and national problems, gave counsel to officials and individuals,— especially to young men who sought advice on knotty questions of everyday life.

The so-called books of wisdom originated in the post-exilic age. They are, specifically, Proverbs, Job, Ecclesiastes; Ecclesiasticus (Wisdom of Jesus, son of Sirach), and Wisdom of Solomon;—the first three being biblical and the last two apocryphal. Proverbs and Ecclesiasticus are concerned with daily conduct or the conduct-problems of life: how to find a formula or formulas applicable to daily living.

Job and Ecclesiastes have a totally different purpose. They have already gone beyond the maxims of Proverbs and Ecclesiasticus, and are wrestling with the question as to God and his justness toward men. The mind is full of questions regarding God's government of this world. Ecclesiastes shows us a pessimist whose intoxication with the pleasures of this world has perverted his perspective of life and its purpose.

284. The Book of Job. No study of the Old Testament is complete without a glance at least, at this wonderful book. We cannot take up its critical problems, but must give some of the results of its study. Job was possibly a God-fearing alien living out on the edge of the desert (Job 1:1). He may have been a prophet (Eccles. 49:9). His fame seemed to be known by Ezekiel (14:14, 20), along with that of Noah and Daniel. He is made the hero of the book, whom the Jewish writer finds and locates in the land of Uz in Edom (cf. Lam. 4:21).

The book is rather semi-dramatic, containing only in the

prologue and epilogue the action required by a drama, while the intermediate poetical part is plainly theological and didactic.

It begins with a prose scene laid in heaven, where Satan was given permission to test Job as to whether he served God merely for personal ends. Sword, fire, cyclone, and fatal calamities smote his property and family. Job, innocent victim of it all, remains loyal, calm and true to the God he knew.

Then the poet appears in another world, with real men about him, to explain the ways of God to man. Job (chap. 3) breaks out in curses against the day he was born, wishing he had died at birth, complaining that he must live when he wants to die. Then the " three comforters " appear at the ash-heap outside the city gate, upon which Job as an outcast is thought of as sitting and moaning.

Chaps. 4–14—cycle one—is a discussion of the character of God, where Eliphaz tells Job about the purity of God (4, 5), to which Job replies (6, 7). Then Bildad the wise, tries his skill on the justice of God (8), to which Job replies (9, 10). Then comes Zophar, a lawyer, setting forth the wisdom of God (11), to which Job sharply replies (12–14). Such theological dogmas Job brushed aside as irrelevant to his case.

Chaps. 15–21—cycle two—aims to picture the real conditions of a wicked man. Eliphaz again takes up the discussion and sets before Job the end of the man who defies God (15). Job's reply denounces all three " friends " as " miserable comforters " (16, 17). Bildad asserts that a wicked man suffers his just deserts when disease catches him, and his family and name perish (18). Job almost collapsed at the charges, but suddenly rises above all their implications by asserting his " trust in the God of the past, his ignorance of the God of the present, and his faith in the God of the future." Henceforth Job's triumph was complete, and his " friends " defeat assured (19). Zophar's retort that the wicked man's prosperity was brief (20), was calmly answered by Job. The result of the second cycle of charges is that Job denied their assertions, while feeling, however, that God and man were not his friends.

Chaps. 22–31—third cycle—the leader, Eliphaz, does the main speaking. He brings a plain, second person singular, " thou "-accusation against Job. He asserts that God does not act arbitrarily, that Job's oppressions, cruelty and arbitrary dealings were carried out because he thought God was not near (22). Job's reply really challenges the justice of God (23, 24). Bildad has little to say to such high-handed execration (25), while Zophar keeps still. Job then resumes with all the assurance of a victor, and gives his " friends " some real parting words that they will not soon forget (26–31).

By this time, apparently a crowd had gathered about the ash-heap, and an unknown Aramæan, Elihu, came forward to give his views of the matter. He took sides with neither party, but wished to be an arbiter in the case (chaps. 32–35). Elihu seems to have been an upstart whose speech was unnoticed in the text, by either Job or Jehovah. In fact, this section may have been inserted later, as it seems to be an interloper in the thought of the poem. This episode closed, Jehovah answered Job out of a cyclone, and asks him two questions: (1) Shall mortal man contend with the Almighty (40:2)? Look at all the wonders of inanimate nature, heavens, light, snow, hail, rain, etc. (38:2-38); and look at animate nature, birds, beasts, etc. (38:39–39:30). Job is aroused and says: " I am insignificant, what can I reply to thee " (40:3-5)? He becomes silent. Jehovah asks: (2) " Should man charge God of injustice in his government of the world? " (40:8). Job is weakening. After God shows him the hippopotamus and the crocodile as his creation, Job humbly confesses . . . " I know that thou canst do all things, Wherefore I abhor myself, and repent in dust and ashes " (42:1, 6), bringing Job to his knees for his harsh words about God. The God of the past and of the present are now identical in his mind.

The epilogue in prose shows the "friends" of Job sharply condemned, and Job himself lauded for his changed attitude (42:7-9). Job was vindicated in that his prosperity was doubled above what it had been before (10–17).

"Discipline precedes blessing" is one of the great lessons of the book. Affliction is the true road to genuine worship. The real lesson of the book, as Godet states it, is, "If the most pious of mankind is incapable of loving God gratuitously, it follows that God is incapable of making himself loved." The problem of the book is, "Why are the wicked prosperous and the righteous in evil plight?" It remains unanswered except by the life of Job himself.

285. The Book of Proverbs. A proverb is a maxim which contains the wit of one but the knowledge of many. Such short, pithy sayings are found among every people and nation and tongue. Especially beloved are they among oriental races. They are found in prose and poetry, and especially in the oral transmissions of the common people.

The ancient Hebrews had a peculiar fondness for such scraps of wisdom literature, as may be seen in the books of the Old Testament. Here and there in the prose books appear such proverbial sayings as, "As is the mother, so is her daughter" (Ezek. 16:44). "The fathers have eaten sour grapes, and the children's teeth are set on edge" (18:2).

The book of Proverbs is a collection of collections of these proverbs, from several centuries of Israel's history. There are at least four main divisions of the book. (1) Chapters 1–9 laud the superiority of wisdom to an imaginative "son," contrasting it with folly in chapters eight and nine. (2) Chapters 10:1–22:16, "The proverbs of Solomon," was built upon the couplet form, either synonymous or antithetic, implying a common origin. (3) Chapters 22:17–24:22, "The words of the wise," where the form of verse is pre-eminently quatrain. (4) Chapters 25–29, "The proverbs of Solomon which the men of Hezekiah copied out." These are mainly couplet in form.

An appendix to these four collections contains three small clusters: (1) " The words of Agur " (chap. 30), a kind of oracle; (2) " the words of King Lemuel, which his mother taught him " (chap. 31:1-9), has a foreign flavour; (3) a poem, praising a noble woman (31:10-31). In this last, each of the verses begins successively with one of the twenty-two letters of the Hebrew alphabet. It is a most beautiful description of the ideal wife of those days.

Many classifications have been made of the subjects mentioned in the book. They cover nearly all the relations of life, and the chief attributes of an individual. They include life in the family, in business, in society, in government; they mention kindness, love, mercy, gratitude, and integrity; also intemperance, unchastity, foolishness, laziness and wickedness.

The proverbs were written and based on the assumption of God's sovereignty in the universe, the violation of whose law was sin. Temple, priesthood, service of Jehovah, are not mentioned. The Hebrew wise men were philosophers, not prophets; they dealt with this moral world and its human kind, leaving out of account the spiritual universe.

286. Literary Activities of the Jewish Colony. The several preceding sections give us some idea of the tremendous activity of the priests, scribes and other writers in the Jewish colony at Jerusalem. Their collecting of historical data, their codifying of laws, their compiling of proverbs, their amplification of the ritual service of the temple, the composition and arrangement of the temple hymns and psalms,—all these literary and worshipful activities gave the colony a certain fixed standard of living that was felt all down through the centuries.

Their commercial relations with surrounding peoples prevented them from entirely closing their door against the outside world. Their contact with Persia likewise enlarged their ideas of religion and its use among men.

More than that, the Hebrew language had been in all the past, and was now, the literary language of the writers.

But Aramaic was the tongue used all about them, and it gradually became the spoken language of the colony. This soon amalgamated them linguistically with all their neighbours. When the Hebrew Scriptures were read to an audience, they were translated into the Aramaic language of the common folk. Indeed, Hebrew in the first century B. C. had become practically an unknown tongue to any but the educated Jew (and Greek).

NOTE ON FIG. 36, tailpiece below: The largest musical instrument pictured on the monuments is the Egyptian Harp of eleven strings. Our modern harps, played only by skilled musical artists, are built on practically the same lines.

PERIOD XI

THE GREEK INVASION AND JUDAISM

CHAPTER XXXIII

ALEXANDER'S CONQUEST AND PURPOSE

287. The Conquest of Alexander (334–323 B. C.). Philip of Macedon trained and inspired his son Alexander with a boundless ambition. In 334 B. C., this twenty-two-year-old young man crossed the Ægean Sea and struck a

NOTE ON FIG. 3, headpiece above: Alexander the Great has his own place in history. His first battle in Asia was at the Granicus River (an affluent of the Sea of Marmora). With unheard-of dash Alexander, almost single-handed, crossed the river and struck the enemy in the centre and utterly dismayed them and won the day. This augured well for all his subsequent clashes with the stupendous Persian empire.

fatal blow at the local garrisons of Persia, at the Granicus in Asia Minor. The next year (333 B. C.), he defeated and put to rout Darius himself at Issus. Down the Phœnician coast he drove, destroying Tyre and sinking the Persian fleet on the Mediterranean Sea. Passing by Jerusalem, he next brought Gaza to her knees and entered Egypt. This age-old land he humiliated. He returned to Asia and swept over into Mesopotamia, taking Babylon, Susa and Perse-polis. Not content with these trophies, he pushed eastward to the Indus, and north into Bokhara, Samarcand and other oriental lands. Back into Babylon he returned, and June 13, 323 B. C., died an untimely death. Ten years had given him the conquest of the civilized world, in which all the Jews had their homes.

288. Alexander's Empire Broken Up. Alexander's death was a signal for his generals and chief men to stake off their claims in the empire. For a generation there was civil strife between those leaders, until there remained only five of them, and each a king in his own sphere. Bloody rivalry for another generation left only three in the lead. We are interested only in Syria-Palestine and Egypt.

The great house of Ptolemy, descendants of a Greek chief in Alexander's army, who was appointed governor of Egypt in 323, held control of that comparatively isolated land until its conquest by Cæsar Augustus. The founding of the city of Alexandria, and its consequent wealth and advantage as a seaport, made Egypt practically master of the Mediter-ranean, as well as of the Red Sea on its eastern border.

One of Alexander's generals, Seleucus, bade fair to suc-ceed his great leader as ruler of the entire empire. But death defeated him. He was succeeded by Antiochus, his son, who, for a time, held all the realm except Egypt and Macedonia. The line was called Seleucidæ or Seleucids, whose sway was finally crushed by the Romans. The realm of Antiochus was trimmed off on all sides by secession and revolution until it embraced little more than Syria, Meso-potamia and parts of Armenia. Its capital was Antioch,

near the mouth of the Orontes River. The two important
ruling houses for our study are the Ptolemies in Egypt and
Seleucids in Syria.

**289. Palestine between the Upper and Nether
Millstones.** Palestine was a corridor between Egypt and

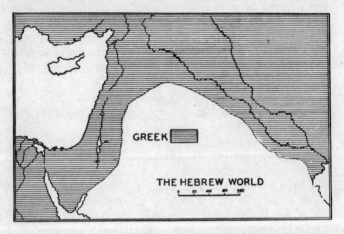

GREEK

THE HEBREW WORLD

Map 14. The World of Alexander's Empire (about 323 B. C.)

Once more the tables are turned, and the Greeks, hated enemies of
Persia, are on the throne of all the known world. But the death of
Alexander was a signal for the partition of that world into smaller
realms. The Jews were the victims of one or other of those small
rulers down to 161 B. C.

Asia. The trade-routes, the caravans, and the invading
armies between those lands had to pass through it. The
country that controlled Palestine held the corridor. The
Ptolemies' only outlets to the civilized world were on the
Mediterranean Sea and across Palestine. To hold the Sea
they needed ship-timber for ships, and that was found only
in the Lebanons, behind Tyre and Sidon. Ptolemy held
this country, with Palestine, the first three years of his reign
(323–320), then for nearly twenty years it suffered under
the depredations of Antigonus, when it again came under
Ptolemy. Seleucus' acquisition of control over Syria did

not, for friendship's sake, disturb Ptolemy's hold on Palestine. Within a generation the Seleucids and Ptolemies met in battle; and for about eighty years, or until Antiochus the Great (223–187 B. C.), harried all Palestine by their contending armies. The poor Jews in Jerusalem, innocent of all wrongdoing, paid tribute, now to Syria, now to Egypt, according to the fortunes of war.

When Antiochus the Great assumed the throne in 223 B. C., he first made peace, and after a few clashes,—finally in 198 B. C., at the battle of Banias,—expelled the Egyptians from Palestine never to return. But the presence of Greeks in all this land was most significant.

290. Alexander's Real Conquest. Alexander's invasion was not merely a series of victorious battles, nor even an obliteration of boundary lines. The conquest of Persia was only the vestibule into his real purpose. Educated under the guidance of Aristotle, he was thoroughly saturated with Greek culture and ideals. These he and his leaders carried with them into the less favoured civilizations of the East. Fully conscious of the superiority of the Greek and Macedonian cultures, Alexander decided by every means to introduce them among the benighted races whom he conquered and who fell under his sway.

Methods of warfare, plans for building cities, conveniences of private homes, appreciation of art in public buildings,—all helped to revolutionize the life of the conquered lands.

The introduction of the Greek language, customs, manners, games, laws, and government gave the East a taste of something they had never before experienced, and satisfied them with the superior character of that civilization. Such a planting of Greek culture has been called Hellenism.

291. Democratic Organization of Cities. The old cities of Babylonia, Syria and Egypt had been generally aggregations of houses without much order, convenience, or plan. The villages were no better. Public buildings were often planned on a magnificent scale, as were the royal and

religious centres. But the homes were little more tnan
unmentionable hovels. Alexander founded new cities on
independent locations in every country, with all the advantages and luxuries of wide avenues, broad squares, and
capacious and beautiful public buildings. Respectable private homes was another feature that made those cities
attractive, populous and prosperous.

The old tyrannical government was displaced by an annual election of a governor by a public vote of the citizens.
A city council passed the decrees that were posted in some
public place for the instruction of the citizens. Slaves did
the real brawn-work, while the freemen as public officers
determined policies and followed the leisure-class occupations and literary pursuits.

292. The Freedom of Greek Life. Of all the peoples of the Near East, the Greeks most enjoyed life and
prepared for its full expansion. Their city life was provided
with especial facilities for enhancing their everyday enjoy-
ment. We usually find a gymnasium for training the body
and for sports. That popular centre became the attraction
of all young men for the building up and hardening of their
bodies, for athletic contests and games of strength and skill.
In this out-of-doors life the Greeks excelled. Their annual
athletic games were patronized by the best men of the times,
and were an exhibit of more than mere physical strength,—
for music, dancing and literary contests were part of the
entertainment.

Each Greek city also had its open-air theatre for the
public presentation of plays; its city hall for public business; its hippodrome for horse races; its market-place for
public trading and social enjoyments; its so-called pillared
hall for those picturesque public men whose leisure gave
them so much joy in the private discussion of questions of
public and private interest. All these buildings were decorated with the artistic productions of the sculptors who were
so highly prized in Greek civilization.

These are some of the attractive fundamental features

that Alexander's conquests introduced into the lands of Egypt, Palestine, Syria and Mesopotamia.

293. The Greek Language and the Bible. The Greek language took root in the wake of Alexander's campaigns. Its nicety of expression, its fine distinctions of tenses, and its wondrous range of vocabulary, gave it an advantage over all the languages of the peoples where it was introduced. The native Greeks of Alexander's army, who made their homes in the newly founded cities and in some of the old foreign centres, became the tireless teachers of their language and culture. In this manner, the tongue struck its roots deep in the soil of the civilizations about the eastern Mediterranean, and in Mesopotamia. Some of the old languages died out, while others were pushed back into the mountains, where they gradually disappeared, or were found only among the poorer peasants. But for all literary or cultural purposes, for business, or government, Greek was supreme.

The growth and power of the city of Alexandria in Egypt attracted not only Greeks, but a large population of Jews who became wealthy and influential. They adopted the Greek language in all their intercourse with the citizens of that thrifty metropolis. Within a few years they observed that the younger generation not only knew little of their mother tongue, Hebrew-Aramaic, but began to neglect the Jewish religious services and the reading of the Old Testament. On their appeal and co-operation, Ptolemy Philadelphus arranged for the beginning of the translating of the Hebrew Old Testament into Greek (about 280 B. C.). Learned rabbis familiar with both tongues first engaged in the task. While begun under the auspices of Philadelphus, the work continued at intervals until completed about 135 B. C. This was the first proper translation of the Hebrew Old Testament into any language. It furnished the Hellenistic Jews in the Greek world their own Bible in their adopted tongue,—the tongue of the highest civilization and culture of that day.

In the first century, the New Testament as we have it was penned in the same language. Alexander's conquests and policies were directly and indirectly responsible for our Greek Old Testament—the Septuagint—and for the New Testament in the same language.

294. The Book of Ecclesiastes. Another book of wisdom. A strange, and by some regarded as the least worthy book of the entire Old Testament. The writer, who calls himself " Koheleth," gives us a picture of the man who apparently " tried everything once," without giving all the specifications. He was practical, experimental, explorational,—endeavouring to find the chief or highest good in life. He searched through all the so-called satisfying things to find a real purpose for living. After he had gone down all the avenues of wisdom, pleasure, wealth, and fame, he concluded that life is a hopeless round, with nothing in view, and that our only relief is to be found in enjoying it all as it passes day by day.

However, after he confesses all his faults and failures, he seems to conclude: " Fear God and keep his commandments, for this is the whole of man " (12:13), and do not wait until old age creeps upon you.

This book of wisdom has likenesses to Job and Proverbs. It has no use for priests, ritual service, or the great truths emphasized by the prophets. The wise men saw the human side of life in a moral world. The contents can scarcely be analyzed, though the thought has a certain definite consecution. Doubtless the book was written by an author who pursued his plan unswervingly to the end.

In his search for the highest good, he seemingly had to pass through all the phases of life where men think they find pleasure and good. In doing this, he is convinced that life is one perpetual grind, that it is all monotony and the same thing over again. Among the various things he tried were: (1) Wisdom (1:12-18) is no comfort, brings no relief,—" in much wisdom is much grief." (2) Pleasure (2:1-1), with all its delights, has no profit whatsoever,—

" all is vanity and a striving after wind." (3) Riches
(2:18–6:12) costs hard labour, and goes in the end to whom
we do not know, and how it will be used we do not know.
Even money is not happiness, and its pursuit is but vanity
and a striving after wind. (4) Renown (7:1–11-8), " a
good name is better than precious oil; and the day of death,
than the day of one's birth." The pessimistic mood of the
seeker after fame permeates all he does. Even fame has
its compromising features which are distasteful to the wise
man. " Whatsoever thy hand findeth to do, do it with thy
might; for there is no work, nor device, nor knowledge, nor
wisdom in Sheol, whither thou goest " (9:10).

NOTE ON FIG. 4, tailpiece below: Alexander conquered Egypt and
founded Alexandria in 331 B. C., an ideal location for a maritime city.
It soon became a seat of learning, especially of Greek and Jewish
scholars. By the first century A. D. it had established a library of
about 900,000 documents as the centre of scholastic Alexandria. The
Jews became so influential that in the third and second centuries B. C.
they translated the Hebrew Old Testament into Greek for the benefit
of their Greek-speaking compartiots. This became so influential by
the first century that it brought about the writing of the New Testament in the same language. Alexandria was one of the intellectual
centres of the Christian Church in the early centuries of our era.

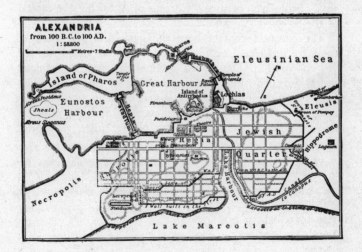

HEAD OF ANTIOCHUS EPIPHANES

CHAPTER XXXIV

JUDAISM'S FIGHT FOR A " PLACE IN THE SUN "

295. Hellenism Flooding Judaism. The so-called Judaism of Palestine was not entirely impervious to foreign influences. The Greek calendar, dating from Seleucus' victory over Antigonus (312), was adopted and used until the middle ages. Many Jews aped the ruling Greeks in names, in dress, and in the celebration of games and festivals. Some even became " Citizens of Antioch," the capital of the Seleucid kingdom.

The constant contact between Greek and Jew made it easy to introduce many customs that appealed to the Jewish youth. The Greek gymnasium and its athletic sports invaded the quiet gentler life of the Jews. Its games and contests gradually degenerated in southwestern Asia from immodesty into debauchery and the grossest evils. These undermined many of the finer virtues of

NOTE ON FIG. 6, headpiece above: Antiochus Epiphanes was the Greek king of Syria whose policy and determination were bent toward the extinction of the Jewish religion. He staked his reputation and his armies on achieving that end. But he met his match in the unparalleled valour of the Maccabæan Jews, who not only defeated his purpose, but wrested from him a guarantee of religious freedom (168–164 B. C.).

Jewish youth, and threatened the religious life of the Jerusalem colony.

The Hellenistic spirit of political preferment and rivalry also inoculated the more ambitious Jews, and damaged the religious life of men who should have resisted such a temptation. If such Greek influence had caught only the peasant, it might have been checked; but it poured its subtle flood of influence over the young, the rich, and the liberal-minded, and led them into ways whose end they did not foresee nor realize. In fact, Hellenism would soon try the virility and endurance of Judaism as it had never before been tested.

296. Hellenists and Devout Jews. The inroads of Hellenism drove the faithful, patriotic Jews to organize into a party called the " Devout " (Khasidim). Their purpose was to checkmate the growth of Hellenism before it should wholly submerge Judaism proper. While most of the wealthy and influential Jews had espoused the new culture, the common people stood for the faith of the fathers. Very soon a sharp line of distinction was drawn between the two parties.

The death of Antiochus the Great (175 B. c.), and the accession of Antiochus Epiphanes, inaugurated a new and aggressive policy for the expansion and strengthening of Hellenism in all his realm.

The " Devout " were not only shocked but alarmed at the godless acts of the Hellenistic Jews. The intrigues of the new party, the seizure by bribery of the high-priesthood, and the assassination of the deposed Onias, drove the " Devout " to desperation. Antiochus had gone to fight Egypt; and the " Devout," taking advantage of a report that he had been slain in battle, fell upon the Hellenists and mercilessly murdered them in cold blood. Antiochus, not slain as reported, returned from Egypt and let loose his wrath on the " Devout," filled Jerusalem with the slain, defiled the temple, and carried off its treasures.

Not satisfied with his efforts to down Judaism, Antiochus

issued a decree to forbid all Jewish religious observances, such as sabbath-keeping, temple sacrifices, circumcision, and distinction of foods. Possession of a book of the law was prohibited on penalty of death. To enforce this revolutionary decree, he sent an army of 22,000 into Judah, who made their attack on the sabbath day, the day on which Jews regularly refused to fight. At their own leisure, they practically destroyed the temple, the homes of the " Devout," and carried into slavery large numbers of the population.

As a further deterrent to Jewish worship, they built on the site of the sacred altar of sacrifice, an altar to Zeus, on which the Jews were forced to sacrifice the flesh of swine; and on the same court they set up an image of that Greek deity, which was " the abomination that maketh desolate " (Dan. 12:11).

This was the depth of disgrace for a Jew. The weaker folk joined the new régime, while the uncompromising fled like Elijah from the edge of the sword into the villages and hills of the land. Antiochus, however, discounted the temper of the fleeing " Devout," to his later dismay and alarm.

297. The Maccabæan Recoil. The attempt to turn all Jews to paganism was so well organized that agents were sent everywhere through the country villages to compel every Jew to sacrifice to, and worship the Greek god Zeus. Among the refugees from the Syrian massacre of the " Devout " at Jerusalem, was one Mattathias and his five sons, who took up their residence at Modin in the hill-country looking toward the Mediterranean Sea. At length the Syrian officer appeared at Modin to ascertain the loyalty of its citizens to Antiochus and his decree. He built an altar for the new worship and commanded Mattathias, as the chief man of the town, to lead the van of worshippers in sacrifice to Zeus, with promise of the king's indulgence and a money reward. Mattathias scorned such an order and promise, and with rage cut down the first man who dared to carry it out, and slaughtered the royal agent who gave the command. Then with an unquenchable zeal he called to the citizens of Modin: " Whosoever is zealous for the law and maintaineth the covenant, let him come forth after me " (1 Macc. 2:27). With that cry Mattathias, his five sons, and other zealots for Judaism, fled to the hills and declared open war against the enemy.

Soon their numbers increased until they were able to carry on guerilla warfare against all Hellenists and their co-adjutors. Mattathias did not long survive the hardships of such a life, but was foresighted enough to name as his successor, his son Judas, and as counsellor, Simon. The intrepid and bold character of Judas soon spread to all the nation. His surname, Maccabæus, " hammerer," soon attached itself to him. His skill as a strategist and military leader of men, the swiftness by which he delivered his blows, the speed with which he appeared and disappeared, bewildered the Syrians. With a complete knowledge of the contour of the country, of the ravines and plains, the caves and the mountains, Judas mystified and confounded every attempt to trap him.

Antiochus decided to suppress such a rebellious band of guerillas. His general, Apollonius, was dispatched with an army to wipe them out. Somewhere near Samaria, Judas and his band met and completely routed the Syrians, and out of the booty replenished their own meagre equipment and supplies. Not to be disgraced by such a defeat, General Seron led another and a greater army, and attempted to reach Jerusalem through the Beth-horon valley. Here Judas trapped and slaughtered them mercilessly, utterly routing the entire army. More booty in the shape of equipment and supplies gave Judas what he needed for further warfare. Antiochus next sent 50,000 troops under his three most noted generals. Attempting to go up from the plain through a wider pass, they went up wady Ali south of Mizpah. Judas, with only 6,000 bold, tried warriors, struck them in the grey of the morning dawn, and caught them off their guard; the Syrians broke and fled, and the whole army was disgracefully defeated.

With characteristic Greek persistence, Lysias, commander-in-chief, personally led another army of 5,000 cavalry and 60,000 infantry to retrieve Syrian honour. Up the valley of Elah they advanced, just north of Hebron. Judas, with only 10,000 veterans, met them at Beth-sura and tragically defeated them, slaying about 5,000 of the foe. Lysias retired to Antioch to recruit another and an invincible host.

298. A Respite and a Restoration. Judas took advantage of the absence of Syrian troops to " clean up " Jerusalem. The Syrian officer of the garrison in the citadel of the city was not equal to an attack on him and his veterans, so they remained safe behind their battlements. When the Maccabæans entered the temple court, they rent their garments and wept at the wreckage and desecration before them. With the spirit of the " Devout " they threw out the pagan image and altar, and all foreign symbols of Zeus worship. They built and set up an altar to God, repaired the gates, court areas and priests' chambers, and prepared new vessels for the service. December 25, 165 B. C., exactly three years after " the abomination that maketh desolate," the repaired temple was re-dedicated to the worship of Israel's God. In the New Testament it was celebrated as the " feast of the dedication " (John 10:22).

As supplementary to this joyful occasion for the Jews' religion, Judas decided to weaken his nearby foes who were sympathetic with the Syrians. He first gave the Idumæans on the south a beating. Then he crossed the Jordan and evened scores with the Ammonites who had maltreated Jewish residents in their country. He swept Hauran as far north as Damascus, and over into Galilee, and returned with a victor's spoils to Jerusalem. Then he captured Hebron from the Idumæans, and devastated the Philistines up to the grand fortress of Ashdod.

Thus far Judas and his hardened and seasoned veterans

had not lost a battle. They had given paganism a blow that stunned it and held it in check for many decades.

299. Judas' Defeat and Victory. As a conclusion to Judas' other victories, he attacked and captured the Syrian citadel in Jerusalem. This gave him control of the city.

Antiochus having died and his successor anointed, Lysias, prime minister, determined to land one crushing blow on the rebel stronghold. With 100,000 infantry, 20,000 cavalry, and 32 war-elephants, all fully equipped, Lysias and the young king arrived in Palestine. Entering the hill-country through the broad pass of Elah, they met Judas and his 10,000 at Beth Zacharias, not far from Beth-sura. Judas soon saw that he would be overwhelmed with that flood-tide of troops, and for his own safety's sake withdrew to, and into Jerusalem, where he defended himself. Lysias, sure of complete final victory, surrounded and laid siege to the city. But it was short-lived, for an alarmist report reached him from Antioch; and, raising the siege, he rushed his army back to the capital. But before leaving, he arranged with Judas a treaty of peace which guaranteed for the Jews religious freedom, even though politically under the sway of Syrian kings.

Judas had achieved the very principle for which Mattathias had opened the war. Paganism was now checked and Judaism had done it. Henceforth the worship of the Jews was apparently safe from interference, and its freedom vouchsafed under Syrian rule. But political independence was still beyond their reach and hope.

300. Religious Freedom and Dissension. Though Judas Maccabæus had won the fight for devout Judaism, the Hellenists refused to abide by the treaty of peace. Their influence with the Syrian authorities gave them the advantage in the contest for leadership. When the king of Syria appointed and sent to Jerusalem a Hellenist as high-priest, the citizens threw him out of the city. The spirit of Syria tried by force of arms, to compel them to accept him, but Judas beat them on the battlefield. A second attempt was made, and Judas, by this time deserted by his worn-out troops, was slain in the fight in 161 B. C.

Thus fell the greatest leader, general, and warrior in all Jewish history. He had rescued the Jewish faith from the pit of paganism. He had, by his cool, calm valour, his indomitable courage, held back the forces of Hellenism, defied their threats, and won the day for the cause of righteousness. He saved his people and their religion from extinction and obliteration. He was more than a Joshua, a Deborah, or a Nehemiah, in his beneficent work for the perpetuation of his race and religion. Henceforth Judaism had a fair field and an even contest with other faiths of the world.

We have now reached the acme of the Maccabæan struggle, and shall leave the rather distressing and inglorious dissensions of the years that follow, for the student of the " Between the Testaments."

NOTE ON FIG. 82, tailpiece below: Gold and silver were media of exchange from the earliest times only by weight. Not until the Persian era was metal regularly coined for money. In the Maccabæan times we have coins struck with an inscription on one side, and a symbol on the other. This coin has on the obverse (left) " Shekel of Israel," about a vase, over which is "year one." On the reverse (right) "Jerusalem the Holy," almost encircling a branch with three buds.

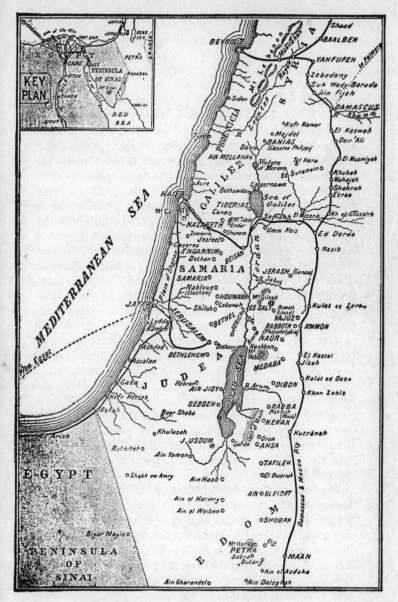

Map 15. Modern Palestine (about 1920 A. D.)

This map answers many questions about Palestine to-day. It shows routes of railways; names, some ancient, some modern, of places; eastern boundary of Egyptian government, from Refah to Akabah; and the general political districts, survivals of the time of Christ. Up in the left-hand corner is a miniature map of lower Egypt.

OLD TESTAMENT CHRONOLOGY

The Old Testament was a product of many writers who lived and wrote in the undated centuries before Christ. Indeed, there was no fixed system of chronology either in their day or in that of ancient oriental history. Events were dated from the occurrence of some great phenomenon of nature, as an earthquake (Amos 1:1), or the fall of an important city, the reign of a king, or other occasion of general interest. Such a variety of methods has left us a heritage of material of very uncertain chronological value. Some of the compilers of the books of Kings and Chronicles have synchronized their dates with those of the neighbour kingdom, and thus have given us a check on the event mentioned. Used in conjunction with those of contemporary peoples, they are useful in constructing a system that can be reasonably established for the centuries of Israel's monarchy and down to the close of the Old Testament.

The greatest light on the chronology of the Old Testament has come to us from the " Assyrian Eponym Canon " (covering 893–666 B. C.), in which we find quadruplicate lists of events and persons, extending over 227 years,—several of them touching Old Testament facts. This Canon practically fixes the dates of those years, all of which fall within the years of Israel's monarchies.

The earliest chronological dates of real value in the Old Testament are the facts found in the books of Kings and Chronicles. But a careful reading of these data shows that care must be taken in estimating the length of each reign. One source of error among earlier chronologers was the custom of adding the lengths of reigns tandem or consecutively. Now, in several cases we know that a king made his son regent while he himself was on the throne. Note particularly

438

the case of Jehoshaphat's appointment of his son Jehoram
(2 Kings 1:17; 3:1) in the eighteenth year of his reign,
though he lived to rule twenty-five years. Another notable
instance was that of Jotham's becoming king when his father
Uzziah became incapacitated (in 750 b. c.) by reason of a
stroke of leprosy (2 Kings 15:5). A still more notable case
is that in which Jotham (in 742), king in place of his leprous father, appointed as regent his son Ahaz (2 Kings
17:1). In other words, the former method of reckoning
the years of reign of any king disregarded these many overlappings of the king and his regent. Another indication of
the looseness of the writer's chronological method is seen in
his counting the years of a king's reign after he had died.
In 2 Kings 15:30 the annalist cites the twentieth year of
Jotham, when his regency and reign altogether totaled only
sixteen years,—a carry-over method of reckoning, which
should have ceased with the death of Jotham. By assigning full value to these overlappings, and a sliding scale to
the beginning and ending of the reigns (according to
whether the reckoning is Babylonian or Egyptian), and by
taking account of the synchronistic data of the historians,
we are enabled to reach a comparatively fixed date for
all events from 893 b. c. down to the close of the Old
Testament.

All dates prior to the beginning of the monarchy are for
the present merely provisional. While some historians give
fixed dates for the early Babylonian and Egyptian kings,
especially around the times of Hammurabi and the twelfth
dynasty of Egypt, we prefer to hold these open for further
light to be dug out of the mounds of the Near East.

Old Testament Chronology

PERIOD II. PATRIARCHAL WANDERINGS

Early Hebrews	Date B. C.*	Contemporary Peoples
Birth of Abram in Ur of Chaldees (Gen. 11:27, 28).	c. 2200	**Hammurabi** (2123-2081) sixth king of first Babylonian dynasty.
Left Harran for Canaan (Gen. 12:4).	c. 2125	Amraphel, prob. Hammurabi, of Shinar warred against kings of the plain (Gen. 14)
Settled in Canaan (Gen. 13:18).	c. 2100	Palestine occupied by Canaanites and Amorites and Hittites.
Birth of Isaac (Gen. 21:5). Abram rescued Lot from raiders (Gen. 14). Birth of Jacob and Esau (Gen. 25:24-26).	c. 2040	Assyrians settled on upper Tigris River.
Death of Abraham (Gen. 25:8), 175 years old; buried in cave of Machpelah. Esau marries Hittite women (Gen. 26:34). Jacob's flight to Paddan-aram, marries Aramæan kinsfolk; after 20 years returns with flocks and herds.	c. 2025	Twelfth dyn. of Egypt (2000-1788).
Birth of Joseph in Aram (Gen. 30:23, 24).	c. 1949	
Isaac's death (Gen. 35:28, 29) 180 years old; buried in Machpelah.	c. 1920	
Joseph premier of Egypt (Gen. 41:46).	c. 1919	
Jacob and family migrate to Egypt.	c. 1910	
Jacob's death in Egypt (Gen. 47:31), 147 years old.	c. 1893	

*Babylonian dates are about those of L. W. King in his *History of Babylon*, 1915. Egyptian dates follow the system of J. H. Breasted in *History of Egypt*, 1924.

PERIOD II. PARTRIARCHAL WANDERINGS (Continued)

Early Hebrews	Date B. C.	Contemporary Peoples
Joseph died in Egypt (Gen. 50:26), 110 years old; buried in Canaan (Josh. 24:32). Sometime in the Hyksos period, bedouin shepherds probably entered Egypt, lived in Goshen, engaged in animal husbandry and business among the Egyptians.	c. 1839	**Thirteenth to Seventeenth dynasties** of Egypt (1788–1580)—the Hyksos period.

PERIOD III. BONDAGE AND WANDERINGS

Hebrews	Date B. C.	Contemporary Peoples
Hebrews (**Habiri**) of the Amarna age.		**Eighteenth dynasty** of Egypt (1580-1350) crushed Hyksos in Syria (after 1501 B. C.). **Nineteenth dynasty** (1350-1205).
	1292–1225	**Ramses II**, probable oppressor of Hebrews, ruled 1292-1225.
Birth of Moses.	1225–1215	**Merneptah**, probable Pharaoh of the Exodus.
Exodus of Israel from Egypt.	c. 1220	
Wilderness wanderings 40 years.	1205–1200	Usurper in Egypt.

PERIOD IV.   TRIBAL ORGANIZATION

Hebrews	Date B. C.	Contemporary Peoples
Hebrews entrance into Canaan under Joshua.	c. 1180	Twentieth dynasty (1200-1090).
Period of Judges; several contemporaries; oppressions local; years of rule round numbers suited to scheme of 480 years (1 K. 6:1), to Solomon's reign.	c. 1050	Twenty-first dynasty (1090-945).

PERIOD V.   THE MONARCHY, c. 1050-931 B. C.

Hebrews	Date B. C.	Contemporary Peoples
Samuel and Saul in authority (1 Sam. 11-15). Saul ruled 40 years (Josephus *Antiq.* VI 14, 9).		
David [40] made king over Judah in Hebron (2 Sam. 2:4).	c. 1010	Egypt and Assyria quiescent.
David made king over all Israel (2 Sam. 5:3-5).	c. 1003	
Solomon [40] succeeds David (1 K. 1: 38, 39)	c. 971	Hiram I, king of Tyre (1 K. 5:1-12).
S. began to build temple (1 K. 6:1, 37).	c. 967	Hiram II of Tyre.
Temple finished (1 K. 6:38).	c. 960	
Hiram displeased with Solomon's gift (1 K. 9:10-13).	945–745	Twenty-second dynasty of Egypt, founded by Shishak.
Solomon's navy (1 K. 9:26-10:22). Uprisings; rebels in Egypt. Solomon's death.	931	

PERIOD VI. DUAL MONARCHIES, 931-722 B. C.

Prophets	Judah	Date B.C.	Israel (Ephraim)	Contemporaries
Shemaiah (of Judah) Ahijah (of Israel) "Man of God" (Israel)	1. Rehoboam [17] at Jerusalem. Shishak's invasion, **5th yr.**	931	1. Jeroboam [22] at Shechem, Tirzah.	Shishak of Egypt (945-924)
		927		
	2. Abijam [3] son of Rehoboam fought Israel	914	**18th yr.** (1 K. 15:1).	
	3. Asa [41], son of Abijam. Relig. reforms. Great army (1 K. 15:25-27). **2nd yr.**	912	**20th yr.** (1 K. 15:9).	
		911	Death of Jeroboam. 2. Nadab [2], son of J. slain by	
Jehu, son of Hanani (Israel)	(1 K. 15; 28-30.) **3rd yr.** Asa Wars with Baasha. Asa bribes Benhadad. Defeated Zerah of Ethiopia.	910	3. Baasha [24], usurper. Wipes out house of Jeroboam, wars with Asa. Benhadad invades Israel	Benhadad I of Syria.
Azariah (Judah) Oded (Israel)		c. 901		Zerah, Ethiopian.
	(1 K. 16: 8-13) **26th yr.**	886	Death of Baasha. 4. Elah [2], son of B. slain by 5. Zimri [7 days] usurper.	
Hanani (Judah) imprisoned by Asa	(1 K. 16:15-19) **27th yr.**	885	6. Tibni and **Omri** [12] 4 yrs. civil war.	Ashurnatsirpal (884-860)
	(1 K. 16: 29) **38th yr.**	874	7. Ahab [22], son of Omri; marries Jezebel of Sidon. Baal cult—state religion.	Mesha of Moab
	(2 Chr. 16:12) **39th yr.**	873		

PERIOD VI. DUAL MONARCHIES, 931-722 B. C. (Continued)

Prophets	Judah	Date B. C.	Israel (Ephraim)	Contemporaries
	Asa had gout, forgot Jehovah. Death of Asa, successor, his son **4. Jehoshaphat** [25] Reformer, political and religious; large army. (2 Chr. 17:7-9). **3rd yr.**	871	**4th yr.** (1 K. 22:41). Famine 3½ years; Elijah slays 450 prophets of Baal; flees to Horeb.	
Elijah's test on Carmel.		868		
	Taught law of God	860		**Shalmaneser III** of Assyria (860-24).
	Tribute from Philistines and Edomites.	856		
		c. 855	Victory over Syrians at Samaria and Aphek. A. in a league against Assyria at Karkar.	
Jehu, son of Hanani (Judah) rebuked Jehoshaphat.	Visits Ahab **17th yr.** Jehoram, son, regent, (2 K. 1:17; 3:1), married	854	**8. Ahaziah** [2], regent with his father Ahab.	
Jahaziel's (Judah) encouragement of the people.	Athaliah, dau. of Ahab **18th yr.** Alliance with Ahab (1 K. 22:44).	853	Ahab slain in battle at Ramoth-gilead. Ahaziah's death; successor	

PERIOD VI. DUAL MONARCHIES, 931-722 B. C. (Continued)

Prophets	Judah	Date B. C.	Israel	Contemporaries
Micaiah (Israel) against 400 prophets (1 K. 22: 5-28). Elisha (Israel)	Defeat of Ammon and Moab at En-gedi. Moab invaded. 5. **Jehoram** [8] son of Jehoshaphat, becomes king, his father still living (2 K. 8:16). Jehoshaphat's death, Jehoram slays his brethren; diseased.	849	9. **Jehoram** [12] his son; joins Jehoshaphat against Moab. 5th yr. (2 K. 8:16).	**Mesha** of Moab attacked by Judah, Israel and Moab.
		847	Siege of Samaria by Benhadad II; flight of Syrians.	**Benhadad** of Syria slain by Hazael (2 K. 8: 7-15).
	6. **Ahaziah** [1], son of Jehoram, who dies of disease. Slain by Jehu near Jezreel (2 Chr. 22:5-9). **Athaliah** [6] usurps throne of Judah; destroys seed royal. Athaliah slain (2 K. 11: 4-20).	842	12th yr. (2 K. 8:25). J. wounded in battle, slain by 10. **Jehu** [28], wipes out house of Omri, and Baal worship; keeps calf-worship. Pays tribute to Shalmaneser III of Assyria.	**Shalmaneser** III battles with Hazael of Syria.
	7. **Jehoash** [40], son of Ahaziah; radical reforms	836	7th yr. (2 K. 12:1). Hazael of Syria takes E. Jordan country.	**Shamsi-Adad** (824-805) of Assyria.

PERIOD VI. DUAL MONARCHIES, 931-722 B. C. (Continued)

Prophets	Judah	Date B. C.	Israel	Contemporaries
	(2 K. 13:1) **23rd yr.** Death of Jehoiada, collapse of reforms; lapse into idolatry. Hazael's army before Jerusalem; bought off (2 K. 12:17, 18).	814	11. **Jehoahaz** [17], son of Jehu. Fell into hands of Hazael of Syria.	**Adad-nirari III** (805-782) of Assyria.
Zechariah (Judah), son of Jehoiada, rebuked Jehoash, was stoned (2 Chr. 24: 20-24).	(2 K. 13:10). **37th yr.**	800	12. **Jehoash** [16], son of Jehoahaz, regent for two years.	(**Mari** of Syria 803)
	Amaziah, regent, with his father Jehoash; Jehoash slain in Millo.	799		
'Prophet' rebukes Amaziah for idolatry. "Man of God" prevents alliance with Israel (2 Chr. 25: 7-10).	8. **Amaziah** [29] slays his father's slayers. Defeats Edom, adopts its idols.	797	**2nd yr.** (2 K. 14:1). Three times victor over Syria. Jeroboam regent with his father.	**Benhadad III,** son of Hazael of Syria.
		790		
	Uzziah regent with his father Amaziah.	787		

PERIOD VI. DUAL MONARCHIES, 931-722 B. C. (Continued)

Prophets	Judah	Date B. C.	Israel	Contemporaries
	Defies Israel, defeated, captured, Jerusalem plundered. (2 K. 14:17) **15th yr.**	785	Death of Jehoash of Israel. 13. **Jeroboam II [41],** first of J. alone (2 K. 14:23); great army officer.	**Shalmaneser IV** (783-773) of Assyria. **Ashur-dan III** (773-755) of Assyria.
	Amaziah slain by his servants at Lachish, succeeded by his son.		Restored former boundaries of Israel.	
Zechariah (Judah) teaches Uzziah (2 Chr. 26:5). **Amos** (Judah) to Israel. **Hosea** (Israel) Chaps. 1-3.	9. **Azariah (Uzziah)** [52], first year alone. Restores former limits of Judah; fortifies country; prosperity everywhere.	c. 770	**27th yr.** (2 K. 15:1) should be **20th yr.** of Jeroboam (from beginning of regency).	**Ashur-nirari II** (755-745) of Assyria.
Hosea (Israel) Chaps. 4-14.	(2 K. 15:8) **38th yr.** from beginning of regency. Uzziah's sacrilege and leprosy. 10. **Jotham** [16], regent in place of Uzziah, a leper (2 K. 15:5).	750	Death of Jeroboam II. 14. **Zechariah** [6 mos.] slain by Shallum. First year of **Pekah** [20], E. of Jordan. Second year of Pekah (2 K. 15:32).	

PERIOD VI. DUAL MONARCHIES, 931–722 B. C. (Continued)

Prophets	Judah	Date B. C.	Israel	Contemporaries
	(2 K. 15:13). **39th yr.**	749	15. **Shallum** [one mo.] slain by	
		748	16. **Menahem** [10], usurper.	
	Ahaz regent with Jotham his father (2 K. 17:1).	742	Menahem's first full year. Tribute to Pul of Assyria (2 K. 15:17-22).	**Tiglath-pileser (Pul) III** (745-727) of Assyria. Rezin of Syria.
	(2 K. 15:23) **50th yr.** 12th yr. of Jotham as reigning king.	738	17. **Pekahiah** [2] son of Menahem, slain by	
Isaiah (Judah)	(2 K. 15:27), **52nd yr.**, death of Uzziah, "leper" king.	736	18. **Pekah** [20], long prior reign in Gilead, about 15 yrs. First yr. in Samaria, 16th from beginning E. of Jordan (see 750 above).	
	16th and death yr. of Jotham, 7th yr. of regency of 11. **Ahaz** [16], his son; appeals to Tiglath-pileser for help.	735		
		734	Pekah of Israel and Rezin defeat Ahaz. Captives carried to Assyria (2 K. 15:29).	
	Ahaz meets Tig. at Damascus; imports Syrian altar to Jerusalem.	732		Damascus falls to **Tig. III.**

PERIOD VI. DUAL MONARCHIES, 931-722 B. C. (Continued)

Prophets	Judah	Date B. C.	Israel	Contemporaries
Micah (Judah)	20th yr. (from beginning of Jotham's regency, old method of dating still in use) (2 K. 15:30). 12th yr. of Ahaz (2 K. 17:1) from beginning of his regency, in 742.	731 730	{ Hoshea slays Pekah (20th yr. from his beginning E. of Jordan in 750 (2 K. 15:30). 19. Hoshea [9] first full yr. (2 K. 17:1).	
	Accession yr. of Hezekiah as regent with Ahaz, his father. 12. Hezekiah [29], first full year, religious reforms; passover observance; temple service restored.	728 727	3rd yr. (2 K. 18:1). Hoshea taken, imprisoned by king of Assyria.	So (Sibe) of Egypt. Shalmaneser V (727-722) of Assyria.
	(2 K. 18:9) 4th yr.	724	7th yr. (old dating, though Hoshea was in prison) Samaria besieged by Shalmaneser V.	

PERIOD VI. DUAL MONARCHIES, 931-722 B. C. (Continued)

Prophets	Judah	Date B. C.	Israel	Contemporaries
	(2 K. 18:10). 6th yr.	722	9th yr. of Hoshea (2 K. 18:10), from beginning of his reign, though a captive. Samaria falls to Sargon II; 28,290 pop. carried to foreign lands; foreigners imported and settled in Samaria.	Sargon II (722-705) of Assyria.

PERIOD VII. PROPHETS PREACHING

Prophets	Judah	Date B. C.	Contemporaries
Isaiah (Judah)		720	Egyptians defeated by Sargon at Raphia.
		717	Sargon takes Carchemish, Hittite centre on Euphrates River.
	Hezekiah's sickness and recovery (2 K. 20:1-11).	713	
	Embassy of Merodach-baladan to Hezekiah (2 K. 20:12-19).	712	
		711	Sargon's "Tartan" captures Ashdod (Isa. 20:1).
		710	Sargon drives Chaldeans out of Babylon.

PERIOD VII. PROPHETS PREACHING (Continued)

Prophets	Judah	Date B. C.	Contemporaries
		705	Death of Sargon, accession of his son **Sennacherib** (705-681).
	Sennacherib overruns E. coast of Med. Sea, Palestine, Philistia Hezekiah pays indemnity (2 K. 18:14-16). Disaster to Assyria's army.	701	Sennacherib fights Egyptians at Eltekeh, claims victory—Tirhakah being Egyptian general.
	Death of Hezekiah, accession of his son	699	
	13. **Manasseh** [55], reaction against Jehovah worship; killing prophets, desecrating temple; did as Ahaz had done.	698	
		688	**Tirhakah** (683-663) Ethiopian ruler of Egypt.
		681	Sennacherib slain by his sons (2 K. 19:37).
	M. pays tribute to Esarhaddon.	670	**Esarhaddon**, his son (681-668), successor. Esarhaddon conquers Egypt, Tirhakah escaping into Ethiopia.
		669	Tirhakah drives Esarh. from Egypt.
	Manasseh pays tribute to Ashurbanipal.	668	Death of Esarhaddon, accession of his son **Ashurbanipal** (668-626) at Nineveh.
		664	**Psamtik I** (664-610) of Egypt.

PERIOD VII. PROPHETS PREACHING (Continued)

Prophets	Judah	Date B. C.	Contemporaries
Hozai (Judah)		663-2	Ashurbanipal retakes Egypt, destroys Memphis and No-Amon (Thebes) (Nah. 3:8-10).
	Manasseh carried captive to Babylon; on penitence restored to throne (2 Chr. 33:11-13). "Cleans up" idolatry at Jerusalem; city fortified.	c. 648-7	Ashurbanipal defeats Elamites, plunders Susa.
	Death of Manasseh, accession of 14. Amon [2], his son, idolater, slain in a conspiracy.	642	
	15. Josiah [31], his son, accession year.	640	
Huldah, prophetess	Josiah's first full year.	639	Assyria in a decline.
		633	Cyaxares founded Median empire.
	Destroys idols and idolatry in the land.	629	Possible Scythian invasion.
Jeremiah	Jeremiah begins to prophesy.	626	Death of Ashurbanipal in Assyria.
Zephaniah		625	Nabopolassar (625-605) king of Babylon (Akkad).
	"Book of the Law" found in repairing the temple; covenant renewed; reforms reaching to Bethel and Samaria; great passover celebration.	621	
Nahum.		612	Nineveh falls before Babylonian and Median armies.

PERIOD VII. PROPHETS PREACHING (Continued)

Prophets	Judah	Date B. C.	Contemporaries
	Josiah slain at Megiddo, by Egyptian army; people crown 16. Jehoahaz [3 mos.] his son; deposed by Necho, carried to Egypt. 17. Jehoiakim [11], a brother, put on throne by Necho.	609	Pharaoh-Necho (609-594) crosses Palestine to help Assyria.
Habakkuk.		608	
	Jerusalem falls into power of Nebuchadr. Daniel and companions carried to Babylon (Dan. 1:1).	605	Nebuchadrezzar defeats Necho and remnant of Assyr. army at Carchemish, drives him back to Egypt; Nabopolassar dies and Nebuchadrezzar II (604-561), his son rules
	Rebels against Babylon (2 K. 24:1). Babylonian army takes Jerusalem, slays Jehoiakim (2 Chr. 36:6; Jer. 22:19; 36:30).	602 598	
Jeremiah. Ezekiel captive to Babylon.	18. Jehoiachin [3 mos.] son, taken captive to Babylon (first proper captivity). 19. Zedekiah [11] son of Josiah, Made trip to Babylon to assure Neb. of his fealty.	597 594	Psamtik II (594-589) of Egypt.
Ezekiel prophesies 591-570.		592	
	Alliance with Egypt; rebels against Babylon. Jerusalem invested by Babylonian army; met and defeated Egyptian allies.	588	Pharaoh-Hophra (Apries) (588-569) of Egypt.

PERIOD VII. PROPHETS PREACHING (Continued)

Prophets	Judah	Date B. C.	Contemporaries
Jeremiah remains with poor peasants; forcibly carried to Egypt. Obadiah.	Jerusalem taken, burnt, razed; Jews taken captive to Babylon; Gedaliah made governor of Judah; slain by Ishmael.	586–581	Nebuchadrezzar besieged Tyre thirteen years (Ezek. 29:17ff.; took it!

PERIOD VIII. THE EXILES

Prophets	Jews	Date B. C.	Contemporaries
Jeremiah in Egypt.	Another captivity by Nebuzaradan (Jer. 52:30).	581	
Ezekiel in Babylonia.	Jehoiachin of Judah released from prison; honored by Evil-merodach.	561	Death of Nebuchadrezzar succeeded by Evil-Merodach (561-559), his son. Slain and succeeded by a brother-in-law, Neriglissar (559-555). Nabonidus (555-538) (Nabuna'id) usurper on throne of Babylon.
		555	
		553	Cyrus conquers Media.
		546	Conquers Croesus of Lydia.

PERIOD IX. THE RETURNS

Prophets	Jews	Date B. C.	Contemporaries
		538	Captures Babylonia, takes over rule of Babylon; Darius made governor for two years.
	Jews, by decree of Cyrus, return to Palestine; to build the temple.	537–36	Cyrus' edict for all captives; aided Jews.
	Jews first return under Zerubbabel; begin to build temple; Samaritan's interference.	536	
		529	Death of Cyrus; succeeded by his son, **Cambyses** (529-522).
		525	Met defeat in Ethiopia, laid waste Egypt.
		522	Cambyses commits suicide.
		521	**Darius I Hystaspes** (521-485) of Persia.
Haggai and **Zechariah.**	Prophets urge temple-building; resumed with protection of Darius.	520	
	Temple completed and dedicated.	516	
		490	Persians and Greeks at battle of Marathon.
		485	Death of Darius, succeeded by his son, **Xerxes I** (485-464) "Ahasuerus."
		480	Persians and Greeks at Salamis.
		479	Persians defeated at Platæa.
		464	Death of Xerxes, succeeded by son, **Artaxerxes Longimanus** (464-424).
	Jews' (second) return under Ezra.	457	
		444	Herodotus.

PERIOD IX. THE RETURNS (Continued)

Prophets	Jews	Date B. C.	Contemporaries
	Nehemiah returns from Persia as governor of Palestine; built walls; reformed law-observance, returned to Persia.	444	
Malachi	Nehemiah's second visit to Jerusalem; new reforms.	432	Pericles in Athens.

PERIOD X. JUDAISM EXPANDING

Prophets	Jews	Date B. C.	Contemporaries
Jonah Joel	Sixth generation after Zerubbabel in 1 Chr. 3:19-24.	c. 350	

PERIOD XI. GREEK INVASION AND JUDAISM

Prophets	Jews	Date B. C.	Contemporaries
	Jews now under Alexander and Greek rule.	334 333 331	Alexander strikes into Asia Minor. Darius defeated at Issus. Alexander's conquest of Egypt. High-priest Jaddua named in Neh. 12:11ff.

PERIOD XI. GREEK INVASION AND JUDAISM (Continued)

Prophets	Jews	Date B. C.	Contemporaries
		330	Alexander takes over Persian empire.
		323	Alexander dies in Babylon, June 13.
	Jews under the Ptolemies in Egypt.	320–198	
	Jews under Seleucid rule.	312–167	
		285–247	Ptolemy Philadelphus in Egypt; translation of Old Testament begun.
	Jews persecuted by Antiochus Epiphanes.	175–164	
	Mattathias starts revolt against Antiochus.	167	
	Judas Maccabeus leader in rebellion.	166	
	Wins liberty of worship for the Jews.	164	
	Judas Maccabeus slain in battle.	161	

THE KINGS OF JUDAH

The year *before* a king's name is either the beginning of his regency or of his proper reign; observe the several overlappings which are necessary to carry out the synchronisms of Kings and Chronicles. For details see each item in the Chronology.

Date	Kings	Prophets	Contemporaneous Kings of Israel
931	1. Rehoboam (17).*	Shemaiah, Iddo.	Jeroboam.
914	2. Abijam (3).	Azariah, Hanani, Jehu.	Jeroboam.
912	3. Asa (41)		Jeroboam, Nadab, Baasha, Elah Zimri, Omri, Ahab.
871	4. Jehoshaphat (25).	Jehu, Jahaziel, Eliezer.	Ahab, Ahaziah, Jehoram.
849	5. Jehoram (8).		Jehoram.
842	6. Ahaziah (1).		Jehoram.
842	0. Athaliah (6).		Jehu.
836	7. Joash (40).	Zechariah.	Jehu, Jehoahaz, Joash.
799	8. Amaziah (29).		Joash, Jeroboam II.
787	9. Uzziah (52).	Zechariah.	Jeroboam II, Zechariah, Shallum, Menahem, Pekahiah, Pekah.
750	10. Jotham (16).	Isaiah, Micah.	Pekah.
742	11. Ahaz (16).		Pekah, Hoshea.
727	12. Hezekiah (29).		Hoshea
698	13. Manasseh (55).		
642	14. Amon (2).	Nahum.	

*Years of reign.

THE KINGS OF JUDAH (Continued.)

Date	Kings	Prophets	Contemporaneous Kings of Israel
640	15. Josiah (31).	Jeremiah. Zephaniah.	
608 608	16. Jehoahaz (3 mo.). 17. Jehoiakim (11).	Habakkuk.	
597 597 586	18. Jehoiachin (3 mo.). 19. Zedekiah (11). FALL OF JERUSALEM.	Obadiah.	

THE DYNASTIES AND KINGS OF ISRAEL
See Remarks under Period VII.

Dynasties	Kings	Prophets	Contemporaneous Kings of Judah
First	1. Jeroboam (22).* 2. Nadab (2). 3. Baasha (24).	Ahijah. Iddo. Jehu.	Rehoboam, Abijah, Asa. Asa. " " "
Second	4. Elah (2).		
Third	5. Zimri (7 days).		
Fourth	6. Omri (12). 7. Ahab (22) 8. Ahaziah (2). 9. Jehoram (12).	Elijah, Micaiah. Elisha.	Jehoshaphat. Jehoshaphat. Jehoshaphat, Jehoram, Ahaziah.

*Years of reign.

THE DYNASTIES AND KINGS OF ISRAEL (Continued.)

Dynasties	Kings	Prophets	Contemporaneous Kings of Judah
Fifth {	10. Jehu (28).		Joash.
	11. Jehoahaz (17).		Joash.
	12. Joash (16).	Jonah.	Joash, Amaziah.
	13. Jeroboam II (41).	Hosea.	Amaziah.
	14. Zechariah (6 mo.).	Amos.	Uzziah.
Sixth {	15. Shallum (1 mo.).		Uzziah.
	16. Menahem (10).		Uzziah.
Seventh	17. Pekahiah (2).		Uzziah.
Eighth	18. Pekah (20).	Oded.	Uzziah, Jotham, Ahaz.
Ninth	19. Hoshea (9).		Ahaz, Hezekiah.

NOTE ON FIG. 87, headpiece below: Shishak's invasion of Palestine in 926 B. C. was a stunning blow to the two new kingdoms of Israel and Judah. Having returned to Egypt with a countless booty, he recorded on the southern pylon of the court of the great temple of Amon at Karnak a record of that campaign. He specifies 156 places, cities, towns, and fortresses, which he captured. Observe the god Amon handing over to him a few of the ten lines of captive cities taken during that sweep into Palestine.

GENERAL INDEX AND REGISTER

Covering the more important names and subjects.

References are to sections (§§) unless otherwise indicated; the asterisk (*) marks an illustration or map; names in CAPITALS are kings or rulers; abbreviations are as follows: (A) Assyria; (Aram.) Aramæan; (B) Babylonia; (C) City; (D) Deity; (Eg.) Egypt; (El.) Elam; (Gr.) Greek; (H) Hittite; (Is.) Israel; (J) Judah; (L) Land; (M) Mountain; (P) People; (Pers.) Persian; (Phil.) Philistine; (R) River.

461

GENERAL INDEX AND REGISTER

(See page 461 for key.)

462

Printed in the United States of America